M000247873

WEYERHAEUSER ENVIRONMENTAL BOOKS

William Cronon, Editor

THE DAWN OF
Conservation Diplomacy

U.S.-Canadian
Wildlife Protection Treaties
in the Progressive Era

KURKPATRICK DORSEY

Foreword by William Cronon

UNIVERSITY OF WASHINGTON PRESS

Seattle and London

The Dawn of Conservation Diplomacy:
U.S.-Canadian Wildlife Protection Treaties in the Progressive Era
has been published with the assistance of a grant
from the Weyerhaeuser Environmental Books Endowment,
established by the Weyerhaeuser Company Foundation,
members of the Weyerhaeuser family,
and Janet and Jack Creighton.

Copyright © 1998 by the University of Washington Press.
Printed in the United States of America

Library of Congress Cataloging-in-Publication Data
Dorsey, Kurkpatrick.
The dawn of conservation diplomacy : U.S.-Canadian wildlife
protection treaties in the progressive era / Kurkpatrick Dorsey :
foreword by William Cronon.
p.   cm. — (Weyerhaeuser environmental books)
Includes bibliographical references and index.
ISBN 0-295-97676-4 (alk. paper)
1. Wildlife conservation — Law and legislation — United States.
2. Wildlife conservation — Law and legislation — Canada.
I. Title.   II. Series: Weyerhaeuser environmental book.
KDZ649.D67   1998   98-3752
346.7104′69516 — dc21   CIP

For

Julie

and

my mother and father

Contents

vii

Contents

Illustrations

Foreword

WILLIAM CRONON

It is customary these days to speak of "global environmental change" as if it were a new problem, a phenomenon unlike anything ever before faced in human history. Certainly we have every reason to be concerned about the effects of greenhouse gases on world climates, the long-term destruction of ecosystems and gene pools that threaten biological diversity, and a host of other environmental consequences of human activities that pose threats to the entire planet. But we misunderstand the nature of these problems if we imagine them to be without historical precedent. In fact, human beings have been altering the face of the planet for a very long time, just as natural processes have been constantly reshaping the earth from time immemorial. The rate of change may have accelerated and its scale shifted dramatically, but in fact current environmental problems almost always have historical analogues from which we have much to learn if only we pay attention both to discontinuities *and* continuities that link past, present, and future.

One of the most persistent continuities in the history of environmental law and policy has to do with boundary-crossing: the tendency of resources and pollutants to transport themselves across the artificial lines—legal, cadastral, national, jurisdictional—that human communities so frequently inscribe upon the land (and air and water) they inhabit. Property boundaries define who does and does not have access to the use of particular natural "commodities," while national boundaries define who does and does not have regulatory power to enforce legal restrictions on such use. Abstract and artificial as these "boundaries" may seem, they are profoundly important to a large majority of environmental conflicts in the modern world. Destruction of ozone by chlorinated fluorocarbons, global warming from the emission of greenhouse gases, deforestation of the tropics, the international migration of exotic pests and new epidemic diseases, the extinction of species from overhunting or habitat change: all of these in one way or another are examples of market forces, new technologies, changing land-use patterns, and complex demographics conspiring to produce environmental changes that express themselves in the form of "boundary-crossings." And there is nothing new about such phenomena. When Alfred Crosby wrote in his classic 1972 book *The Columbian Exchange* about the "ecological consequences of 1492," he was essentially narrating what happened when the Atlantic Ocean ceased to be a stable boundary separating the people and organisms of Eurasia and Africa on the one hand from the people and organisms of the Americas on the other.

It is therefore not surprising that some of the earliest international environmental treaties in North America, negotiated at the outset of the twentieth century, were about redefining legal obligations and responsibilities for organisms whose life cycles ignore national boundaries. In his fascinating book on the origins of environmental diplomacy, Kurk Dorsey has produced the first full-scale scholarly study of three key treaty negotiations that helped lay the foundations for all subsequent diplomatic efforts to deal with international environmental problems in North America, especially those involving wildlife. Scrupulously researched, carefully argued, and always clearly told, the book describes the nature of these early conflicts and reveals the ways in which diplomats and scientists struggled to come up with new solutions to the difficult legal and environmental challenges they faced.

More important, though, Dorsey offers a comparative perspective that is most suggestive in helping us understand why some treaties succeed and others fail. In fact, these three early negotiations between the United States and Canada differed dramatically in the extent to which they solved the environmental problems their sponsors sought to address. The Inland Fisheries Treaty of 1908 was more or less a total failure, doing nothing to alter the depletion of fish stocks on the Great Lakes and Puget Sound by commercial fishing. The North Pacific Fur Seal Convention of 1911, on the other hand, can be given credit for rescuing coastal fur seals from the near-certain extinction they were facing by the first decade of the twentieth century . . . though this positive result was achieved only when the commercial seal hunt was already on the brink of collapse. Finally, the Migratory Bird Treaty of 1916 had a far-reaching impact in protecting waterfowl species traveling between the two nations, so much so that it remains in effect to this day.

One of Kurk Dorsey's great strengths as a historian is that he pays close attention to the practical political circumstances that produced these very different results. Readers will not find in this book a pat set of social scientific models or formulae that "explain" or "predict" whether a particular type of treaty will fail while another succeeds. What emerge instead are the complex events, personalities, and political-economic forces that shaped environmental diplomacy during the first two decades of the twentieth century. Individuals are not the blind pawns of vast disembodied forces in this book. In Dorsey's view, individual people make a big difference to the way history unfolds, and readers familiar with environmental controversies today will instantly recognize the kinds of arguments that brought diplomats and scientists like David Starr Jordan and William Hornaday into such deep and persistent conflict in the debates surrounding these early wildlife treaties. Reading this book, one will never be tempted to regard environmental problems as abstract or pragmatic politics as irrelevant: instead, one quickly comes to understand that success in protecting an endangered resource depends utterly on the particular political realities associated with that resource.

How, then, should one understand the different outcomes of these three case studies? If one were to try to simplify Dorsey's complex story, a quick answer to this question might run as follows. Crucial to the failure of the Inland Fisheries Treaty was the fact that there was no large-scale public outcry for protecting the fish of the Great Lakes and Puget Sound. Fish, one might say, were a classic example of "uncharismatic minifauna," the kinds of animals that Americans and Canadians refused to take to their hearts as willingly as the "charismatic megafauna" — the large doe-eyed ungulates, the intelligent marine mammals, and eventually the heroic predators — that became objects of public concern at an earlier date. Scientists arguing on behalf of the fisheries treaty had sound reasons to be concerned about the health of Great Lakes and West Coast fishing stocks, but these long-run concerns were no match for the strong economic interests of commercial fishers trying to protect their profits in the here and now.

In the case of the North Pacific Fur Seal Convention of 1911, a complex negotiation between the United States, Canada, Great Britain, Russia, and Japan took nearly a quarter century to finally produce a viable compromise capable of protecting a key endangered species in the northern Pacific. Crucial to the controversy was the fact the United States, in owning the Pribilof Islands, controlled the lands on which fur seals reproduced, and therefore had special access to the easiest and most concentrated form of fur-seal hunting. Other nations involved in the hunt had to rely more heavily on pelagic sealing: killing the animals on the open sea. For many years, heated debate revolved around whether declining seal populations at coastal and island nurseries like the Pribilofs were in any way linked to hunting at sea, since nations involved in the pelagic hunt had a strong vested interest in denying such a connection. The 1911 treaty became possible only when all seal-hunting nations recognized that seals were disappearing in both locations and that the industry was doomed if dramatic steps were not taken immediately. This opened the way to compromise and finally resulted in a treaty that did in fact save fur seals from extinction by ending the pelagic hunt via the simple mechanism of cash payments to nations affected by its closure. This result was undoubtedly aided by the fact that public sympathy for seals was so much greater than it had been for fish.

Public sympathy was likewise crucial to the most successful of these negotiations, the Migratory Bird Treaty of 1916. A broad coalition of hunters, birdwatchers, women's clubs, and scientists argued effectively that commercial hunting of songbirds and migratory waterfowl was disastrously depleting breeding stocks, and that without systematic international protection many extinctions would occur in the near future. The recent demise of the passenger pigeon undoubtedly underscored the seriousness of this threat. Strong evidence was mobilized that migratory birds made a major contribution to agricultural prosperity through their role in consuming insect pests, and this, coupled with overwhelming public sympathy for birds in general, produced the political will to negotiate an effective treaty.

The struggle to protect biological diversity of course continues right down to this day, and there is no way to foresee its ultimate outcome. The treaties described in this book, whether successful or unsuccessful, were merely opening battles in a much longer war. Defining the legal and political responsibilities of nations to each other and to the natural environment in protecting the wildlife species that cross international boundaries remains an issue in which all of us have a crucial interest. That is why we can be grateful to Kurk Dorsey for tracing so carefully the early roots of a diplomacy in which nothing less than the biological future of the world may be at stake.

Acknowledgments

It is impossible to thank everyone who deserves mention, and I apologize to those whom I have forgotten. As an undergraduate at Cornell University, I was fortunate to have Walter LaFeber as a professor in three classes. His excellence as a teacher encouraged me to choose U.S. diplomatic history as my field of study. I first began to combine my interests in history and birds as a graduate student at Northwestern University, where I met Arthur McEvoy, a wonderful teacher and writer. Arthur helped make me a better historian in many ways. While at Northwestern, I benefited from discussions about combining diplomatic and environmental history with Walter Hixson, Michael Sherry, Drew Isenberg, Petra Gödde, and Andrew Hurley. Drew also took the time more recently to analyze and critique my arguments, which forced me to strengthen them.

I owe many thanks to my colleagues and professors at Yale University. Mark Shulman, director of the Yale International History Colloquium, twice allowed me to present my research in a public forum. On both occasions, I received much helpful advice. In particular, Fred Logevall and Steve Schwartzberg took the time to make in-depth comments. Early in the process, Garry Brewer and Robin Winks provided insight on the problems and opportunities that my research area presented. William Cronon also deserves a great deal of thanks for his suggestions, encouragement, and knowledge. Bill helped to strengthen the environmental history angle in my research, and he was always a source of valuable advice and bibliographic citations. I am especially grateful to my advisor, Gaddis Smith, who was consistently supportive as I attempted to determine how to approach this topic. He was patient while I changed topics, he was enthusiastic about my attempts to bring environmental issues into diplomatic history, and he provided excellent editorial criticism.

My research was made considerably easier by a Graduate Student Fellowship from the Canadian Embassy and an Andrew Mellon Dissertation Year Fellowship from Yale University. The College of Liberal Arts at the University of New Hampshire provided me with summer fellowships in 1995 and 1996 to help me complete the manuscript. Michael Keller at the Yale library helped immensely, and the staff at the Yale library's Manuscripts and Archives department was always helpful. I also owe thanks to Bill Cox at the Smithsonian Institution Archives, Dane Hartwell at the United States National Archives, and Roanne Moktiar at the National Archives of Canada, as well as the staffs of the Manuscripts and Archives division of the New York Public Library, the Rare and Manuscript Collections at Cornell University, the Department of Special Collections at Stanford University, and the American Heritage Center at the University of Wyoming.

Listening to stories from friends and colleagues, I had grown to fear the publishing process, but my friends at the University of Washington Press have made this a pleasurable experience. Kim McKaig helped improve the writing substantially, and Julidta Tarver has done a wonderful job of shepherding the manuscript and the author along the way. Also, Bill Cronon and Arthur McEvoy reviewed the manuscript and provided advice on its direction.

Finally, I would like to acknowledge my deep gratitude to members of my family for their unfailing support. My parents, Anne and Robert Dorsey, provided financial, intellectual, and, most important, moral support throughout graduate school. I cannot thank them enough. I wish especially to thank my wife, Julie O'Brien Dorsey, for her constant love, understanding, humor, and patience. I dedicate this book to them.

THE DAWN OF
Conservation
Diplomacy

The Intersection of
Diplomacy and Conservation

As we near the end of the twentieth century and begin to comprehend fully the impact of the end of the Cold War, environmental protection has emerged as an important item on the world's diplomatic agenda. At the Earth Summit in Brazil in 1992 and in national discussions about the impact of free trade on the environment, Americans have been trying to find an appropriate place for environmental protection in our dealings with other nations. As a society, we engage in crucial debates about the costs and benefits of various laws and treaties designed to preserve the environment. We have a natural inclination to accept sacrifice in order to preserve certain species or natural formations that we enjoy, and we also recognize that we must limit ourselves in order to ensure adequate supplies of renewable resources such as clean air and water. Yet we worry not only about the impact of our actions on the biosphere but also about the impact of environmental protection on our economy and our ability to compete in the global marketplace. Thus, modern environmental protection, especially on an international level, often depends on the ability of various interest groups to bargain and exert political leverage on governments.

It may be tempting to look at this modern horse-trading and conclude that it is a new phenomenon, a post–Earth Day manifestation of the importance of the environmentalist movement. But, in fact, modern environmentalists are following in the footsteps of the conservationists of the Progressive era, who themselves learned tough lessons about placing their issues on the diplomatic agenda. Between 1890 and 1920, scientists and conservationists in the United States and Canada found themselves blazing a new trail. For the first time, they had an opportunity to cooperate with diplomats in the creation of treaties to protect resources that spanned the Canadian-American border. They seized that opportunity, and their accomplishments

3

included the first three comprehensive wildlife conservation treaties in history: the Inland Fisheries Treaty of 1908, the North Pacific Fur Seal Convention of 1911, and the Migratory Bird Treaty of 1916.[1]

Those who pushed for international agreements to save threatened wildlife did so because of the discontinuity between environmental and political boundaries. Progressive era conservationists recognized that state and national governments were often unable to undertake sufficient protective action for resources that crossed borders. In proposing a North American conference on conservation, President Theodore Roosevelt zeroed in on the fundamental issue: "It is evident that natural resources are not limited by the boundary lines which separate nations, and that the need for conserving them upon this continent is as wide as the area upon which they exist."[2] Roosevelt's conference was not particularly successful, but his comments suggested a newfound awareness that nations had to cooperate to promote conservation.

Although the fisheries, fur seal, and bird treaties were conceived of and executed independently, they shared some basic similarities. Each dealt with commercially valuable vertebrates that migrated across international boundaries. Overharvesting of the animals in question threatened imminent extinction and subsequent irreparable economic and environmental damage. In each case, there was no viable alternative to a scientifically based diplomatic solution. Finally, and at the heart of this book, the ability of scientists and conservationists to shape the treaties and influence public opinion — in the face of economically driven opposition — determined the success or failure of all three agreements.

THE CONTEXT: CANADIAN-AMERICAN RELATIONS

There is some irony that these cooperative agreements came from one of the most power-oriented periods in Great Power relations. Arms races, imperial scrambles, and saber-rattling characterized the diplomacy of the time, when even allies distrusted each other. It was a time of such rivalry and militarism that Roosevelt, who was not squeamish about warfare, won a Nobel Peace Prize. Culminating in the carnage of the First World War and the failed search for a new world order, this phase of Great Power relations seems hardly the time for groundbreaking international conservation agreements based on cooperation.[3]

But in the face of the general global tension that characterized the era, the United States and Great Britain began their famed rapprochement. Spurred by expanding German power and a growing sense of cultural similarity, British leaders saw in the rising United States a potential ally. They decided that it would be better to accommodate the growing power of their former colony than try to contain it. After years of tension and antagonism, Americans were justifiably suspicious. Some politicians were determined to twist the lion's tail just a few more times, playing to their Irish and German constituents. In frustration, Secretary of State John Hay, who had quite a record of winning concessions from London, complained that Anglophobic politicians criticized his diplomacy because he did not crown his victories by saying, "To hell with the Queen." Over time, though, American leaders recognized their favorable position and used it to win concessions from London, such as the Hay-Pauncefote Treaty regarding the Panama Canal.[4]

One factor complicating the rapprochement was the unique position of the third player in the North Atlantic Triangle, the Dominion of Canada, which was slowly moving toward complete political independence from Britain. Many Canadians feared that their independence would lead to subservience, political or economic, to the United States. Since 1776, London usually had sided with Canada in North American disputes and had rebuffed repeated American attempts to annex the Dominion. Because Canadians had stayed in the empire while Americans rebelled and then continued to make trouble, London had reason to favor Canada. But the power realities of the day dictated that American strength was at least as important as Canadian loyalty.[5]

Under the British North America Act of 1867, which served as the constitution for the Canadian government, Canada was dependent on London for its foreign policy. The Canadian head of state, the governor general, served at the pleasure of the monarch and was London's representative at Ottawa. Although the Canadian Parliament had a basically free hand on domestic issues, Canadians had no official voice in making foreign policy. The governor general did consult with cabinet ministers on external issues, but he alone was responsible for making recommendations to British leaders at Whitehall. Of course, the British foreign secretary was free to ignore Canadian opinion while formulating policy for the empire.[6]

This system of conducting foreign policy lacked a direct channel for official contact between Ottawa and Washington, which hindered the resolution of Canadian-American disputes. The historian Oscar Skelton noted that "Miss Ottawa had a voice, but etiquette forbade her speaking to Mr.

Washington except through Papa London."[7] Proposals from the United States regarding Canada took a tortuous path: from the State Department to the British Embassy to the Foreign Office to the Colonial Office to the governor general to the Canadian government—and then back again. The migration of diplomatic initiatives between Washington and Ottawa was far more arduous than that undertaken by any wild animal. Thus, from across the Atlantic Ocean, London created a foreign policy to deal with the United States, and Canada had to live with the results.

British willingness to put rapprochement ahead of Canadian desires was never more apparent than in the resolution of the Alaska boundary dispute, which stood as the defining incident of British-American-Canadian relations at the turn of the century. The crisis began in 1897, when word spread that prospectors had found gold in the Klondike region of Canada, and people from around the globe poured into this remote, inhospitable area. The least dangerous route took prospectors across the Alaska panhandle at the towns of Skagway and Dyea, over the mountains at Chilkoot or White Pass, and then down the Yukon River to Dawson. Miners faced an uncertain future, if they survived the journey, but the lure of instant wealth drew tens of thousands of men.[8] Not only were local authorities unprepared to handle the deluge of rough characters, but there also was a great deal of uncertainty about who actually had sovereignty over the ports of entry. Leaders in Washington, Ottawa, and London read different borders into the Anglo-Russian Treaty of 1825, which the United States had inherited with the 1867 Alaska purchase. With thousands of prospectors pouring into the region, control of access to the goldfields was at stake. A neighborly disagreement about a fence line had become a point of national honor.[9]

Hoping to avoid a dispute, the British, Canadians, and Americans convened a Joint High Commission to discuss the border and other issues in August 1898 in Quebec. Six months later, the meeting adjourned without a treaty, because the delegates could not reach an agreement on the Alaska boundary issue. The Canadians and British believed that the Americans would yield on the border in order to make progress on the other subjects. The American delegates, however, perceived that resolution of the other problems mattered to Canadians too. Because of their strong belief in the legality of their position on the Alaska boundary, the American delegates were in fact willing to let the conference collapse over that one issue. In words that the American commissioners might have echoed, the diplomatic historian Samuel Flagg Bemis described the Canadian position: "It was a ridiculous and preposterous claim, just as weak as it could be. . . . [It] derived its only strength from the fact that a great government was willing to espouse it."[10] Not only was the State Department unimpressed by the Canadian position, but the British government was obviously reluctant to confront one of its few remaining allies over the questionable claim of a wayward dominion. Canadian intransigence left London scrambling for a face-saving way to concede the point to the United States.

Finally, in January 1903, Great Britain and the United States agreed to arbitrate the dispute. Along the way, President Roosevelt warned that he was "going to be ugly" with Canada if need be and moved troops to Alaska to reinforce his commitment to the American position. In the words of the historian Charles Tansill, "The British Government resented these Rooseveltian tactics, but the changing scene on the stage of world politics made Lord Lansdowne give the President the leading role in this drama of Anglo-American relations."[11] The 1903 treaty stipulated that each side would name three "impartial jurists of repute" to a six-person panel that would resolve the border dispute. Determined to win, Roosevelt appointed Republican Senators Henry Cabot Lodge of Massachusetts and George Turner of Washington, as well as Secretary of War Elihu Root, none of whom could be described as impartial. Ignoring Roosevelt's brash moves, the British government chose Lord Alverstone, the Lord Chief Justice of England, to accompany the two Canadian jurists. When the final decision came in October 1903, Alverstone voted with the Americans to award most of the disputed territory to the United States. Rather than risk losing an ally in an increasingly dangerous world, Britain had chosen to sacrifice Canadian interests.[12]

Canadians' reactions to this perceived betrayal of national honor reflected a range of opinions about the United States. Some blamed Americans for treating them unfairly and expressed fear that Washington aspired to annex the rest of Canada. But other Canadians believed that the United States was no longer actively in the real estate market.[13] As the Montreal *Herald* suggested, "Canada is that portion of North America the United States doesn't want."[14] In addition, many well-informed Canadians understood that the United States had the better case and that Canada had to accept some blame for its inept handling of the dispute. A few years later, the governor general, Lord Grey, summed up the ambivalence that many Canadians felt about their southern neighbor: "We have the friendliest feelings toward the United States; . . . we do not intend to discriminate against them; we don't intend to be bullied."[15]

The tribunal's decision also strengthened the Canadians' desire to distance themselves from London. Canadians directed their hottest fire at Great Britain for ignoring the Dominion's loyalty. If Canada could not trust Britain to protect its interests, then Canadians demanded the right to fend for themselves diplomatically. Partially in response, in 1909 the Dominion government established the position of undersecretary of state for external affairs to give Canada a voice in foreign affairs. Cooler heads realized that the Dominion was not ready to be cut adrift in shark-infested diplomatic waters. But Canadians did want a more active role in negotiations with the United States.[16] This new Canadian willingness to take charge was evident in the three impending wildlife protection treaties. In each case, Canadians took the lead to mold the treaties to their own interests.

The Canadian demand for more autonomy coincided with a British desire to teach the Canadians some responsibility. In part, the British had been appalled by Canada's disorganized approach to the boundary dispute; as a frustrated Lord Grey noted, there was "no record, no continuity, no method, no consistency" in Canadian foreign policy. Granted some autonomy, however, "Canada would be prompt and satisfactory to deal with, instead of the swollen impossible cork, the extraction of which almost bursts a blood vessel."[17] But they also believed that Canadians did have a right to more self-government. Grey and Sir James Bryce, ambassador to the U.S., played key roles in facilitating Canadian efforts to shape relations with the United States. Grey, who came to Canada in December 1904, and Bryce, who came to Washington in March 1907, worked closely with each other and with Secretary of State Elihu Root to find equitable solutions to Canadian-American differences.[18] Thus, the Alaska boundary dispute, which marked a low point in Canadian-American relations, led to the creation of mechanisms to improve communication between the two nations, which in turn facilitated the completion of the treaties.

Under this new system, Americans and Canadians began to deal directly with each other, although Great Britain still held responsibility for ratifying all treaties. The first well-known agreement to come out of this arrangement was the 1909 Boundary Waters Treaty, which established the International Joint Commission (IJC). The treaty was a model of cooperation and fair play; an arbitration panel handled points of contention, and the negotiators gave the IJC a mandate to manage the boundary waters for the common good of both countries. Given the ultimate failure of the 1908 Inland Fisheries Treaty, this was the first successful conservation accord, and the IJC remains a functioning agency.[19]

About the same time, the two nations also resolved the status of the Grand Banks fisheries off the crown colony of Newfoundland. For centuries, Europeans had pursued the vast schools of cod that congregated in this prolific fishery. With the end of the American Revolution, American and British negotiators made the first attempt to divide the fishery. For decades, they disagreed about what rights each side should have. After accords in 1818, 1854, 1871, and 1888 failed to provide a permanent and equitable solution, Root, Bryce, and Grey agreed to submit the dispute to the Permanent Court of Arbitration at The Hague, Netherlands. In 1910 the arbitrators created a compromise, the centerpiece of which was a commission to establish reasonable rules. The longest running feud in North America had reached a peaceful conclusion.[20]

One final point of contention was the ongoing debate about reciprocal trade. In Canada, and to a lesser extent in the United States, reciprocity brought out fierce emotions. People realized that opening up the border to even more trade would bind the two countries almost inextricably. In the early 1890s, both Canadian political parties supported reciprocity, but the United States was in a protectionist mood. By 1910, President William Howard Taft had made reciprocal trade a major goal, and he found an ally in the prime minister, Sir Wilfrid Laurier of the Liberal party, who advocated free trade as advantageous for Canada because it would open up a huge market and lower prices for consumer goods. But the Conservative party, for both economic and political reasons, argued that free trade threatened to make Canadians "hewers of wood and drawers of water" for American industry, and they repeated some of Taft's less astute comments on the accord as proof that the United States wanted mainly to separate Canada from the empire and absorb her into the Union. In the elections of 1911, Laurier staked his campaign squarely on support for reciprocity and got crushed. The Conservative victory indicated that, although Canadians liked Americans well enough, they did not wish to *be* Americans.[21]

All of these conflicts were fundamentally about how Canadians and Americans used common property resources. The cod fishery and boundary waters were obviously shared natural resources. Perhaps more surprisingly, many Canadians saw reciprocal trade as a resource use question. They had front-row seats to watch Americans rip through their natural bounty at a dismaying pace. Canadians feared that freer trade would put all of their resources at the mercy of that same destructive force. On the other side of the border, reciprocity appealed to many Americans as a means of gaining duty-free access to Canada's natural wealth. In reality, Canadians were about as destructive as Americans, but the smaller population base and vast inhospitable areas lessened their impact on nature.

Despite the perception that the two nations had fundamental differences in resource policies, some observers noted that the United States and Canada had much in common. Writing in 1907, the scholar Samuel Moffett spoke for many when he argued that "the Americans and the English-speaking Canadians have been welded into one people." Canadians and Americans read the same magazines and books, attended the same types of schools, shared currency denominations, and used the same slang, "that most delicate test of a people's unity." But most important, the undeniable fact of proximity tightened the Canadian-American economic relationship at the expense of the Canadian-British linkage. These similarities gave Americans and Canadians a basis for mutual trust and a sense of shared identity that prevented disputes from spiraling out of control.[22] Despite some questionable assertions, such as his claim that Canadian political development basically imitated that of the United States, Moffett understood that the links between Americans and Canadians were unbreakable.

The existence and resolution of these various problems indicated two important themes in Canadian-American relations that directly influenced the outcome of the three wildlife protection treaties. First, Canadians and Americans had almost no interest in serious conflict with each other. The great political and cultural similarities defused tension and encouraged governments to search for common ground. Second, those similarities were, however, the source of strong competition for natural resources. Both expanding economies, which were linked to the political and cultural systems, demanded the same kinds of raw materials. Thus, while common national aspirations and beliefs caused disputes over resource use, they also prevented true animosity between the two peoples. The United States and Canada had a unique opportunity to allow their proximity and common interests to create conservation agreements that overrode economic competition.

THE CONTEXT: THE GROWTH
OF THE CONSERVATION MOVEMENT

In addition to the cultural and diplomatic forces pushing the two nations into cooperation on natural resource issues, both nations witnessed the growth and development of the international conservation movement. In the United States, conservationism existed as a branch of the general Progressive movement of the early twentieth century. It had adherents throughout society, although it was largely a movement of the middle class. Among Canadians, the conservation movement was not as popular, but it did have important supporters within the national government.[23] Most important, conservationists in the two countries were in close contact with each other.

The first conservationists were scientists who wanted to use their knowledge to attack the waste of natural resources. Early adherents, such as the famous forester Gifford Pinchot, focused on the need to manage renewable resources for the use of future generations. Foresters and hydrologists, especially, worked together to improve planning and increase efficiency. Even with nonrenewable resources, such as minerals and petroleum, conservationists tried to reduce waste so that supplies would last longer. They urged efficient use and scientific control of America's natural resources. Generally known as utilitarians, they did not aim to save natural beauty or appealing animals but rather to ensure the long-term health of the American economy.[24]

Another branch of the movement was preservationism, led by people such as John Muir. Whereas the utilitarians tended to be elite scientists with government connections, preservationists were a broader group of biologists and other concerned citizens who strove to protect natural beauty from wanton destruction. While not eschewing economics, they tended to agitate for the legal protection of areas and species of aesthetic value, and they excelled at education and public relations. Preservationists often took the lead on wildlife issues, which rarely seemed to attract the interest of the utilitarians.

As trends, preservationism and utilitarianism often intertwined, and in fact conservation as an effective political force depended on strong links between the two. The prime example of the combination was Theodore Roosevelt, who not only had close ties with the utilitarian leaders but also appreciated the beauty of birds and such formations as the Grand Canyon.[25]

Although few people had TR's breadth, certain issues were able to bring people together from throughout the movement. Supporters of the Migratory Bird Treaty and the North Pacific Fur Seal Convention came from across the conservationist spectrum, as they combined aesthetics and economics to justify international action to save these animals.

As a movement, conservationism arose in opposition to the myth of superabundance widely held in American society. From the days of the first European settlement of North America, nature's bounty seemed unlimited, especially in contrast to depleted Europe. For centuries, Americans had found more resources whenever the need arose. Over the next ridge or beyond the next river, one could always discover more land, more trees, or more game. The existence of a vast area of unclaimed frontier discouraged resource users from showing prudence. Loggers removed huge swaths of trees, industrialists polluted air and water, and farmers and ranchers pushed the land beyond its productive capacity, usually without any sense that their practices were not sustainable. While conservationists derided shortsightedness, they generally recognized that capitalistic development was inevitable. A leading conservationist named John Burnham blamed the demise of the bison on "the advance of civilization, which nobody wants to stop, but which couldn't have been stopped if it had been wanted."[26]

Improved transportation and technology, inseparable from industrialization and population growth, compounded the problems caused by the belief in unlimited resources. Railroad expansion opened once pristine wilderness to economic activity and hunting, and improved engines gave sealing and fishing vessels greater range and power. Better firearms and fishing apparatus allowed people to take more resources for the same effort. Because the Canadian economy and society faced many of the same pressures, these patterns repeated themselves in the Dominion. The biologist Aldo Leopold summed up the situation well: "The conquest of nature by machines has led to much unnecessary destruction of resources. Our tools improve faster than we do."[27]

The combination of optimism, improved technology, and economic competition led to what economists call "the fisherman's problem." Fish, seals, birds, and many other types of natural resources are common property—a resource used by many but owned by no one until killed, captured, or extracted. Because there is no sole owner, common property has, almost by definition, many users. These users have no economic incentive to show forbearance in their harvesting because, as the historian Arthur McEvoy has explained, "every harvester knows that if he or she leaves a fish in the water someone else will get it, and the profit, instead."[28] Such behavior, while economically rational, is environmentally unsustainable. Some fish, seals, or birds must be left behind in order for the species to replenish itself, as most harvesters well know. The fisherman's problem, then, is that most fishermen feel compelled to sacrifice the long-term health of their common property unless society, often acting through some level of government, imposes restraints on all users.

The demise of two species of highly mobile, formerly countless animals served as the alarm that roused the wildlife protection impulse in the American conservation movement. The extermination of the passenger pigeon and the destruction of the bison herds caused many people to rethink their attitudes toward the environment. When hunters and scientists could no longer find species once thought to be indestructible, it was a clear signal that nature could no longer take the beating Americans were dishing out. One writer expressed the hope that the extinction of the passenger pigeon "should forever teach us that our wildlife is ours only in trust and that we owe much to succeeding generations."[29] Belated action by conservationists barely saved the bison from extinction, but the passenger pigeon survived only in the imagination of birdwatchers, who occasionally mistook mourning doves for the extinct *Ectopistes migratorius*.[30]

The destruction of these and other species indicated that, in a radical change in earth's history, the market determined which species became extinct. As John Burnham assessed the situation, "The buffalo and the wild pigeon went because of commercialism."[31] Nature continued to eliminate species that could not adapt to a changing environment; now the market removed those that had more value dead than alive, including food animals, fur bearers, and predators. At the turn of the century, many species of birds, mammals, and fish carried a price tag. Under the basic law of supply and demand, as a species became more scarce, individual animals became more valuable, and hunting pressure increased. Hunters and fishermen usually did not set out to destroy their target species, but market forces did nothing to encourage restraint.[32]

Therefore, conservationists searched for alternatives to these market forces in an effort to regulate shared resources. They sought to safeguard natural resources by combining scientific knowledge with government power. This combination was supposed to ensure impartiality. In theory, scientists pursued only the truth and government officials desired only to serve the national interest. In the words of the historian Samuel Hays, "Conservationists envisaged . . . a political system guided by the ideal of efficiency and dominated by the technicians who could best determine how to use it." [33] This attitude prevailed in both Canada and the United States, thus easing the way for bilateral cooperation.

In a culture that enriched, or at least tolerated, those who ruined common resources, the only recourse for conservationists was government action. Beginning in the 1880s, a small group of dedicated people lobbied state legislatures to protect wildlife, but for a variety of reasons they gradually concluded that only the federal government could do an adequate job. First, state regulations were often no better than the unregulated market. Like individuals, states saw themselves as competing with each other. A state that restricted the hunting of migratory animals only left more in the pool for other states' hunters. Second, in order to get complete, uniform coverage throughout the United States, conservationists had to pound laws through more than forty state legislatures instead of one Congress. Third, some resources, such as the fur seals, did not fall under any state's jurisdiction.

The next step, then, was to legitimize federal control over those species that, because of their range, migratory movements, or economic value, the states could not protect. With its forestry, fishery, mining, and other bureaus, the federal government had in fact been active in natural resource policy for decades. But conservationists wanted Washington's intervention into traditional states' rights areas. The first step in this direction was the Lacey Act of 1900, which used federal police powers to regulate interstate commerce in game birds.[34] From that point on, conservationists waged a steady battle to broaden federal authority.

The search for a means to broaden federal power led to the use of the national treaty power to centralize conservation policy. Some resources, such as the fur seals, were beyond state control and demanded an international solution. Others, such as the inland fisheries and migratory birds, had traditionally been the domain of the states. But with international competition destroying these resources, which were themselves migratory, the only solution was to seek international, cooperative agreements. U.S.-Canadian treaties could ensure the uniformity of regulations—and therefore the means to protect common property—throughout the whole area north of the Rio Grande.

Introduction

The growing conservation movement combined with shifting Canadian-American relations to create an atmosphere for international environmental cooperation. In 1908, the two governments signed the Inland Fisheries Treaty to regulate the fisheries of Puget Sound, the Great Lakes, and other boundary waters. In 1911, they joined with Russia and Japan to halt the destructive practice of pelagic sealing in the North Pacific. In 1916, they agreed to the Migratory Bird Treaty, which established protective regulations for most of the species of birds north of the Rio Grande. But the mere signing of an agreement did not guarantee actual protection for the designated species. Real protection came only when treaty proponents could convince citizens and statesmen that such protection mattered.

The final outcome of these efforts to internationalize wildlife conservation depended on the intersection of scientific evidence, sentimental regard for wild animals, and the economic interests of opponents and supporters of a particular treaty. There was no magic formula for success or failure, but treaty supporters recognized the importance of having scientific, ethical, and economic justifications for protecting certain animals. All three treaties generated opposition from those who predicted economic hardship or questioned the constitutionality of the agreements, and conservationists had to muster a broad base of support to counter the opponents. Treaty supporters also had to worry about the politicians and majority of the population who were fundamentally apathetic about conservation issues, people who needed to be shaken from their lethargy by compelling arguments. Thus, as with the modern environmentalists, the Progressive conservationists found themselves grasping for any weapon in complex political battles in which no one factor determined victory or defeat.

Scientists provided much of the basic groundwork for the treaties, as most parties accepted their impartiality. In the Progressive era, scientists had the respect of their nation, which often heeded their warnings. By documenting and protesting the decline of fish, seals, and birds, they assured that those species would not slip away quietly, as the passenger pigeon had. All three treaties depended on evidence that government scientists gathered. Scientists also provided a valuable model for diplomats in their ability to emphasize professional collaboration over nationalistic competition. Organizations such as the American Fisheries Society spanned the Canadian-

American border and encouraged cooperation, although scientists were certainly not immune to jingoism.

Scientific evidence also helped conservationists make utilitarian arguments about the economic importance of these treaties. For most citizens, the decline of fish, seals, or birds did not seem to have any direct impact on their lives. It was up to conservationists to persuade people that, in fact, the demise of these species would siphon money out of their wallets. The opponents of each treaty complicated that task by fighting to protect their own economic interests, usually by pointing out the hardships such an agreement would impose. Thus, in the battle to win the rational economic minds of legislators and voters, treaty supporters found themselves relying on scientific evidence to suggest the benefits of protection.

But utilitarian arguments alone could not determine the ultimate fate of each treaty, as aesthetics played a crucial role. The preservationist wing of the movement focused naturally on the beauty of the animals to be protected and, at times, anthropomorphized them wildly. Some conservationists worried that sentiment, like dynamite, could be dangerous if used improperly. Burnham summed up this ambivalence: "Sentiment is one of the finest of human attributes if converted into constructive activity — otherwise it is an unmitigated curse." [35] Still, they turned to it, because constructive use of aesthetics was crucial in mobilizing the rank and file of the conservation movement and the general public.

In the end, the success or failure of each treaty came down to the ability of conservationists to justify it on both sentimental and economic grounds. In the case of the Inland Fisheries Treaty, supporters had no aesthetic arguments to use — because few people found fish beautiful — and few conservationists rallied around the agreement. Therefore the advocates, consisting mainly of a few government scientists and state fisheries officials, focused on economic arguments that were largely hypothetical. Their opponents were able to counter by emphasizing the immediate economic hardship that the treaty's regulations would bring. With little support and fierce opposition, the treaty never became law.

The North Pacific Fur Seal Convention succeeded when conservationists were able to convert public concern for the species's welfare and scientific proof that the seal was endangered into an economic arrangement that was beneficial to both sides. Because conservation coincided with long-term American economic interests, once proponents of cooperation convinced American diplomats of the merits of their approach, there was very little opposition in the United States to the concept of seal conservation. But in Canada, where economic interests and legal precedents did not mesh easily with American concepts of conservation, the reasons for conservation did not become so apparent until the seal teetered on the brink of extinction. Fortunately, the Canadian government relented, and the seal population rebounded within ten years.

Finally, the Migratory Bird Treaty was the natural product of the growing popularity of birds in both countries and the mounting scientific evidence that bird protection made good agricultural policy. When combined with the weakening of the economic powers that opposed tough bird protection laws, these forces produced the strongest of the three Canadian-American wildlife protection treaties — one that is still in force today. Treaty opponents tried to argue that it violated the constitution, removed a vital source of food from America's tables, and encouraged elitism, but they had no argument as powerful as the basic aesthetic appeal of birds and their yeoman work as insectivores.

The debates over science, sentiment, and economics were, below the surface, about whether to take a short-term or long-term view of the resource use problems. Diplomats on both sides found it very easy to take a short-term approach, as they viewed these issues as minor impediments to the larger Anglo-American rapprochement. The existence of an agreement often meant more to them than its effectiveness. Likewise, those with direct economic interests also took a short-term view of these questions. Those who live on the whims of nature can rarely afford to plan their resource use years in advance; rare has been the fisherman who begs for more regulation to guarantee the future of his livelihood. Fortunately, the resource users and diplomats often clashed, allowing their conflicting attitudes about the need for treaties to overwhelm their mutual interest in avoiding thorough, long-term solutions.

In contrast, conservationists and scientists were able to take a long-term approach to these resource issues. For scientists, the advent of Darwinian theories certainly cemented the understanding that life on earth was ancient and not to be destroyed frivolously. They could see beyond immediate economic concerns, in part because they needed to save species for future scientific studies. For their part, conservationists were, by their nature, concerned with maintaining resources for posterity. The famed scientist, conservationist, and president of Stanford University David Starr Jordan knew that "there is scarcely any issue of greater importance before the American people, because if we do not save the birds and the game while they are living we can never get them back again."[36] If scientists and conservationists could convince the American people that, in fact, planning for the future was crucial, then they could win their battles for the treaties.

Whether or not these treaties hold lessons for the modern counterparts of the Progressive conservationists is up to those who currently work for international conservation. It would certainly be easy to dismiss these agreements as conservative solutions to simple problems in a distant era. Compared to the biodiversity agreement signed in 1992–93, the Migratory Bird Treaty seems almost quaint and certainly flawed. But without that treaty it is easy to imagine the extinction of several species and hard to imagine the many subsequent steps to preserve habitat and broaden bird protection. And, just as important, the leaders of the Progressive conservationists faced many of the same hurdles that loom today — dissent in the movement, fierce economic opposition from people fearful for their livelihoods, apathy among the general public, favoritism toward certain issues and species, skepticism from diplomats, and legal challenges. While the environmental problems today are different, and certainly more complex, their solutions still require cooperation among various professions, good public relations, and economic and sentimental rationales.

PART I

THE INLAND

FISHERIES TREATY

Nothing has caused more tension in U.S.-Canadian relations than disputes over fishery rights. With voracious appetites for seafood on both sides of the border, adjoining coasts on two oceans, and steadily improving fishing methods, Americans and Canadians have been in constant competition for fish. This competitive use of aquatic resources has often pushed the relationship to the breaking point and just as frequently forced the United States and the British empire to devise some new method to resolve their differences — at least temporarily. Although the boundary water fisheries never produced the same level of controversy or received as much attention as did the Grand Banks off Newfoundland, concern for their status led to one of the earliest efforts to promote international conservation of wild animals.

The Inland Fisheries Treaty of 1908 stood as the first attempt to combine a scientific approach to conservation with a diplomatic approach to easing international tension. The treaty covered the Great Lakes and Puget Sound, as well as a few other minor fisheries, including Lake of the Woods, Passamaquoddy Bay, the St. Croix River, Lake Champlain, and Lake Memphremagog. The political borders that bisected these bodies of water hindered the uniform regulation of the fisheries but did nothing to prevent the movement of fish and fishermen. Canadian fishermen came to American ports to sell their catches for higher prices, while American fishermen crossed into Canadian waters in pursuit of fish. Both practices angered the Canadian government and certain economic interests, which led to aggressive policies toward American fishermen. In an atmosphere of increasing tension and declining fisheries, treaty proponents hoped to create a set of common rules that would resolve the dispute.

The treaty grew out of a two-part problem. First, all along the border fishermen overtaxed the fisheries. Both Americans and Canadians were guilty of expanding their operations beyond the carrying capacity of the waters. Like most people in the two countries, fishermen operated under the assumption that they could not exhaust such a vast resource base. The depletion of the boundary water fisheries was consistent with the general unregulated, unplanned exploitation — at times destruction — of natural resources in North America.

Second, multiple political jurisdictions caused regulatory chaos on the boundary waters. Each body of water had at least two, and as many as five, governments with some sort of jurisdiction. States and provinces were reluctant to impose strict regulations on their taxpaying, voting fishermen, who might then find themselves at a competitive disadvantage. Particularly in the United States, legislators tended to outlaw only those methods that fishermen from neighboring states and provinces preferred, and enforcement on both sides of the border was usually lax. Under these circumstances, the various local governments were not likely to come to any sort of agreement on efficient, uniform controls. There was no incentive to toughen laws, and states and provinces could not legally enter into conventions stipulating cooperative control. Only an international agreement could provide the necessary uniformity.

The fisheries' status as transnational common property resources made regulation difficult. The ability of fish to cross boundaries put them beyond ownership until caught, and the large number of fishermen encouraged competition instead of cooperation. A state or province that might have been willing to regulate a resource wholly within its borders, such as timber or minerals, could do little with a fluid resource forever flowing across its borders. That fundamental difficulty was compounded because fish had no aesthetic value to most people, so no preservationist force emerged to lobby for their protection. Unlike birds and seals, fish were solely a commodity, swimming nuggets of gold free to the taker. The inability of any one government to control international common property made fisheries conservation a diplomatic issue, but the inability of private citizens to see the need for fisheries conservation prevented diplomatic success.

In the end, the Inland Fisheries Treaty failed because the American government and fishermen were unwilling to accept cooperative restrictions on the right to catch fish. Politicians in Congress and the White House were unable to see beyond the short-term national interest of maximizing gain at another nation's expense. In contrast to the vocal opposition of many fishermen—who actively encouraged congressional opposition to fisheries regulation—conservationists and scientists failed to speak out about the treaty. At a time when leaders in Washington needed someone to counter the influence of the fishermen, scientists were too few and conservationists uninterested.

1

A Problem of Scale,
1892–1897

The fisheries along the Canadian-American border are a diverse lot. On either coast, they include bays and rivers, with species that move between salt water and fresh. Between the coasts, lakes of varying sizes and depths straddle the border, from tiny Lake Memphremagog to giant Lake Superior. Each body of water has its own ecosystem, with differing carrying capacities and species mixtures. And each body of water has its own problems and opportunities. The freshwater lakes and saltwater coastal bays are quite unlike each other. Passamaquoddy Bay on the East Coast has little in common with Puget Sound on the West Coast. Lakes Huron and Superior have some things in common, but conditions are much different in Lake Erie. The one thing they all hold in common is a path of development from subsistence use by Native Americans to destructive commercial fishing as part of an industrializing North American society.

In the competitive market economies of Canada and the United States, people had incentives to practice unsustainable methods of fishing. As a result, tension among fishermen was high, especially among groups separated by local or national boundaries. Fishermen from one state or province were quick to blame their problems on fishermen from other locales and slow to consider changing their own methods. It became especially easy to fault those on the other side of the international border, who were both competitors and foreigners. From the Atlantic to the Pacific, tempers flared as fishermen sought to restrict their foreign competition. By the 1890s, control of the fisheries had become a diplomatic issue.

In 1892, Canada and the United States responded to the increasing animosity among fishermen by establishing a two-member scientific commission to address the decline of the fisheries. This diplomatic approach revealed two important, and partially contradictory, assumptions about the place of these fisheries in diplomacy. First, unlike the long-running feud over the cod fishery off Newfoundland, this issue did not intrigue high-ranking diplomats, who were happy to leave it in the hands of scientists. Second, by wrapping all of the boundary waters into one package, the diplomats indicated that they were more interested in a political resolution — a sort of magic wand approach — than in a rational scientific solution to an old and complex problem. Two scientists, no matter their diligence, could not hope to tackle the political, economic, and ecological problems inherent in overfishing along such a huge international border.

The two scientists had their mandate, however, and after four years they filed an exhaustive report that confirmed the unsustainability of the prevalent fishing methods and presented some suggestions for regulations. But they left unwritten one conclusion that might have made a difference: the boundary water fisheries could not be regulated by one treaty, law, or commission. The diversity and complexity of the fisheries and the economic and political strength of fishermen combined to make one uniform approach unfeasible. Perhaps the scientists understood this central problem of their effort, but it was not their job to establish the diplomatic framework to solve the problem.

THE BOUNDARY WATERS

Beginning on the East Coast, the first body of water on the border is an inlet of the Bay of Fundy, Passamaquoddy Bay, between Maine and New Brunswick. Dramatic tides and a rocky shore make fishing dangerous in these largely Canadian waters, but the American lobster (*Homarus americanus*) has rewarded fishermen for their efforts. In addition, common ocean fish, such as the mackerel, come into the bay when the tide is high. The St. Croix River empties into the bay after running for seventy-five miles, mostly along the Maine–New Brunswick border. A number of anadromous species cross through the bay to head up the river to spawn. Historically, the most important of these have been the Atlantic salmon (*Salmo salar*), which was quite prolific prior to the 1850s, the alewife (*Pumolobos pseudoharengus*), smelt (*Osmerus mordax*), and various fish from the herring family.[1]

Moving inland, glacier-carved Lake Memphremagog and Lake Champlain provide the next international fisheries. The former is mainly in Quebec but reaches down into Vermont, while the latter stretches for 125 miles along the New York–Vermont border and into Quebec. Both lakes are oligo-

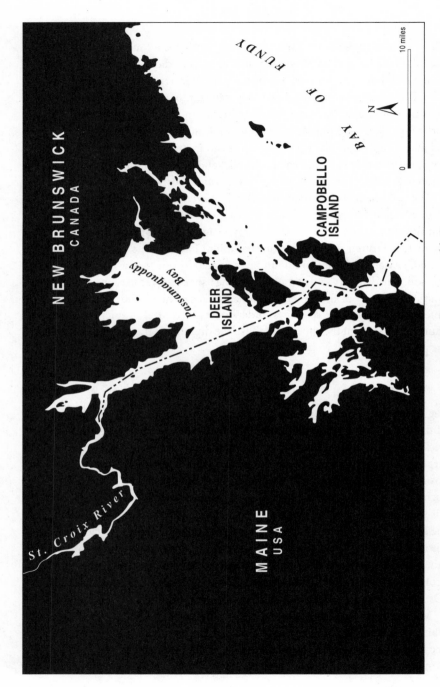

MAP 1. St. Croix River and Passamaquoddy Bay

trophic, meaning that they are nutrient poor and too deep for sunlight to reach the lake bed in most places, so that they cannot support much life. Neither lake has an abundance of fish, but both have schools of perch, pike, and a local variation of the whitefish, all of which spawn in feeder streams. A few commercial fishermen have made a precarious living on Lake Champlain, but the general scarcity of fish and the species distribution make the lakes better suited for sport fishing.[2]

Farther inland, the Great Lakes lie as the great source of freshwater fish. A product of the Wisconsin Glaciation about 15,000 years ago, they assumed their current form only 5,000 years ago. At 95,000 square miles and 67 trillion gallons of water, they are the largest body of fresh water on the planet. Approximately 150 species of fish from the Arctic Ocean, the Atlantic Ocean, and the Mississippi River filled the niches available as the new aquatic midwest of the continent formed. Of the five lakes, only Lake Michigan does not form part of the U.S.-Canada border.[3]

At the close of the nineteenth century, the two most important species were the whitefish (*Coregonus clupeiformis*) and the lake trout (*Cristivomer namaycush*). Both were excellent market species because they were big, numerous, and tasty. The whitefish commanded such culinary praise that it even inspired a poem of dubious merit:

> All friends of good living by tureen and dish,
> Concur in exalting this prince of a fish;
> So fine in a platter, so tempting a fry,
> So rich on a gridiron, so sweet in a pie,
> That even before it salmon must fail,
> And that mighty *bonne-bouche,* of the land-beaver's tail.[4]

Whitefish could weigh as much as thirty pounds and tended to stay in large schools throughout the year. Trout attained twice that weight and generally dispersed more. Whitefish were more common than trout, especially in the two eastern lakes.[5]

Two other species lived in the lakes in sufficient abundance to make them commercially and ecologically valuable. The lake herring, or cisco (*Argyrosomus artedi*), may well have been the most numerous species in the lakes. It was not, though, an ideal market species. A really big cisco might reach twenty-four ounces, but the vast majority weighed less than one pound. In addition, herring were not especially palatable, and they spoiled easily.

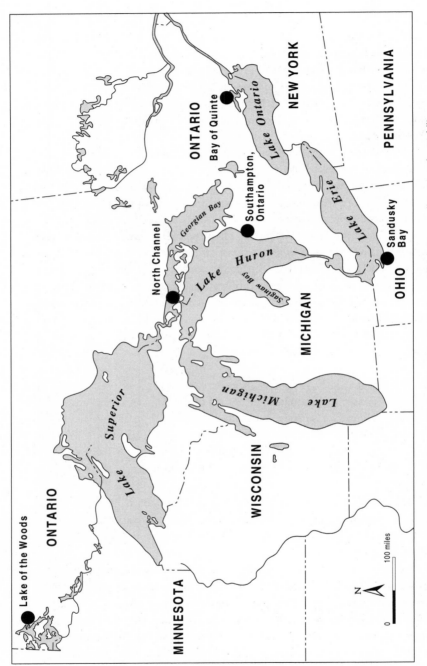

MAP 2. Great Lakes and Lake of the Woods. (Adapted from Bogue, "To Save the Fish")

They were, however, easy to catch, because they were abundant and congregated in large schools. Facing both human and piscine predators, a herring's life was short and dangerous. Yet their prodigious capacity to reproduce allowed them to withstand overfishing a few generations longer than either the trout or whitefish.[6] The final of the four most valuable lake species was the sturgeon (*Acipenser rubicundus*), the largest species by far, with adults weighing up to 400 pounds. Covered with something akin to armor plates, mature sturgeon face no predators, yet they are mainly bottom-feeding omnivores—a sort of fish equivalent to the brontosaurus. Because of their feeding habits, they prefer shallow water, and they do not, therefore, frequent the deeper lakes. Sturgeon supply caviar and isinglass, a gelatinous substance used in jellies and glues.[7]

A number of other edible species populated the lakes before commercial fishing became common. The Atlantic salmon lived in Lake Ontario, their path into the other lakes blocked by Niagara Falls. Black bass, a popular sport fish, were widespread but not very numerous. Catfish were also common in Lake Ontario, although not in the other lakes. Other common but not especially valuable species included pike, pickerel, perch, saugers, suckers, sheepshead, carp, and eels.[8]

The easternmost of the lakes is Ontario, which lies east of Niagara Falls bounded by New York, Ontario, and the St. Lawrence River. From a fisheries standpoint, Ontario has been the least productive of the Great Lakes. The smallest of the lakes at 7,339 square miles, Ontario bottoms out at over 750 feet. Generally oligotrophic, it has one highly productive area, the shallow Bay of Quinte, off the northeast end, which is completely surrounded by Prince Edward County, Ontario. In most places, though, the bottom falls off abruptly from the shore, reducing the productive waters to a small portion of the lake's total volume.[9]

Next along the border is Lake Erie, the most productive part of this freshwater sea, bordered by Ontario, New York, Pennsylvania, Ohio, and Michigan. The lake has an area of about 10,000 square miles, and it is the shallowest of the five, never deeper than 210 feet. In contrast to the other lakes that seem cut from stone, Erie is in a sandy basin. Sunlight penetrates to the lake bed and combines with rich nutrients to provide a solid basis for fish populations. One scientific study described the lake as "practically one continuous fishing grounds."[10] The part of the lake west of an imaginary line between Point Pelee, Ontario, and Sandusky, Ohio, is especially productive and usually no more than a few fathoms deep. The western end still has the remnants of a vast marsh where the Maumee River enters the lake and numerous islands and shoals, all of which make for excellent spawning grounds. The eastern part of the lake is deep enough to accommodate those fish that need cool water during the hot summer months. In the middle of the south shore, Sandusky Bay provides another shallow, productive fisheries area.[11]

Biologically, Lake Erie's fisheries resemble those in the other lakes, with two important differences. First, Erie herring are significantly larger than the herring of other lakes — although still smaller than trout or whitefish — making them much more valuable commercially. Second, there is a major behavioral change in response to the vast shallow area at the western end of the lake, which is subject to temperature extremes. Summer heat and winter ice force most of the fish into the more stable deep water in the eastern part of the lake. Consequently, almost every species undertakes a regular migration that follows the path of the international border, moving west for the spring and fall and east for the summer and winter.[12] In the other Great Lakes, fish move between inshore spawning grounds and deeper water mid lake.

North and west of Lake Erie, between Ontario and Michigan, lies Lake Huron, with its vast Georgian Bay. Huron reaches depths of 750 feet and covers 23,000 square miles. Because of the lake's great depth, Georgian Bay and Saginaw Bay (in Michigan) account for most of Huron's fish production. Until the early twentieth century, both whitefish and trout were fairly common in the lake, and an unusually slim subspecies of herring was abundant in Saginaw Bay. As with Lakes Ontario and Superior, fishing in Lake Huron has always been best along the shallow edges when fish come inshore to spawn.[13]

The last, deepest, and largest of the Great Lakes, Superior, proves that the size of the lake does not correlate with the value of the fishery. Bordered by Ontario, Minnesota, Wisconsin, and Michigan, the lake covers almost 32,000 square miles and reaches depths of 1,300 feet. Its rugged coastline provides a few shallow sandy areas, such as Thunder Bay, for fish to spawn, but the lake bottom drops off quickly. From east to west, the vast middle of the lake holds very few marketable fish, so that less than 25 percent of the lake's surface is productive for fishermen. Like Huron, Superior is an aquatic desert, but a few species thrive in certain regions, especially lake trout and whitefish.[14]

Due west of Lake Superior, filling 1,500 square miles between Minnesota and the western extremity of Ontario, is Lake of the Woods. With thousands of islands scattered around the central area, known as the Big Traverse, and a shallow, sandy bottom, "there can be few, if any, sheets of water its size in the world which give a greater annual yield of fishery products."[15] Like Lake Erie, the lake is naturally eutrophic, with huge summer algal blooms that shut down fishing for weeks. The dominant fish in the lake is the sturgeon, which thrives in shallow, eutrophic lakes. Whitefish and trout are present, but the dearth of deep water—which they need to withstand summer heat and winter cold—limits their numbers.[16]

The final boundary water fishery is on the West Coast, between Washington and British Columbia, where the Fraser River enters the Strait of Georgia, which in turn enters Haro and Rosario straits—an area which for convenience is sometimes referred to as the greater Puget Sound region. Hundreds of species of fish live in these waters, but the six types of salmon dominated the fishing economy. The salmon pass through the boundary waters on their way from the ocean to their spawning grounds along the upper reaches of the various streams and rivers that empty into Georgia, Haro, and Rosario straits. All of the salmon species return to their natal streams to spawn and die after a life span of two to six years, depending on the species.[17]

Of the salmon species, the sockeye salmon (*Oncorhynchus nerka*) reigns as the commercial fisherman's favorite. It weighs only five to eight pounds—compared to twenty to thirty for the chinook salmon—and is considered especially palatable. The sockeye that come through the Strait of Juan de Fuca confine their spawning runs largely to the Fraser River and its tributaries, which run more than 700 miles into the interior of British Columbia, thus concentrating the species at the mouth of the river. Because they have to travel farther upstream than other salmon species, the sockeye begin their spawning runs earlier, thus leaving them in excellent condition as they enter the river mouth. The sockeye also have difficulty adjusting to the lower salinity level of the sound and river, so they stay near the mouth of the Fraser from twelve to twenty-four days before heading upstream.[18] They have evolved a life cycle that concentrates them near a point of human habitation when they are at the peak of their value but have not yet reproduced. In other words, they are vulnerable to disaster.

The boundary waters between the United States and Canada, then, contained valuable fisheries, but they were also limited in potential productivity. The various lakes were either fairly small or had vast unproductive areas. The two coastal boundary fisheries were based on a small number

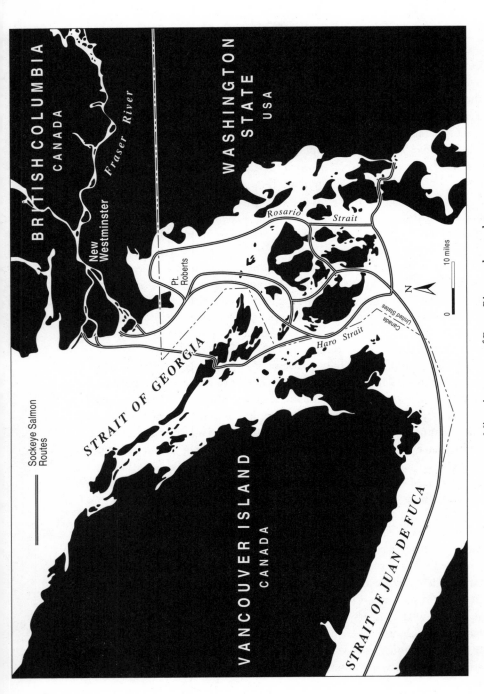

MAP 3. Migration routes of Fraser River sockeye salmon.
(Adapted from Roos, *Restoring Fraser River Salmon*; Stein, *Archaeology of San Juan Island*)

of species concentrating for a short time before each headed up a single river. There were times and places of abundance, but there were more times and places of paucity. And more important, the boundary water fisheries exhibited a diversity that ensured that no single set of rules could govern them. From fresh water to salt water, from anadromous salmon to bottom-dwelling sturgeon, the boundary waters were complex, economically valuable, ecologically important, and in danger.

EARLY FISHING EFFORTS

As long as they have lived near the boundary waters, humans have taken advantage of fish as a food source. Because the fish come inshore to spawn on a regular basis, they are easy to catch. Their predictable patterns of movement allowed Native American tribes to plan on using fish as a food source during certain parts of the year. Early European explorers and settlers found the fish to be an abundant and necessary source of sustenance. As the country around each of the fisheries became more settled, a predictable pattern of increasing use set in. Within just a few decades, most of the fisheries had reached their sustainable limits.

The early development of each of the Great Lakes fisheries followed a similar course. In each case, white settlers found seemingly unlimited fishing opportunities in the inshore waters, and they used seines to trap the fish. As local populations and commercial possibilities grew, some people turned to full-time fishing and more elaborate nets. The ease with which the first settlers had captured fish apparently deluded subsequent generations into believing that the lakes were full of fish, when in fact the large concentrations were seasonal and local. In each lake, then, the early period of fishing ended when commercial fishermen located the best places and methods.

Before Europeans came to the lakes, Native Americans had already discovered the best fishing places. Along the less productive lakes, such as Superior, Indians positioned their villages to take advantage of the spawning grounds and other inshore areas where fish were abundant. Some used dip nets to catch whitefish, others used spears to kill sturgeon; whatever species were present, the local tribes found ways to harvest them. Unlike the other lakes, Erie offered riches that drew Native Americans from hundreds of miles away. According to the historian Harlan Hatcher, people came from as far as present-day Kentucky to fish among the islands of western Lake Erie.[19]

Europeans in the region marveled at the abundance of fish in the spawning grounds and took advantage of the knowledge and fishing techniques of the local Indian tribes. French explorers in the seventeenth century reported that the lakes were teeming with huge fish that were easy to catch. In the next century, British trappers and military officers found similar conditions. During the War of 1812, British and American soldiers in the Detroit region had no problem surviving on fish when their supplies failed. In the 1840s, the settlers at Sault Ste. Marie, on the north tip of Lake Huron, lived through the winter by ice fishing. According to one report, a person could catch fifty trout in a day, many of them "weighing half as much as a man." [20] Given the harsh weather and remote locale, probably many communities along the western and northern shores of the lakes lived comfortably through hard winters on fish alone.

On both sides of the border, people learned quickly the commercial possibilities that the schools of fish presented. As settlers established farms, trading posts, and other activities along lakeshores, they knew that they could depend on fish as a source of food. Like the Indians before them, they used simple tools to catch a few fish when they needed them. In addition, they began to use seines to corral larger schools. [21] Although they were not especially elaborate devices, seines did allow people to enter the market on a part-time basis. By 1795, there was already something of a commercial fishery developing on Lake Erie. Twenty years later, seiners in Maumee Bay were selling their catch to the growing town of Detroit. By 1833, seven vessels were working the western end of the lake with seines and lines. [22]

In 1831, Alexander MacGregor settled on the Fishing Islands, just north of Southampton on the Canadian side of Lake Huron. With a few men, he perfected a system for shoreline fishing. One man acted as a lookout in a tall tree; when he spotted the clouds of silvery fish coming toward shore, other men would row out a short distance and cast their seines around the school. The fishermen then brought the nets close to the shore, where they would throw the fish onto land for others to cure and pack in barrels. One such excursion could net 400 barrels of herring. Repeating a scene from previous years on Lakes Erie and Ontario, MacGregor found that his men were taking far too many fish for their own use, and he needed a commercial outlet. He too found a market in Detroit, selling 3,000 barrels at a dollar each. [23]

Similar events occurred on Lake Superior, where agents of the American Fur Company were contemplating the potential value of whitefish. As early as 1823, they recognized that they could give Ohioans whitefish rather than cash for eggs and butter. In 1839, they shipped 1,000,000 pounds of fish eastward and had fishing camps at a few places around the lake. The company's failure in 1842, in the wake of the panic of 1837, temporarily halted commercial fishing on the lake, but settlement of the area in the 1840s led to a resurgence by 1850.[24]

On Puget Sound, fishing followed a pattern similar to that on the western Great Lakes. For Native Americans, the salmon species were "the most important and most dependable food source of the region."[25] Tribes held communal fishing grounds, which they inhabited seasonally. From land and canoe, they caught salmon with harpoons or dip nets, depending on the depth and speed of the spawning streams. Early European explorers marveled at the size and abundance of the fish, as well as the skill of the native fishermen.

Agents of the Hudson's Bay Company took an interest in Indian techniques of drying the catch. By 1823, they were experimenting with similar methods and packing the salmon for export. Their first few shipments to London arrived as a rancid soup, leading to a general dampening of enthusiasm for the idea. They continued to ship salmon to Canton and Hawaii, but this first attempt at commercial fishing off the Fraser River showed little profit. Thus, well into the 1850s, the salmon were a food source primarily for the locals, both whites and Indians.[26]

Across the border, then, people developed the fisheries along a common path. It began with Native Americans, who practiced standard subsistence fishing in a manner that probably did little harm to the ecosystem. European explorers then came upon Indian villages, learned of the productivity of the waters, and proceeded to eat well. When settlers arrived, they took advantage of the abundant inshore fisheries to support themselves. Before long, they began to turn to small-scale commercial fishing using seines. Roughly simultaneously, an ambitious entrepreneur would dare to fund full-time commercial fishing. Success, whether by him or a successor, was usually the first step toward the full-scale commercialization of fishing on that body of water.

THE END OF SUSTAINABLE FISHING

Although each fishery followed a unique path, they all headed for the same destination. A combination of entrepreneurial spirit, rampant competition, technological development, pollution, and misperceptions about fishery ecology helped push the various species into decline. As the areas around the boundary waters became more populated, pollution and demand for fish both increased rapidly. Aquatic ecosystems, especially those of the Great Lakes, were more fragile than most people recognized, and they could not withstand increased human pressures. From coast to coast, the fisheries peaked quickly and then began a slow decline.

Fishing on the St. Croix River was the first to fail. Fishermen had been enthusiastic about building weirs on the river and its upstream tributaries, and they had caused some damage. In 1825, however, entrepreneurs built a dam across the river at the edge of its tidal waters, making any spawning run up the river nearly impossible. By 1894, three more dams blocked the river, although each had a poorly maintained fish ladder. Hypothetically, a salmon could find its way from the Atlantic into the St. Croix and up to an ancient spawning ground, but there were very few left to try it.[27]

An increase in pollution added to fish woes. Bark and sawdust from decades of lumbering covered the bottom of the river and floated out into the bay, suffocating plants and animals alike and disrupting the ecosystem. In addition, large logs scoured and destroyed the river bottom spawning beds. Industrialization also brought a collection of tanneries that lined the banks of the river and its tributaries. The final threat was from the St. Croix Cotton Mill at Milltown, New Brunswick, which dumped both chemicals and cotton fibers directly into the river.[28] Between the industries and the dams, fish had almost no chance in the St. Croix River by the turn of the century.

The real problems, though, were in the Great Lakes, where new types of nets, industrial pollution, and the rapidly increasing number of fishermen were destroying the fisheries. In many ways, the fundamental culprit was ignorance. Ignorant of ecology and ichthyology, many people believed the early pioneers' reports that the lakes were teeming with fish. Few understood that Superior, Ontario, and Huron were actually not that hospitable for fish.[29] Fishermen quickly learned that only a few places in those deeper lakes, usually the shallow bays, had enough food and shelter to be good fishing grounds, but even they did not always grasp the idea that the lakes' productivity was limited. Likewise, most people did not realize the extent of the damage caused by pollution, erosion, and industrial development. Changes were occurring on the bottoms of the lakes and in the feeder streams that people could not see or imagine, and the fish were in decline.

All throughout the Great Lakes, fishermen switched from seines to gill nets as they moved from inshore to deeper waters. Fishermen made gill nets of twine, which was tarred once or twice per year to keep it from rotting.

They attached stone sinkers on the bottom and wooden floats on the top to keep the net suspended vertically. For such a simple instrument, the gill net's premise was rather complex. A fish that swam into the net would not be able to squeeze through the mesh; as it attempted to back out, its gills caught on the twine, thus entrapping it. Although similar in appearance to a seine, the gill net made fishing much more efficient. Seines were good only at scooping up large schools of fish, but gill nets could be left in the water to catch any passing fish of a particular size. Seines, then, were useful only when manned, but gill nets would continue to catch fish as long as they were in the water.[30]

Fishermen varied the size of the mesh depending on the species pursued, which made regulating gill nets difficult. In pursuit of sturgeon, fishermen used a mesh of nine to thirteen inches; for whitefish and trout, three to six inches; for herring, two to three inches. Decreasing yields caused fishermen to gradually adopt smaller meshes. In the 1830s, Lake Superior fishermen used six-inch mesh to catch whitefish and trout; by 1900, they were down to three- or four-inch mesh.[31] Of course, the nets could not distinguish among different species of fish, so the mesh really determined only what size of fish got caught. Herring nets often caught undersized, immature whitefish, which fishermen could not save. The fish in the gill net had trouble breathing, and they tended to die quickly. Decomposition then became a problem, especially with herring, so fishermen had to bring their catch to market as soon as possible; they could not stop to sort out the young whitefish and return them to the water.

Gill net fishermen needed a sturdy boat to get to the deeper waters where their nets were most effective at certain times of the year. At first, Great Lakes fishermen used sailboats, but in the 1880s they began to convert to steam-powered tugs. Tugs could operate in rough weather, had a greater range, and had a larger carrying capacity. Depending on the weather conditions and types of fish pursued, tugs deployed anywhere from four to twenty miles of nets. Under the same conditions, sailboats could carry only half as many nets. Individual nets were anywhere from 200 to 600 feet long, and the fishermen set them in groups of two or four. Even a few tugs so equipped could eliminate a large school of fish. Those fishermen who stayed with sails often added steam winches to allow them to haul in more and bigger nets. The growing use of tugs and steam winches, along with smaller-meshed nets, increased the strain on the fishery.[32]

Gill netting throughout the lakes began in earnest in the 1850s as a result of increased demand for fish and improved methods of transportation.

35

Through trial and error, fishermen learned to follow the fishes' seasonal migrations. In the 1880s, the use of nets in the lakes doubled. American fishermen dominated Lake Erie by 1894, with almost 300 boats and 6,000,000 linear feet of nets. At about the same time, fishermen used about 5,000,000 linear feet of gill nets in Superior. There were not enough fish to keep those nets full.[33]

While fishermen were blanketing the open waters with the gill net, they covered the shallow inshore waters with the pound net, which was basically a seine set as a maze and fixed in place by stakes driven into the bottom. A fisherman needed a small boat to maintain a pound net and collect its catch, but the expense of operating such a net was much less than casting gill nets. Still, pound nets were not for part-time fishermen, as seines had been. Like gill nets, pound nets required frequent tending. Depending on the temperature, fishermen had to empty the nets every one to three days, or else the fish would be unmarketable. With a full-time commitment to fishing, pound netters had to run several nets at once to turn a profit.[34]

There are three major parts to a pound net. The lead is a long, large-meshed net set across the fishes' migration route that diverts them from their path into the heart and crib of the net. The pound net works because a fish that encounters an obstacle will seek a way to maneuver around it and return to its normal course. The fish will follow the lead into the heart, which is basically a large funnel with an opening into the crib, also known as the pot. The crib serves to hold the fish until the fisherman checks the net. Some fish will catch their gills in the lead or heart, but most fish are caught swimming in the crib, which, like a seine, has a very fine mesh.[35]

Pound nets work only in shallow water where the bottom is soft enough to set stakes. In the Great Lakes, except for Erie, such places were fairly limited, so the pound nets tended to be clustered. To compensate, fishermen tried to improve their chances both by increasing the size of their nets and by setting a number of nets together. In some cases, the lead extended for a mile out into the lake; in others, the crib totaled over 64,000 cubic feet. Because one net was insufficient to cover overhead costs, most fishermen relied on multiple nets, all set near each other.[36] Most states and Ontario required a minimum spacing of a few hundred feet between nets, but otherwise pound nets were unregulated.

In suitable areas, pound nets were as numerous as gill nets. Shallow Lake Erie, with its muddy bottom, was ideal for this technique. Fishermen first used the nets on the lake in 1850 in Maumee Bay; by 1890, there were more than 1,500 on the American side and nearly 200 on the Canadian. On Lake Huron, there were about 600 pound nets in 1894, and more than 350 of those were in Saginaw Bay. With so many nets competing in such a limited area, it was not uncommon for fishermen to string ten or even twenty nets together. As they had with the gill nets, fishermen followed a general trend toward a smaller mesh size in order to improve their productivity. Throughout the lakes, fishermen were using more and bigger nets with smaller meshes.

Society compounded the fishermen's self-inflicted wounds, as pollution became a widespread problem throughout the Great Lakes. Each year, logging, one of the region's oldest industries, dumped tons of organic matter into the lakes, especially Superior and Huron. In Huron, in fact, logging pollution was truly an international issue because of the large amount of timber that Canadians floated to Michigan. As the logs ground together, the bark stripped off and sank to the bottom. As common, and perhaps more damaging, was the practice of sawdust dumping. Mill operators around the Great Lakes found it easy to dispose of their piles of sawdust in the water.

Industrialization also degraded the lakes. In cities like Cleveland, Hamilton, and Buffalo, heavy industries used the lakes both as a source of fresh water and as a free sewer. In addition, most of these municipalities dumped their garbage and sewage into the lakes, which seemed vast and capable of swallowing up refuse with no ill effect. As late as 1909, an Ontario provincial commission thought that if garbage scows traveled at least ten miles offshore before dumping the refuse would cause little damage.[37]

Farming and logging added to the problem by increasing erosion, which damaged spawning grounds. Massive fires often broke out in the debris left behind by the loggers, thus finishing the job of stripping the land. Without vegetation to hold water, runoff washed soil into the shallow water and ruined spawning grounds. Especially in the area around the Maumee River, draining wetlands and subsequent agricultural practices encouraged runoff that collected the topsoil. This muddy water then washed out to the previously clear spawning beds that whitefish favored. Carp, sauger, and sheepshead — all commercially worthless — could tolerate turbulent water and took over the spawning areas. The result, then, was not a diminution in overall fish production but an alteration of species composition that harmed commercial interests and the ecosystem.[38]

Even without overfishing, the combination of municipal waste, industrial pollution, erosion, and logging debris would have been enough to destroy the natural balance in the lakes. Yet there was no great outcry against the destruction. That silence grew, in part, from the general American and Canadian inability to see fish as wildlife with more than economic value. Framing the issue in purely pecuniary terms, people could surrender the interests of the fisheries to the interests of industrialization. At the time, pollution was just one of the social costs of creating wealth on both sides of the border, and few people advocated government interference in the working of industrial plants. In the words of the historian James Tober, "The driving force of expansion and growth" would have prevailed over any attempt to place wildlife first.[39]

West of the Great Lakes, the decline in fisheries could be traced solely to overfishing, not pollution. For instance, in Lake of the Woods, unregulated fishermen needed less than ten years to damage the most prolific species. Sturgeon dominated the lake in 1895 to the point that there were not enough other fish to sustain a viable industry. Local fishermen had caught 77,000 sturgeon in 1895 alone, at an average weight of twenty-five pounds each. In addition to the fish flesh, they exported 186,700 pounds of caviar and over 5,000 pounds of air bladders. Fishermen set their first pound net in 1887; eight years later, 259 dotted the lake. All of the good spawning and feeding grounds were covered with nets. Although the fishery was still producing sturgeon, the fierce competition had created an unsustainable use of resources.[40]

On the West Coast, the industrialization of the fishery increased pressure on the salmon. Early salmon fishermen had little trouble catching their prey, but selling it was a problem. In 1871, entrepreneurs solved the problem by building a cannery along the Fraser River. Canned salmon became a large piece of the British Columbia export economy within just a few years, and by 1902 there were about fifty canneries along the Fraser. Canneries opened in the less-regulated atmosphere of Washington as well, often with financial backing from Canadian canners. Canned salmon became a very popular export commodity throughout the world, with cases bringing as much as $11 each.[41]

To meet this burgeoning demand, canners turned to technology and management to overcome a number of limiting factors. In 1902, Canadian canners formed the B.C. Packers Association to reduce competition. They signed contracts with independent fishermen and operated their own nets to ensure a constant supply of fish, and they diversified their holdings to protect against bad years. To increase efficiency and decrease labor trouble, in 1903 owners introduced a canning machine known as the "Iron Chink" because it replaced Chinese laborers. In the Pacific Northwest, salmon fishing had truly become an industry, complete with horizontal and vertical integration.[42]

As the industry grew and competition intensified between Canadian and American canners, regulations failed to keep pace. Until 1891, British Columbia had allowed 500 gill nets around the mouth of the Fraser River at New Westminster. In addition, the province limited the size, operation, and placement of each net to ensure that enough fish got through to maintain the stock. In 1891, though, the provincial government loosened the licensing standards, allowing local canners up to twenty nets each. Soon, there were 1,700 gill nets in Canadian waters.[43]

Most likely, British Columbia relaxed its laws in response to a growing American presence in the salmon fishery. While most American fishermen still used the seine, a growing number had switched to the trap net, "the most effective form of apparatus for the capture of the sockeye salmon."[44] First introduced in 1885, there were only twenty-one of this type of pound net in use in 1895, but any wise observer could see that they represented the future. The state of Washington had a reputation for not policing its fisheries, and Canadians worried that that would not change. The American salmon industry was still young, but the incentive for its development was great, and officials in Olympia would not erect obstacles. In 1895, American canneries processed more than five million pounds of American-caught salmon, a fraction of the twenty-five million pounds packed on the Canadian side. But by 1899, Americans packed as many cases as did Canadians.[45]

As was so often the case, improving technology and declining productivity were intertwined in a complex manner throughout the boundary water fisheries. As yields declined, fishermen faced a choice—get out or try harder. Most chose to increase their effort, either setting more and better nets or buying bigger boats. A ruinous cycle set in and destroyed the fisheries. After the initial boom, fishermen had to work harder to maintain their catch levels. But that meant taking fish faster than a species could replenish itself. Fishermen then turned to smaller-meshed nets and other methods to increase their catch. Eventually, with large investments in gear—nets, boats, and so forth—fishermen had to look for some other species upon which to make a profit. The pattern then repeated itself.[46] Some outside force had to break the cycle.

Thus, by the 1890s, fisheries all along the border were expanding rapidly, but the fish populations were not growing. Fishermen often found themselves hoping and believing that they could catch more if they tried harder, and they quickly pushed the fisheries past the point of safe harvesting, or sustainable yield. At the same time that fishermen were exerting more effort, pollution was destroying spawning grounds and altering the lakes and streams that supported fish. Without effective regulations, the fisheries were doomed to a quick demise.

THE FIRST ATTEMPT AT COOPERATIVE REGULATION

The decline of the fisheries was no secret, but it seemed that the solution was. In retrospect, it is apparent that strict international regulations were the best antidote to the fierce international competition that exacerbated the problem of declining fish populations. At the time, some British and American diplomats recognized that the specter of a nasty diplomatic dispute lurked in the boundary waters, but their efforts to vanquish it generated yawns from people who failed to see the need for any action. Those statesmen who tried to eliminate a source of tension by regulating the fisheries had first to persuade others that the issue was important, and then they had to fashion a system that would actually defuse the tension. They hoped that they could address the problems of all of the boundary water fisheries in one fell swoop, but that strategy served in the long run to complicate matters even further.

The first attempt to regulate the boundary water fisheries began in 1892 with discussions between Secretary of State John W. Foster and several Canadian representatives. In October of that year, Foster formally proposed that Canada and the United States conduct a scientific study of the waters in question. The United States Fish Commission and its Dominion counterpart would share information, resources, and manpower in an attempt to satisfy "the mutual interests of their respective citizens and subjects as regards their equal and common benefit in the conservation of food fishes." [47] Foster suggested that he and the British minister to the U.S., Sir Julian Pauncefote, should exchange formal notes on the subject, with the understanding that the scientists' conclusions would be only a basis for future discussions, not binding regulations. On 5 December 1892, Pauncefote informed Foster that Canada agreed to the American proposal.

By stressing conservation and common benefit, Foster acknowledged that the boundary water fisheries were a common property resource in need of cooperative protection. In 1892, his was an enlightened view. Fishermen, in particular, were prone to see their prey as an indestructible bounty to be taken at will. If they needed to reduce their take, in the unlikely event that the fish began to decline, fishermen often believed that they could control themselves without recourse to government regulations. In reality, such restraint was highly unlikely. The presence of the boundary line, and the reality of international rivalry that came with it, exacerbated the natural competition among fishermen. Foster, to his credit, recognized the nature of the problem and pushed for Canadian-American cooperation to save the fisheries and reduce tension.

Each country assigned a competent scientist to the commission. The United States chose Dr. Richard Rathbun, a government ichthyologist who spent his career with the Fish Commission and the Smithsonian Institution. The Canadians appointed Dr. William Wakeham, a leading Dominion fisheries expert, captain of a fisheries patrol vessel, and medical doctor. By picking qualified scientists with no direct political affiliation, the two governments suggested that they were serious about finding an equitable solution based on scientific fact, not political dealing. Foster and Pauncefote had agreed that the two men would meet within three months of the exchange of diplomatic notes and that Wakeham and Rathbun would then have two years to complete their investigation.[48]

The scientists faced an impossible task with the four goals Foster laid out for them. First, they were to devise a plan for "the limitation or prevention of exhaustive or destructive methods of taking fish . . . in the territorial and contiguous waters" of Canada and the United States. Second, they were to examine the feasibility of preventing "the polluting or obstructing of such contiguous waters to the detriment of the fisheries." Third, they were to propose adequate closed seasons—that is, times when fishing would be illegal—to protect the fisheries. Finally, they were to determine "practical methods of restocking and replenishing" the reduced species.[49] Even with two years, no mere mortals could have possibly fulfilled such a broad mandate. As a diplomat, Foster wanted a quick solution to a potentially thorny problem, but, as scientists, Rathbun and Wakeham wanted a thorough inquiry; the two goals were incompatible.[50]

Rathbun and Wakeham believed strongly in the need for a complete understanding of the boundary water ecosystems.

> In seeking to determine the actual cause of decrease in a fishery product, or even to establish the possibility of its decline, it is necessary, above all

things, to become thoroughly acquainted not only with the form in question, but also with its surrounding and associated species.[51]

Even with the accumulated records of both countries, a scientist in the 1890s would have needed two years to gain a thorough knowledge of even one of the Great Lakes. It was a noble but impractical goal. Foster and Pauncefote had asked too much of the scientists.

Wakeham and Rathbun did not come close to meeting their March 1895 deadline. In 1893, they managed to cover only the Atlantic coast, the St. Croix River, and the northern shores of Lakes Erie and Ontario. Under pressure from Canadian fishermen who blamed Americans for their difficulties, the Dominion government urged Wakeham to focus on the Great Lakes. Therefore, he and Rathbun spent all of 1894 on the four boundary lakes. At the end of that year, Rathbun asked for an extension and promised Secretary of State Walter Gresham that the scientists would submit their report by June 1895. He underscored the need for thoroughness by reminding the secretary of "the extent and value of the industries that may be affected thereby."[52] Perhaps to postpone dealing with the scientists' reports, both governments agreed to extend the deadline until 1 June 1896.

In March 1896, Wakeham came to Washington to meet with Rathbun and prepare their report. Between them, they had compiled 15,000 typed pages of information, as well as copies of state legislation and previous scientific work. Suddenly, June did not seem that far away. The scientists asked for, and received, one last extension. On 31 December 1896, more than four years after the Foster-Pauncefote agreement, Wakeham and Rathbun turned in their "Report of the Joint Commission Relative to the Preservation of the Fisheries in Waters Contiguous to Canada and the United States."

Secretary of State Richard Olney correctly summed up the report as "valuable, interesting, and exhaustive."[53] Wakeham and Rathbun provided a thorough summary of the scientific knowledge of the boundary waters. For each body of water they provided descriptions of the geography, food fishes, and fishing methods, as well as statistics on the types and amounts of fish caught. Finally, they assessed the level of risk for each of the major food species and made some recommendations, although they could not fulfill Foster's four goals. Despite their tireless effort, they admitted that "we have found it impossible to consider fully all of the questions which the subject presents." In fact, they began their report by calling for "more complete inquiries."[54]

Perhaps overwhelmed by the pile of data and the huge mandate, Rathbun and Wakeham presented a conservative report. They wrote about each body of water in turn, moving from east to west. The report was full of statistics and charts demonstrating the decline of the boundary water fisheries, and the commissioners did identify culprits. But they generally confined themselves to reporting the facts, while offering only a few basic recommendations. Most important, they did not delve into the underlying economic incentives for overfishing.

Their analysis of the decline of Lake Erie, the most important freshwater fishery in the world, revealed the limits of the commission's report. The evidence of Lake Erie's decline was overwhelming. Between 1885 and 1890, the fishery peaked in terms of pound nets in use, total output, and whitefish, sturgeon, and herring caught. By 1893, sturgeon catches were down 84 percent from 1885, and herring were off almost 50 percent from 1890. Whitefish had declined so much that they made up only 9 percent of the lake's output. Between 1890 and 1893, total catch dropped from 72.8 tons to 52.4, and pound net fishermen were going bankrupt. But perhaps the most telling statistic was the catch per pound net on the Canadian side. Between 1872 and 1894, annual yield per net dropped from over 10,000 pounds to under 1,200. All Rathbun and Wakeham could suggest was that the industry "requires an entire revision, but it is certain that nothing effectual can be accomplished without recourse to heroic measures."[55]

Rathbun and Wakeham concluded that the culprit was overfishing. Whitefish, the scientists reported, suffered from too many gill nets and pound nets. On their migratory paths, whitefish encountered so many pound nets the scientists found it "almost surprising any should reach their spawning grounds." Then they ran into more gill nets in all parts of the lake. The herring faced so many nets on their old spawning grounds that they moved to unsuitable locations, where they failed to reproduce. While pollution and habitat destruction were problems, they "can not have ranked as a very potent factor in comparison with the fishing practices above referred to."[56]

To counteract the rapidly increasing damage, Rathbun and Wakeham recommended some controls on fishing on Lake Erie. "Relief is to be sought, first," they wrote, "through a reduction in the amount of fishing, and, second, by the correction of certain practices which may be regarded as pernicious." They called for a 50 percent reduction in both types of nets, which would lead to "an increase of the supply of fish and greater individual prosperity among the fishermen who continue in the business." In addition, they recommended spreading out, reducing, and rearranging the pound nets. Finally, they demanded a serious effort to increase the mesh size of all nets. They recognized that their suggestions were arbitrary restrictions to bring the industry in line with the resources on which it was based, but they also knew that it was "imperative that a sufficient number of the fish should have the opportunity of spawning to insure the perpetuation of the species." As secondary parts of their scheme, they urged an end to sewage and garbage dumping, as well as increased hatchery efforts.[57]

The two scientists noted that five political units—Ontario, Ohio, New York, Michigan, and Pennsylvania—had jurisdiction over parts of the lake.[58] Making no attempt to cooperate with one another, they produced five sets of laws and customs for one lake. Wakeham and Rathbun concluded that "the discord produced by the five separate and wholly dissimilar codes of law which apply to this region emphasizes the necessity for some unity of action."[59] The lack of any clear boundary line between the regions compounded the problem and led the scientists to recommend that one of the highest priorities had to be fixing the border on official maps. Their experience suggested that fishermen thought that everything more than three miles offshore was "a high sea . . . to which the fishermen from both sides are privileged to resort in common."[60]

The scientists also commented that the lake's fish presented a difficult regulatory challenge. Most of the freshwater fish followed seasonal migrations, taking to deeper water in the winter and summer. Unlike the fish in the other lakes, which tended to migrate from inshore waters to the middles of the lakes, the fish in Lake Erie moved from one end to the other. Because they crossed state boundaries on the southern edge, these "extensive periodical movements . . . render difficult the harmonizing of the many interests concerned therewith."[61]

The commissioners' recommendations regarding Lake Erie reflected their general attitude toward the problems along the border. As they saw it, the basic problem was the disruption of fish reproduction by the large numbers of nets, their small mesh sizes, and their placement. For each of the Great Lakes, they focused on tactics that would allow the fish better access to their spawning grounds, and they openly admitted that the number of fishermen would have to be reduced. For Lake of the Woods, they called for a serious reduction in the number of pound nets. And for the Fraser River they suggested strict rules for the placement of nets in order to simplify the formidable maze that the rather dimwitted salmon faced. For each body of water, they called for an enlargement of the minimum mesh size as a means to allow undersized fish to escape. They did not recommend banning any particular practice, nor did they single out any group of people for blame. There was just too much fishing.

Besides calling for various restrictions on times, methods, and locations of fishing, Wakeham and Rathbun emphasized hatchery work as a means to counteract the decline of valuable species. The first attempt to propagate valuable species on Lake Erie came in the 1870s, when Ohio opened a hatchery on the Maumee River. By 1887, Ohio's fisheries experts were releasing 100,000,000 whitefish fry annually, as well as millions more of other species. The commissioners credited such efforts with salvaging the whitefish and urged more governments to expand their programs.[62] But millions of young fish produce only a few thousand adults, even without aggressive fishermen. Among vertebrates, fish produce an unusually high number of offspring because fry rarely survive in the fish-eat-fish aquatic world. Those that dodge the climatological and predatory bullets have to avoid fishermen who catch immature fish. Only then can they go on to reproduce. Hatcheries may not have been the answer for Lake Erie, but they made excellent political sense. Instead of stopping fishermen from catching undersized or spawning fish, the government could spread a little pork and claim to be doing its best. In the 1890s, hatchery work was just beginning, but by the 1900s it had become the backbone of most government fisheries policy.

Despite their orders, Rathbun and Wakeham did not emphasize the problems posed by obstructions and pollution. They briefly mentioned the dams on the St. Croix, but they did not insist on the construction and maintenance of adequate fish ladders. Likewise, they noted that pollution had damaged the St. Croix fisheries and was present in Lake Erie, but they generally downplayed its impact. For instance, in 1893 Rathbun visited a tannery near Cheboygan that was drawing a great deal of criticism from local fishermen who believed that it was polluting Lake Huron. In his opinion, the "tan liquor" that the plant dumped into the lake was "worn out."[63] Perhaps the overall efficiency of the plant beguiled Rathbun, or perhaps he, like many of his contemporaries, believed that flowing water cleansed itself. In any case, it is hard to imagine that that "tan liquor" was not still a toxic soup. Even if that tannery had been especially clean, it was just one of hundreds — if not thousands — of factories dumping waste directly into the lakes. In addition, erosion, municipal pollution, fish offal, and lumbering waste added to

45

the environmental damage. The commissioners acknowledged all of these problems, but they confined themselves to general calls for the reduction of pollution; there was a stark contrast between the thoroughness of their proposed fishery regulations and the cursoriness of their comments on pollution.

Wakeham and Rathbun also chose not to discuss the role of fish merchants in promoting overfishing. A large number of fishermen, especially on the Great Lakes, were either in the direct employ of fish merchants or operating under lien systems similar to sharecropping arrangements. The rest had to deal with fish merchants throughout the season. The natural inclination of dealers to sell larger fish often served as the only means to prevent fishermen from taking undersized fish. Rathbun discovered that "the men who buy the fish . . . are in favor of larger fish and larger mesh, while those that have thousands of dollars invested in twine are very fearful."[64] As long as they had some fish coming to market, merchants could better afford to think about the long-term effects of destructive fishing techniques.

But dealers rarely exercised that power for restraint. For instance, the Sandusky Fishing Company gained control of all of the fish coming out of Lake of the Woods. With no other potential buyers for their fish, the fishermen of the lake were at the company's financial mercy. The company, though, did not stop the explosion of nets in the lake. The owners had cornered the German market for American caviar, yet they did nothing to ensure the long-term health of their resource. If anything, dealers pressured fishermen to catch more fish in order to pay off debts.[65]

The fisheries of Lake Superior were under the similar, although not quite so monopolistic, control of the A. Booth Packing Company of Chicago. Alfred Booth's company had packing stations around the lake and owned several vessels. In addition, its strong position allowed the company to buy the catch of independent fishermen in remote parts of the lake and work to shut down competitors.[66] In later years, Booth's expanding enterprise wriggled its tentacles deep into the Canadian industry, the most egregious example of clandestine control of Canadian fishing by American businessmen.

At the core of the problem, though, fish merchants' profits depended on moving as much fish as possible. In most places, the twenty-four ounce whitefish — generally known to be undersized — found a buyer, and fishermen knew it would. One shipment from Georgian Bay that Rathbun checked carefully contained 272 whitefish. The fish weighed a combined

360 pounds, or only twenty-one ounces on average, but the merchants took them.[67] In other cases the price placed on nature's bounty was absurdly low. On Lake Superior, merchants paid one dollar for 100 herring until the local market was saturated, at which point they paid nothing for them. The Sandusky Fishing Company paid seven and a half cents per 100 pounds of Lake Erie sheepshead destined for a fertilizer factory. The Canadian fishermen on Lake Erie received six to seven cents per pound for whitefish shipped to Toronto. But a pound of herring brought only three quarters of a cent in Buffalo and one and a half cents locally.[68] The price a fish brought depended on the proximity of the market and the desirability of the species. Still, if it had fins, the dealers and fishermen would try to find a market for it.

The role of fish dealers in promoting destructive practices, especially in penetrating the Canadian fishing industry, raised a larger question about which nation was better at protecting its fisheries. The Canadians had a reputation for being stricter, at least partially because of a combination of geography and political structure. Geography left all of the international Great Lakes under Ontario's jurisdiction, thus lessening the confusion that reigned on the American side. The Canadian political structure granted the Dominion the right to regulate the fisheries, even though they were technically provincial property. In addition, the Dominion had 100 wardens in the field at most times, fighting tough battles to enforce regulations.[69] In contrast, the American states had earned their reputation as lax enforcers of weak regulations, and the federal government could regulate only through the use of a treaty.

Fishermen from around the Great Lakes, both Canadian and American, told the scientists that Canada's rules encouraged conservation. One fish merchant from Cheboygan told Rathbun that "there is no better law than the Canadian law for saving fish."[70] On the other side of the border, a Canadian fishing captain asserted that the northern half of Lake Erie would produce 100 times more fishing if Canada had American laws. A fisherman from Mackinaw Island suggested a closed season, "as they have in Canada," and he summed up the nature of the American attitude toward fishing the Great Lakes: "This country has gone to the Devil on just that account, . . . they have gone to an excess in everything."[71]

On the surface, the evidence suggested that Ontario did a better job than any of the American states. Above all, Ontario had clear limits on mesh size for different types of nets. In addition, there were several places where fish seemed to be holding their own on the Canadian side of the border, while rapidly declining on the American side. For instance, on both Lakes Huron and Superior, sturgeon were down 80 percent on the American side but holding steady on the Canadian side. Also on Superior, Canada's whitefish catch was actually increasing in the 1890s despite the steep declines on the American side.[72] Throughout the Great Lakes, Canadian fishermen and fisheries seemed to be in better shape than their American counterparts.

But a closer look at the report suggests that Canadians were just as capable of stripping the lakes as the Americans. The fisheries of both the Bay of Quinte and Georgian Bay, which were entirely under Canadian jurisdiction, had collapsed by 1896. In particular, the whitefish catch in Georgian Bay had crashed despite increasing efforts by Canadian fishermen. While the Canadian catch on Huron and Superior generally held steady, certain areas such as Thunder Bay on the north shore of Lake Superior had been completely fished out.[73] At least in part, Canadians continued to have success on these two grand lakes because pollution and competition were less intense on their side. Perhaps Canadians were as capable as Americans of abusing the Great Lakes — there were just fewer of them.

CONCLUSION

The unwritten message of the Wakeham-Rathbun report was that Foster and Pauncefote had asked the scientists to do too much. They had no precedent with which to work, because cooperative efforts to conserve fisheries on such a broad scale had never been tried before. Most of the fisheries in their mandate had not been the subject of extensive research efforts, leaving the men with the task of basic field research before they could even begin to address the four broad questions that the diplomats had put to them. The boundary water fisheries were so diverse and complex that two scientists could not possibly have understood all of the angles. Finally, there were some issues, such as pollution control and the influence of fish merchants, that were not really in the purview of fisheries experts.

Wakeham and Rathbun had done all they could to tackle this huge problem. They had committed nearly four years of their lives to the project, had employed several assistants at various times, and had compiled a vast amount of data; yet, they were unable to offer a complete response to the diplomats. They had been thorough and unbiased in their search for the truth; when confronted with conflicting testimony, they had conducted experiments and gathered data. Their final report was exhaustive and informative without being political. They limited themselves to scientifically based recommendations about regulations, probably because that was their area of expertise.

Although they were very competent scientists, Rathbun and Wakeham were really not qualified to make evaluations of pollution sources, political boundary lines, or economic trends. Other scientists, economists, diplomats, or politicians should have had responsibility for these issues. Presumably, Foster and Pauncefote feared that a larger commission would just bog down in endless debate; they may have believed that if Wakeham and Rathbun accumulated the facts about the economic and political conditions in the boundary water fisheries, then diplomats and political leaders could create the necessary solutions. In any case, no two people could have done everything that the diplomats had asked.

Given the lack of precedent and the great complexity of the issue, all parties would have been better off if Pauncefote and Foster had scaled down the commission's mandate. The commissioners wasted their time studying Lake Champlain and Lake Memphremagog, which had insignificant fisheries. The St. Croix was a dead river, and that section of the report served only to warn about the dangers of pollution and obstruction. Lake Ontario was fished out, and Huron and Superior were clearly not as productive as Lake Erie. Lake of the Woods was very productive but very small. Lake Erie and the greater Puget Sound region, therefore, were the only large-scale, productive fisheries along the whole border. A good first step would have been to limit the commission's study to those two areas. Given the complexities inherent in each, a better step would have been to establish different commissions for each body of water. A Lake Erie commission, including a diplomat from each side and a chemist or two to go with the biologists, would have had plenty to do and might have been able to propose adequate regulations.

Despite the flawed process, Rathbun and Wakeham succeeded in compiling a vast quantity of valuable information. They recorded what others had suspected, that the boundary water fisheries could not sustain the level of fishing then prosecuted. And they at least indicated that pollution, obstruction, and the fish merchants were matters of international concern. They advanced the cause of Canadian-American cooperation by putting scientific objectivity ahead of national interest, and they demonstrated that diplomats could trust international scientific commissions to provide necessary expertise. On the other hand, their efforts also suggested that diplomats and scientists often had different approaches to complex international problems. Most important, they set the stage for more serious efforts to corral the runaway boundary water fisheries.

2

The Jordan Rules,
1898–1909

After submitting their report, Richard Rathbun and William Wakeham left the next move to diplomats. They could follow the lead from the commission and attempt to create strict regulations; they could hand the problem back to scientists for further review; they could aim for a political solution that buried the underlying scientific concerns; or they could ignore the problem and hope that it went away. The last two options were the most appealing, and they prevailed for the next ten years. By 1906, though, it was clear that organized apathy would not solve the problem and that any solution had to have at least a thin veneer of scientific credibility.

In that year, diplomats reopened discussions on the fisheries problem, and they did not distinguish themselves with fair play. After two years of petty disagreements, they finally produced a treaty that handed the problem back to scientists, led by David Starr Jordan. To a certain extent, Jordan had more authority than his predecessors, because he had the power of a treaty behind him. Also, as a man adept at putting himself in the public eye, Jordan had the public relations skill necessary to sell his ideas to the public and politicians. With a Canadian counterpart, Jordan drew up a set of rules to save the boundary water fisheries.

Still, Jordan's position could not overcome the fundamental flaw of the whole process: the inability of scientists and diplomats to truly embrace each others' expertise. Diplomats never completely shook the idea that the dispute was political and therefore demanded a political solution. Scientists never quite accepted that the ultimate judges of their efforts, the voters and their representatives, would ignore scientific logic and evidence. With these blinders, all parties made mistakes, usually in the form of bad compromises, which damaged the already slim chances of protecting the fisheries. Thus the Jordan rules represented a strong effort to make the best of a bad situation. Despite the various snags along the way, Jordan's regulations had a chance to become law in 1909 if the scientists could complete their work before Theodore Roosevelt left office.

HIGH COMMISSION AND LOW RETURNS

Although Wakeham and Rathbun's work did not spawn an immediate effort to solve the problem, it did find its way onto the agenda of the Joint High Commission (JHC) meetings in 1898 and 1899. Despite generally amicable and very lucrative ties between the U.S. and Canada, the Alaska boundary and Bering Sea disputes stood in the way of complete cooperation. With the hope of resolving all outstanding points of contention, and with encouragement from London, the two nations agreed to convene a JHC in Quebec in August 1898.[1] The ultimate failure of these talks prevented any progress toward joint conservation of the boundary water fisheries.

The main obstacle to success at Quebec was the number of issues on the table. At preliminary meetings, diplomats established a list of a dozen topics in need of resolution, most of which the historian Samuel Flagg Bemis later dismissed as "minor frontier and navigation questions." Although the diversity of issues might have allowed a broad compromise, it prevented the commissioners from addressing the true complexities of any one issue. To handle the work load, the commissioners divided themselves into subcommittees, thus diverting attention from the most pressing crises.[2]

The meetings began on 23 August 1898 in an atmosphere of secrecy and optimistic press reports. The leader of the American delegation, Senator Charles W. Fairbanks of Indiana, made it clear that the United States was prepared to meet Canada halfway. He incorrectly anticipated a similar conciliatory mood on the part of the British commissioners. Another commissioner anonymously compared the meeting to "a number of grown-up cousins sitting down to settle up a rich uncle's estate." Just a month after the conference began, the *New York Times* reported that, except for the formalities, most of the major issues had been resolved.[3]

In reality, the conferees were like adolescent brothers fighting for the last piece of cake. By early October, both sides agreed that they needed a few weeks to consider their various positions, especially on the Alaska boundary. They reconvened in November in Washington, D.C., hoping to break the impasse. Instead, negotiations ground to a halt while the two sides tried to reconcile their different appraisals of the sealing fleet based in British

Columbia.[4] When that crisis passed, the negotiators stumbled over reciprocity in December. Finally, the whole conference ended in ruin when attendees were unable to find any common ground on the Alaska boundary dispute. Despite much hard work, the Joint High Commission succumbed to the issue that brought about the conference in the first place.

Apparently, the commissioners had reached an agreement, based on the Rathbun-Wakeham report, on part of the boundary water fisheries. Without giving a reason, the commission had chosen to limit its fishery discussions to the Great Lakes. After the American commissioners met with two Great Lakes fishermen in September, the *New York Times* reported, "Both sides desire the better protection of the fresh-water fish, and no doubt this part of the proposed treaty will be disposed of readily."[5] In 1901, Senator Fairbanks recalled that the commission had come close to final agreements on every issue except the border.[6] All progress was in vain, though, and the Great Lakes were left without any joint regulations.

The diplomatic deadlock meant that the depletion of the fisheries would remain unchecked. On both the Fraser River and the Great Lakes, catches continued to decline. Canadian statistics revealed that the 1906 salmon catch was down 50 percent from 1902, and the Great Lakes catch was "light." Employment in the industry was sliding as boat owners looked to more efficient methods, and scarcity was driving fish prices higher. Knowledgeable observers foresaw catastrophic results unless each side adopted "such fishing regulations as will permit a sufficient number of adult fish to reach the spawning grounds . . . to carry out their work of procreation."[7]

The experience of the fishermen of Southampton, Ontario, illustrated the deteriorating conditions. 1905 was a lean year on Lake Huron. On 14 October, with the closed season for fishing only two weeks away, several men wrote to Richard Prefontaine, Canadian minister of marine and fisheries, asking for an extra two weeks of legal fishing. Given their light catch, they felt that they had "to make some provision for the coming winter."[8] They offered no explanation for the poor season, but like most fishermen they believed that just a few more days would change their luck. Prefontaine refused their request because of a lack of extenuating circumstances. Instead, he noted that the long-term good of the fisheries and fishermen required strict adherence to the laws.[9]

The next year was even worse, but a political campaign provided hope for the fishermen. They wrote to their member of parliament, his opponent, and the ministry looking for assistance. This time, Prefontaine's assistant,

R. N. Venning, agreed to an extension to 5 November 1906. In explaining this reversal, he cited several factors. First, the local government had been tardy in issuing licenses, so some fishermen had only one week of legal fall fishing. Second, local merchants reported a shortage of fish. And third, because the provinces actually owned the fish under Canadian law, Venning believed that he had to yield to Ontario's interests. While he understood the implications of extending the open season into the spawning period, he also understood that good politics makes for bad fishery management. The fishermen got a short-term gain, and the fisheries took a long-term loss.[10]

Conditions were not good on the other side of the border either. Citing "the rapid depletion of the fish supply in Lake Erie," the Cleveland Chamber of Commerce appointed a committee in 1905 to consider ways to revitalize the local fish industry. The committee members quickly recognized the problem. Nothing had changed since Rathbun's fieldwork, especially the lack of cooperation among the various governments on the lake. In addition, they concluded that the regulations in force were wholly inadequate, except for those put forth by the great state of Ohio. Ironically, they recognized the problem by criticizing the regulatory hodgepodge but demonstrated it by absolving Ohio's fishermen and government of any blame.[11]

The Clevelanders did recommend a course of action, but they had little hope for its implementation. Sensing the ruin of a vital local industry at the hands of foreign and interstate competition, the businessmen "reached the conclusion that the ideal, and perhaps the only adequate method of dealing with the situation, was by means of an international agreement governing all of the Great Lakes." Perhaps with a tinge of Progressivism in their blood, they believed that only such an authority could bring order out of the regulatory chaos. They disbanded in 1907 with "grave doubts as to the legality of an international treaty on the subject."[12] Legality was not the problem, politics was.

The decline of the Great Lakes fisheries also caught the attention of a leading professional organization. At its annual meeting in July 1906, the American Fisheries Society (AFS) passed a general resolution supporting Canadian-American efforts to conserve the border fisheries. At the 1907 meeting, A. Kelly Evans of Ontario forced the AFS to enter the political fray.[13] Evans introduced two strongly worded resolutions with explicit calls for action. The first demanded that the border states and provinces surrender their rights to regulate the fisheries. The second called for representatives from Ottawa, Washington, Ontario, and the relevant states to meet and formulate uniform regulations for the Great Lakes. In a letter to President Roosevelt and Governor General Grey, an AFS official reported the resolutions and noted that "the absence of such legislation causes confusion and dissatisfaction among fishermen and is not for the best interests of the fisheries."[14]

By actively supporting the negotiations, the AFS made a positive impact on the progress of the treaty and conservation diplomacy in general. As scientists and conservationists from both sides of the border, AFS members spoke with authority for the best interests of the fisheries as economic and scientific entities. The society's recommendation for a multilevel, international conference focusing solely on the Great Lakes was the best advice either government received on the subject. The society's actions reinforced the belief in both capitals that international regulation of the boundary fisheries was both necessary and feasible. But perhaps more important, the American Fisheries Society set a precedent by daring to offer its expertise in a field about which the negotiators knew little. For the first time, a scientific and conservation organization was attempting to influence the course of international natural resource protection.

The hard times in Cleveland and Southampton were symbolic of fishermen's struggles and attitudes all along the border. From lobstermen on Passamaquoddy Bay to fishermen on Puget Sound, most were fishing more and catching less. In response, they increased their efforts and sought to wiggle out from under the few existing government controls. In their minds, someone else deserved the blame for the decline of the fisheries, and they should not have to pay for the mistakes of others. Even those governments willing to take action faced fishermen who were unwilling and unable to look beyond their short-term needs. The only hope for real long-term reform of the system lay in cooperative diplomacy based on science.

ELIHU ROOT'S DIPLOMATIC INITIATIVE

The diplomatic impasse remained unbreakable until President Theodore Roosevelt chose Elihu Root as his new secretary of state in 1905. Roosevelt's appointment sent a mixed message to Canada. Root's service as one of the "impartial jurists" on the Alaska boundary tribunal did nothing to enamor him to Canadians. On the other hand, as the historian Richard Leopold has argued, Root was committed to a "sober realism," a position that Canadian leaders could appreciate.[15] His legal experience encouraged him to pursue compromise, his ties with corporate America allowed him to see the importance of American economic might abroad, and his deeply held conservatism made him more of a problem-solver than a visionary. A few months after becoming secretary of state, Root wrote, "The main object of diplomacy [is] to keep the country out of trouble."[16] Above all, Root strove to reduce friction that might hinder the normal development of American commerce. Given the huge volume of Canadian-American trade, it is not surprising that Root looked northward early in his term.

In March 1906, Root proposed to the British ambassador, Sir Mortimer Durand, that Canada and the United States should finally resolve their outstanding differences. He focused on three particular issues: the Grand Banks fisheries off Newfoundland, navigation and construction along the boundary waters, and the boundary water food fisheries. Root included a draft treaty for the boundary fisheries. With traditional diplomatic restraint, he suggested "that some more effective measures should be adopted for the protection and preservation of the food fishes in the contiguous waters of the two countries."[17] In reality, the fisheries needed more than "more effective measures" — they needed a complete regulatory overhaul.

Root had no idea how hard it would be to negotiate and implement such a treaty. He reminded Durand that the two nations had come close to an agreement on the subject in 1899, and he hoped that negotiators could build upon that foundation. Durand reported to London that Root's optimism in general was based on "the entire absence of any friction between the two governments."[18] But Root's optimism was misplaced. The boundary fisheries were different from anything else he had encountered.

As Root sent off his draft treaty proposal, the omens were mixed. First, the need for bilateral action was present but not generally accepted. Second, although a substantial amount of the scientific work had been completed, the Rathbun-Wakeham report was ten years old and by no means perfect. Third, U.S.-Canadian relations were free of major distractions, but diplomats on both sides still had lingering suspicions of each other. Finally, Root expected little opposition, but he had no reason to expect a groundswell of support either. Presidential will and congressional attitude would determine the fate of the proposal.

Root foresaw a quick and painless three-step process. First, the diplomats would draw up the treaty, including a definition of the boundary waters, the establishment of a two-member scientific commission to study the fisheries, and a fixed completion date for their work. Second, after the treaty had been ratified, the two scientists would draft a set of protective regulations. Third, the Canadian Parliament and U.S. Congress would pass laws encompassing the commission's recommendations. Root believed that the whole matter could be resolved before he left office in 1909.

The negotiations for the treaty proved more difficult than they should have. Root's draft had only four articles, none of which appeared to be very controversial. Yet the Canadian government hesitated to accept the American offer and challenged Root repeatedly. In principle, both sides espoused fisheries conservation, but each was suspicious of the other's motives and ability to deliver. The resulting delay did nothing to help the fisheries and only ensured that the process could not be completed during Roosevelt's administration.

Root believed that diplomats could provide only the framework for broad fisheries conservation. The central feature of the plan was a two-member International Fisheries Commission (IFC) staffed by one Canadian and one American. Root planned for these two to produce a comprehensive set of regulations, using the Rathbun-Wakeham report as a starting point. The negotiators believed that the bilateral nature of the IFC would guarantee evenhandedness and domestic political support in both countries. In addition, the existence of a commission freed the diplomats from the difficult and lengthy task of developing regulations.

The time frame that the negotiators granted to the IFC revealed the basic motives behind Root's proposal, which were similar to Foster's from 1892. The commissioners were to submit their proposed regulations within six months of ratification of the treaty. The impending deadline was meant to force the commissioners to complete their work rapidly, but it ruled out any serious attempts at conducting scientific fieldwork along the border. Had Root and his colleagues been interested primarily in conservation, they would have allowed the IFC much more time to ensure a thorough study of the resource. Probably, the diplomats feared that an open-ended commitment would yield another four-year study ending with infeasible recommendations. They wanted a quick political solution, not a thorough scientific inquiry.

The treaty proposal stipulated that the IFC recommendations would become law. Most participants accepted that both Congress and Parliament would have to enact legislation to that effect, but some believed that the president and prime minister could simply proclaim the regulations and begin enforcing them. Certainly Roosevelt was capable of taking such a direct approach.[19] Given the volatility of the U.S. Senate, both sides would have preferred a presidential proclamation, but Chandler Anderson, State Department Counselor, warned against such a move.[20] Therefore, both sides tacitly agreed to allow their legislative bodies the final say on the IFC proposals.

The Canadian government responded to Root's proposal on 23 April 1906. Governor General Grey informed Ambassador Durand that his government supported the general idea of the treaty, but his ministers had two concerns. First, they were skeptical that the American federal government could get the cooperation of the border states and their senators. Second, they requested that the treaty include Rainy River, Rainy River Lake, and Lake Michigan. Root had followed Secretary Foster's lead and included Passamaquoddy Bay, Lake Memphremagog, Lake Champlain, the four international Great Lakes, Georgian Bay, Lake of the Woods, and Puget Sound. But the Canadians wanted Lake Michigan included under the theory that it was similar to Georgian Bay.[21]

Root rejected Canada's proposal to include Lake Michigan because it was "wholly within United States territory." Anderson had warned Root that inclusion of the lake in the treaty might be unconstitutional and would certainly put the treaty at risk in the Senate.[22] Of course, Canadians felt the same way about Georgian Bay, but Root could point out that John Foster and Julian Pauncefote had established a precedent by including the bay and excluding the lake. Root also assured Durand that the states would comply with such a treaty. He quoted from a Justice Department report of 1898: "The fact that a treaty provision annuls and supersedes the law of a particular state upon [the regulation of fisheries] is no objection to the validity of the treaty."[23] Root did not have, however, any direct knowledge that the states would acquiesce.

For a year, the two sides refused to budge on Lake Michigan. They occasionally exchanged notes reiterating their positions or disputing the merits of including Lake Memphremagog, but there was no real progress until June 1907, when Canada's ministers finally offered to exclude Lake Michigan in exchange for leaving out Georgian Bay.[24] Root agreed in December only after Anderson noted that "Georgian Bay would be adequately regulated by Canada, independently of any treaty obligation."[25] Still, Root believed that "the best fishing grounds lay along the shores of the chain of islands separating Georgian Bay from Lake Huron."[26] He demanded inclusion of at least the portion of the bay known as North Channel.

The two nations then descended into squabbling about how much of North Channel should be included. Root wanted all of this area, arguing that "separate regulations of the different parts of the same body of water must necessarily be ineffective."[27] Root believed that "North Channel" was an arbitrary human distinction, not one that the fish recognized. The Canadian government considered North Channel to be a part of its sovereignty, just as the United States controlled the area where Lake Michigan emptied into Lake Huron. Finally, on 5 March 1908, Lord Grey authorized the new ambassador, Sir James Bryce, to accept Root's definition of North Channel.[28]

There was no evidence that North Channel was any more productive than any other part of Georgian Bay. Rathbun and Wakeham reported nothing unusual about that area; in fact, they commented that fishing was unusually even throughout Georgian Bay. They also observed that there was little data indicating that fish migrated from the bay to Lake Huron, or vice versa. Root probably did not have access to some source that suggested otherwise, but he refused to back down. The waste of time involved in this dispute offset any gains made by including this limited area in the treaty waters.

Not only did the petty nature of the North Channel disagreement delay the conclusion of the treaty for nine months, but it also undermined the very spirit of cooperation necessary. Both sides tried to limit their territory covered by the regulations, and they thereby engendered distrust. Canadians believed that the United States was trying to exempt as many fishermen as possible from the scheme, while Chandler Anderson had a hunch that Canadians were trying to parlay gains on the fisheries treaty into a stronger position on the boundary treaty.[29] Both nations negotiated as if the status of North Channel were a point of national honor, causing them to overlook the greater principle of conservation of shared resources.

While the Georgian Bay disagreement perked along, another problem came to a head in the spring of 1907 on Lake Champlain, where local animosity had become a "most exasperating bit of international friction."[30] Lake Champlain serves mainly as the border between Vermont and New York, but a small portion known as Missisquoi Bay extends into Quebec. The U.S. government had established a fish hatchery on a stream that passes through Canadian territory on its way to the bay. Fishermen from the two states and Quebec all competed for the perch that traveled through the bay on their spawning runs. In addition, as Rathbun and Wakeham had indicated, there was considerable sentiment on the American side in favor of banning commercial fishing in the lake.[31]

The point of contention was the Canadian practice of using seines to scoop up large schools of perch as they headed from the largely American lake to the entirely American hatchery. In April 1907, Senator Redfield Proctor of Vermont wrote to Root that the Quebec minister of fisheries had failed to fulfill his promise to end seining on the bay. Root passed along the complaint to Bryce, noting that even the Canadian Privy Council had recommended a cessation of seining. He then indicated that the entire package of inland fisheries negotiations "may be seriously interfered with if the existing feeling in Vermont is not allayed." [32]

Root's comment was both a threat and a warning. On one hand, he was threatening to halt progress on a treaty that Canadians wanted. Protection of the fisheries, especially in the Great Lakes, was more important to Canada than to the United States. If Ottawa could not deliver on a simple matter like Lake Champlain, then Washington would prevent action on the Great Lakes. Simultaneously, Root was warning Bryce and the Canadian government that senatorial intransigence could be the biggest obstacle to progress. The "existing feeling in Vermont" was no doubt a reference to Proctor's anger, which could turn the Senate against Canadian interests. While Root saw the value in attaining an inland fisheries agreement, he also knew that the United States held the upper hand in the negotiations.

In December, pressure to resolve the Lake Champlain problem rose. New York's Republican governor, Charles Evans Hughes, proposed that New York, Vermont, and Quebec agree to a common set of regulations for the lake. Whatever Hughes's goal may have been, he succeeded in getting the attention of the State Department. Acting Secretary of State Robert Bacon wrote a soothing letter, assuring Hughes that the department was doing everything in its capacity to ameliorate the situation. Bacon urged Hughes to have patience and reminded him of the "instability and lack of permanence" of state legislation in this type of matter. To support his argument, Bacon cited the July 1907 conference of the American Fisheries Society, which called on the states and provinces along the border to relinquish their fishery rights to their respective federal governments. [33] The department heard no more complaints from the Lake Champlain area as it worked toward completion of the treaty.

Although the Lake Champlain dispute seemed to be relatively unimportant in the larger scheme of boundary waters fishing, it had become a diplomatic bargaining chip. One Vermont official pointed out to Senator Proctor that what the Quebecois were doing on Missisquoi Bay was really no different from what Americans were doing in the greater Puget Sound region—poaching another nation's fish as they returned to their natal streams. He was convinced that both sides needed a treaty to prevent these local problems from becoming national issues.[34] Just days later, Root and Bryce came to the same conclusion. Bryce reported to Ottawa that Root believed that the tension on Lake Champlain "made the early conclusion of the treaty . . . a matter of urgency."[35] Root must have wondered how such a simple treaty had become so complex.

Before accepting the final draft of the treaty in March 1908, the British and Canadian governments sought assurances that the treaty was constitutional in the United States. On 12 March 1908, only one week after accepting the American proposal in regard to North Channel, Ambassador Bryce informed Root that the Canadian Privy Council still had doubts about the role of the states after ratification of the treaty.[36] Obviously frustrated, Root replied that *somebody* would enforce the treaty. Even if the federal government could not do so, state fishery officials overwhelmingly approved of the principle behind the treaty.[37] But Root's answer hardly reassured. He could not guarantee that Congress would accept the treaty. Nor could he explain how those enthusiastic fishery officials—who were overseeing the destructive practices then in vogue—would have more power and foresight in the future than they currently had.

In London, officials continued to express apprehension about the feasibility of the treaty. With the image of the senatorial mangling of the Hay-Pauncefote Treaty in 1901 fresh in his memory, Lord Elgin of the Colonial Office suggested that the empire should hold out for the assent of each of the states bordering on the treaty waters. An assistant in Elgin's office wrote, "It is well known . . . how limited is the power of the Government of the United States to enforce the permanence of treaty obligations by the several States of the Union."[38] He concluded by calling on diplomats to be certain that Canada did not fall prey to Washington's inability to deliver as promised.

Despite these concerns, both sides pressed on and finally completed the treaty more than two years after Root initiated it. Root and his good friend Bryce signed the agreement on 4 April 1908 in Washington. Within two weeks, both the Canadian Parliament and the U.S. Senate had approved it. Once Congress passed the appropriations bill to pay for the needed scientific studies, the formalities were resolved. Assistant Secretary of State Alvey A.

Adee concluded, "This seems to finish up the inland fisheries convention." [39] The gross inaccuracy of his assessment indicated the difficulty that the State Department had in grasping the realities of shared resource conservation.

THE RETURN OF THE SCIENTISTS

Ratification of the treaty brought scientists back into the ring, but it did not mean that they had complete control. The diplomats needed scientific expertise both to create regulations and to strengthen their credibility. But they did not want impractical technicians meddling in political questions. There was the problem. Decisions on such delicate matters were inherently political, and even a politically savvy scientist would annoy some powerful interests.

The State Department wanted someone who did not exist: a topflight scientist with strong political instincts who would suppress his scientific training in the interests of smooth diplomatic relations. American diplomats kept for themselves the power to make political decisions, at least in part because they feared the power of boundary states' congressmen. Scientists were a necessary evil. Instead of choosing David Starr Jordan for his strengths and then fighting hard on his side, they chose to settle for Jordan and hope to contain him.

Although no one appeared to be rushing, urgency might have helped. Theodore Roosevelt had announced that he would not run for another term as president; therefore, his powerful support would be available only until March 1909. With that deadline in mind, Root had granted the commissioners only six months beyond their date of appointment to complete their task. This decision prevented the scientists from being thorough, crushed flexibility, and forced both governments to choose commissioners quickly. As it turned out, the IFC failed to meet the target date, but its proposals still suffered from the unwarranted haste.

Ottawa and Washington then set out to find two men competent to act as the members of the commission. Both sides stalled, hoping, in Bryce's words, to determine whether the other would appoint a "prominent official or impracticable scientific expert." [40] Bryce's comment suggested that diplomats did not usually appreciate scientists' efforts to be thorough and that scientists did not always appreciate the need for rapid action. Not fearing scientists, Fisheries Commissioner George Bowers recommended David Starr Jordan as the American representative. Almost simultaneously, the

Canadians settled on Samuel T. Bastedo. The United States had found both a prominent public figure and a scientific expert, but the Canadians had found neither.

David Starr Jordan was an excellent choice. Bowers described him as "more familiar than anyone else in this country with the natural history and economic questions involved."[41] Jordan was well known on both sides of the border as the president of Stanford University and a noted social critic. He promoted democracy, temperance, pacifism, free trade, educational reform, and conservation in a series of books, articles, and speeches. Jordan commanded an audience wherever he traveled.

By training, Jordan was an ichthyologist. He received his education from Cornell University and briefly served there as a professor. He moved on to Indiana University, where in 1885 he became president at the age of thirty-four. In 1891 the trustees of Stanford recruited him to serve as the first president of their institution, and it was there that he first gained national recognition. Throughout his career, Jordan continued to travel the globe to study fish. Like most of his colleagues, Jordan saw fish as both natural and economic actors, and he understood fishery management techniques.[42] He was a conservationist, but he wrote, "It is not best for sentiment to stand in the way of actual need."[43] Therefore, he fit in with the scientists in the U.S. Fish Commission.

Jordan also had diplomatic experience. In 1896, President Grover Cleveland had appointed him chair of the American commission to study the fur seal herds of the Pribilof Islands. At the time, the United States and Great Britain were locked in a struggle over access to the seals, and Jordan's job was to determine the true status of the herds. Starting almost from scratch, Jordan produced an exhaustive, authoritative four-volume study of the animals that guided federal policy for years.[44] By any standard, Jordan was the best person in the United States for the IFC.

In contrast, Samuel Bastedo had a clouded and undistinguished career. In July 1906, Bastedo left his position as Ontario's deputy minister of fisheries amidst allegations of partisanship. In early 1908, the Dominion government appointed him to break a deadlock over fisheries policy among Ottawa and the provinces of Ontario and British Columbia. He failed at that assignment. Even Ambassador Bryce admitted to Root that Canada would have been better off with a scientific expert, impracticable or not.[45]

Root, recognizing Jordan's multiple talents, agreed with Bowers's recommendation. On 3 June 1908, he wrote to Jordan asking for his services on the

IFC. In the letter, Root laid out his vision for the completion and enforcement of the treaty. In the first step, Jordan would draw up the regulations and assist in passing the necessary legislation. For this period, Root noted that "the Government desires to obtain the benefit of your special knowledge and ability." Then the government would enforce the regulations. Root specified that he was not requesting Jordan's services in enforcement, although he hoped that Jordan's handiwork could become the domain of a National Fish Commission.[46]

Jordan enthusiastically "accepted the position as a matter of pleasure and honor, and also as a matter of duty."[47] As an assistant, he chose Dr. Barton W. Evermann of the Fish Commission, his coauthor on the weighty *American Food and Game Fish* (1908). Evermann served not only as a skilled field researcher but also as a listening post in Washington while Jordan was in California. Jordan knew that time was his enemy, and he immediately set out to learn "the defects of the existing statutes . . . if such exist, and of the hardships real or supposed to which fishermen, in either nation are now subject."[48] It was the beginning of a dedicated effort on Jordan's part to prod the federal government into protecting the food fish of the boundary waters.

In that first summer, Jordan and Bastedo traveled extensively in their attempt to gain at least a superficial understanding of the problems at hand. Amazingly, on 24 August Jordan notified the State Department that the commission had visited all of the treaty waters, although there were many natural history questions left unresolved. In fact, there were probably more unanswered questions about migration, spawning grounds, and so on than there were known facts. For instance, Jordan reported without surprise that he had found a new species of fish in Lake Erie, one of the most studied bodies of water in North America.[49] Even with previous scientific work and their combined experience, there was no way that Jordan and Bastedo could gain a thorough knowledge of the boundary water fisheries.

Further complicating matters was Bastedo's lack of commitment to the project. In late August, he learned that Prime Minister Laurier had appointed him a deputy minister in charge of annuities. In his autobiography, Jordan politely wrote of Bastedo, "Pension work was more to his taste than fisheries regulations." In October, while Jordan was drafting the regulations, Bastedo was campaigning for the Ontario provincial elections and creating new annuities forms.[50] Bastedo did not resign from the IFC, however, until November 1908. At heart, Bastedo was a Liberal Party hack who had somehow won a reputation as a fisheries expert.

While Jordan worked, he tried to elicit input from Bastedo. He informed the Canadian that he was drawing up a list of recommendations and showing them to trustworthy individuals. Bastedo replied that he could make no comments until he discussed the matter with the minister of marine and fisheries, L. P. Brodeur, who coincidentally never seemed to be in his office. Trying a new tactic, Jordan invited Bastedo to visit him in California for a brainstorming session. Bastedo held out for New York. In exasperation, Jordan warned Evermann that, between the tight deadline and Bastedo's absence, the treaty might fail.[51]

As it turned out, Bastedo caused less trouble than the State Department did. In his effort to draft suitable regulations, Jordan quickly discovered that the biggest obstacle was going to be the department, which had very particular ideas as to what belonged in the regulations. Over the next three years, Jordan engaged in a turf war with several ranking officials, especially Counselor Chandler Anderson. As the legal voice of the American foreign policy apparatus, Anderson expressed legal opinions that held as much weight as did Jordan's scientific views. Though they spoke of each other with respect, they usually failed to agree in their treaty interpretations. Jordan thought that the department was settling for "the lowest common denominator," while Anderson believed that Jordan was naive about political realities.[52]

In late August, Jordan tested his limits by proposing that the government create a new branch of the Fisheries Commission to enforce the IFC regulations. If this "Protection Division" was not in the cards, then the Division of Scientific Enquiry — under Evermann's direction — should have the necessary power. In any case, Jordan wanted Evermann in charge of his rules.[53] Central to this scheme was Jordan's attempt to establish a national warden force, paid for by a system of licenses, under the control of scientists.

Anderson responded quickly with a warning memo to Root and Robert Bacon. Although he did not explicitly address Jordan's request, he did set out to establish a strict interpretation of the treaty. He began by stating his assumption that, out of obligation to Great Britain, the administration had to expedite federal legislation because "there does not seem to be the least probability that the necessary legislation will be adopted by the several states." Therefore, Congress had the power to legislate within the scope of the treaty. He then delivered his counterpunch: even though the treaty included an article that gave the commissioners some discretionary power, the Constitution clearly did not allow a federal license and fee system.[54]

A few days later, Jordan received an official ruling from the State Department to guide him in drafting the regulations. First, state laws would remain valid unless they conflicted with IFC recommendations. Second, individual states were free to make additional restrictions based on local conditions. Third, no national licensing system was "practicable." The first two decisions pleased Jordan because they freed him from the anxiety that his rules might accidentally eradicate a number of useful state laws. But the third, as he suggested to Evermann, made things easier — not better. He encouraged Evermann to convince Anderson of the need for a federal warden service in the treaty waters.[55]

Jordan called the licensing system "the most important part" of his plan, but Anderson refused to budge. In Jordan's mind, licenses were necessary for a number of purposes. First, they were a simple way to regulate access to the fisheries, thus making conservation easier. To serve in this capacity, though, the licensing scheme had to be more rigid than the one then in use in Canada, under which "it is possible to issue a license to do something otherwise illegal." Second, licenses also served as a means of uniform registry common to both sides of the border. Third, licenses provided revenue for conservation activities. Jordan tried to convince Anderson that the fees could be used for fish hatchery purposes, if a federal warden service was not acceptable. But Anderson opposed the whole idea of licensing. As Jordan wrote to Bastedo, "We therefore have no licenses to issue and no money to receive."[56]

Their sparring suggested that Anderson and Jordan represented two schools of thought regarding the use of federal power in conservation. Anderson believed that in foreign policy the federal government was bound by the same constitutional restraints that it faced in making domestic policy. As a conservative, he had no desire to test the Supreme Court's tolerance level. On the other hand, the progressive reformer Jordan wanted a broader application of federal powers.[57] He thought that the whole point of the treaty was to wrest control of the fisheries from incompetent state management and grant it to the federal government.

In particular, Anderson and Jordan found themselves disagreeing about states' rights. Jordan wrote, "Our difficulties in dealing . . . with the relation of state rights to government control . . . are greater than those connected with the protection of the fisheries."[58] He wanted a broad mandate to protect the fisheries, but Anderson would grant him only limited authority. Anderson appeared to be drawing an arbitrary distinction between legitimate and illegitimate uses of federal power. For instance, he never explained to Jordan how a license system was more unconstitutional than the establishment of a federally mandated closed season on Lake Erie.

Jordan's battle with Anderson revealed the limitations on his power. His desire to have free reign conflicted with Anderson's need to limit the political damage brought on by this treaty. Whereas Jordan saw the treaty as an opportunity to fix the fishing industry, the diplomats saw it as an opportunity to erase a political headache, not create more of them. Despite the department's effort to control him, Jordan still had more power than Rathbun had had. And he intended to use it.

CANADA FINDS A PRINCE

In November 1908, the Laurier government chose a real scientist, Professor Edward E. Prince, to replace Bastedo. Prince had served on a number of fisheries commissions, and, unlike his predecessor, he cared about fishery conservation. In 1906, Laurier's government had appointed Prince to study the fisheries in Georgian Bay and the Fraser River, and he worked for two years on both. During his time in British Columbia, he worked with officials from the state of Washington in an attempt to coordinate provincial and state laws. His recommendation that each government adopt tough regulations earned the opposition of powerful interests on both sides of the border. For instance, the New Westminster (B.C.) Board of Trade claimed his ideas would "discriminate in favor of trap operators, foreign investors and the aliens who carry on the Gulf fishery."[59]

Prince also served as the chairman of the Dominion commission that studied Lake Erie's waters from 1907 to 1909. Prince and his colleagues suggested that Canadian fishermen not be allowed to hand over their catch to American vessels for transportation to the American market or in any other way yield their rights. They also concluded that a number of standard fishery regulations were necessary, such as closed seasons and equipment restrictions. Most striking, though, was Prince's understanding that external factors were contributing to the destruction of the fisheries. To that end, he urged stricter regulations on the dumping of municipal garbage and the establishment of Dominion fish reserves free from all types of disturbance.[60] Unlike Bastedo, Prince had ideas for improving the quality of the fisheries.

But Prince needed some time to acquaint himself with the particular problems he would face on the IFC. Jordan and Bastedo had agreed to meet in New York around 20 November, and Prince wanted to honor the commitment. But Bastedo had left him nothing in the way of notes or correspondence.[61] Prince had only his own experience and Jordan's word as his base of information. He was torn between expediting the process for the sake of the fisheries and asking for more time in order to bring himself up to speed with Jordan.

While Prince considered his options, the border fishermen began to get nervous about "the Jordan proposal." Of course, very few of them actually had seen his draft regulations, but they knew that the IFC was nearing its deadline and many had met the scientist in the previous few months. Jordan anticipated a response from commercial fishermen and state fish commissioners who might consider some of his restrictions to be drastic, but he also believed that "none of them will come as a surprise to any of these people."[62] He had underestimated the vehemence of their outcry.

In October 1908, the first blow came from the noted conservationist John Burnham of the New York State Forest, Fish, and Game Commission, which had received a copy of Jordan's proposed regulations. Burnham was already annoyed with Jordan because he had not shown up for a meeting in July, but the proposals increased his anger. In a seven-page report, Burnham argued that "the proposed statutes would let down the bars for indiscriminate and illegal fishing . . . and while containing some good features, are as a whole not to be compared with the protective laws now in force in New York." Among other errors, Jordan had regulated fish in lakes where they did not live and dabbled in areas beyond his expertise or commission. In doing so, he lost a powerful voice in a powerful state.[63]

Senator Knute Nelson, a Republican from Minnesota, followed up with complaints of his own. He reported that the fishermen of Lake of the Woods were "up in arms" about the impending regulations. They claimed that there had been a huge increase in the number of fish taken in the past few years, indicating not a decline but successful management. In support, Nelson included affidavits from four local fishing captains, all of whom swore that the IFC regulations—which were still largely hypothetical—would drive them out of business.[64] Nelson's letter was an ominous sign. Not only did it suggest the depth of fishermen's hostility toward regulation, but it also indicated that congressmen of Root's own party were inclined to follow their constituents instead of the administration on this issue.

Canadian opposition also arose in November. J. H. Todd, a powerful salmon packer from Victoria, British Columbia, wrote to Brodeur with a series of complaints about "the American proposals." Todd believed that Jordan had recognized that Canadian methods of catching salmon were nondestructive, yet the IFC proposal made no distinction between American and Canadian practices. Todd thought it was absurd that Canadians and Americans should face the same restrictions, although he admitted that Americans might have a different perspective. If the regulations did not make any exceptions for the British Columbian methods, he warned, there would be a great loss of canneries and capital.[65] As a man with much capital invested in the industry, Todd should have had a long-term view of the need for conservation, so his opposition came as another blow to the still unwritten regulations.

The upwelling of complaints coincided with a State Department plan to have Jordan meet with concerned individuals in Washington in November. Originally, Jordan was to have met with state fish commissioners after he met with his Canadian counterpart in New York. On 17 November, presumably in response to the growing complaints, Assistant Secretary Robert Bacon decided to invite commercial fishermen to the meeting.[66] Given how late he made the decision, it was as much an insult as a favor. Neither Jordan nor the government kept any record of the meeting, perhaps because no one could make it to Washington on such short notice. One fisherman from Lake of the Woods had to write to Jordan with his opinions because he received the invitation on 23 November, the day of the conference.[67]

The meeting in New York between Prince and Jordan failed to produce a complete set of regulations by the November deadline. The two men came to an agreement on forty points, but they were unable to agree on some of the more important issues. Primarily, Prince wanted a three-month extension to compensate for his late start. Jordan felt pressure to finish the regulations, but he understood Prince's predicament. Therefore, the two agreed to go to Washington to discuss the matter with the diplomats. After meeting with Bryce, Root, and Roosevelt, the scientists agreed to submit their regulations by April 1909. Any hope of completing the process before Roosevelt left office had evaporated.[68]

With extra time now available, Jordan and Prince could afford to thoroughly consider the remaining problems. Both men wanted to meet in California, but the Dominion government ordered Prince to wait until he got more responses from the provinces. While waiting for Prince, Jordan tinkered with specifics and allowed himself to become overconfident. He thanked Anderson for his help in trimming the regulations and noted that "there appears to be in no quarter any objection to the acceptance of these regulations." [69] One wonders if Jordan was reading his mail.

Meanwhile, angry British Columbians were pressuring Prince and Brodeur. The first complaint came from J. D. Taylor, the M.P. from New Westminster, the heart of the salmon industry. He believed that in the past corporations had succeeded in shaping provincial policy in such a way that individual workers always lost out. Taylor feared that Prince and Jordan were making the same mistake, thus leaving normal people out of the IFC's considerations. Surprisingly, the British Columbia Packers Association voiced the same opinion. Its members expressed a willingness to shut down operations for two years for the long-term good of the fishery, but they warned Prince that such a move would most harm those who worked in the plants and on the boats.[70]

The majority of the complaints to Ottawa, though, came from packers more concerned with American competition. These petitions expressed a common fear that American regulations were so lax that strict Canadian regulations served only to fatten American wallets. The British Columbia Packers Association lamented that Canadians had lived with conservation policies for years, and now Jordan asked them for more restrictions. Todd pointed out that in 1908 the American canners packed 50,000 to 75,000 more cases than anyone expected. Then they lowered the price and dumped the excess on the British market, thus cutting Todd's profits.[71] The Fraser River Canners' Association expressed the feelings of many Canadians: "Canada provides the fish supply. Your Honourable Government has placed and enforced most stringent regulations upon her subjects; BUT WHAT RECIPROCAL REGULATIONS HAVE BEEN ENACTED BY THE UNITED STATES?"[72] The Canadian fishing industry was not going to accept these regulations without a fight. But the fear of American influence prevented Canadian fishermen from seeing that the IFC had the only chance to corral the maverick Puget Sound trap-men.

In response to the angry letters that Prince was getting from the West Coast, Jordan decided to remove certain proposed regulations to meet Canadian requests. On Christmas Eve, Brodeur ordered Prince to go west and meet the leaders of the British Columbia opposition to the treaty. The Canadian government still had doubts about the current IFC recommendations, though, which were mostly Jordan's work. Perhaps believing that the differences had been resolved, Jordan sent Prince a signed, finished set of regulations in late December.[73]

Still, Jordan continued to work on the regulations. On 1 January 1909, he asked Root for further appropriations to allow him and Prince to conduct fieldwork through August. Root agreed reluctantly because Jordan wanted the time to improve his understanding of the issues at hand, and the secretary could hardly object to that. Meanwhile, Jordan continued to pester Anderson with questions. Despite Anderson's note on states' rights from the spring, Jordan still worried that the IFC regulations might not mesh well with state statutes. Hypothetically, a combination of state and IFC close seasons might outlaw fishing for the entire season in certain areas.[74] Anderson ignored Jordan's request to make the regulations even more specific.

By early February, Jordan concluded that only Washington State really opposed the IFC's concept of fishery protection. As he wrote to Evermann, "Everybody seems satisfied with our program, except the state of Washington, which is trying to forestall by adopting most of our reforms in advance."[75] The key words were "most of." Washington's legislature hoped to avoid the stricter IFC rules by adopting watered down variations. Still, Jordan pressed on.

Jordan actually had bigger problems in Washington, D.C., than in Washington State. To his surprise, Anderson had altered some of the proposals that Jordan had lifted straight from the Pennsylvania and Ohio statutes. Jordan complained to Anderson that state commissioners around Lake Erie had requested that the IFC create sweeping regulations because "fishermen had much more respect for national than state law." If the IFC restrictions were not complete, they had warned, the states could undermine federal fisheries protection by allowing their laws to wither. Now, months after his appointment, he found himself asking Anderson whether his job was "to remedy the most serious evils" or "to prepare a general, broad uniform code to touch all fishery interests."[76]

The ongoing struggle between Jordan and the State Department shed light on one of the most basic flaws of the treaty process. The major actors on the American side had different concepts of what the end product should look like. Root wanted an agreement that would quickly resolve an outstanding U.S.-Canadian conflict. Anderson sought one that did not offend constitutional purists, such as himself. Jordan hoped to fix a suffering fishing industry. The three visions were not compatible: Root's did not grant

Jordan enough time, Anderson's stifled innovation, and Jordan's challenged constitutional standards.

While Jordan fine-tuned his proposals, he waited for Prince to visit Palo Alto. The Canadian commissioner had promised to come to California to create a final version of the regulations in early March. By the terms of the treaty, the two men had only until early April 1909 to submit their work. Yet as late as 22 March, Jordan wrote to a friend, "I am waiting, more or less patiently, for the arrival of my British colleague." A fishery official in British Columbia had warned Jordan that Prince did not seem to have much sense of time.[77] Jordan was left waiting until late March, when Prince told him that he would arrive in California on 6 April. By way of explanation for his silence, Prince admitted, "I had a rather serious nervous attack."[78]

Before he left for Palo Alto, Prince received orders from Brodeur regarding the Canadian government's position. First, the Ministry of Marine and Fisheries was to have exclusive control of fisheries regulations in Canada. Second, Brodeur had to approve any departures from current Canadian regulations before Prince could agree to them. Third, he reminded Prince that the regulations needed the approval of the Governor General's Privy Council, and, therefore, he should not give away control over anything that was already Canadian. Fearing the worst from his American counterparts, Brodeur ordered Prince to send coded summaries of the IFC meetings in California.[79]

Brodeur's orders revealed the contrast between the Canadian and American approaches to the IFC. Jordan took his orders from diplomats, but Prince took his from fisheries officials. Brodeur kept a much tighter rein on Prince than Root or Anderson could keep on Jordan. While American officials pursued separate agendas, Canadians had one goal: reduce American pressure on the boundary water fisheries. Despite the Bastedo appointment, the Canadian government took the treaty much more seriously than did its American counterpart. At the same time, Brodeur revealed a stubborn belief that Canada was blameless for the decline of the fisheries. It may have been reasonable to expect two biologists to judge competing regulatory schemes without bias, but diplomats and legislators would never do the same.

Before reaching Palo Alto, Prince stopped at Vancouver to meet again with local salmon fishermen and packers. Despite his assurances that he would not accept regulations that would favor the Americans, Prince felt the wrath of the British Columbia salmon men. They complained about the three most basic parts of the restrictions: minimum mesh size, the weekly closed season, and the general closed season of 25 August to 15 September. In their opinion, Jordan was, at best, misinformed or, at worst, typically American. Prince reiterated his belief that the state of Washington was at fault, not Jordan. But Jordan was not a well-liked figure in the area. His work to eliminate the Canadian practice of catching seals on the high seas made him unpopular in the sealing ports of Victoria and Vancouver. One fisherman went so far as to complain that those seals were the cause of the problem because they ate so many salmon.[80]

When they met, Jordan and Prince knew that they could no longer procrastinate. They both understood that the more quickly they moved, the faster Congress and Parliament could take action. As a starting point they "adopted the policy of considering the future of the fisheries as paramount, thus setting aside all questions of advantage to either nation."[81] They worked for several days trying to reconcile different approaches to some of the problems. For instance, Prince wanted to expand closed seasons on the Great Lakes to cover all of the spawning season because Ontario had no fish hatcheries. Jordan, however, thought that raising the lower weight limit of most species would allow individual fish to spawn at least two years before being caught. As a solution, they included both proposals in their list. Jordan wrote that "Professor Prince and I agreed on the scientific and economic issues involved," but when they disagreed on some point, they simply left it off the list.[82] One major omission was a licensing system, which the Canadians desired but Jordan had been told was unacceptable.

Jordan was quite optimistic that their regulatory scheme would win approval. He was good friends with Ambassador Bryce, who bore a "remarkable resemblance in personality and to some extent appearance [to] John Muir."[83] After Bryce came to visit the commissioners in California, Jordan was "very well satisfied with the possible outcome."[84] But Jordan knew that the biggest obstacle to the ultimate success of the treaty could be found on Capitol Hill. Ever the optimist, Jordan told Prince that with State Department backing, the IFC regulations would slide through Congress. As Jordan would later discover, the department's backing was more hypothetical than real.

CONCLUSION

On 22 April 1909, Jordan and Prince finally concluded their set of regulations and sent copies off to their respective superiors. They recommended sixty-six rules covering all of the waters from Passamaquoddy Bay to Puget Sound, with specific regulations for each body of water. Most of them were straightforward attempts to control the type of equipment that fishermen could use, when they could use it, and what kinds of fish they could catch. These regulations were quite similar in rationale and effect to those that Wakeham and Rathbun had suggested thirteen years earlier. In addition, the commissioners scattered several radical proposals throughout the document. The most striking would have prevented individuals or corporations from polluting the boundary waters "unless permitted . . . under any law passed by the legislative authority having jurisdiction." [85]

Despite the hurried nature of their work and the insufficient scientific basis available, Prince and Jordan presented an admirable set of recommendations. Their suggestions would have imposed some hardships on the boundary fishermen on both sides, but, as Jordan argued later, "There can be no resuscitation . . . unless we cut out about half the fishing." [86] Prince and Jordan would not settle for regulations that merely managed the decline; they wanted to begin rebuilding fish stocks for the long run, even if that entailed short-term suffering. The commissioners also endeavored to treat each side evenly, although the different methods used on opposite sides of the border often made that task difficult. The two men recognized that the fisheries were doomed unless they could put aside competition for national advantage. In submitting the draft regulations to the State Department, Jordan wrote, "I think that our proposed series of regulations represent about all that can be done on the basis of present knowledge." [87]

Although Jordan and Prince did admirable work, they were unable to complete their regulations by the time Roosevelt left office. The fault was not theirs alone. Root and the Canadian authorities failed to expedite negotiations and spent far too long quibbling over minutiae. Had they accepted the spirit of cooperation, they could have concluded an agreement in a few months. Instead, their attempt to gain national advantage hindered progress. Thus, negotiations that could have been finished in 1906 lingered on into 1908. Once the treaty was wrapped up, the great mistake was the Bastedo appointment. Instead of appointing a competent, dedicated scientist like Prince in the first place, Laurier made a horrendous choice. Bastedo's subsequent resignation—and the necessity for extending the IFC deadline—ensured that Roosevelt would not see the regulations presented during his term.

The late completion date prevented Roosevelt from taking action on behalf of the IFC regulations. As one of the most powerful conservationists of his day and a leader committed to efficiency and long-range planning, Roosevelt probably would have proclaimed the regulations without waiting for congressional assent. His successor, William Howard Taft, was neither as dedicated to conservationism nor as strong a leader as TR. Unlike Roosevelt, he would not risk any political capital on a potentially unpopular set of fisheries regulations. Had the regulations made it to Roosevelt's desk, the future of the boundary water fisheries might have been substantially brighter. As it was, Jordan's rules would have to wait for someone to step forward and shepherd them through the political pound nets in Washington.

3

The One That Got Away,

1909–1914

Edward Prince and David Starr Jordan's report forced their governments to choose between the short-term interests of fishermen and the long-term interests of the fisheries. In Ottawa, the Dominion government quickly brought its laws into compliance with treaty stipulations. In Washington, D.C., however, President William Howard Taft led a government that resisted the scientists' efforts. Congressional leaders and State Department officials feared the profound implications of the International Fisheries Commission's proposals. In the ensuing attempts to craft suitable enabling legislation, they removed the most restrictive regulations in an attempt to dilute the treaty's impact. In the end, their obstructionist policies succeeded in destroying the IFC's work.

The attempt to get congressional approval of Jordan and Prince's work was a test of the appeal of conservationism to the new administration. Conservationists had high hopes that Taft would continue his predecessor's work in that direction. But Taft was no Theodore Roosevelt, and he chose to pursue more limited conservation goals than had the Bull Moose. In speeches, he pledged to fight for Roosevelt's policies, but when pressed for controversial action he took refuge behind a strict interpretation of the Constitution.

By avoiding a leadership role in fisheries conservation, the administration left Jordan almost alone in his struggle to win approval of the IFC regulations. His best argument — that things would get much worse without the proposed restrictions — was largely theoretical and unpopular. Jordan could not prove that the fish would be more numerous under the IFC plan, and the vast majority of Americans were ignorant of the situation. Other than the small, elite American Fisheries Society, there was no organization working to promote fisheries protection in the way that the National Association of Audubon Societies lobbied for birds.

If pressed, conservationists might have accepted the need for preserving supplies of food fish, but few individuals rallied to the "Save the Fish!" banner. Led by the likes of the forester Gifford Pinchot, the utilitarian wing of the movement sought to end the waste of natural resources. A sense of national duty and a desire to protect the basis of the economy motivated them to push for better control of common property resources. As a supply of inexpensive, nutritious food, fish were an asset as valuable as any of the prominent items on the conservationist agenda. But they were, by nature, in an inhospitable environment, there were few educated ichthyologists, and the complexity of fish ecosystems was daunting. Utilitarians did not worry about fish.

For the preservationists, fish simply did not have the appeal of other wild animals. Aesthetically, fish had three shortcomings: they were hard to find, they had neither fur nor feathers, and they did not sing. In short, in most people's eyes, they were not beautiful. Preservationists who already stretched to protect mammals, birds, and parks had little energy left for mere fish. To be fair, Jordan did little to rally them to the cause. Without pressure from conservationists, Taft and Congress were free to ignore the long-term needs of the fisheries.

In contrast to the conservationists, fishermen brought energy and organization to the struggle over control of the fisheries. With their jobs at stake, they had more motivation than anyone else, including Prince and Jordan. They hired lawyers and rallied behind their civic leaders in efforts to derail unfavorable regulations. Jordan received stacks of letters protesting everything from specific local restrictions to his whole program. In addition, congressmen and members of parliament from the border states and provinces heard negative comments from their fishing constituents. This fight was one that fishermen would not lose easily.

Fishermen claimed that the IFC regulations threatened their jobs, ignoring the fact that unregulated fishing threatened to destroy the entire industry. Many believed that they could continue fishing indefinitely at the same level of effort, if only the government would leave them alone. They were right that the IFC wanted to reduce the number of fishermen, but they refused to admit that declining fish populations were already having the same effect. The industry as a whole would survive only with the benefit of some long-term planning. But only resolute politicians could pass a law eliminating jobs, even if it was good in the long run.

Opponents in the U.S. also argued that the treaty and the commission's regulations were unconstitutional. This idea usually came from the lawyers and congressmen who represented the fishermen, and it carried a significant threat. From the very beginning, State Department Counselor Chandler Anderson had expressed concern about the precept of the treaty—that the federal government had the right to intervene in local resource issues—even though he was paid to defend the State Department's actions. His reservations were, no doubt, also held by those two conservative lawyers, Taft and Secretary of State Philander Knox. With this issue in particular, the fishermen's defenders had hit an exposed nerve in the administration.

For more than three years, Jordan and occasional supporters fought on, knowing that unless they succeeded the boundary water fisheries were doomed. Without any public support, they had to rely on warnings of future disaster. But the immediate concerns of the fishermen trumped the hypothetical concerns of a handful of scientists.

TROUBLE WITH THE TAFT ADMINISTRATION

The new administration in Washington brought with it a new set of foreign policy goals. Whereas Roosevelt and Root had been interested in maintaining order and strengthening the U.S. position among the Great Powers, Taft and Knox lacked a strategic vision. Their policy of "dollar diplomacy" involved opening areas for American business, with the belief that American strength would follow. This focus damaged Jordan's chance to push the regulations through Congress. Roosevelt and Root could have framed the regulations as a step in cementing Anglo-American relations, but the new administration did not see any important link between the fisheries and larger diplomatic goals.

Taft's State Department was no more committed to the treaty than it absolutely had to be, which was not very. With Elihu Root and Chandler Anderson gone, no major player remained from the group that oversaw the negotiation of the treaty. Taft's choice for secretary was Philander Knox, a lawyer best known for his work at Carnegie Steel and his service as U.S. Attorney General. Knox had two failings. First, his experience as a lawyer encouraged him to seek victory over compromise in negotiations. Second, he failed to cultivate the Senate's desire to be involved in foreign policy.

In addition, Knox chose as his assistant Francis Huntington Wilson, who, among other things, was a personally unpleasant Anglophobe.[1] Neither Wilson nor Knox had Root's desire to smooth U.S.-Canadian relations, and neither had a good relationship with the British ambassador, James Bryce.

Although Anderson had stepped down as department counselor, he still kept a semiofficial eye on the proceedings of the IFC. On 29 April 1909, Anderson sent Knox his opinions of the recent IFC draft. Mainly, he warned that Jordan had expanded the scope of the treaty beyond its proper limits. Although he did not specify the problems, Anderson told Knox that Jordan had failed to make several changes that the department had requested. He advised the secretary that, if Jordan did not heed the department's wishes, the United States should withhold approval of the regulations.[2] Almost immediately, then, the new regime was undermining Jordan's efforts.

Anderson informed Jordan that Jordan's signature on the regulations was meaningless without the approval of the State Department. He reminded Jordan that he had overstepped his bounds by not bringing the IFC report in line with the official American position. In particular, Jordan had opened the regulations with a paragraph that implied that the treaty power superseded local authority. Jordan had reason to believe that he was correct, but Anderson worried that such a brash statement would anger Congress. Anderson maintained a friendly tone, but he made it clear that the IFC proposals would not be acceptable to Congress or the State Department. An upset Jordan decided that "the present State Department wishes us to dodge responsibility whenever possible."[3]

Perhaps sensing skepticism in the new administration, in June Canadian Minister of Marine and Fisheries L. P. Brodeur took the unusual step of writing directly to Knox, circumventing the traditional channels. He wanted to proclaim the regulations, but he desired to act simultaneously with the Americans. Therefore, Brodeur asked Knox to move quickly and keep the Dominion government informed of changes in the American position. Knox advised Brodeur that the regulations would not be made public until Congress had time to review them, and Congress was in recess until December.[4]

Despite Knox's commitment to staying quiet, the regulations were receiving publicity in border fishing communities, and little of it was good. Many fishermen had met Jordan and Prince while they were conducting field research, and Jordan had sent others preliminary drafts of the regulations, so fishermen had an idea of the eventual outcome. On Saginaw Bay, fishermen complained that the regulations on mesh size "will virtually re-sult in killing this portion of the fishing industry." From Lake Huron came a petition saying, "Many of us depend entirely on fishing for a living and have considerable amounts invested in outfits which would be valueless if the proposed action were taken." [5] But one fish merchant from New York understood why the regulations were necessary: "The fisherman has always been his worst enemy and never provides for the future." [6]

With Congress out of session and Taft uninterested in unilateral action, Jordan and Prince left their offices in June 1909 to pursue further fieldwork and improve the regulations. [7] Their decision revealed a fundamental weakness in the mechanism that Root had established to promote cooperative fisheries protection. Prince and Jordan received their appointments because they were good scientists. Their major task was to draw up scientifically based protective regulations, and they headed back to the border to produce more effective rules without much concern for the political difficulties that their proposals already faced. More than extra research, the IFC recommendations needed a political guardian angel to provide safe passage through the U.S. Congress. Jordan was not qualified for that job, but Root's scheme left no alternative. Root had counted on Theodore Roosevelt's assertiveness to get the valuable conservation measure passed on Capitol Hill, but there was no one in Taft's administration who wanted to fight for the treaty.

Jordan and Prince did learn a great deal during their field trip. From Passamaquoddy Bay to the West Coast, they corrected previous mistakes, updated their information, and attempted to explain themselves to suspicious fishermen. As scientists, they had to admit when something was incorrect, but in so doing they committed political suicide. If they were outwardly dissatisfied with their own work, then they would have a difficult time persuading congressmen to ignore their constituents and vote for the measure.

On 19 August, Jordan informed Knox that the two scientists felt obligated to make some changes in their proposal. He foresaw six minor adjustments and three substantive regulatory improvements. He hinted that two of his concerns were trap nets in Sandusky Bay and salmon fishing in the greater Puget Sound region. The third was probably minimum mesh sizes for nets in Saginaw Bay. He wanted advice on the procedure he should pursue, but he received no help from anyone in the State Department. The American commissioner wrote to Evermann that "Mr. Knox, through Mr. Anderson, refused to do anything more than what we have already done for fear that he might get into a conflict with state rights." [8] Jordan could only hope that

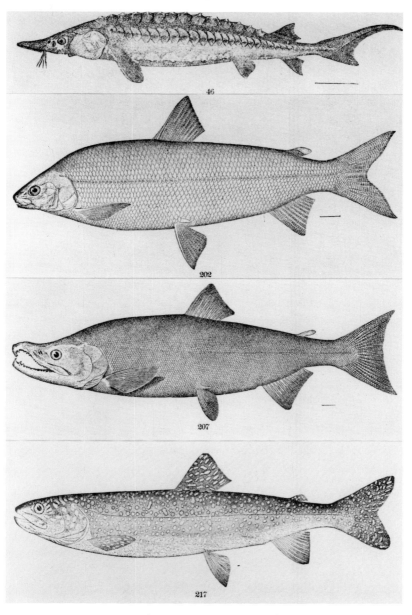

From top: Lake sturgeon *(Acipenser rubicundus)*;
lake whitefish *(Coregonus clupeiformis)*;
sockeye salmon *(Oncorhynchus nerka)*;
lake trout *(Cristivomer namaycush)*.
From Jordan and Evermann, *The Fishes of North and Middle America*, vol. 4

Salmon fishing fleet at the mouth of the Fraser River.
National Archives of Canada PA-51350

William Wakeham, 1897.
National Archives of Canada c-84720

Secretary of State Elihu Root in his office.
Library of Congress

David Starr Jordan about 1910.
Stanford University Libraries, BP Box 13, 4760

(Top) Richard Rathbun.
Carl A. Kroch Library, Cornell University

(Bottom) Senator William Smith of Michigan.
Senate Historical Office 5481-10

Fishing on Lake Superior.
Department of the Interior (Canada) 1936-271, 0-4-2-4, Box 2702

Salmon catch.
Photo by S. J. Thompson.
Geological Survey of Canada 1970-88, T2-36

he could avoid negative repercussions by making the changes "privately and quietly." [9]

Unlike Prince, Jordan was sensitive to the political pressure to kill the regulations. The adaptations he wanted for Saginaw and Sandusky bays were scientifically and politically motivated. He believed that the original proposals were not entirely fair to fishermen in those regions, because they were based on bad science. Prince, however, was suspicious that his American counterpart might be yielding solely to political pressure. Jordan warned him, "Sooner or later we must correct some of our errors or omissions, or else they will cause us trouble." [10]

In January, while Jordan and Prince waited for some sign of support from the moribund Taft administration, Senator Shelby Cullom of Virginia introduced a bill to implement the IFC regulations in the United States. The bill never made it out of the Senate Foreign Relations Committee. [11] Its fate came as no surprise, because it received no support in Congress or from the executive branch. Knox urged Jordan to lobby the Senate on behalf of the bill. Jordan, however, perceived this invitation as a set-up, because Chief Forester Gifford Pinchot, another holdover from Roosevelt's days, had just been fired for similar actions. [12]

The State Department's abandonment of Jordan further buried the chances of any serious progress on fisheries protection. Jordan had accepted Root's offer to be the American half of the International Fisheries Commission with the understanding that he would be free to leave when the regulations were turned over to the State Department. He had assumed that the department would, at that time, be glad to get his proposals. But Knox and Huntington Wilson were apathetic, at best. Jordan had sunk hundreds of hours into this work, but he was stuck. If he resigned, fisheries conservation would be set back; if he continued, he had no reason to expect success. He could only hope that his luck would change while the bill was in Congress.

JORDAN BATTLES CONGRESS

Recognizing that the administration had no intention of helping him, Jordan decided that he would in fact have to take the battle to Capitol Hill in 1910. A major procedural problem had arisen that further threatened the already weak prospects for fulfilling the intent of the treaty. The Senate would not accept the regulations without significant revisions, but Sir Wilfrid Laurier's government would not consider any revisions until Congress approved the initial rules and the principle behind them. Logically, Jordan had to focus on his countrymen and worry about Canada later.

In trying to break the impasse, Jordan warned that if the regulations "are thrown back simply because the American fishermen are not satisfied, Canada will hardly consent to do anything about it."[13] The Canadian government demanded that, pursuant to the treaty, Congress make the proposals law before either side considered amendments. In fact, the Privy Council decided that Canada would not accept any changes to the regulations until they had been in force for one year.[14] The Foreign Relations Committee never seriously considered such a scheme. It simply tabled Senator Cullom's bill and waited for rules more to its liking. In direct opposition to its treaty obligations, the State Department officially agreed. The Canadians held the moral high ground, but the Senate held the high cards.

The regulations faced opposition from four main sources. Ohio senators protested the elimination of trap nets in western Lake Erie. Michigan senators were irate about the mesh size of nets in Saginaw Bay. And Washington senators were just plain angry. An unexpected opponent was Senator Henry Cabot Lodge of Massachusetts, who, for reasons unknown, hated the IFC regulations as if they were a gift from the Kaiser. Jordan was willing to work with the senators from Ohio and Michigan, and he understood the opposition from Washington, but he had no idea how to deal with Lodge. Even though all of these senators were Republicans, neither Taft nor Knox brought their weight to bear on them.

The earliest protests came from the Ohio senators. Republican Senator Theodore Burton told Knox, "I have received a great number of strong protests against certain of the proposed regulations which it is claimed promise to inflict hardships upon American fishermen."[15] Burton also told Huntington Wilson, "It really seems to me that these regulations were not matured with that degree of care which is requisite to safeguard the interests of the fishermen of the Lakes."[16] Senator Charles Dick informed Jordan that in his opinion the loss of trap nets would cost Ohio 150 jobs and $500,000.[17]

Jordan sought a compromise. He pointed out that he was only following the lead of the Ohio Fish Commission, which had recommended that the state outlaw the use of trap nets. In addition, he argued, trap nets were illegal everywhere else on the continent, because they were placed entirely underwater and therefore hard to regulate.[18] Still, Jordan recognized that fishermen in that region had limited means for catching fish, and he was also aware that Burton and Dick could influence any Senate vote on the IFC rules. He tried to convince Prince that the Ohioans had a point, but the Canadian would not agree.

Jordan also had to deal with Senator William Smith of Michigan, who had Lodge's ear on the treaty. While he was not an especially powerful member of the Foreign Relations Committee, Smith had enough influence to turn many senators against the treaty. He ferociously refused to accept the regulations that Prince and Jordan had devised for Lake Huron. The item that most angered Smith was the restriction on small-mesh nets in Saginaw Bay. Many voters there lived by catching the slim and abundant subspecies of lake herring that populated the bay, and the large mesh would drive them out of business. Smith was angry, he had influence, and he intended to protect his constituents.

Both Jordan and Knox heard impassioned pleas from Michigan to alter the rules. The state game and fish warden called the regulations for Saginaw Bay "absurd."[19] He continued, "The regulations seem to have been framed by someone who had no knowledge whatever of conditions on the Great Lakes." Likewise, a local fisherman expressed his appreciation to Jordan for his friendly attitude but reminded him that his livelihood was on the line. Anticipating Jordan's answer, the fisherman asked, "Having no assurance of immediate assistance from you to whom, then, should we go but to the Congress?"[20]

Jordan believed that Smith and the Saginaw area fishermen had a legitimate complaint, and he felt that those fishermen were subject to a "distinct injustice . . . through my own fault."[21] Jordan tried to persuade Prince to accept a revised version of Section 46, which restricted the sizes of meshes on pound nets in Lake Huron, but Prince refused to budge. The Canadian government had made its position clear. Jordan complained to his friends about the Canadian attitude, because "with the hold [the Saginaw Bay fishermen] have on the Senate I do not think that anything will be done until in some way they are dislodged."[22] The commission's error meant that Smith or Brodeur would have to compromise on principle, and neither was likely to do so.

Jordan's subtle attempt to blame Canadian stubbornness was not entirely fair. It was true that Sir Wilfrid Laurier's government did not go out of its way to accommodate American objections, but then Canadian fishermen had built up a reservoir of resentment towards their American counterparts. Not only did Americans operate in a basically lawless environment, but Americans owned a large portion of the Canadian fishing industry.[23] Canadian lawmakers, especially Brodeur, believed that they finally had the upper hand in their long-running attempt to force some restraint on their American counterparts. They were not about to start making exceptions that might turn the tide against them. While Jordan understood Canadian discontent, he feared the Senate's record of mangling treaties that it did not like.

Out west, the American salmon industry clearly stated its position to its elected representatives. Attorneys for one group of fishermen argued that "the treaty has the effect of destroying the American industry for the purpose of exploiting a British industry." [24] Another group of Puget Sound fishermen chose to challenge the constitutionality of the regulations. They informed Senator S. H. Piles that "we are proceeding upon the theory that these fisheries belong absolutely to the state, and that the Federal government has no power or authority to take them away." [25] Their attorney had done his homework well; in late May he asked Anderson for a copy of his internal report, "The Scope of Treaty-making Power of the United States," which he believed would support his contention that the treaty was unconstitutional.[26]

Despite the talk about challenging the constitutionality of the IFC regulations, the real issue was the use of the jigger in salmon pound nets. The jigger is a long, J-shaped section of netting that reroutes fish to the net's crib if they miss the opening. Some fishermen thought that the jigger made no difference, but the majority—and the IFC—believed that it improved a net's efficiency by 50 to 100 percent. In addition, the placement of the jigger could wipe out any advantage given by forcing fishermen to shut down their traps for a weekly closed season.[27] A shrewd fisherman could set up the jigger in such a way as to place the fish in an infinite loop until he reopened the trap, at which point most of the fish would swim right into the crib. Jordan and Prince decided to outlaw it. The continued protests from Puget Sound tested Jordan's good nature; he confided to Prince, "If I were to write the statutes again I should feel like making them more severe." [28]

The bad news from the American capital stood in contrast with the good news from Ottawa. In March 1910, William Templeman, minister of inland revenue, introduced a three-part bill to Parliament that included authority for the Privy Council to promulgate the regulations when it so chose. As the minister explained, the government would wait until the U.S. government was ready, at which point the two governments would simultaneously proclaim the regulations. In stark contrast to the American enabling legislation, which contained each of the proposed regulations, the Canadian bill was a simple authorization measure. The M.P.s could either accept the regulations or refuse them. Given the nature of the parliamentary system — in which a majority government almost never loses a vote on a bill — the outcome was not in doubt.

Debate on the bill focused more on American reliability than on the merits of federal intervention into fisheries conservation. J. A. Currie from North Simcoe, Ontario, argued that the treaty was a waste of time. He knew that many American citizens had begun to call for amendments to the regulations, and he took that to be a bad sign. The U.S. government would not, in his opinion, approve the treaty without the consent of the states. Because the Taft administration had done nothing to gain such consent, he predicted that somewhere along the line the treaty would go down in flames. In rebuttal, John Conmee of Thunder Bay and Rainy River could offer only that Mr. Currie "has water on the brain today." [29]

From the West Coast, another voice rose in opposition. This time, the assailant was J. D. Taylor of New Westminster, British Columbia, at the heart of the Fraser River salmon industry. After listening to lengthy defenses of the treaty, Taylor had heard enough. Upset about the wording of a regulation meant to render salmon traps inoperable for forty-eight hours each week, he vented his anger:

> We are not in this section doing anything to help conserve the salmon . . .
> I say that in all seriousness, because so far as we on the Pacific Coast are concerned, we are apt to experience nothing but calamity from the operation of these regulations.[30]

In his final statement, he noted that Washington State could not enforce the law and the U.S. federal government would not; therefore, the Dominion risked subjecting its own fishermen to overly stringent laws. Even a treaty proponent, G. H. Bradbury from Selkirk on the north shore of Lake Erie, admitted that "for many years the Americans have always got the best of us." [31] Canadians from fishing towns simply did not trust the United States to be responsible.

Even though the outcome was never in doubt, Templeman had to reply to the carping. He agreed that the American record of fisheries protection was shabby. He recognized that previous attempts at a cooperative arrangement had failed. Yet he held out the hope that the Dominion finally had a breakthrough, because this time the U.S. government had agreed to a treaty that would bring its rules in line with Canada's. If fishermen determined that the rules were unfair, the IFC principle of joint control included a mechanism to resolve their problems. Finally, in an attempt to win over Taylor and impress upon the House of Commons the magnitude of the opportunity, Templeman said, "If we did not have this treaty with the United States government to regulate fishing in Puget Sound . . . we might just as well conclude that fishing on the Fraser River would be absolutely destroyed in another ten years."[32] Parliament then passed the bill.

With Parliament on record, Jordan and Prince scheduled one more meeting to create a strategy for bridging the gap between Congress and Parliament. Jordan arranged to come to Ottawa around 20 June, after attending to some business in New York. In order to emphasize the urgency, he told Prince that he was leaving for Europe in July and would not return until the end of October. On the day Jordan arrived in Ottawa, Prince sent a letter to Palo Alto canceling their meeting. As a rationale, he pointed out that he did not agree with most of Jordan's proposals, writing, "I could not fail to note how little regard was paid to the interests of Canadian fishermen."[33] In addition, he suggested that he did not have the authority to agree to any changes even if they were agreeable. The burden was no longer on Ottawa's conscience, because it was the U.S. government that was not upholding its end of the obligation.

A few days later, Prince sent another letter to Jordan in an attempt to atone for his odd behavior. He lamely apologized for "a mix-up in timing" that had led him to leave town during Jordan's visit. As a consolation prize, he noted that the governor general, Lord Grey, was "taking a personal interest in the matter."[34] Unfortunately, Grey's appointment was about to expire, so Prince really had no good news at all. Ever the optimist, Jordan wrote from Europe that he would still like to meet in November in order to present a united front to anyone who might wish to test the law in the Supreme Court.[35] Perhaps Jordan had forgotten that there still was no law to challenge.

Jordan's persistence probably stemmed from his misapprehension that Brodeur had forced Prince into rejecting concessions to American political realities. In reality, Prince was almost as staunch as his minister on the need for a firm stand. In early March, he told Brodeur that amending the regulations before they were even implemented would open the floodgates: "Fishermen would object, as they always do, to every regulation ever devised."[36] Prince knew that Jordan faced many complaints, but he did not agree with Jordan that concessions would help the IFC in the long run. He also made it clear that he felt no sympathy for Jordan's plight, because he too had faced resistance from every fishing region in the Dominion.[37]

Prince did waver a little, but Brodeur did not. On 27 May, Prince had sent a memo to Brodeur outlining the situation in the United States. Senators Lodge and Smith were in a take-no-prisoners mood, and Jordan was desperate. Without giving it any official endorsement, Prince passed on a suggestion from Barton Evermann, who counseled that the IFC should yield on the three major points of contention — mesh size in Saginaw Bay, trap nets in Lake Erie, and jiggers in the greater Puget Sound region — in order to get the positive benefits of the other sixty-two regulations. Prince noted that he had held firm, but he also left Brodeur an opportunity to take the offer. On the bottom of the memo, Brodeur wrote, "No changes should be made and the negotiations should not go on."[38]

Brodeur's strong commitment to keeping the regulations intact was morally admirable and politically foolish. Unlike so many other people involved, he would not compromise the long-term health of the fisheries. But in holding the line Brodeur was blind to the realities of American governance. The original Jordan-Prince report was dead in the water. Instead of trusting Prince and Jordan to cut the best deal they could, he attempted to try his hand at diplomacy. In August, bypassing diplomatic protocol, he approached the American consul in Montreal with an appeal to Secretary Knox. His letter told the secretary of the embarrassment and hardship that Canada suffered waiting for American action.[39] Jordan could have told him that begging was counterproductive; Knox did not bother to reply.

As Jordan sailed for Europe in late July 1910, supporters of the IFC had no reason to be optimistic. The only advance toward effective international control of these valuable fisheries was passage of the appropriate legislation in the Canadian Parliament. While a positive step, that act of the House of Commons was never in doubt. In Washington, Senator Cullom's bill gathered dust. No one had stepped forward to help Jordan break the deadlock, and there was no reason to expect any reinforcements before the 1912 elections. The one glimmer of hope was that Jordan fought on, unwilling to quit while there was still even a slim chance of success.

JORDAN'S LAST STAND

Amidst the gloomy prospects for the future of fisheries protection and international conservation efforts, David Starr Jordan got a second wind. From his reentry into the fray in December 1910 through another setback in February 1911, Jordan was at his most impressive. In what was, in retrospect, the end of the open season for this treaty, Jordan made his most impassioned effort to convince his opponents of the need for U.S.-Canadian cooperation, even if it entailed some sacrifice. In the end, Jordan could not overcome the obstructionism of the State Department, the obstinacy of the Senate, and the indifference of conservationists.

In all of his previous efforts to gain support for the regulations, Jordan had not tried to present a rationale for the regulations. Given his strong performances as a social critic on so many issues, this failure to convert his expertise into public support was surprising. To be fair, his job, as Root had defined it, did not include winning debates on the subject of international fisheries conservation. At some point while he was touring Europe, Jordan apparently decided that it was now his duty to fight the political battles.

Upon his return, Jordan traveled to Ottawa to meet with Prince and Brodeur to plot a strategy. Both men actually showed up. Afterwards, Brodeur wrote to Jordan: "I wish to congratulate you on the harmonious working of the International Fisheries Commission. . . . It is pleasing that such a fair and effective system of regulations . . . has been agreed upon."[40] Brodeur then reported to Jordan that Laurier's cabinet was willing to amend the contested regulations regarding Saginaw Bay and Sandusky Bay as soon as Congress passed Cullom's bill.

With that commitment in hand, Jordan turned to the State Department. In mid-December 1910, Jordan wrote to several people in the department trying to rally action. First, he wanted "the President to issue a proclamation promulgating our fishery regulations."[41] With enthusiasm, he explained his position to the newly reappointed counselor, Chandler Anderson: "The Canadian Government feels, very justly, I think, that—the Saginaw matter now out of the way, this whole measure should be pushed as rapidly as may be."[42]

Jordan then got down to the business of building an intellectual case for the internationalization of shared resources, based on the state of the salmon on the West Coast. The facts were simple: Washingtonians could step up their activities and destroy the fishery, but British Columbians could do the same thing. Spending most of their time on the high seas, the salmon did not belong to either state or province, but their survival depended on cooperation between the two. Washington, in particular, could not claim ownership of a species that spent about one week of its four-year life in the state's waters. Therefore, the treaty did not transfer ownership from the state to the federal government. Nobody could *own* the fish. The treaty was not an extension of federal power but rather a recognition of the international nature of the fisheries.[43]

Jordan then proceeded to lecture Knox and Anderson on the true merits of his work on the treaty. He reminded them that the goal of fisheries conservation was "of the greatest importance." Root's treaty aimed to unify the statutes with the larger goal of enhancing the supply of food fish in the region. The boundary waters contained, in Lake Erie and in the greater Puget Sound region, two of the most important fisheries in the world, which "can be protected only through joint action of the regions concerned. Such joint action, in the machinery of nations is attainable only by treaty." Up to that point, though, only Canada had carried out its international obligations.[44]

The American commissioner demanded immediate action to put the regulations into place. He admitted that regulations on such a grand scale had to contain some flaws, especially in the first draft, and he was willing to entertain complaints. Despite the shortcomings, he wrote, "it will readily be seen that these regulations as a whole are not arbitrary nor severe, but rather that they represent a minimum of the preservation necessary for the conservation of these most valuable fisheries." Jordan pledged to right any wrongs, but he also emphasized his duty to reduce overfishing. He argued that the opponents of the regulations were self-interested or shortsighted: "These regulations are a measure of conservation. Enlightened opinion of men concerned is in their favor, but as they mean less promiscuous fishing, there are men whose interest is in opposition — and that all along the line."

Knox did not blink. On 20 January 1911, just two days after receiving Jordan's demand for action, he ordered Jordan to cable four amendments to Ottawa, all of which allowed more ways to catch or use fish. Jordan acknowledged the request the next day by noting that Knox's proposals were all quite minor. Then, on 26 January, Knox took a bolder step. He sent four more amendments to Jordan to be passed on to the Canadian authorities, and he had the audacity to tell Jordan that the fishermen liked the new wording better in each case; Knox had probably never met a fisherman. Jordan objected to one, which shortened the weekly closed season from forty-eight to thirty-six hours for nets in the greater Puget Sound region, but he thought Canada would accept the changes if they meant immediate passage by Congress.[45] Jordan was taxing his own political skills and tolerance.

The Canadian response to Knox's ultimatums was muted. On 25 January, Brodeur presented an amended version of the regulations to the House of Commons, but he did not submit another after Knox's second set of amendments. Jordan recorded a small tremor from Prince, but that was the extent of the Canadian reaction. Prince did not object directly to the changes, but he did comment that the amendments "ignore uniformity and are disastrous to fish conservation." [46] Over a month later, Prince commented more explicitly to Jordan. He expressed concern about the impression in Washington that the two IFC commissioners had struck some sort of deal. He cautioned Jordan that there would be an uproar if the Canadian public thought that the Dominion government was bowing to American pressure.[47]

On 7 February 1911, Knox took the step that he should have taken in May 1909: he sent the newly amended IFC report to Taft and Congress. He urged Congress to act quickly both to satisfy America's treaty obligation and to stem the tide of depletion of the boundary water fisheries. From the tone of the letter, the average reader might have concluded that Knox was a champion of U.S.-Canadian cooperation and conservation. On 10 February, President Taft sent a message to Congress that stated, "I cannot too strongly urge upon Congress the importance of taking prompt action to put into operation the conservation measures provided in the regulations." [48] In the interest of accuracy, Taft should have replaced "cannot" with "will not."

While Knox continued his calculated assault on the treaty, Anderson seemed to be warming up to Jordan. He reported that Jordan was willing to go to Ottawa to make sure that Canada would accept Knox's final alterations. In Anderson's opinion, the State Department owed Jordan a full-fledged lobbying effort on Capitol Hill if he actually got Canadian assent. In fact, Anderson argued that Taft should immediately promulgate the regulations as a sign of good faith. If Taft and Knox did not support him, then there was really no reason for Jordan to make the trip. Anderson added as an afterthought that Jordan had the unofficial support of the State Department in his endeavors.[49] While hardly a ringing endorsement, Anderson's memo was the most backing that Jordan had received from the department since his appointment.

The only legislative debates about the regulations, however, were taking place in Ottawa. On 10 March, Taylor and one of his allies challenged Brodeur to show some sign of progress south of the border. The minister had to admit that Congress had not made any visible progress, but he pursued a course of moderation. He reminded the assembly of "the great importance to Canada of having a treaty on this subject with the United States." He concluded with the comment, "The regulations, though not so severe as I would like to see them, have, nevertheless for the first time brought the fishery regulations of the United States under the control of a central power."[50] On the other side of the continent, one of Taylor's constituents had a different reading of the situation: "The Americans certainly have no sense of honor or regard for their obligations."[51]

Part of Jordan's problem was that the only input on the treaty came from representatives of the fishing interests, such as Charles Bullymore, an attorney from Buffalo. He, better than any other person, summed up the two basic objections to the IFC regulations. First, he demanded to know what gave the United States the authority to take control of Lake Erie from Pennsylvania and New York. Second, he pointed out to Anderson the problems of the size limit for lake whitefish. "These small fish run into nets," he wrote, "and cannot be prevented by printing something on a piece of paper."[52] When he got no satisfaction from the State Department, he turned to pestering Jordan.

Unlike some of the other people who contacted Jordan, Bullymore was not vindictive. He thanked Jordan for being consistent, even if they disagreed: "It is just a question of looking at things through different glasses."[53] He admitted that the fishermen he represented might prefer the uniformity of federal regulations, but they had no idea who was in charge. In his opinion, the fishermen wanted "the big, broad, liberal policy of the Federal Government." He also promised Jordan that, if he got a couple of adjustments, "there is nothing that I will not do, even to standing on my head" to support the IFC regulations.[54]

Still, Bullymore forced Jordan to defend the contention that the federal government had the right to make such a treaty. Jordan was cautious, writing that "the United States should take part in these things, I think, only when it is essential to the public welfare."[55] While he believed that the federal government had to do what the states legally could not, he admitted that he would leave to others the question of whether the country "would rather wait until the fisheries are still further depleted." In the end, Jordan recognized that Bullymore's two main points were inseparable: "I am not by choice a constitutional lawyer, but I have been forced into the profession in trying to save the 1½ pound whitefish."[56] There was the fatal flaw; Root had asked a scientist to tackle a legal and political problem.

This exchange with Bullymore proved to be Jordan's last act as commissioner. On 19 April 1911, Secretary Knox ordered him to "kindly suspend action. Other arrangements under consideration."[57] Two days later, Huntington Wilson wrote to Jordan to explain that he had been fired "for reasons of economy and administration." Congress had the regulations and Jordan's work was, in Wilson's opinion, accomplished. "The Department appreciates to the fullest extent," he wrote, "the distinguished scientific ability which you have brought to the service of the Government."[58]

Jordan accepted the ax with grace, although he did make a reference to "feeble-minded senators."[59] He agreed with Wilson that Root's offer of June 1908 had expired, perhaps because he thought that he could no longer do anything constructive. He admitted to some failings as commissioner, but he also noted that "the Government evidently thought that a clever man who knew something of fishes would know all about the local interests in every one of the thousand fishing ports along the border."[60] He might also have mentioned the pressure to be a political genius as well. Finally, as he told Richard Rathbun, "Congress is very sensitive whenever anybody says that he is going to lose a little money through an act of Congress."[61] Jordan had done the best he could within the limits and saw no reason to apologize.

Jordan did try one last trick to keep his goals alive. In July, he nominated Dr. Evermann as his replacement. Secretary of Commerce and Labor Charles Nagel had come to know Jordan during the negotiation of the North Pacific Fur Seal Treaty, and the two men respected each other. Jordan confessed that, "having put my spare time for nearly three years on these regulations, I do not want to see them thrown away."[62] Nagel, therefore, agreed to recommend his subordinate Evermann to Knox.

In his correspondence with Nagel, Jordan could not maintain his optimism. Although he saw signs of support in Ohio and Michigan, he feared that the Puget Sound fishermen were still quite stubborn. "The fisheries of Puget Sound," he wrote, "are doomed if the present conditions go on very much longer."[63] Nagel suggested that the treaty might still be salvageable, but Jordan replied that "it does not look likely to me."[64] When Knox announced that a New York politician, Job Hedges, was his choice for the IFC instead of Evermann, Jordan called it "a cynical perversion of authority." He described Hedges as "an excellent citizen and charming after-dinner speaker [who] knows nothing whatever of the Fisheries."[65]

Knox's treatment of Jordan clearly annoyed the loyal Nagel. When the fishermen of Puget Sound complained that Canadian fishing wardens were seizing boats that strayed into Canadian waters, Secretary Nagel lashed out at Knox about the status of the treaty. He began by giving a more coherent rationale for the regulations than any other administration figure had. The treaty, he argued, would have conserved "at maximum productivity" both countries' fisheries and fishing interests. But the salmon interests had fought the treaty. If they "had exerted their influence in favor of federal control of international fisheries instead of against it, it is altogether probable that the federal government would now have a well-equipped patrol on Puget Sound, which would have prevented the growth of the deplorable conditions now existing." [66] Perhaps now, he commented, the salmon fishers were beginning to see the merits of the treaty they had fought so bitterly.

The end of Jordan's service on the IFC removed the last strong voice in the United States in favor of scientifically based centralized control of the border fisheries. Whoever replaced Jordan would not have his combination of scientific knowledge, social vision, and public influence. Knox did not give an explanation for Jordan's dismissal, although Wilson used the original terms of Jordan's appointment as justification. In reality, he probably grew tired of dealing with Jordan's persistent attempts to place the long-term good of the fisheries ahead of the short-term interests of American fishermen.

THE LINGERING DEATH OF THE INLAND FISHERIES TREATY

Despite Jordan's dismissal, the two sides continued to discuss means of implementing the treaty, but all real chances of success were gone. Beginning in the spring of 1911, both the executive and legislative branches of the U.S. government took inflammatory action in the form of altering the regulations. In response, the Canadian government and Ambassador Bryce threatened to withdraw from the treaty. Unfortunately for Canadian authorities, the American government was willing to allow the treaty to perish. For two years, Ottawa searched without success for a magic wand to resolve the problem. In the end, the Canadians had to abandon the treaty.

On 17 May 1911, Senator Smith of Michigan took the first action on the Senate floor on behalf of the enabling legislation. He called for rapid action on the bill in order to grant fishermen as much time as possible to adjust to the regulations. Since Cullom had introduced the bill in February 1910,

Smith had "corrected the details" and consulted with people in all parts of the country on the proper wording. He had removed the regulations that contained the toughest restrictions on fishing methods. He now believed that all interested parties were satisfied with the regulations as they stood in the bill. On 22 May, the Senate passed it.[67]

The passage of the bill sparked the first diplomatic activity regarding the treaty in almost three years. On 6 June, Ambassador Bryce declared that the Senate Foreign Relations Committee had mutilated the regulations. The bill, which was pending in the House of Representatives, did not have an adequate appropriation, and the committee had removed every regulation opposed by local interests. Bryce was enraged that senators had used individual regulations as bargaining chips for other legislative issues, but he admitted, "It is not the first time in which the Senate has shown itself actuated by such motives and neglectful of international obligations." The only real surprise, in Bryce's mind, was Senator Elihu Root's silence on the Foreign Relations Committee. The ambassador had expected that Root "would do his best to prevent the repudiation of the contract he had himself concluded." Bryce resolved to make a strong diplomatic charge to save the treaty.[68]

Ten days later, Bryce challenged Knox to stand up for the treaty. He began by reminding Knox that the treaty stipulated that the two countries had to have identical regulations. The Senate, however, had removed ten vital pieces of the legislation, including the four that Jordan had deemed to be the most important. The result was "a diversity which would be both inconsistent with the Treaty and highly inconvenient, indeed impossible in practice." As a solution, Bryce urged the administration to either persuade the Senate to reconsider its actions or veto the bill.[69]

After six weeks of insulting silence from the State Department, Bryce tried again to get some satisfaction. This time, he explicitly stated that the Privy Council had decided to renounce the treaty if the Taft administration could not produce any progress on the legislation. Bryce argued that the boundary water fisheries were still productive only because of Canadian restraint; if Canada adopted the American attitude, "the fisheries would be very seriously depleted to the injury of the United States as well as Canada." Finally, he called Knox's attention to the president's many speeches about the great opportunities afforded by Canadian-American cooperation. The fisheries treaty was just one part, "designed both to develop a great industry and to increase the supply of food for the people of both countries." He concluded by again asking Knox to take a firm stand.[70]

Knox's refusal to respond to Bryce's request was petty. The secretary did not particularly like the ambassador, but he still owed him the respect due to the representative of both the most powerful nation on the globe and America's northern neighbor. Also, the Taft administration was already in danger of losing its coveted trade reciprocity deal with Canada, and a more conciliatory line might have helped the Laurier government.[71] But Knox was not much of a statesman, and he was even less of a conservationist. He had no interest in wrestling with powerful senators over a question of fisheries preservation, and he did not see how the treaty might fit into the larger picture of U.S. foreign policy.

Given the central position of natural resources in the reciprocity debate, the administration would have been wise to demonstrate conservationist inclinations. Many Canadians feared that freer trade would give Americans the chance to strip Canada of its resources as they had denuded the United States.[72] Already, American companies had purchased control of large pieces of Canada's economy in the form of forests and fishing equipment. Willingness to accept the IFC regulations would have been a sign of good faith on the administration's part. If the U.S. government could not even honor a straightforward natural resources treaty that it had instigated, however, then Canadians had reason to fear American action under the reciprocity pact. The American inability to show good faith no doubt played a part in the downfall of the Laurier government in the 1911 elections.

In March of 1912, the new Canadian government contemplated its options. Calling the current system "one-sided, unfair, and productive of disastrous results," the authors of a summary memorandum vindicated Canadian actions on the treaty. The original IFC proposals were, at best, a compromise, but they served two purposes. First, they were an improvement over the current situation, and, second, they supported Canada's claim that previous American rules had been unfair. Now, though, the Senate had butchered the bill, and Canada faced a dilemma. Based on the assumption that "it would be regrettable in the highest degree if the present effort failed," there were three options. First, Canada could pressure the United States for another year; second, Canada could accept the abused version and hope for the best later; third, the Dominion could try to shock Congress into action by annulling the treaty. While the authors left the choice to be debated, they warned that the Senate was "stimulated by a very small body of selfish and reckless fishermen and fish merchants who have no care for the future."[73]

In 1913, Woodrow Wilson's new administration renewed hope in some circles that the treaty might be given one last chance. Job Hedges turned out to be a personal friend of the Canadian prime minister, Robert Borden, who persuaded the Privy Council to grant Wilson some time to work on Congress. Ambassador Bryce suggested that the new administration deserved a year to try "a little of that tact in which the Taft Administration was conspicuously deficient."[74] Bryce, though, warned his government that Canada should offer a compromise regarding Lake Huron only; if that failed then it was time to quit.

Jordan wrote directly to Wilson to advise him on the best course of action. Mainly he complained about "senatorial dullness" and the "neglect of the Department of State."[75] But he did make it clear that the basic problem was heavy overfishing. He also recommended that Wilson should appoint Evermann to replace Hedges, who had recently resigned. Finally, just to make clear his allegiance, Jordan praised Secretary of State William Jennings Bryan and the new State Department as a "centre of peace" that would avoid dollar diplomacy.[76]

The summer of 1913 saw two important developments that raised hope that the IFC regulations might make a miraculous recovery. First, the State Department chose Dr. Hugh Smith, the director of the Bureau of Fisheries, to be Prince's counterpart. Unlike Hedges, Smith was a scientist, and unlike Jordan, he could devote all of his time to the effort. Prince was quite pleased and wrote to Smith that he had begun "to be very depressed about the outcome of the many years' work of the International Commission."[77] Smith quickly arranged for the two commissioners to meet President Wilson to explain "the somewhat firm attitude taken by the Government of Canada."[78] The second important development of that summer was Canada's decision that it could no longer work single-handedly to save the fisheries. The government warned the United States that if no regulations were forthcoming, then "the Canadian Government will, to its regret, be forced by circumstances for which they must declaim all responsibility to resume their liberty of action."[79] The Privy Council chose to hold the ultimatum until 28 November, at which point the government set a 1 March 1914 deadline.

In December 1913, the treaty proponents rallied for one last charge up Capitol Hill. Prince urged his government to drop its hard-line position and accept the best possible deal. He wrote, "It would be a calamity ruinous to the great Boundary Fisheries of both countries *if nothing were accomplished under the present treaty.*"[80] Both the State and Commerce Departments pledged to support the original regulations in Congress, and Wilson also announced his support. Finally, for the first time, American conservationists called on the president to support stringent fishery conservation measures.

The awakening of the conservationist leaders to the merit of the fisheries treaty was truly too little, too late. In two strongly worded letters, the New York Fish, Game, and Forest League — which included the noted conservationists T. Gilbert Pearson, William T. Hornaday, and John B. Burnham — called on the "special and selfish interests . . . to stand aside for the common good."[81] But they made it clear that their major concern was a possible Canadian backlash against the Migratory Bird Treaty, not the plight of the fish. Birds trumped fish. Also, in writing to the administration, they failed to lobby the true culprits in the Senate, where the treaty needed help. Had Burnham, Hornaday, and Pearson come to Jordan's aid in 1909 they might have made a difference.

Despite the concentrated support for the treaty, the necessary bills did not reach Congress until February 1914. On 10 February, Elihu Root emerged from his five-year slumber to introduce a bill based on Jordan's initial report to the Senate. Two days later, the same bill came before the House of Representatives. On 27 February, senators friendly to the treaty requested that the bill be discussed ahead of schedule in order to comply with Canadian demands.[82] For the first time in years, the treaty seemed to have more supporters than detractors. Assistant Secretary of State J. B. Moore believed that "as a result of the admirable work done by the American and Canadian commissioners since last summer, there is now no opposition in the United States."[83] The Privy Council chose to let the deadline pass.[84]

Moore's assessment of the support for the treaty in the fishing community was wrong. By the end of March, three important observers had tallied the potential for economic damage that the treaty might cause. A state senator from Ohio estimated that the prohibition of trap nets would cost \$1,000,000 annually.[85] The president of a Puget Sound packing company said his plant would have to close, costing 600 jobs and his \$365,000 investment. Finally, the Washington Fish Commissioner claimed that the rules would shut down the \$13 million salmon industry and throw 12,000 people out of work.[86] "The Canadian fishermen," he wrote, "gain practically everything if these regulations become effective, while nothing is conceded to the United States."[87]

Although some of these statements stretched the truth, this sentiment still dominated Congress. When the Senate brought the bill up for consideration on 27 February, some senators called for more time to study the regulations. This audacious request earned a rare rebuke from Senator Root, who said, "The whole thing has dragged along now for five years without the Government of the United States complying with its obligations."[88] The ensuing debate revealed one major surprise. Senator Poindexter of Washington supported the regulations because the canning industry had decided that federal control was the only safe way to regulate "the great silver horde [as it] goes to the spawning ground."[89]

While the Puget Sound senators showed a conciliatory side, those from Ohio and Michigan fought on. One of the first questions to arise was whether or not to exclude Saginaw Bay from the regulations. Senator Porter McCumber of North Dakota argued that such action set a precedent that would allow each nation to alter the extent of the treaty's power. In response, Henry Cabot Lodge pointed out that Canada agreed to exclude the bay, and "if Canada does not object, certainly there can be no other good ground for objection." Besides, Lodge continued, Senator Smith wanted the bay excluded: "I think it ought to be made as a matter of good faith to the senior Senator from Michigan."[90] In the end, the Senate agreed to exclude Saginaw Bay, then passed the bill.

The next obstacle was the House of Representatives, which had never seriously discussed the regulations in the past. Congressman Henry Flood of Virginia was the sole voice for the regulations as he attempted to get the bill passed on 2 March. He faced an almost impossible task. Not only did he have to win a vote on the bill, but first he had to get a two-thirds majority in order to suspend the rules and bring up the bill for debate early. Flood argued that Canada had already waited for four years and the bill was necessary for effective fisheries protection.[91]

Flood never had much of a chance. Congressmen from Ohio, Minnesota, Michigan, Maine, and a number of other states opposed the bill for a variety of reasons. Some argued that the regulations would harm their constituents. One stated that Canadian desire for quick action revealed that the treaty was a bad deal for the United States. Another clever opponent compared the fisheries bill to the Weeks-McLean migratory bird protection act of 1913, which he said was just the first step toward building a million-dollar bureaucracy to enforce the law. Flood tried to fight back, but he was almost alone. When the Speaker of the House finally called for a vote on whether or not to suspend the rules, Flood fell far short of the two-thirds margin.[92] The House never resumed debate on the bill.

Canada waited silently all summer. The British ambassador, Sir Cecil Spring Rice, reminded Assistant Secretary Robert Lansing in May that "so important a measure in the direction of the conservation of the natural resources of the continent" deserved action, but Lansing was powerless.[93] The Commerce Department searched for some means of compromise but could find nothing. Finally, on 8 October 1914, the governor general told Spring Rice that Canada would resume its liberty of action. Eleven days later, the ambassador passed along the message to Secretary Bryan. In his note, he absolved Canada of any blame. At the bottom of the note, an American official wrote: "The expected has at last happened."[94]

In late 1914, several people examined the treaty for signs of life. Secretary of Commerce William Redfield and Secretary Bryan thought that Canada might change its mind if Congress would pass the legislation. Even the governor general supposedly wanted to give the regulations another attempt. But IFC commissioner Hugh Smith knew that the game was over: "This is a regrettable outcome of an effort to preserve an international industry by international regulations after the inability of the States to cope with the situation had been amply demonstrated. . . . In my judgment the further agitation of this matter is useless.[95] The Inland Fisheries Treaty had failed.

CONCLUSION

Although the principles of the Inland Fisheries Treaty never became law, the treaty was an important first step in the development of international cooperation to conserve natural resources. Supporters of the treaty made, and suffered for, just about every mistake imaginable. Those who wished to stop this early attempt to organize transnational conservation of a shared resource had a fairly easy task. But the supporters learned lessons that would pay off down the line with future agreements, and the strength of the conservation movement suggested that there were more to come.

Advocates of international cooperation could not overcome the desire for direct ownership of common property resources. In both Canadian and American societies, ownership of private property was an almost sacred right. Ownership defined how someone could use a resource; almost everything of economic value had to have an owner. If no individual could own a resource, such as fish in a large body of water, then people took solace in assigning group ownership. But even group ownership was theoretical, both because the fish routinely crossed borders and because states hesitated to regulate users. At least in the United States, state ownership actually stood in the way of conservation and regulation.

Jordan recognized this problem, but few heeded his words. State ownership had been a means to manage the use of common property by protecting the interests of all users within a political jurisdiction, but now Jordan was suggesting that state ownership only exacerbated competition. The answer had to be cooperative international control that recognized certain rights without granting final say to any local or national owner.

The methods of ownership and regulation of the boundary fisheries pursued by state, provincial, and national governments were incompatible, which raised the second problem. Different governments could, in good faith or bad, impose conflicting sets of regulations on the same resource. Particularly in the United States, where one body of water often bordered several states, rules often worked at cross-purposes. This problem intensified when the political units belonged to separate nations, no matter how friendly. Diplomats and scientists, then, had two tasks before them. First they had to make the states and provinces agree to protect their fisheries, then they had to create rules that actually protected the resource.

A treaty was the logical means available to solve both major problems, and a few minor ones, at once. From a conservation standpoint, the goal of the treaty was to answer the question of ownership. Had the boundary fisheries treaty survived, it would have established that the fish were the common property of all citizens of both countries. The citizens, through their representative governments, then would have empowered the International Fisheries Commission to protect the fisheries for the good of the majority, not local interest groups. In addition, the treaty would have served as a model for similar problems between the United States and Canada.

The treaty itself was a reasonable document, with no obvious flaws. At only four articles, not much could go wrong. In fact, its simplicity was a virtue. Once Root and the Privy Council stopped haggling over which waters to include, there was not much left to debate. The one condition that might have been a mistake was the six-month limit on the IFC's time. In retrospect, the scientists needed more time to truly understand the conditions that prevailed on the border. Rathbun and Wakeham's report was valuable. But if the negotiators had wanted regulations based on their work, then they should have just appointed the two elder scientists to the IFC and let them rewrite their recommendations. On the other hand, had the IFC commissioners accomplished their tasks within the six-month time frame, President Roosevelt could have taken action on behalf of the regulations.

The fundamental flaw of the treaty, then, was not in its structure but in its vague purpose, which led to different expectations in Ottawa and Washington. Root instigated the negotiations with an eye toward reducing Canadian-American tensions. His endorsement of fisheries conservation was at best a secondary concern, and at worst it was a ruse to gain Canadian acquiescence. Canadian authorities believed that fisheries conservation meant controlling American fishermen, but conservative American diplomats could not endorse federal intervention in the traditional realm of the states. Canada would not accept anything short of strong federal intervention, but Root and his successors believed that such action might be unconstitutional and unpopular in Congress. In fact, the same Senate that had approved the treaty would not approve the logical regulations that it generated. Root had sold to Canada a treaty that he and Congress could not deliver; it was the old bait-and-switch maneuver.

Root and the Canadian authorities could have given the treaty a better chance had they limited its scope to just Lake Erie and the Fraser River salmon fisheries. Diplomats demanded the inclusion of every fishable boundary water on the assumptions that fish moved across the border naturally and that such migration caused political problems. They believed that protection for Canadian fishermen could come only under an arrangement that brought all American fishermen under strict control. In reality, though, only the Lake Erie species and the West Coast salmon showed signs of damage brought on by international competition. In some areas, such as the deeper Great Lakes, Rathbun and Wakeham had suggested that the fish rarely crossed the border. Other areas were just not important enough to risk losing Lake Erie and the Fraser River. Had they protected these two, treaties for the others could have followed.

Restricting the treaty to those two major fisheries would have produced three benefits. First, with substantially less ground to cover, the IFC might have completed its work before Roosevelt left office. Prince had served on Dominion commissions that had studied both areas, and he probably would not have needed much time to catch up with Jordan. Second, by concentrating on those two areas, the treaty would have generated fewer opponents in Congress, especially Senator Smith, the relentless defender of Saginaw Bay. Third, those two fisheries, more than any others, lent themselves to constitutionally acceptable federal control. Lake Erie, bordered by four states, needed uniform regulations, and the state of Washington had a weak claim to ownership of the Fraser River salmon. Had the treaty been smaller in scale and the various players quicker to act, new regulations might have been in force in 1909.

Root's successor as secretary of state, Philander Knox, was the closest thing to a villain in the whole story. Knox refused to consider the merits of conserving the boundary water fisheries, and he did nothing to help the treaty when it was in danger. Jordan commented that, when the Senate chopped up the regulations in 1911, "the State Department made no protest, held no hearings, and, in fact, did nothing."[96] Knox had many reasons to dislike the treaty—it was Root's idea, Jordan was a little too progressive, it meant restrictions on free enterprise, American fishermen would be the main losers, Bryce supported it—and all of them probably encouraged him to allow the treaty to wither. Had he accepted Jordan's advice and twisted a few senatorial arms, the regulations might have passed intact.

Senators William Smith and Henry Cabot Lodge also did their best to block the treaty's progress. Of course, many other congressmen deserved blame for selfishness or shortsightedness, but these two were the worst offenders. Smith could not see beyond the short-term self-interest of a small band of constituents. He refused to consider the long-range impact of the treaty's failure on fishing in Michigan or the availability of cheap fish for all of his constituents. As bad as Smith was, Lodge was even worse. He was a leader of the Republican party, a friend of Theodore Roosevelt's, and a man proud of his vision, yet he stooped to trading pieces of a bill of national importance without weighing the impact of his actions. As members of the Foreign Relations Committee, these men set the tone for the rest of the Senate.

The body of American fishermen, too, did their best to inhibit the treaty's success. In some ways, their concerns were understandable, because their jobs and lives were on the line. Scientists knew that the fishermen were slowly destroying their own resource base, but the fishermen chose not to see it that way. In their eyes, they were following an honorable profession as well as they could. The IFC regulations would succeed only in giving their business to Canadians, who were a convenient scapegoat for the declining yields the fishermen were witnessing. Still, like their senators, they failed to see that their short-term focus was the root cause of the decline of their resource base. True, Jordan's plan promised a loss of jobs, but in the long run it was a means of saving some part of the industry.

The treaty failed not only because of the stubbornness or selfishness of its opponents, it was also the victim of apathy on the part of its supposed allies. The growing conservationist movement contained a number of influential people who could have had an impact on both the executive and legislative branches in Washington. In later fights, William T. Hornaday would prove to be a master of rousing public opinion and pummeling Congress into submission, but he never got involved. Theodore Roosevelt might have asked Senator Lodge what he intended to accomplish with his belligerent attitude, but he probably never did. There was no groundswell of public support for fisheries protection, and without it there could be no conservation.

The Canadian government also made some egregious errors. The appointment of Samuel Bastedo as the Canadian representative to the IFC was truly uninspired. His indifference and possible incompetence slowed Jordan's progress and left Prince in a difficult situation. Throughout the process, the Dominion government did a poor job of dealing with the American method of government. Instead of trying to understand and work with the concerns of American fishermen and senators, the Canadians chose to remind their American counterparts of the superiority of Canadian ways. Canadian fishermen did their share of damage to the fisheries but were quick to blame the Americans for any problems. While they were right to be angered by American intransigence, they were far from perfect.

Finally, even David Starr Jordan deserved just a little criticism mixed with praise. He put in hundreds of days crafting the regulations and fighting for the treaty, and he rarely complained about the mishandling of his work in Washington. He made conservation the highest priority of his work on the treaty. He admitted his mistakes and worked hard to justify his controversial decisions. He did everything that anyone could expect him to do to advance the treaty and fisheries protection in general. But his one failure was his inability or unwillingness to state clearly why the treaty deserved support in Congress, in the executive branch, or among the general public. Jordan, more than anyone else, was capable of drawing up scientifically sound regulations *and* presenting the case for them to an audience. Had he worked to drum up public support for the treaty, the outcome might have been different.

In the end the treaty failed for a number of closely connected reasons. The lack of public support, especially from the prominent conservationists of the day, allowed congressmen to listen only to their constituents who fished for a living. The obvious economic consequences of the regulations turned most fishermen against the treaty, even though it was in their best long-term interests. Fish themselves did not engender much public sympathy. And, finally, the nature of fisheries as common property made them a difficult subject for most diplomats to control. But while the treaty was a failure by most standards, it set the stage for negotiations to protect both fur seals and migratory birds.

PART II

THE NORTH PACIFIC

FUR SEAL CONVENTION

Simultaneous with, but separate from, their doomed efforts to regulate the boundary water fisheries, Canadians and Americans searched for a diplomatic means to save the North Pacific fur seal (*Callorhinus ursinus*). As with the fisheries, the conflict involved issues of ownership and use of a migratory, valuable resource exploited by various nations. The seals in question were born on American-owned islands, but they spent most of their lives in international waters. American officials claimed permanent ownership of these valuable fur-bearers because of their place of birth. Canadians countered that they had a natural right to pursue and capture the seals on the high seas. Therefore, the American government saw the seals as national property, while the British and Canadian governments emphasized that they were in fact common property.

The crisis emerged in the 1880s, when Canadians began taking seals on the high seas, a practice well within their legal rights. The United States government, which was turning a tidy profit from harvesting seals on land, protested that these British subjects were committing acts of piracy by stealing American property. Canadian sealers and British statesmen argued that their sealing methods were legal and no more damaging than the American practice of harvesting seals on land. At a time when the British and American governments still viewed each other with some suspicion, both sides eschewed conciliation for confrontation. While the two sides quarreled, the seal population crashed 90 percent.

The initial recourse to confrontation hindered negotiations for years and obscured the common interest that British and American diplomats had in attaining a long-term solution. As the seals disappeared, British leaders recognized that extinction would have repercussions both in Anglo-American relations and in the fur-dressing industry in London. Likewise, American leaders knew that seal harvests were generating hundreds of thousands of dollars per year for the U.S. Treasury, and the only way to maintain that income would be to reach an accommodation with London. From a financial standpoint, Canada was the wild card, because Canadian sealers stood to lose the most in any settlement that restricted pelagic (at-sea) sealing. Eventually, the Canadian government concluded that the seal herd was so depleted that it was in the Dominion's interest to stop sealing and reach a deal with the United States.

But the sealing compromise was not simply a matter of number-crunching in three capitals until all sides liked the results. It would not have been possible without the intercession of scientists and the sentimental appeal of the fur seal itself. In an attempt to strengthen their case, American diplomats had brought in scientists during the 1890s to prove that pelagic sealing was threatening the species and therefore the industry it supported. When the Americans' legal case went up in flames, they were left with only the scientists, who came through with evidence of decline due to pelagic sealing. As the dispute gained public attention, a few shrewd private citizens, such as the noted conservationist William T. Hornaday, took up the cause of seal conservation and won great sympathy for the embattled creatures. Such sentimental concern reached into the highest levels of the American, British, and Canadian governments and facilitated the protection of the species.

Finally, in 1911, Canada and the United States joined with other concerned powers to outlaw pelagic sealing and divide the proceeds from land sealing. Unlike the fisheries treaty, the sealing convention was a general success. The ingredients for conservation were all present in the fur seal dispute: the seals were cute enough to appeal to the public, scientists had accumulated massive amounts of evidence that pelagic sealing was not sustainable, and eventually it became clear that all parties could benefit financially from international regulation. First the Americans and then the Canadians overcame the inclination to take a shortsighted approach to the issue, and their long-term vision produced financial and environmental dividends.

There were two stages to the diplomatic activity to save the seal and the seal fur industry. Beginning in 1886, the United States and Great Britain pursued the diplomacy of threats and confrontations meant to intimidate the other into surrender. Recognizing the legal and diplomatic weakness of their position, American diplomats were the first to break the pattern with their offer in 1898 to purchase Canadian interests. The failure of the two sides to resolve their differences at the Joint High Commission in 1898–99 led to the second phase of the negotiations. After a period of deadlock, the United States, Canada, and Great Britain spent the years from 1903 to 1911 searching for common ground, aided by a growing recognition of the importance of science and sentiment in evaluating the sealing crisis.

4

Conflict in the Bering Sea, 1886–1899

Whan the United States and the British empire first clashed over sealing rights in the North Pacific in the 1880s, both relied on international law to justify their positions. Great Britain, with full support from Canada, stood fast on the principle of free use of the seas, which had long been the gospel of the empire's naval might. The United States countered with a number of weak arguments meant to exempt the seals and their habitat from accepted law of the sea. What the Americans lacked in legal reasoning they made up for in tenacity. Neither side saw the sealing dispute as a matter of conservation of a resource; both sought a quick victory that would terminate the dispute.

The inability of the United States to succeed using traditional diplomatic tactics forced an appeal to science. Throughout the 1890s, American diplomats turned increasingly to science for arguments against pelagic sealing and justifications of government policies. As scientists compiled evidence that revealed the evils of pelagic sealing, it became clear that diplomats could also appeal to public sentiment in their efforts to end the killing of nursing female seals. After losing the legal battle at the Paris Tribunal in 1893, American diplomats gradually found themselves using nontraditional arguments to counter London's position.

In this shift, Americans received help from British leaders, who for three reasons moved toward compromise. First, they increasingly saw the need to maintain the friendship of the United States in a dangerous world. Second, American scientific evidence suggested that continued pelagic sealing might destroy the species and, therefore, undermine the London fur industry. Third, believing themselves the most civilized people in the world, the British had difficulty sanctioning the killing of female seals. Still, they could not easily yield on freedom of the seas. And until Americans accepted the idea that seals were common property, not national property, Canadians believed that they were simply being muscled out of a productive business by jealous Americans. Compromise would not come easily.

THE NORTHERN FUR SEAL

Unlike the boundary water fisheries, fur seals lent themselves to a diplomatic solution. Seals appealed to the public, they were well understood scientifically, and their skins were a valuable resource. In addition, located in a remote corner of the globe, the fur seal was not a concern for state governments or threatened by the complexities of habitat loss, and access to the species could be regulated. The historian Samuel Flagg Bemis provided a pithy summation of our scientific knowledge of the fur seal in a sentence famous to students of diplomatic history: "Amphibious is the fur seal, ubiquitous and carnivorous, uniparous, gregarious and withal polygamous."[1] The scientist and rabble-rouser William T. Hornaday, who knew a thing or two about bitter conflict and contention, best captured the nature of the historical dispute surrounding the seal when he wrote that the fur seal "has been the cause of more years of bitter conflict and contention between nations . . . than any other wild animal species."[2]

The life of an individual fur seal follows a predictable cycle. Pups are born on the rookery islands in June and July. For a few months they stay on land while their mothers forage for food in the surrounding seas. During this time, pups are subject to a number of threats. On sandy areas, parasitic worms will drain the life out of many. In some cases, raging bulls defending their territory trample the pups. Sea lions, orcas, and other large predators may devour those that wander into the water. Still others die of starvation if their mothers are killed. By November, the survivors can fend for themselves and begin to leave the barren beaches where they were born. Their first winter in the water is the most trying time of their lives, as they must survive on instinct alone. They must swim thousands of miles, catch enough food, and avoid predators, all without touching land for months. Under these pressures, the average life span of a male seal is only two years, for a female less than five.[3]

Beginning in April, fur seals return to their rookeries. The largest of the herds uses the fog-encased Pribilof Islands in the eastern Bering Sea as its base, while the other main herd goes to the Russian-owned Commander Islands. Smaller groups of seals use Robben Island and the Kurile Islands

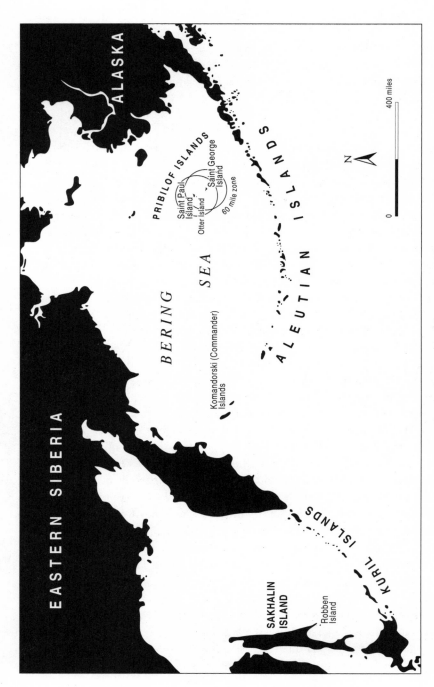

MAP 4. The northern part of the North Pacific Ocean

as their rookeries. The Pribilof rookeries are on two small islands, St. Paul and St. George, about 200 miles from the nearest land. The first seals to return are the bull males, who battle to establish territories on the breeding grounds. Soon after, the mature females return to give birth and mate again. Polygamy is the rule, with bulls having harems averaging thirty to fifty females. The young seals will spend most of their summers in the water, although they will haul out—or come on to land—away from the breeding grounds.

The fur seal's social structure, then, facilitates the harvest on land of young male seals. Males and females are born in even numbers, but on average only one male is needed to breed with thirty females. Such an evolutionary strategy encourages older males to engage in fierce fights over available females. Young males, with little chance of mating success, do well to gather in pods well clear of these hormonally charged behemoths. From a human standpoint, the best fur in the entire species is on the backs of the young males. Thus, fur seal evolution produced a breeding regime that accidentally created a large, separated pool of economically valuable, but biologically expendable, individuals.

The seal's habits also made pelagic sealing especially damaging. A nursing female often covers 200 miles—mostly in international waters—in her search for sufficient food to feed herself and her pup, while a breeding male stays on land to guard his harem. Young females also stay in the water, having no particular reason to come onshore; but young males often haul out in the hope of getting a rare chance to mate. Thus females spend much more of the summer in the water than males, and, therefore, they are more likely to be caught by pelagic sealers. It is widely accepted in game management that killing young females is the best way to destroy a species.[4]

The source of the seal's commodity status has always been its thick fur coat, which protects it from the elements but also made it a target for intense economic exploitation. With a density of 300,000 hairs per square inch, the seal's fur provides excellent insulation against chilly waters. Those insulative qualities also make sealskins attractive to people. Seal fur has guard hairs, which are longer, stiffer, and less desirable quills that detract from the economic value of a fur. Once humans learned how to remove the guard hair, seal fur became a hot commodity. The same qualities that made the fur perfect for the Bering Sea made it desirable on Fifth Avenue.[5]

Over the years, the value of sealskins has fluctuated, depending on the market for fur and the location of the sale. In the late 1700s, Russian and

American traders often got no more than a dollar per skin. But after hunters demolished sea otter populations, the demand for warm fur turned to fur seals. By the 1870s, the skins fetched about $14 in London, the center of the industry. Between 1890 and 1910, Pribilof sealskins averaged about $27 each. By 1920, when seal fur became more fashionable, prices peaked around $140. Even as late as 1982, skins sold for $64. But fashion is fickle, and the animal rights movement of the 1980s spawned a backlash against the fur industry that finally destroyed the market for fur seal coats.[6]

Seal fur lost its popularity largely because the seals are undeniably cute by most human standards. Other than the large and aggressive breeding males, most seals are smaller than human beings and rather harmless. One early investigator, Henry Elliott, referred to the "exceeding peace and dove-like amiability" of female seals. Their large brown eyes and soft fur—two traits that people usually associate with lovable animals—led him to comment on the seals' "attractive, gentle, and intelligent" expressions.[7] As something of an artist, Elliott was skilled at depicting those traits in his sketches of fur seals, which were the sole visual image most people had of the species. In the water, seals epitomize grace and skill, and people often mistake their normal behavior for playfulness. Over the years, defenders of the seals have used their natural appeal to rally public opinion many times.

Despite such rampant anthropomorphism, seals are really no different from most predatory species. When not sleeping, a seal is usually foraging for fish and squid. Seals eat as many as fifty species of the former and ten of the latter, some of which are commercially valuable. The most notable are the various species of *Oncorhyncus* salmon that spawn in the rivers of the northwest coast of North America, but seals also eat mackerel, smelt, and anchovies. In addition to being voracious predators, seals can be "snappish creatures, uncivil to each other, cruel to pups not their own." They have excellent instincts for survival, but they are not intelligent nor in any way capable of emotions. In short, they are wild animals under severe evolutionary pressure to adapt to a harsh environment.[8]

Over the years, seals have been the subject of extensive scientific inquiry. At the turn of the century, fur seals were probably one of the easiest aquatic animals to study. Their rookeries were more accessible than those of other pinnipeds, they spent more time in one place than did cetaceans, and they were certainly more interesting than fish. In addition, their economic value and the associated diplomatic crisis encouraged governments to support scientific studies. The business records of the companies that hunted seals

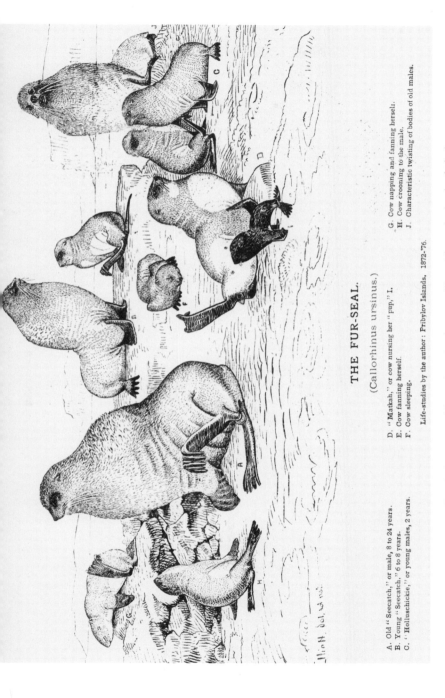

THE FUR-SEAL.

(Callorhinus ursinus.)

A. Old "Seecatch," or male, 8 to 24 years.
B. Young "Seecatch," 6 to 8 years.
C. "Holluschickie," or young males, 2 years.

D. "Matkah," or cow nursing her "pup," I.
E. Cow fanning herself.
F. Cow sleeping.

G. Cow napping and fanning herself.
H. Cow crooning to the male.
J. Characteristic twisting of bodies of old males.

Life-studies by the author: Pribylov Islands, 1872-'76.

Henry Elliott's depiction of fur seals on land. From Elliott, *The Seal-Islands of Alaska*

PELAGIC ATTITUDES OF THE FUR-SEAL.

1. Position when sleeping. 2. Position in rising to breathe, survey, etc. 3. Positions in scratching, etc. 4. "Dolphin jumps."

The village of St. Paul in the distance, and the Black Bluffs to the right on the middle ground.

Elliott's depiction of seals in the water, with the village of St. Paul in the background. From Elliott, *The Seal-Islands of Alaska*

THE KILLING-GANG AT WORK.

Method of slaughtering Fur-seals on the grounds, near the village, St. Paul Island.

The drove in waiting.

Sealers knocking down a "pod."

Natives skinning.

Elliott's depiction of killing seals on the Pribilofs. From Elliott, *The Seal-Islands of Alaska*

Sealing schooners laid up for the winter in Victoria, 1891.
National Archives of Canada PA 110161

Seized Canadian sealing schooners, 1886.
Photo by N. B. Miller, from Jordan and Clark,
Seal and Salmon Fisheries . . . of Alaska, vol. 4

Pelagic sealers, 1894.
Photo by Charles Townsend, from Jordan and Clark,
Seal and Salmon Fisheries . . . of Alaska, vol. 4

(Top) Henry Elliott, self-portrait, 1910.
Library of Congress

(Bottom) Sir Joseph Pope.
National Archives of Canada PA 1108

William T. Hornaday at his desk at the New York Zoological Society.
American Heritage Center, University of Wyoming

also provided important information about the seal's migratory path and food preferences. In 1902, David Starr Jordan mistakenly declared that further scientific study was unnecessary.[9]

The northern fur seal, then, was well positioned for both a diplomatic crisis and a scientific solution. Because it split its time between international waters and national territory, the seal was susceptible to two competing methods of hunting pursued by citizens of different countries. The ensuing competition sparked an international conflict that lasted twenty-five years. But the ease with which people could study seals allowed scientists to come to strong conclusions about methods of preserving the animals. In later years, the scientific evidence allowed Americans and Canadians to agree on both the need for and the means of conserving seals.

THE RISE OF PELAGIC SEALING

The European discovery of a market for sealskins in the late 1700s sparked competition for the vast herds. For decades, people of various nationalities took advantage of the remote locale, harsh conditions, and lax law enforcement to avoid obeying sealing regulations. The steady toll of foreign sealing forced first St. Petersburg and then Washington to search for means to protect the seal herds from foreign depredation. International law, scientific uncertainty, and unimaginative diplomacy foiled both Russian and American attempts to maintain control over a resource that did not fit into any clear category.

Sailing in the sea that bears his name, the Danish explorer Vitus Bering first sighted the Pribilof Islands in 1740 while on a voyage of exploration for Russia. The islands were uninhabited except for a few million seals and a smattering of other marine mammals and birds. As Russian traders learned of the rookeries and the potential market for sealskins, they began to move into the area. In 1787, they relocated 137 Aleuts to the Pribilofs to work skinning the seals. With this force of serfs at hand, the Russians proceeded to harvest between two and four million seals over the next eighty-five years.[10]

Over the course of almost a century, the Russians learned lessons of seal management the hard way. In 1803, the Russian-American Company, which held an exclusive lease to the islands, apparently had to discard 700,000 skins that had rotted in its warehouses in Alaska. On several occasions in the first half of that century, the Russian government had to order a halt to sealing activities to allow the herds to rebuild their numbers. Finally, around 1850, the "Slavonian sealers," as one American termed them, recognized that killing female seals was not an intelligent long-term management strategy. For the next fifteen years, with scattered protective measures in place, the Pribilof herd regained strength.[11]

Besides regulating its own citizens, St. Petersburg also tried to protect its sealing interests by excluding foreign competition. Despite attempts to exercise authority in the Bering Sea, the Russian government was almost powerless in the area. The famed Ukase of 1821, issued by Czar Alexander I, was supposed to prevent foreign economic penetration of the North Pacific, but it was merely an empty pronouncement. In addition, the czars granted monopolies at various times to companies with palace connections, but the territory was so vast and the management so poor that even Russian subjects often violated the grants. By the time of the Alaska Purchase, American merchants had taken steps to control economic activity in the Pacific Northwest.[12]

The Alaska Purchase in 1867 sparked a brief period of uncontrolled exploitation of the Pribilof Island seals. There were probably 2,500,000 animals in the herd at that time, although no one made a reliable estimate. With no rules regulating their activity, many Americans were eager to take over where the Russians had left off. In the summer of 1868, sealers killed 250,000 seals of all ages and both sexes in an atmosphere that the historian Briton Busch has compared to the most lawless of gold rushes. The U.S. government put a halt to commercial harvesting in 1869 while it searched for a way to protect its seal interest.[13] The presence of the seals on federal land turned out to be crucial to their conservation because it meant that the government had both a pecuniary interest in sustaining the species and direct legal control.

Congress and the administration of President Ulysses S. Grant chose to follow the Russian example by issuing an exclusive lease for twenty years. The Alaska Commercial Company (ACC), which had been one of the leading despoilers of the Pribilofs in 1868, won the first lease. The terms were fairly simple. The company could take up to 100,000 young male seals each year; in return, it paid the government $55,000 annually plus a fee of $2.625 per skin. Over the course of twenty years, the government earned over $10,000,000, and the ACC paid more than $22,000,000 in dividends. The deal made both sides rich, but it also drove other entrepreneurs to look for ways to take the seals without violating the lease, and that meant taking them at sea.[14]

At first, the ACC had no problem fulfilling the terms of its lease. There were plenty of three- and four-year-old males, carrying the best fur in the species. In fifteen of the twenty years of the lease, the company took more than the allowed 100,000 skins. But by 1889, the situation on the islands had changed, and the ACC was struggling to fill its quota. In desperation, the company's employees resorted to killing yearling males, which were not particularly valuable. The seal herd could no longer produce 100,000 adolescent males each year.[15]

Although the ACC held a virtual fiefdom out to the three-mile territorial limit around the islands, the company had no authority over the pelagic sealers who were largely responsible for the herd's decline. During their seasonal migration up and down the Pacific coast, the seals attracted hunters looking to make a few dollars in the fur trade. Killing the seals was rather easy, because they slept on the surface and were fairly tame. By 1880, entrepreneurs in Victoria and Seattle began outfitting schooners to follow the seals from their wintering grounds near San Francisco to the Bering Sea. As long as seals stayed in international waters — where they spent most of their time — they were never safe from the sealer's rifle.

Pelagic sealing, though legal, earned vilification for its wastefulness. Because of weather conditions in the North Pacific and the rough nature of the schooner crews, quality control was less than ideal. Sealers shot the animals as they slept or came to the surface from feeding. A dead seal sinks quickly, though, and sealers were unable to recover 50 to 80 percent of seals killed. Even worse, in the water it is almost impossible to distinguish males from females, and females made up 80 to 90 percent of the pelagic harvest. In addition, many of those females were pregnant and had pups back at the rookery.[16] Thus, a sealing crew that brought back 1,000 skins might have killed a few thousand more adults, caused untold hundreds of pups to die of starvation on the islands, and damaged the next generation. In the long run, the killing of females at sea was the greatest threat to the species, and it made pelagic sealing unsustainable.

The wasteful nature of pelagic sealing, combined with the anthropomorphizing of seals, forced many people to the conclusion that the practice was immoral. Conservationists liked to describe the practice as brutal and barbaric, and in later years they took to graphic descriptions of starving seal pups. In particular, many observers criticized the killing of female seals as incompatible with rational use of the species. The *New York Times* called pelagic sealing "wanton and promiscuous slaughter for the profit of a few persons . . . unworthy of a civilized country."[17] No doubt, this opinion was closely linked with the financially motivated efforts of the American gov-ernment to stop Canadian sealers, but it was accurate. Pelagic sealing, then, sowed the seeds of its own demise by offending both the utilitarian and preservationist impulses in Americans—it was just a matter of telling citi-zens about the realities of hunting seals at sea.

Pelagic sealing had existed on the fringes of civilization for decades, but it first became an international problem in 1882. In that year, pelagic sealers sold over 20,000 skins to the London markets for the first time. Through-out the decade, sealers increased the number of seals taken at sea until it was almost as high as the land kill, causing unimaginable waste. American and Canadian sealers operated under a laissez-faire system. They were free to kill when they wished, and they were not restricted to certain types within the species. The British empire held as a fundamental tenet that capturing wild animals on the high seas was a natural right that could not be restricted, and Canadian sealers took advantage of that position.

As the depredation of the herd increased throughout the 1880s, Washing-ton looked for some method to protect both the seals—as American prop-erty—and the government's profits. In 1886, Revenue Service cutters began to confiscate Canadian sealing vessels caught in the act, even if they were in international waters. The British government formally complained and made plans to dispatch its own warships to the area. With pelagic sealing now a diplomatic issue, American statesmen proposed a multipower con-ference to determine who had rights to the seals. Desirous of improving re-lations with Washington and guarding the interest of London furriers—and perhaps sickened by pelagic sealing—Lord Salisbury, British prime minis-ter and foreign minister, was prepared to outlaw sealing in a wide area, but the Canadian government killed the proposal in July 1888. Salisbury was in a bind. As he later wrote, "The Canadians have the strict law on their side: the Americans have a moral basis for their contention which it is impossible to ignore."[18]

With negotiations paralyzed, the government faced uncertainty as the ACC's lease came to an end in 1890. The ACC lost its renewal bid to the newly formed North American Commercial Company (NACC), which had suspiciously extensive ties to Benjamin Harrison's administration. The new deal reflected the uncertainty of the herd's future. The NACC could take no more than 60,000 skins per year, but it had to pay $60,000 annual rent, plus $9.625 per skin—$7 more than the ACC. In addition, the secretary of the treasury had the right to impose any regulations that he deemed necessary.[19] The steady decline of the seal population necessitated the lower limit on skins taken, and the rising costs of protecting the herd forced the higher rent payments. Both of these factors were direct results of increased pelagic sealing.

While the government's actions were based on the idea that the species was dwindling, the science to prove that point was very thin. A naval officer visiting the islands in 1872 guessed that there were six million seals, which seems like a wild exaggeration. One of his colleagues, and one of the first government agents to visit the Pribilofs, Henry Elliott, estimated that there were about 4,500,000 seals in the herd, which became the official government standard for normality for nearly twenty years. Elliott defended his figure tenaciously, but later scientists had no trouble demonstrating that his number was about two million too high. One critic—and he had many—called Elliott's number "an estimate multiplied by a guess." By 1890, sealers had reduced the herd to approximately 800,000, although there was still no good scientific inventory of the Pribilof herd.[20]

Despite his mixed reputation, Henry Wood Elliott served both to bring the sealing controversy to the public and to make the role of scientists prominent in the decision-making process. He lived near Cleveland, Ohio, but his heart was with the seals in the Pribilofs. Within three months of his arrival on St. Paul Island in 1872, he married a woman of Russian descent, Alexandra Molivdov, which served to strengthen his ties to the seals and islanders even more. He liked people to refer to him as "Professor," although he worked mainly as an artist and had no college education. More than anyone else, Elliott fought for stricter limits on sealing. He believed that his initial visits to the Pribilofs between 1872 and 1876, and a subsequent visit in 1890, made him the preeminent expert on fur seals in the world. His friends referred to him as "Henry Elliott, the fur seal expert," and even his enemies admitted that his combination of language skills and scientific interest made him uniquely qualified to work on the Pribilofs. But anyone who disagreed with him risked his wrath, and he was willing to use any tactic to save the fur seal. In particular, he grew to despise trained scientists who came to conclusions that differed from his. Elliott's actions led many scientists, diplomats, and bureaucrats to decide that he was hopelessly irrational, but he could be very persuasive.[21] His persistent effort on behalf of the seals won him some powerful admirers in Washington, and he parlayed their admiration into action.

Elliott's visit in 1890 came as the government sought more evidence that pelagic sealing was destroying government property. Upon his return from the North Pacific, Elliott wrote a scathing report for the Treasury Department that focused not on pelagic sealing but rather on the management of the land sealers. He observed that the seal herd had declined dramatically since 1872, and he predicted that its "utter ruin and extermination is only a question of a few short years." He admitted that his first instinct had been to blame the pelagic sealers, but he then concluded that the land sealers bore a majority of the blame. In particular, he asserted that driving a young male seal from the beach to the killing ground caused the animal to lose its "virility and courage." The seal, he decided, was not designed for land travel, and those that the sealers released had suffered from internal injury, overheating, and stress. Therefore, he concluded that the process of land sealing was destroying the seals' ability to reproduce successfully.[22]

While it is true that fur seals did not evolve to move on land, Elliott's theory was wrong. To prove his point, he would have had to have shown that fewer females were giving birth—evidence of a loss of male virility—or have dissected enough males to demonstrate widespread internal injury. He did neither, because that was not his style. Rather, he imagined a potential cause and then concluded that it was true because he could not possibly be wrong. After all, he was the expert. This version of the scientific method made Elliott enemies throughout the scientific community. But this confidence also made him very persuasive with the naive.

Shocked at Elliott's strange hypothesis and accusatory tone, Secretary of the Treasury William Windom chose not to publish the report for three reasons. First, he claimed that Elliott was secretly in the employ of the ACC and attempting to harm the NACC. Second, he believed that there were basic defects in the report that harmed the American diplomatic position. Third, "it was pervaded by the spirit of aggressive criticism instead of being a dispassionate statement of the facts."[23] As far as Windom was concerned, Elliott had undermined both his credibility as a scientist and the government's position.

Secretary Windom's decision made Elliott an angry crusader against the government's policies. In a typical response, he sent his report to newspapers in Cleveland and New York and accused the government of hiding the truth. For the rest of his years, Elliott hounded any government official or scientist who had the independence to question his judgment. His refusal to reconsider his positions and inability to tolerate dissent made him a poor scientist, and his belief that he alone understood the seals drove him to strange behavior. In later years, he took to sending anonymous letters to opponents, although his handwriting was distinctive, and even went so far as to toy with blackmailing David Starr Jordan. His dedication to the fur seals was admirable, but his actions were often inexcusable.[24] Still, he continued to find receptive audiences among the powerful people of Washington.

In the first twenty years of regulated sealing under American jurisdiction, conditions on the Pribilof Islands had deteriorated. In 1870, the herd had been around its probable carrying capacity of 2,500,000, and land killing operated under reasonable restrictions. By 1890, the herd was down to one-third of its former size and killing on land and sea was indiscriminate. The United States government, looking to safeguard its seal endowment, had made sealing a diplomatic, legal, and scientific issue, but as of 1890 none of those avenues looked promising.

A CONFRONTATION IN PARIS

Despite Elliott's damning report and the diplomatic impasse of the 1880s, President Harrison and the State Department launched a new diplomatic offensive to handcuff Canada's pelagic sealers. Out of this effort came the Bering Sea Arbitration Tribunal of 1893, which managed to annoy both sides with its decision. Although the tribunal's ruling has often been held up as an example of the benefits of arbitration, it was also responsible for forcing American diplomats to upgrade the importance of science and conservation in their strategy.

The maneuvering that took place in 1890 and 1891 led to the formal introduction of scientists to the diplomatic process. Secretary of State James Blaine and Lord Salisbury did not like each other, but neither did they want to add strain to Anglo-American relations. After a confusing and exasperating series of proposals and counterproposals, the two sides settled on a compromise in June 1891. They came to a *modus vivendi* that halted pelagic sealing until May 1892, limited the NACC to 7,500 seals killed for food for the Pribilovians, and agreed in principle to submit to arbitration if necessary. Most important, the United States and Great Britain established a joint commission, with two scientists from each side, to visit the Bering Sea.[25]

British willingness to undertake a joint study was an important breakthrough. The original Anglo-American dispute was about property rights in international waters, not the scientific justifiability of sealing, and London had the stronger case. By agreeing to widen the terms of the debate, the British were risking defeat. The investigators might just conclude that pelagic sealing was scientifically indefensible, no matter its legality. Perhaps the British sought such a defeat as a means to preserve London's fur industry without obviously abandoning Canada. Theoretically, the Americans also risked an adverse decision, but the years of Russian and American harvesting had confirmed that the young males were, from a management standpoint, superfluous. With a weak legal case they had nothing to lose; a full investigation could only help the Americans and the seals.

The commission reflected the two governments' lingering suspicions, however. The British and Canadian delegates, Sir George Baden-Powell and Dr. George Dawson, had orders to concentrate on issues of international law and economics. But the Americans, the respected government scientists C. Hart Merriam and Thomas C. Mendenhall, tried to focus on the "preservation and perpetuation" of the species. The four men visited the Pribilofs in August and September of 1891 and then reconvened in Washington in February 1892. After several fruitless meetings, they issued a brief statement declaring that fur seals were in decline as "the result of excessive killing by man." Then they disbanded, unable to agree on anything else. The period for study was so short and the diplomatic consequences were so important that the investigators chose only to reinforce their original positions.[26]

In April 1892, the American delegates filed their own report, which contradicted Elliott's 1890 submission. They concluded that the herd's health depended on a secure birth rate. Because of the harem system, the killing of excess males could not harm the animal's ability to reproduce; therefore, "the deterioration of the herd must be attributed to the destruction of female seals." Given the strict regulations against killing females on the Pribilofs and the inability of pelagic sealers to discriminate between males and females, Mendenhall and Merriam recommended a complete ban on pelagic sealing as the only measure that could save the herds.[27] They left no room for compromise, but then they were basically correct.

The breakdown of the scientific conference forced Blaine and Salisbury to return to diplomacy. Like the scientists, the diplomats could see no middle ground and were therefore headed to arbitration. Salisbury simply could not surrender the right to free use of oceanic resources, and Blaine would not back down from the position that the United States owned the herd and the eastern Bering Sea. The Americans were angry because they believed that the British had done nothing to enforce the 1891 agreement. For their part, the British held out for American agreement to pay damages if the arbiters ruled against the United States. In February 1892, they agreed to continue the *modus vivendi* through 1893 and to meet before an arbitration tribunal a year later.[28]

The tribunal convened in Paris on 23 February 1893, although both sides had begun the process of submitting written arguments months before. There were seven arbitrators on the panel — one Canadian, one Briton, two Americans, and three independent Europeans. They had three decisions to make. First, they had to consider the legitimacy of American inheritance of Russian claims in the North Pacific. Second, they had to decide if the United States could claim ownership of the seals. And third, they had to establish regulations that would diffuse the situation. For most of July and August the arbiters deliberated before they finally lowered the boom on the American arguments.[29]

The centerpiece of the American position was the rather ridiculous idea that the Bering Sea was a *mare clausum,* or closed sea. Blaine decided that the Alaska Purchase included exclusive rights to the eastern part of the sea, which Russia had claimed in its time. According to this theory, the United States could treat the Bering Sea as an inland lake, with the right of complete economic control. Of course, the United States had protested against and violated that claim when it had been made by Russia, and there was no good reason to think that independent arbiters would accept it in 1893. In his postmortem, one American agent to the tribunal, John W. Foster, admitted that the Americans knew that this part of their case was weak.

Second, the Americans pursued the strange argument that seals were just like domestic animals. Foster argued that, unlike most marine mammals, seals had a particular legal citizenship based on their island of birth; in fact, one American delegate claimed that seals could not be marine mammals because they were born on land. Thus, the Pribilof herd belonged to the United States no matter where it traveled. As a consequence, the seals were more like sheep that strayed from an owner's property than wild animals. Foster believed that the United States had a strong case on this point, but only a biased jurist could have accepted the proposition that seals were not free-ranging wild animals.[30]

American representatives did argue that pelagic sealing was scientifically unjustifiable, but they failed to develop that point into a usable doctrine, perhaps because the practice was still legal in the United States. Instead of bringing Merriam and Mendenhall with them, the American team chose only to submit the scientists' report, which became just a minor part of the sixteen volumes of proceedings. A case of such importance, with such a weak diplomatic basis, should have spurred some creative thinking. The Americans had an opportunity to acknowledge that the seals were common property in need of international cooperation, which only the tribunal could provide. Had that argument been convincing, it would have forced the arbitrators to look at the scientific basis for banning pelagic sealing, which was quite strong. There was no guarantee that a common property line of reasoning would have succeeded, but it was better than anything else that Blaine could offer.

For their part, the British held to an accepted precept of international law, the primacy of the three-mile territorial limit. They argued that no one, Americans included, had ever accepted the concept of *mare clausum* in any other case. The Bering Sea, in particular, was hardly closed in reality. As to the national property theory, the British pointed out that straying and migrating were not equivalent actions; the seals were just like any other wild game animal that naturally wandered beyond property lines. Finally, just to take the sting out of Merriam's and Mendenhall's conclusions, the British dug up Elliott's 1890 report as testimony to the danger of land sealing.[31] The ease with which they disposed of the American positions embarrassed the United States.[32]

After weighing the facts and sifting through the mounds of debris left by the plaintiffs, the arbitrators managed to reach a decision that annoyed the Americans and Canadians. They rejected both American claims and ordered the United States to pay more than $470,000 in damages for seizing sealing vessels. They then turned to the problem of how best to protect the seals. The three independent arbitrators designed a sixty-mile buffer zone around the islands that the Canadians could not enter. They also proposed an annual closed season from 15 April to 1 July in the eastern Bering Sea and outlawed the use of firearms in pelagic sealing. Neither the American nor the British arbitrators had the votes to amend the proposals, which were then adopted.[33] Although both governments expressed moderate pleasure about the workings of the arbitration panel, within a few years both sides were working hard to revise the ruling.[34]

Canadian sealers were angered because the decision made their jobs harder. The principle of freedom of the seas meant nothing to them compared to the actual ability to catch seals. They had objected to the *modus vivendi* as an economic hardship, and they had hoped to return to unrestricted access to their livelihoods. Now they could no longer use guns, and the best sealing areas were off-limits. In their opinion, the Paris regulations reduced their annual take by half. In addition, the Americans made no motion to pay the indemnity until 1898. Years later, citizens of Victoria still cursed the injustice of the Paris award.[35]

Americans, on the other hand, were disappointed that the arbitrators had not halted all pelagic sealing against the Pribilof herd. Merriam claimed that the buffer zone and the closed season were unenforceable. Canadian and British authorities were not about to invest energy in enforcement, and the Revenue Cutter Service was no match for the wild North Pacific. Given the persistent fog and navigational difficulties, even the sixty-mile buffer zone was hard to patrol. Elliott believed that, as long as Canadians were allowed to seal at all, the commercial extinction of the herd was assured. Others engaged in hyperbolic accounts of the Canadian depredation of the herd. One American commentator remarked that had a Victorian sealer drawn up the Paris regulations, "he could scarcely have made them better suited to his needs." [36]

The tribunal's award was not, however, a total defeat for the United States. In attempting to accommodate both sides, the arbitrators had acknowledged that the status quo was unacceptable. The neutral jurists had created their regulations as a compromise, but their efforts revealed that intelligent, independent people believed that Canadian sealing methods were not sustainable. Pelagic sealing was a legal right, but a moral wrong. In addition, their restrictions did work to make sealing in the Bering Sea much less profitable.

The real losers were the seals. The ruling left a number of gaps besides those that concerned policymakers in Ottawa and Washington. First, Canadian sealers were free to increase their efforts on the other side of the Pacific, where the smaller herds on the Commander Islands, Robben Island, and the Kuriles were very vulnerable. Second, the ruling did not apply to Japanese sealers, who were just beginning to cross the ocean. And third, all of the seals were still vulnerable at some time to pelagic sealers. This threat was especially relevant to the lactating females, which sometimes traveled beyond the buffer zone to feed.

The arrival of the Japanese sealing fleet was probably the least predictable result of Anglo-American fur seal diplomacy. In 1884, Tokyo had outlawed pelagic sealing, and three years later the Japanese foreign minister had called for international cooperation to save the fur seal. But the restricted sealing in the eastern Bering Sea forced Canadian and American sealers to look westward for a source of income. A few sealers operated out of Japanese ports, under Japanese flags, to avoid the tribunal's rules. Others simply crossed the Pacific each year as part of their annual expeditions. As a result, they destroyed the Kurile herd and damaged both Russian herds. In response, the Japanese not only lifted their restrictions on pelagic sealing but then subsidized the industry.[37] What had been an Anglo-American problem had now spread to Asia.

From the standpoint of traditional diplomacy, the Paris award was the epitome of rational arbitration of an otherwise insoluble crisis. Two sides with no common ground allowed neutral parties to create a compromise that diffused tension. With the buffer zone, the chance that a confrontation between a Canadian schooner and an American cutter might spark an international incident was greatly reduced. Neither side had been humiliated by publicly backing down, and peace had been maintained.

But from the standpoint of international conservation, the Paris award was an example of how traditional methods were inadequate. American delegates argued that fur seals were national property, as if the seals were no more wild than sheep. British representatives pursued the argument that sealing was a natural right, even though many of them recognized the unsustainability of Canadian practices. Above all, the regulations did not stem the tide of destruction, and the fur seal herds continued to shrink. Both sides saw arbitration as a chance to gain national advantage, not as an opportunity to promote wise use of a shared resource. It was only coincidental that American national advantage would have been more beneficial to the fur seal herds.

A NEW APPROACH

The defeat at Paris forced the American government to reconsider its approach to the seal problem. Because ownership was no longer a feasible claim, American officials had to find some new way to stop Canadian sealers. Their response was to return to science, which they had nearly ignored in 1893, for a justification to end pelagic sealing. The growing societal beliefs in conservation and the power of applied science led trained scientists and statesmen to seek means of maximizing profits through management of the herd. The process of blending science with diplomacy was slow and arduous, but American diplomats had to begin separating themselves from the failed ownership theories.

Between 1893 and 1896, neither the United States nor Great Britain made any serious proposals regarding sealing, but the dilemma had not gone away. Both sides were bound to accept the tribunal's decision until 1898, so there was little reason to press the issue. In addition, the Venezuela crisis of 1895 forced all other differences off the table while the two nations came to an understanding about the meaning of the Monroe Doctrine.[38] Meanwhile, Canadian and American sealers had pretty much wiped out the western Bering Sea herds and continued to take tens of thousands from the Pribilof herd. It was only a matter of time before American diplomats put sealing back on the agenda.

For most of the 1890s, the leader of American efforts to resolve the sealing crisis was the former secretary of state, John W. Foster. According to the historian Charles Campbell, Jr., Foster threw himself into a thorough study of the fur seal problem and became a master of the details of sealing. His knowledge was impressive, but his stubbornness irritated British officials. Ambassador Sir Julian Pauncefote disliked Foster, and Salisbury called him "a tricky lawyer." But more than any other American diplomat, Foster had a scientific understanding of the sealing dispute.[39] Perhaps the British disliked him because he was not tied to tired and easily dismissed ideas the way that Blaine had been.

In 1896, the United States and Britain agreed to send scientists to the eastern Bering Sea in 1897 to conduct thorough studies of the fur seal situation. To lead the American group, President Grover Cleveland chose David Starr Jordan, a friend of Foster's from their days at Indiana University. Stanford's president was not particularly knowledgeable about the seal, but he was a highly regarded scientist and a prominent public figure. In addition, as a fisheries biologist, Jordan believed in the power of science to promote management of natural resources. To assist him, Jordan chose a number of scientists familiar with seals who shared his views on maximizing returns through conservation activities.[40]

The appointment of Jordan instead of Elliott revealed that scientists did not necessarily think with one mind. The two men did share many ideas: they opposed pelagic sealing as barbaric; they saw aesthetic and economic value in the fur seal; and they believed that land killing was not inherently incompatible with conservation. They differed, though, in that Jordan was much more cautious and rigorous in his scientific technique, while Elliott tended to estimate and leap to conclusions. Whereas Elliott seemed to treat the seals like family, often praising their intelligence and gentle expressions, Jordan was able to separate emotion from science. Jordan believed that people could manipulate the seals to improve the herd's profitability, but Elliott argued that the seal's condition was "not within the power of human management to promote." Their different approaches led to conflicting views on harvesting male seals. Elliott had no doubt that the lessons of history demonstrated that, when the herd got too small, it needed a closed season for several years. Jordan believed that humans could always harvest a certain percentage of the young males, because they were biologically extraneous to the herd.[41]

By choosing Jordan to lead the scientific inquiry, the Treasury and State Departments revealed their desire for a report that would not only condemn pelagic sealing but also support continued land sealing. Foster knew that Jordan appreciated the utilitarian rationale and would separate sentiment from fact. Jordan would not recommend the cessation of land sealing unless the evidence proved that the lessees bore some responsibility for the decline of the Pribilof herd. Elliott, in addition to his odd behavior, was unacceptable because he had already concluded that there should be a multiyear moratorium on harvesting the young males. For the next sixteen years, Elliott and Jordan competed for influence in Congress and in changing administrations, and their differences drove a wedge into the group of scientists, statesmen, and conservationists working to save the seals.

Part of Jordan's appeal to the government might have been his ability to match Elliott's publicity campaign. Unlike Elliott, who was obsessed with the seals, Jordan was interested in a number of subjects and therefore had more balance. He spoke and wrote eloquently, and he was earning a national reputation as a scientist and reformer. Jordan also had a flair for fiction; in 1897 he wrote a popular children's story about the seals, *Matka and Kotik; A Tale of the Mist-islands,* that had a sad ending.[42] He did not crave publicity, but he certainly knew how to get it.

Jordan did not disappoint his patrons. Under his name, the Treasury Department published a four-volume set of information on the species.[43] Following up on Merriam and Mendenhall, Jordan and his colleagues investigated the seal's life and the various methods of ending it. Without hesitation, they concluded that pelagic sealing took females faster than the herd could replace them and was therefore unsustainable. As an added bonus, Jordan edited a separate four-volume set that included an assessment of Elliott's 1890 report. After a ten-page summary of the scientific errors of that document, Jordan concluded, "We must express our regret that it was ever written or printed."[44]

For their part, London's two scientists also submitted a report, although their version contradicted that of the American scientists. James Macoun (a Canadian) and D'Arcy Thompson (a Briton) waited until the American government published Jordan's report before releasing theirs, leading the American scientists and diplomats to charge that Canadian national interests had interfered with scientific objectivity. Despite privately agreeing with the Americans that the herd could never grow under the pressure of pelagic sealing, Macoun and Thompson publicly absolved the pelagic sealers of blame for the Pribilof herd's decline. In anger, Charles Townsend, the director of the New York Aquarium, actually engaged in fisticuffs with Macoun.[45]

Reflecting the clash of the scientists, Foster and British diplomats were having difficulty reaching the basis for diplomatic discussions. Early in 1897, the United States asked Japan, Russia, and Great Britain to agree to four-power talks with a goal of imposing uniform regulations on sealing throughout the North Pacific. In order to strengthen the American position, Congress outlawed pelagic sealing by American citizens. Russia and Japan agreed to send representatives to Washington, and three-power negotiations opened in October 1897. London did not send diplomatic representatives, although the Canadian prime minister, Sir Wilfrid Laurier, did accompany Thompson and Macoun on their mission to meet with American scientists about the same time. However, Laurier refused to participate in the diplomatic discussions.[46]

These talks were significant because for the first time American diplomats acknowledged the vital role that sentiment could play in breaking the deadlock. The treasury official Charles Sumner Hamlin asked Japan to agree to at least one of three American proposals — none of which benefited Japan — even if Great Britain did not, because "if we take action in the matter to prohibit pelagic sealing, the whole moral force of humanity will be brought to bear on Great Britain and she cannot stand out against it." Likewise, Jordan pointed out that in the nineteenth century much of the large wildlife had lost out to man in a competition for land, but fur seals "occupy territory that man does not need and cannot use." The only moral recourse was to end pelagic sealing and allow the species a margin of safety.[47]

The Imperial government faced a dilemma. In the aftermath of its victory over China in 1895, Japan wanted to prove further that it belonged among the elite powers. Attacking pelagic sealing would win favor with the rising United States and provide an opportunity to restore the small herd on the Kuriles. But at the same time, defending pelagic sealing would strengthen relations with the British empire, still the most powerful force in the world. In addition, Tokyo had begun to subsidize citizens who wished to pursue high seas fishing and sealing operations. The program had proven to be quite popular and had helped alleviate the depletion of the country's inshore fisheries. Therefore, neither the government nor public opinion would accept a treaty on sealing that restricted Japanese rights unless Great Britain agreed to the same terms.[48]

Foster was able to make some progress with Russia and Japan. On 6 November 1897, the three nations agreed to establish a closed season throughout the North Pacific and a ban on pelagic sealing in the Bering Sea for 1898 if Great Britain would join them.[49] The problem, as Foster knew, was in Ottawa, not London. As early as March 1897, George Clark, Jordan's secretary, had urged McKinley and Secretary of State John Sherman to buy out Canada's sealing interests. Clark believed that such a purchase would appeal to the sealers in Victoria, because "pelagic sealing is a suicidal industry since it must necessarily destroy its own capital." In addition, he believed that Canadians would be happy to stop a practice that was "a menace and disgrace to both nations." In exchange for an American agreement to pay a fair price for the sealing fleet, he predicted that the Canadian government would outlaw pelagic sealing.[50]

American consideration of a plan to compensate Canadian sealers helped revitalize efforts to resolve the sealing dispute. In December 1897, American diplomats proposed a conference linking sealing with U.S.-Canadian disputes over fisheries, the border, and reciprocity. Laurier expressed willingness to participate in such a meeting if the United States and Canada could reach a preliminary agreement on the level of compensation for the sealers. Foster and Pauncefote allowed their dislike for each other to undermine their discussions. In March 1898, with the proposed Joint High Commission in danger, President William McKinley intervened by offering to meet without prearranging anything. Laurier reluctantly accepted.[51]

When the JHC opened in Quebec in August 1898, the plan to compensate Canadian sealers was still in its infancy. Of the four members of the sealing subcommittee, only Foster knew anything about the industry or the species. The negotiations hit an immediate snag, then, when the British members called for a two-month recess to allow them to travel to Victoria to learn about sealing firsthand. When they returned, both sides agreed to the concept of compensation for the sealing fleet, but they disagreed on how much the vessels were worth. The members hit upon a compromise solution; each side had a naval officer appraise the sealing fleet. There was some surprise when the two officers estimated the fleet to be worth approximately $500,000. Both sides had anticipated that the total value might be in the millions of dollars, but the naval officers had revealed that Canada's sealing industry had declined significantly.[52]

After the naval officers submitted their reports, a final agreement seemed to be at hand. The United States offered 10 percent interest in the Pribilof herd, and the NACC "was prepared to pay $500,000 in consideration of the benefits which it would derive from the discontinuance of pelagic sealing." Canadians asked for $750,000 and a 25 percent share, but they had little basis on which to demand so much.[53] Not only had their own naval officer appraised the fleet at less than $750,000, but 1897 and 1898 had been the two worst years ever for the Victoria sealers. Total catch had declined, and it was becoming apparent that pelagic sealing was no longer profitable. Still, the Canadian government believed that the public opposed a deal on principle. Laurier had to find a solution that guarded traditional Canadian interests while still resolving the problem.

The British delegates expressed a willingness to settle for $500,000, but they insisted that the Americans make some concession of "national importance" to balance out Canada's sacrifice of the right to pelagic sealing. This demand led to the collapse of the conference. Foster and the leader of the American delegation, Senator Charles Fairbanks of Indiana, believed that granting Ottawa a percentage of the NACC's skins was the major concession. But Laurier needed a victory on another front to balance out the perceived defeat on the Bering Sea issue. Specifically, he wanted the United States to change its position on the Alaska boundary. When Fairbanks refused, the Canadian government withdrew from the negotiations.[54]

The breakdown occurred because each side thought it was doing the other a favor. Americans believed that "it ought to be possible to agree upon terms which would induce these men to go out of a losing business."[55] The United States government was willing to pay half a million dollars to sailors and investors whom it viewed as pirates, just to avoid an open conflict. But from the Canadian perspective, Foster was asking Victorians to give up a perfectly honorable profession for a pittance of the herd and market value of the gear. As one British delegate reminded Fairbanks, fishermen from New

England would not accept a similar offer, nor would Americans want them to. If Canadians were to make such a sacrifice, then they deserved some reward.[56]

Meanwhile, the seal population continued to decline. Jordan estimated that in 1897 there were only 400,000 seals left, of which 129,000 were breeding females. Through his studies of seal biology, he estimated that an undisturbed herd would grow at only 6 to 7 percent per year when one accounted for the 10 percent of adult females that die naturally each year. Pelagic sealing increased that loss an additional 10 to 35 percent. Even in 1897, when Canadian sealers sold only 20,000 skins from the Pribilof herd, Jordan estimated that they had killed 14 percent of the breeding females.[57] Jordan considered the Canadian assertion that the Paris regulations had left the herd in equilibrium at 15 to 20 percent of its natural size. He concluded, though, that the Canadian sealing effort was still too great to allow for such a balance. In addition, he had not anticipated the growing impact of the Japanese sealing fleet.[58]

Given the peril that faced the herds, Canada would have profited from the American financial offer. Pelagic sealing was no longer a lucrative enterprise for most Canadian sealers. From 1892 to 1897, the number of schooners clearing Victoria for the sealing grounds had declined from 65 to 31. Between the Paris regulations and the scarcity of seals, the average catch per schooner had dropped from 2,000 in 1886 to 950 in 1897. But Canadians held out for more than just economic compensation; they wanted an acknowledgment that pelagic sealing was a legitimate means of exploiting common property.

From the American standpoint, after only four years the deal would pay for itself. Maintaining the revenue cutters cost about $150,000 per year, compared to gross receipts from the islands of about $250,000 annually. When added together, then, over four years the government would pay Canadians roughly $600,000 — the $500,000 lump sum plus 10 percent of the gross receipts each year — the same amount it would save by keeping the cutters at home. In addition, with no pelagic sealing, the herd, the NACC's profits, and government revenues would rebound. The only problem was Canada's demand for a *quid pro quo*. The United States would not link pelagic sealing to its position on the Alaska boundary.

The failure of the JHC to solve the sealing crisis could not obscure the significant gains the American government had made toward its goal of eliminating pelagic sealing. By breaking free from the ownership theories and embracing science, American diplomats were able to get past the confrontational attempts used from 1886 to 1893 to resolve the problem. Diplomatic initiatives also revealed that the United States could come to a satisfactory arrangement with Japan and Russia without difficulty. Even co-operation with Canada was no longer inconceivable, especially if Canadians would consider the scientific, economic, and moral bases for ending sealing.

CONCLUSION

Between 1867 and 1898, the Pribilof Islands fur seal herd declined from approximately 2,500,000 to 400,000 individuals. There were two reasons for this alarming trend. First, from 1868 to the late 1880s, there was simply too much killing of young male seals on the islands. Between the lessees and the freelance sealers of 1868, land sealers took almost 2,500,000 animals in thirty years. Second, but of far more importance, pelagic sealers collected at least 600,000 seals from the vast Pacific, a figure that does not include the hundreds of thousands of mammals that were shot but not recovered.[59] Most of those taken at sea were mature females, whose deaths impaired the ability of the species to regenerate.

Fearing that pelagic sealing would ruin its property rights in the seal herd, the United States launched a diplomatic offensive to guard the species. Had pelagic sealing not threatened the herd's reproduction, Washington still would have equated it with piracy. International law was not in agreement with that position, however. In a stinging rebuke to the Americans' unimpressive legal theories, the Paris Tribunal of 1893 delivered the message that traditional diplomacy would not bring a satisfactory outcome. Gradually, then, the United States moved away from its national property theory and towards a scientific approach to the sealing crisis that would emphasize sentiment and economic cooperation. If Canadians had a legal right to seal, they also had a legal right to sell. American diplomats, then, tried to persuade Canada that continuing sealing was both bad and bad business.

Still, the negotiations revealed that the seals' salvation was not immediately at hand. The scientific discussions that took place in Washington showed that Canadians refused to acknowledge American evidence that pelagic sealing was harmful to the herd. In turn, the negotiations at the Joint High Commission faltered because Canadians continued to see relinquishing pelagic sealing as a sacrifice that deserved more than financial compensation. In addition, the proposed Canadian-American deal would have opened questions of how to deal with Japan. With the double benefits of government subsidies and freedom from the Paris regulations, Japanese sealers were becoming more of a threat than their Canadian counterparts.

The solution to these problems would be difficult to achieve. The United States had to accept the fact that seals were not government property with purely financial value. As long as either Canada's or Japan's government thought that the United States was trying merely to increase its profits by nudging out the competition, there was no chance for success. At the same time, Japanese and Canadian leaders had to accept that, legality aside, pelagic sealing was a destructive and condemnable activity. American, Japanese, and British diplomats had to treat the seals as common property in need of conservation for the benefit of all. Until they met those requirements, there was no chance for the international cooperation necessary to save the northern fur seal.

Still, by 1899, with the seal herds in dangerous decline, American and British diplomats had laid the foundation for a cooperative, long-term solution to the disagreement that would protect the seal and the industry that it supported. They could see that science convicted pelagic sealing of wastefulness and sentiment convicted it of brutality. All they needed was some reasonable method of inducing Canadians to yield pelagic sealing without undermining the framework of the empire.

5

Conciliation and Conservation, 1900–1912

The failure of the Joint High Commission temporarily obscured the progress that the United States and Canada had made toward an equitable solution to the fur seal dilemma. So long as Canada held out for some important concession on another issue, there would be no progress; in fact, at times the crisis seemed to worsen. But the momentum for conservation was building on both sides of the border and in the Old World, and both governments felt pressure to save the species. Although the American offer changed only slightly over the next several years, Canada declared it acceptable in 1911, having finally reached the conclusion that further intransigence was detrimental to Dominion interests.

Canada's—and Japan's—acquiescence and American patience demonstrated the power of preservationist sentiment and the equanimity of the proposal, both of which were reinforced by scientific evidence. Years before the conclusion of the convention, government officials from all interested powers admitted that conservation of the species was a worthy goal in itself. No nation wished to carry the blame for driving the fur seal to extinction. But at the same time, none wished to be the only country making a sacrifice to save the seal. Thus the American proposal to share the proceeds to be gained by seal conservation was the logical, and perhaps only, foundation for an agreement that saved both the species and the sealing industry. All interested scientists agreed that seals were in decline, and the only reasonable explanation was the mass killing of female seals by pelagic sealers. The seals and the pelagic sealers could coexist no longer, and the governments had to choose which to drive to extinction.

For years the Canadian and Japanese governments believed they had to choose between citizens and seals, which was not hard to do. But eventually they recognized the real complexity of choosing between sealers who were destroying their own industry and powerful foreign governments that were offering financial and moral inducements to end pelagic sealing. Canada, in particular, faced pressure from Britain to save the seal and, consequently, the seal-fur industry in London. That choice was not so easy, but ultimately they agreed to yield to scientific evidence, moral outrage, and economic reality.

That the United States was still interested after so many years was a testament to the power of the economic, scientific, and moral arguments for seal preservation. At times of exasperation the government flirted with the idea of destroying the species in order to be done with the disagreement, but that idea was economically shortsighted, scientifically indefensible, and morally abhorrent. When resolution of the crisis seemed near, Americans actually agreed to give away even more of their proceeds in order to salvage the species and the fur harvest. Thus a diplomatic resolution came at the darkest moment, when the herds were at their lowest, because the costs of failing to cooperate had become so high.

Those costs had risen because of the work of scientists and conservationists in promoting protection of the fur seal. Led by David Starr Jordan and his government scientists on one side and Henry Elliott and William Hornaday on the other, defenders of the seal had built a compelling case to outlaw pelagic sealing. Their ultimate success in banning pelagic sealing came despite a serious split in how they perceived the seals and nature in general. Jordan, the rational scientist, wanted to manage the seals to increase productivity, while Elliott, the impulsive raconteur, advocated leaving the seals to their own devices. When they combined behind their mutual antipathy toward pelagic sealing, they made a powerful force; when they divided over management plans, they revealed the weaknesses of the conservation movement.

ELLIOTT'S DAY IN THE SUN

The resolution of the Alaska boundary dispute in 1903 opened the way for more negotiations on the Bering Sea controversy. But lingering bitterness in Washington and Ottawa from the collapse of the Joint High Commission distracted diplomats from the cooperative solution that seemed possible in 1899. Secretary of State John Hay and the British ambassadors agreed in 1903 and 1905 to restrict sealing, but Canada rejected both deals as contrary to its national interests. Out of the impasse came a proposal from Henry Elliott to share the herd with Canada. In contrast to the diplomatic failures, this idea provided the basis for a settlement in the future.

Like his predecessors, Hay viewed the fur seal controversy more as an impediment to better relations with Canada and Great Britain than as a question of conservation. Still, he worked for Theodore Roosevelt, who took "a lively interest in the question from a Natural History point of view." He could not have misunderstood the importance of protecting a valuable and interesting resource to the administration that set new standards for conservation. At the same time, he had a low opinion of Canada's role in Anglo-American relations, comparing the Dominion to "a married flirt, ready to betray John Bull on any occasion, but holding him responsible for all her follies." He sought a solution as diligently as any of his predecessors, but he would not abandon the precedent established at Quebec.[1]

In July 1903, Hay renewed the American offer to purchase the Victoria sealing fleet. Given their recent defeat on the Alaska boundary, Canadians were immediately suspicious. One fisheries official warned his colleagues that Hay's action was meant "to catch Great Britain and Canada rather rusty on the subject, and is only a part of the *persistent endeavours . . .* to weary the British Government into acquiescence." The British ambassador, Sir Michael Herbert, encouraged Ottawa to reopen negotiations, but Canadians ignored him as a rebellious teenager might ignore a stern parent. Herbert's death in London in the fall relieved Laurier's government of the burden of rejecting his suggestion, and Hay's proposal went unanswered.[2]

While Hay waited for some response, Henry Elliott seized the opportunity to reinstate himself as the government's preeminent seal expert. Perhaps sensing that Roosevelt was more interested in conservation than previous presidents, the determined lobbyist began a campaign to change policy in the Departments of Treasury, Commerce and Labor, and State. He charged that previous government work succeeded only in boxing in the United States so that "Mr. Hay is absolutely powerless to make a single move for the better . . . unless it is agreeable to the Canadian hunters." He reiterated his controversial belief that "*the land killing on the islands has been far more deadly to the existence of the fur seal herd than has been the pelagic hunters' work.*" He then went on to accuse David Starr Jordan of hallucinating, and he savagely attacked the work of government agents on the islands.[3]

Despite his headstrong attitude and libelous comments, Elliott found an audience in the White House. Roosevelt liked strong-willed men who were not afraid to challenge conventional wisdom. At first glance, the two had much in common: they both railed against waste and greed in the use of America's natural resources, and both were unyielding in defense of what they thought was right. Perhaps encouraged by William Hornaday—a distinguished zoologist and supporter of Roosevelt's "strenuous life" ideology—the president asked Elliott for his insights on the sealing issue. Based on the favorable reports from the White House, even Hay was willing to consider Elliott's advice.

In memoranda to Roosevelt in December 1904 and Hay in March 1905, Elliott revealed how little he actually knew about seal diplomacy. He informed Roosevelt that "we are being held up at Ottawa by the erroneous and mischievous work of our own agents." He continued on to say that Laurier was really an ally of seal protection in need of support from Washington, a conclusion not in line with Canadian diplomacy. Elliott offered to go to Ottawa as an unofficial representative of the American position. He felt confident that he understood "Canadian officialism" because in the 1860s he had spent several months with "the Governor General of British Columbia." He wrapped up his request by suggesting that in his presence the Canadian cabinet "will be free to enquire, talk and argue all points without going on record." In a meeting, the president gently informed Elliott that he could not serve in such a diplomatic capacity.[4]

Although Elliott lost his bid to make seal policy in the White House, he was always able to command a following among the neophytes on Capitol Hill. In early 1904, with no sign of cooperation from Ottawa, one of Elliott's leading allies in Congress, Senator William Dillingham of Vermont, called on the federal government to reduce the seal herd to 10,000 animals. The reasoning for this so-called mercy killing was quite simple: the growing expense of the Revenue Cutter Service had made the Pribilofs a money-losing proposition. Senators in support of the bill reasoned that killing most of the seals would remove a source of friction between the two North American neighbors, eliminate the expensive patrol, and produce a financial windfall for the Treasury. With nothing left to chase, pelagic sealers would quit the business, leaving the seals to slowly rebuild their numbers.[5]

In February 1905, with Dillingham's proposal under consideration, Secretary Hay and the new British ambassador, Sir Mortimer Durand, discussed possible alterations of the Paris regulations. After being treated so rudely in 1903, Hay was no longer interested in making any financial arrangements. Based on the scientists' reports, the American wanted to extend the closed season until October, when the pups were weaned, and expand the buffer zone to include all of the major feeding grounds. Durand pointed out that neither of those additional restrictions would be acceptable to Canada, but he was willing to pass along more equitable changes. After further conversations, the two men agreed to move the closed season from May and June to August and September in an effort to cut down on the number of pups starving to death on the beaches, which was at least a concession to public opinion. Durand, however, needed Canadian approval for his actions.[6]

Upon receiving the Hay-Durand agreement in March, the governor general emphasized that the Laurier government would not reply until it had surveyed the sealers. Canada had no obligation to change the rules, and the government suspected that Americans were trying to blame Canadian sealers for deaths due to natural causes. In the muddied language of the Privy Council, Americans were angry "because it was found that the sealers could still pursue their calling which it was at first thought would be sufficiently hampered . . . to cause a voluntary relinquishment thereof." After consulting with the sealers, the Canadian government reported that the American proposal exchanged the best sealing months for the worst. In doing so, it would cause the end of the Canadian sealing industry. The Hay-Durand agreement died in October, shortly after Hay did.[7]

Roosevelt and some leading senators had hoped that the threat to reduce the herd would help the State Department's negotiations, but Canadians saw through the bluff. Despite Elliott's public endorsement of "killing that life down to the small nucleus sufficient alone to preserve the species," few scientists supported such drastic action, and the possible reaction of the public was intimidating. It was one thing to harvest surplus males for economic reasons, but it was another to wantonly destroy nursing females just to spite a few hundred Canadians. In addition, both sides knew that the breeding seals to be killed were less valuable than the young males. Destroying the herd would be an act of desperation, not a good business decision.[8]

As if to show that the threat had been meaningless, in March 1905 three senators who had supported killing off the seals now proposed to share the herd with Canada. Dillingham, Knute Nelson of Minnesota, and Henry Burnham of Vermont supported the idea of granting Canada 25 percent of the Pribilof proceeds in exchange for 25 percent of the costs and an end to pelagic sealing. Only such cooperation could provide the necessary "care and conservation" that the herd needed. Because Congress had just concluded a session and Hay's diplomacy was taking another path, the time for action on this proposal had not yet arrived. In later years, however, it would serve as the basis for an equitable settlement of the sealing dispute.[9]

This good idea came from Elliott. In an unusually rational state of mind, he surmised that the only way to stop Canadian pelagic sealing was to give Ottawa some form of joint control over the islands. He believed that Canada would also accept a ten-year moratorium on all sealing to allow the herd to regain its former abundance, at which point it might return $1,000,000 annually.[10] This proposal marked an important step forward, because it was based more on granting rights to Canada than taking them away.

Elliott took the fate of this proposal personally. Almost immediately, he began to refer to the Hay-Elliott plan, which he seemed to confuse with the Hay-Durand plan. Always at the center of his own universe, he did not realize that the plan to which Hay and Durand had agreed was not based on his idea at all. After 1903, Hay refused to consider a pecuniary settlement with the Canadian sealers, because it seemed too much like a reward for bad behavior. In addition, he and Elliott had had a falling out over Elliott's demand for reimbursement for his work on the seals. Elliott, though, continued to believe for years that Hay had based his diplomacy on Elliott's input. He would base his later hostility toward government policy on this misapprehension.[11]

In some ways, then, Hay's death opened the door for a settlement based on Elliott's proposal of joint ownership of the seal herd. Hay's bitterness toward the Canadian government prevented him from offering terms that would recognize Canada's legitimate claim to the seals. At the same time, his feud with Elliott diminished the chances that he would espouse an idea so closely tied with the rambunctious lobbyist. The combination of a new secretary of state, the failure of past American offers, and the continued decline of the species forced the United States government to look more seriously at Elliott's proposal to share the seal herd with Canada.

CHANGING OF THE GUARD

Between the cold reception for Elliott's proposal in 1905 and early 1908, four important changes occurred that opened the way for a rational settlement of the Anglo-American sealing crisis. First, both in reality and in the minds of American diplomats, Japanese sealers replaced Canadians as the main threat to the Pribilof herds. Second, Canadian sealers recognized that a combination of Japanese competition and the Paris regulations made their business unprofitable. Third, David Starr Jordan again displaced the volatile Henry Elliott as the U.S. government's scientific expert on sealing.[12] Fourth, three new players entered with the goal of strengthening the Anglo-American relationship: Governor General Lord Grey, Ambassador Sir James Bryce, and Secretary of State Elihu Root.[13] None of these developments produced immediate results, but they all increased the opportunities for a cooperative settlement.

The new secretary of state emphasized the need for Anglo-American cooperation and strove to remove impediments to friendly relations between the two nations. Root recognized that clearing away sources of U.S.-Canadian friction was a high priority, and by early 1906 he had made several proposals to London and Ottawa. Unlike Hay, Root seemed to have a streak of conservationism in his blood. Along with Theodore Roosevelt, he had been a founding member of the Boone and Crockett Club, which supported both hunting and conservation. Root, therefore, believed that conservation was a legitimate goal of American diplomacy.[14]

On 18 April 1906, Root made a formal offer to the Canadian government to resume sealing negotiations. Along the lines of the Elliott-Dillingham idea of March 1905, he expressed a willingness to grant Canada 20 percent of the proceeds from the Pribilofs in exchange for cessation of pelagic sealing.[15] Then he waited. The complexities of triangular diplomacy and the innate caution of Laurier's government in dealings with the United States slowed the progress of every diplomatic initiative between Washington and Ottawa.

Root received Laurier's inevitable rejection in December. The prime minister called 20 percent "hardly adequate pecuniary compensation" and suggested that Root was unaware of the Canadian position held since 1898. He explained that, at the Joint High Commission, Canada had insisted on money and "some substantial national concession, which would go far to remove all international differences between the two countries." Laurier expressed disappointment that Root had asked Canada to surrender a natural right without offering some equally important national concession. A few months later the influential *Toronto Globe* reiterated the ideology behind Laurier's response: "The importance of the ocean as an international right is far too great to be disregarded, and Canada can never consent or be a party to the surrender of rights on the high seas."[16] Actually, Root saw his offer in the reverse. He believed that the 20 percent was a substantial national concession, but he was unwilling to pay for the increasingly useless Victoria sealing fleet. Laurier, however, could see sealing only in terms of international rights and his political fortunes, not economic folly.

One of the great ironies of Canada's rejection of Root's offer was that Elliott never forgave the secretary for it. Somehow, Elliott got the idea that "Root, to serve those greedy private interests, *has been secretly holding my treaty down.*" Root, like Hay before him, refused to beg Canada to continue negotiations. Elliott, however, blamed Root for Canada's rejection of the 20 percent offer and the subsequent decline of the seal herds. In 1909, he even wrote for a magazine, "The mills of the Gods . . . are pulverizing the Root of all evil for our fur seal herd!"[17] As he had since 1890, he failed to see the problem inherent in Canadian intractability. Instead, he refueled his publicity machine and planned for a new confrontation with the government's agents.

Elliott's growing belligerence toward government policy finally caused an open rift between him and most other scientists who studied the seal. In particular, he excoriated Jordan and Walter Lembkey, the government agent on the island, for supporting continued land sealing. Lembkey's job was to maximize the government's profits from the seal herd without damaging the herd's long-term stability. But Elliott accused him of harvesting protected seals and altering the books to cover his tracks. While Lembkey may have been overzealous in his prosecution of sealing, he was neither corrupt nor secretive in his harvesting methods.[18]

Elliott also grew to hate Jordan because he believed that Jordan did not pay him sufficient homage. The break had actually occurred in 1898, when the Treasury Department gave Jordan the task of deflating Elliott's previous work. But by 1906, Elliott's spite became so overpowering that he could find nothing good to say about Jordan's work or character. He criticized Jordan's desire to describe new species as "*mechanical work . . . best done by men who have wooden minds.*" He unfairly accused Jordan of plagiarizing a chart from his 1890 report, and he asked his friend Hornaday "how a man having so little common sense could be in charge of that big California University."[19]

The source of Elliott's immediate anger was Jordan's renewed status as the government's seal expert. Elliott thought that he had regained that perch in 1904, when Roosevelt had asked for his advice. But for the second time in fifteen years, his irrational behavior, questionable judgment, and record of instability cost him his influence in the executive branch. In contrast,

Jordan and his associates were neither publicity hounds nor amateur states-men. Jordan had established himself as both a better scientist and a more stable and reliable person. Elliott still had his connections in Congress, but he wanted influence on both ends of Pennsylvania Avenue.

Jordan's followers worked hard to apply their scientific knowledge in an effort to break the pelagic sealers' siege on the Pribilof herd. In an unintentionally amusing series of experiments, government agents tried rearranging rocks on breeding beaches to foil parasites, penning in male seals at a small lake, and branding pups in an effort to rebuild the species' numbers. That all of these attempts failed—sometimes fatally—did not undermine their significance. As good Progressives, the scientists believed that their expertise provided the best means to resolve the dispute. Certainly, they could do no worse than the diplomats.[20]

With or without seal branding, the Victoria sealers were heading toward extinction. In 1905, seventeen vessels collected about 13,000 skins, drastic declines from 1900, when thirty-six schooners brought in 34,000 skins. By 1908, there were only eight schooners in operation, and they caught only 4,400 seals. Every year, fewer vessels sailed for the sealing grounds, and they brought back fewer skins per vessel (table 1). The evidence was overwhelming; the Paris award and the decline of the herd were strangling Canadian pelagic sealing.

On their economic deathbeds, the Canadian sealers struggled for a miracle cure by nullifying the Paris regulations. Beginning in 1906, Joseph Boscowitz, vice-president of the Victoria Sealing Company (VSC), orchestrated a campaign to overturn the rules or, better yet, recoup his company's capital. In a stunning display of audacity, he offered Root a halt in sealing for a term of years if the United States would pay an annual subsidy on the VSC's capital. If Root refused, Boscowitz threatened to sail his ships under the Japanese flag to avoid the regulations. Cynically, Boscowitz adopted the language of conservation: "It seems a thousand pities that the Governments interested could not formulate a *modus vivendi* by which the seal life could be saved." Root coldly replied that there was no chance that his government would consent to such blackmail.[21] To Canadian officials, Boscowitz suggested that under eminent domain laws the government owed the ship owners some form of compensation.[22] Grey and Laurier ignored him.

But Boscowitz did correctly identify as one of the causes of the VSC's decline the influx of Japanese sealers into the Bering Sea. By 1906, the once small fleet had grown to more than thirty vessels. Unlike the Canadians, the

Table 1

Pelagic Sealing Catches by Canadians

Year	Boats	American Coast	Eastern Bering Sea	Russian Coast	Japanese Coast	Total
1887	22	12,084	21,716			33,800
1888	20	11,041	16,940			27,981
1889	23	16,985	16,585			33,570
1890	29	26,238	18,165			44,547
1891						52,365
1892	65	31,557		14,805		46,362
1893	55	28,613		12,013	29,206	69,832
1894	35	11,703	26,341	7,437	48,993	94,474
1895	40	6,066	35,918	6,281	18,687	66,952
1896	54	8,350	25,700	1,306	17,968	53,324
1897	31	5,082	15,607	1,382	7,321	29,392
1898	31	9,646	16,943	50	360	26,999
1899	25	10,471	23,284	699		34,454
1900	36	16,438	17,513	208		34,159
1901	37	7,265	10,362	3,397	2,130	23,154
1902	31	4,936	5,193	1,340	3,331	14,800
1903	21	3,865	8,161	1,910		13,936
1904	19	3,118	8,237	1,790		13,145
1905	17	2,779	8,576	1,081	510	13,006
1906	17	2,184	6,324	1,098	553	10,159
1907	15	1,934	2,858	263	185	5,240
1908	8	1,282	2,277	677	216	4,452
1909	4	1,493	1,439	623		3,555
1910	5	1,303	2,293	626		4,222

Source: RG 25, vol. 1108, File 40, vol. 2, pt. 2. (The source did not explain the gaps in information for 1891.)

Japanese did not have to honor the sixty-mile buffer zone, the ban on firearms, or the closed season. Boscowitz argued, "The practical and effective result of the enforcement of these regulations has been to transfer the business heretofore carried on by the Victoria Sealing Company to the owners of Japanese sealing vessels."[23] Although his point was not totally accurate —

the VSC had been created eight years after the Paris tribunal met—his basic reasoning was. Canadian sealers could not compete with the Japanese fleet.

Japanese sealers filled the niche that the Canadians had unwillingly vacated in 1893. Initially, the Japanese honored the three-mile limit around the Pribilofs. But as the species declined and more sealers took advantage of the large government subsidies, competition for the few remaining seals increased. According to one naval officer on the scene, the crews of the schooners were of various ancestry, but they were all "desperate men." Among the Native Americans living in coastal regions of Alaska, one schooner earned the nickname "Terror" because of its piratical acts. With no more than four revenue cutters responsible for an area of hundreds of thousands of square miles, there was no way to guard the rookeries and the Alaskan coastline. Japanese sealers had almost free reign throughout the Bering Sea, just as the Canadians had had years before.[24]

The increasing scarcity made Japanese schooner captains more aggressive than the Canadians had ever been. Generally, the main vessels remained anchored beyond territorial waters, while small hunting boats with three or four men came close inshore. These tactics made it difficult for the crews of the American cutters to confiscate the mother ship. In 1906, the Japanese began to come ashore on foggy days and kill the seals on land. On 16 and 17 July, five different schooners landed crews on St. Paul Island, prompting a firefight. In the melee, American guards using a Gatling gun killed five sealers and captured several more. After that confrontation, the sealers devised a new technique. Instead of landing, they approached the rookeries and fired their shotguns. The gunfire scared the seals into the water, where the sealers could get to them with little trouble. When American guards had the time to respond, they had to be careful not to kill or disturb the seals.[25]

The brazenness of Japanese methods prompted some in the U.S. government to urge a strong response. When the "Terror," officially known as the *Kinsei Maru 2*, was hauled in for violating territorial waters in 1908, the owners tried to avoid paying the assessed fines. Fishery Commissioner George Bowers called on the government to confiscate the ship and the skins that were on board to send an appropriate message. In summation, he wrote, "Every consideration of justice, every rule of efficient administration, every instinct of national independence and conservation advise the enforcement of the Court's decision."[26] Going further, some urged the administration to shift its diplomatic focus from Ottawa to Tokyo. Walter Lembkey explained the problem: "A settlement with Canada, which does not at least involve Japan, would be of no advantage to this country, and would be simply a waste of money." His superior, Secretary of Commerce and Labor Oscar Strauss, concurred. He told Root that Japan should be the target of diplomatic initiatives because of her much larger fleet and freedom from the 1893 regulations.[27]

But American diplomatic contact with Japan on the sealing issue had been almost nonexistent since 1897. The Japanese had made it clear then that they would reject regulations that did not also apply to Canadians, and that sentiment may have inhibited American initiatives. Still, American diplomats should have tried to apply the Paris regulations to Japanese-flagged vessels, a goal that the New York Times had identified way back in 1893.[28] Even after Japan won the Russo-Japanese War and became a rookery-owning power, Root failed to challenge Tokyo to restrict pelagic sealers.[29] By 1909, the Japanese interests were so valuable that Tokyo had a right to expect some sort of diplomatic concession from the United States.

The failure to take aggressive action toward Japan was the greatest blunder of American seal diplomacy. While American statesmen concentrated on buying out the aging and declining Canadian sealing fleet, the Japanese were expanding their fleet of newer schooners. In contrast to Canadians who operated under the Paris regulations, subsidized Japanese sealers found the pursuit quite lucrative. Both Japan and Canada considered sealing to be a question of national policy, but, unlike Canadians, Japanese investors had a rational economic motive to continue sealing at sea. The United States would have been better off concentrating its financial offers on Tokyo and allowing the tribunal's award to strangle Victoria's sealers.

BREAKING THE DEADLOCK

In April 1908, the British Ambassador, Sir James Bryce, came to Root with a proposal to reopen sealing negotiations. Root was skeptical, having seen no evidence of a change in Canada's position, but Bryce prevailed on his friend. He believed that pelagic sealing was a fading and unacceptable industry and that the Dominion government would soon be willing to discuss terms for its cessation. He also sought to halt the decline of London's seal-fur industry. The challenge for Canada would be negotiating a deal that saved face, while that facing the United States would be finding a solution quickly enough to save the Pribilof Island seals.

Despite Root's skepticism, especially about the added complexity of Japanese interests, there were signs that negotiations might be fruitful. The scientific evidence of decline was irrefutable, and the moral opposition to sealing was growing. In July, the British demonstrated their commitment by extracting from Laurier Canadian requirements for a satisfactory treaty. First, he requested a complete ten-year closed season; second, he expected the adherence of Japanese sealers to the same restrictions; and third, he demanded adequate compensation for Canadian sealers.[30]

On the other side of the Pacific, the Russians and Japanese were opening negotiations on the problem despite the animosity left over from their recent war. Spurred on by the seizure of a Japanese schooner just outside of Russian territorial waters, the two governments wanted to prevent the escalation of a minor incident into a crisis. The Russians argued that banning pelagic sealing would benefit both countries now that Japan had the rookeries on Robben Island, which it had won in the Russo-Japanese War.[31] The Japanese government responded cautiously, but editorials in two English-language newspapers pointed out that pelagic sealing both increased the risk of an unnecessary confrontation with the United States and Russia and was bad long-term economic policy. In addition, they called the industry "decidedly immoral as well as inhuman." As one argued, Japan's continued pursuit of such a questionable activity made her look selfish in the eyes of the world.[32]

With these positive signs coming in from the other sealing nations, on 21 January 1909 Root called on Japan, Russia, and Great Britain to join with the United States to resolve the Bering Sea dispute. He suggested that Japanese interests might now be more in line with those of America and Russia, because all three had declining—but potentially lucrative—seal herds. The demise of the herds, he observed, would also harm Canadian interests. Unless all four nations on the North Pacific could agree on protective measures, the species would be destroyed. The scientific evidence, he concluded, demonstrated "that any permanent solution of this difficult question should include an international agreement absolutely prohibiting pelagic sealing."[33]

Even before Root had issued his circular, the Canadian government had reentrenched itself in opposition to a sealing agreement. In December 1908, R. N. Venning, the assistant commissioner of fisheries, presented Canada's options to the Privy Council. He acknowledged that the rise of the Japanese sealing fleet had put Victoria's sealers at such a disadvantage that they were willing to sell out. He also admitted that "seals were now so reduced the question was no longer as to whether the sealing business was of any value to anyone engaged in it; . . . but the question today was whether the seals could be saved from utter extinction." But he also expressed the typical Canadian position that the United States had won the Paris award and should, therefore, leave Canada alone.[34]

In the end, Venning concluded that the Dominion should reject any American offer of compensation for the right to catch seals in international waters. The most important historical lesson of the previous twenty-two years, in his opinion, was that "Canada has consistently and with the greatest care combated the many ingenious and persistent efforts of the United States to suppress pelagic sealing." Therefore, Canada should not change its position just because sealing was temporarily unprofitable. Typically, he claimed, Americans saw sealing as a question of dollars and cents, but Canadians regarded sealing as an issue of rights on the high seas. Taking a long-term view of the situation, Venning suggested that the United States could never offer acceptable terms.

Venning's intransigence reflected not only his lack of training in the ways of diplomacy but also the shortcomings of Canadian diplomacy. No government should rely on a fisheries official to craft diplomatic policy single-handedly. Venning's job was to help Canadians catch more marine animals, not to weigh the international consequences of the Dominion's policies. In May 1909, however, the new Canadian Department of External Affairs came into being, with Sir Joseph Pope in charge. For the first time, the Canadian government had an official whose primary responsibility was to consider the impact of Ottawa's policies beyond the Dominion. Pope's authority promised a new approach to the sealing problem, if only because Canada could no longer rely on London to take care of its foreign policy.[35]

It took all of Pope's confidence, intelligence, and professionalism to bring order out of the chaos that was Canada's approach to diplomacy. Both Whitehall and the State Department wanted Canada to take a stand, but Pope had to wait for the British Colonial Office to send copies of all pertinent documents, because the Dominion's records were so poorly maintained. With Bryce pushing for a compromise, Pope faced a delicate situation. He believed in the primacy of the empire and was generally suspicious of American motives. But his service as an aide to the Joint High Commission had taught him that Canada had to prepare to fend for itself in case London could not. In his first test, he had to choose between a traditional Canadian interest and the wishes of his empire's respected ambassador to the United States.

While Pope considered his options, Ambassador Bryce continued to discuss terms with the State Department. In May 1909, Bryce reminded the department legal advisor, Chandler Anderson, that Canada considered the 20 percent offered in 1906 to be inadequate compensation. Anderson reiterated the American contention that the skins were not compensation for abandoning sealing, because such an offer would set a bad precedent for American negotiations with Japan. Bryce deduced that the United States wanted to share the herd so as to create "a joint interest in the future of the herd in order that a cordial cooperation in measures for its preservation might be secured." In other words, 20 percent of the herd was not compensation, but rather a means of bringing Canada into the ranks of countries that had reason to oppose pelagic sealing.[36]

In their talks, Bryce and Anderson laid down the terms that eventually served as the basis for the U.S.-Canadian agreement. The core of the settlement remained Canadian acceptance of 20 percent of the skins taken each year on the Pribilofs in exchange for outlawing pelagic sealing for fifteen years. Bryce expressed his concern that American conservationists might force a ten-year closed season on all land sealing, which would leave Canada without compensation. Anderson, then, agreed that Canada should receive a lump sum every year in which seals were not harvested. Anderson also explained that the United States intended to come to an arrangement with Japan that would halt pelagic sealing, and he hoped that Great Britain would cooperate in that venture.

As the Taft administration and Bryce were coming to terms, Pope had accepted Venning's advice that Canada should oppose any agreement with the United States on sealing. In October, he reported to the Privy Council that "the only reason that could possibly justify our Government in prohibiting Pelagic sealing would be the threatened extinction of the herd." He worried that if the seals were not as endangered as Washington claimed, then the Canadian government would look foolish for having surrendered its rights to a resource on the high seas. He reported the following American estimates of the herd's size: in March 1908, Henry Elliott put the herd at 50,000; in January 1909, Root estimated the herd at 150,000; in May 1909, Anderson placed it at 200,000. Together, Pope commented, these numbers showed "a gratifying increase for the recent year."[37] Jokes aside, his point seemed valid — the status of the seals was not as certain as American diplomats and scientists wanted to believe. But he had also hinted that he accepted the sentimental argument that the species had to be preserved.

Pope's position clashed with that of an increasingly impatient British government. In early November, the American ambassador to Great Britain, Whitelaw Reid, piqued the interest of Sir Edward Grey, the British foreign secretary, in the sealing question by lecturing him on the evils of pelagic sealing. In response, "Sir Edward agreed that it would be a great pity to let the herd be destroyed."[38] About the same time, Grey received a report from Commander E. H. Edwards of HMS *Algerine,* which patrolled the Northern Pacific. Edwards concluded that pelagic sealing should not be tolerated "in any civilised country whose inhabitants have any consideration for animal life and animal suffering." Drawing on Edwards's and Reid's appraisals, the Foreign Office called on Canada to cooperate with the United States to end "the extreme cruelty of the present system of pelagic sealing." In addition, Ambassador Bryce made it clear to Canadian officials that destruction of the species meant economic hardship in London. Canada's financial interests were now directly up against British sentiment and the interests of the London furriers.[39]

The Canadian government finally bowed to Whitehall's pressure to agree to a four-power conference, but not until Pope and Laurier had placed conditions on their attendance. Pope still believed that the United States was "inviting Canada to limit the freedom of her people in order to build up the fortunes of the lessees of the Pribyloff Islands." He feared that if the other conferees all opposed pelagic sealing "we may . . . find ourselves, at any rate morally, bound to accept prohibition, perhaps *without any compensation.*"[40] Therefore, the Canadians made their attendance conditional upon a preliminary agreement about the financial terms. This very small step forward shrewdly put the burden on the United States, but it also revealed that Canada had worries about sentimental opinion throughout the English-speaking world.

With the demise of the seals outpacing the progress of the diplomats, American scientists again found themselves as the best hope to save the seal. On 15 January 1909, Secretary Strauss appointed David Starr Jordan to chair the new Fur Seal Advisory Board (FSAB), consisting of the distinguished naturalists C. Hart Merriam, Charles H. Townsend, Leonard Stejneger, and Frederic Lucas, as well as Edwin Sims, the former legal counsel of the Department of Commerce and Labor. As a group, they were as distrustful of pelagic sealers as they were of Henry Elliott, who was not invited to participate. Strauss specified that the FSAB's goals were the "rehabilitation and preservation of the fur-seal herd." As the government's panel of experts, the group had to consider the renewal of the North American Commercial Company's lease—due to expire in April 1910—and devise methods of controlling pelagic sealing.[41]

The steady decline of the herd under the pressure of Japanese sealers worried the board members. In a report later printed in *Popular Science,* George Clark, Jordan's trusted assistant at Stanford and a recent visitor to the islands, estimated that the herd was down to 140,000 animals—with 50,000 breeding females—only one-third of its 1896 size. The number of harems on one of the rookeries frequented by the Japanese had declined by 80 percent in the same period. On St. Paul, 6 percent of the pups had starved to death by July, presumably because pelagic sealers had killed their mothers. The NACC was having a harder time than ever fulfilling its quota of only 15,000, although Clark verified that the company was not killing females.[42] Even for these veterans of the sealing dispute, Clark's report must have been very troubling.

In November, the committee members made two major recommendations to the new secretary of commerce and labor, Charles Nagel. First, they suggested that the government should alter the lease system to ensure closer control of the land-sealing operation, including the option to halt the harvest. The two alternatives were either to place the government in complete control or to allow the lessee only to sell skins collected by the government agent. Second, the scientists recommended that the United States should call a conference of diplomats and scientists from the four sealing nations. Jordan and his colleagues believed that a diplomatic exchange based on the scientific evidence would lead to an agreement to cease pelagic sealing.[43] In *The Call of the Nation,* a book about reforming politics and economics, Jordan argued, "If Canada and Japan cannot be shamed into abandoning this right, it is for our plain financial interest to pay them to do so."[44]

The FSAB's report was not well received in the State Department. An angry Anderson demanded that the board members refrain from making foreign policy recommendations, probably on the theory that he did not tell them how to conduct scientific research. Several months later, he suggested that "in case we succeed in arranging for a conference it seems to me desirable that no experts on either side should be included."[45] Anderson's reaction was ungrateful. The accumulation of scientific evidence had served both to show the unsustainability of pelagic sealing and to build up public resentment against the Canadian sealers. Without years of input from the scientific community, the American diplomatic position would have been untenable.

Nagel, on the other hand, appreciated the advice. Legally, he had to issue a lease, but he searched for other options. After consulting with the State Department, he asked Taft to support legislation placing total control of the Pribilofs under the Department of Commerce and Labor. He suggested that "the herds have been reduced to such an extent that . . . the controlling question has become one of conservation." Nagel also anticipated that placing the seals under government control would assist American diplomats in their efforts to end pelagic sealing. He told Congress that he "would like to have the fur-seal business put in such a position that it may be pressed forward or receded from—just as the exigencies of the case call for." [46] In other words, government control would be a useful bargaining tool.

Nagel received broad support from foes of sealing, including Henry Elliott, who found himself agreeing with Jordan. By this time, Elliott had allied himself with William T. Hornaday, the master fund-raiser and manipulator of the press and Congress. Under Hornaday's recommendation, Elliott steered away from public pronouncements on the bill and allowed the smoother Hornaday to handle the public relations. As an officer of the New York Zoological Society and a veteran public speaker, Hornaday could, on occasion, tone down the rhetoric in a way that Elliott could not. Having mesmerized the editors of the *New York Times* years earlier, Hornaday had his way with the press and launched a vigorous campaign to raise public awareness of the importance of the sealing bill. Testifying to Congress, he emphasized that he wanted to bridge the gap between Elliott and the government scientists, because both sides agreed that the seals would be better off without the NACC around. Congress responded by passing "An Act to Protect the Seal Fisheries of Alaska." [47]

The Elliott and Jordan factions soon had a falling out, though, over the meaning of the act. It clearly stated that the secretary of commerce and labor had the authority to regulate the land sealing operations in a manner consistent "with the preservation of the seal herd." The FSAB called for continued harvesting of surplus males in order to reduce the number of extraneous bulls that might trample seal pups. The State Department also wanted to continue the harvest to maintain pressure on the pelagic sealing nations.[48] But Hornaday countered that conservation and diplomacy required a complete halt to sealing. In his typical rhetoric, he observed that by "clearing our hands of fur seal blood" the government would have the moral high ground in dealing with the other sealing powers.[49]

In May 1910, Secretary Nagel chose to accept Jordan's advice instead of Hornaday's. He authorized Walter Lembkey, who now had almost czarist powers on the Pribilofs, to harvest approximately 12,000 young male seals while leaving 2,000 young males as a breeding reserve.[50] Jordan and his colleagues envisioned rational management of the herd through the well-regulated culling of most young males. They reasoned that the young males were superfluous but valuable, and the old males were potentially dangerous to the herd but worthless. Therefore, it made sense to them to prevent most of the young ones from becoming old ones.

Hornaday and Elliott struck back in anger. They charged Nagel and his subordinates with violating the public trust by extending the seal harvest. In a seething letter, Hornaday screamed "DID THE PRESIDENT . . . OR THE UNITED STATES SENATE, INTEND FOR ONE MOMENT THAT YOU SHOULD GO RIGHT ON IN THE BLOODY KILLING BUSINESS? NO!" he answered rhetorically, "A THOUSAND TIMES, NO!" In lengthy letters to the *New York Times,* and in editorials that he inspired in the same paper, Hornaday questioned the integrity of the secretary and his advisors. He also warned Nagel that the public would not stand for more sealing after he had done so much to rally public support for the bill to end the leasing system. He implicitly threatened Nagel with the same fate that had recently befallen Secretary of the Interior Richard Ballinger.[51]

Hornaday also attacked the science behind Nagel's decision. He accused Jordan of having only a superficial knowledge of the fur seals and harboring a desire to assist the pelagic sealers. More to the point, he argued that there could be no scientific basis for the hypothesis that harvesting male seals helped the herd. Hornaday testified, "There is not a single species in the world which has required the intervention of man for the purpose of killing its surplus males."[52] If males had to be killed to improve the herd's health, then the seal had not done a very good job of evolving. Such control implied that seals were now no more than domestic animals. On Elliott's advice, Hornaday denounced any killing of seals as dangerous to the future of the species.

Although his basic point was reasonable, Hornaday made two mistakes. First, he attacked Jordan's integrity. Like Elliott, Hornaday was incapable of tolerating other views, even when honest, prominent scientists espoused them. To accuse Jordan of helping the pelagic sealers was absurd and vicious.

In so doing, he only alienated Nagel further. Second, Hornaday refused to acknowledge that the seal herds were no longer isolated from human activity. In an undisturbed state, the seals would not have needed human intervention to regulate breeding, but years of killing had disrupted the whole environment. Humans had so altered nature that scientists had to consider options other than a *laissez-faire* approach.

In the end, Hornaday and Elliott failed in this attempt to stop land sealing because they had no influence over Nagel. Like Philander Knox, Nagel was a corporate attorney with little use for Hornaday's tactics or Elliott's hypothetical science. Jordan, no matter what his political beliefs, appealed to Nagel as a rational scientist capable of separating truth from speculation. The FSAB provided the secretary with the evidence necessary to indicate that pelagic sealing was bad business, while well-managed land sealing could continue indefinitely. Nagel recognized the importance of conservation, but he was not overwhelmed with sentiment about the species; at one point he ordered a seal fur coat for his wife. His first goal was to restore the profitability of the land-sealing operations.

The imminent extinction of the herds, the rising outcry against pelagic sealing, and the passage of the seal conservation bill all encouraged the Americans to become more liberal in their offer to Canada. In February 1910 the United States agreed to pay Canada $200,000 as an advance on the Dominion's share of the skins, which would remain at 20 percent. The money would allow Canada to compensate the remaining sealers for leaving the enterprise. The governor general admitted that the American draft treaty was reasonable, but Laurier's government quivered with indecision. Fearing a mistake, Pope and various fisheries officials searched for technicalities that would allow them to reject the American offer. For instance, Pope worried that the seal herds might move to some other island and free the U.S. government of its responsibilities under the treaty.[53]

By July 1910, the British government had lost its patience with Canadian delay. Referring to the February offer, Bryce reminded Ottawa that "there might appear to be a lack of courtesy on our part if I fail to make some reply." Further, he mentioned that the Americans might "even drop the whole matter in despair." When Bryce failed to elicit a response, Lord Crewe of the Colonial Office notified the governor general that the Dominion should stop dallying lest the "sealing industry . . . become extinct, in which case Canada would lose the advantage which it is proposed to obtain for it by the agreement under consideration."[54] The Canadians stood their ground.

In particular, Canadians held out for one more change in the treaty's language. The American draft had an article that committed the signatories to outlaw pelagic sealing everywhere at all times. Minister of Marine and Fisheries William Found argued that Canada should approach the treaty as a good business deal for a limited amount of time. When the treaty expired, he anticipated, pelagic sealing would be "a more attractive venture." Pope put it more succinctly: "The acceptance of this article would put us in the position . . . of being paid for refraining from committing an immoral act!"[55] The State Department agreed to rewrite the article to limit its scope to the eastern Bering Sea.

Finally, on 7 February 1911, Great Britain and the United States signed a preliminary agreement to outlaw pelagic sealing. The United States would give Canada 20 percent of the skins taken on the islands in exchange for a fifteen-year suspension of Canadian pelagic sealing in the eastern Bering Sea. In addition, the United States would advance Canada $200,000, to be repaid out of Canada's share of the skins. The agreement also included safeguards in case the American government chose to halt land sealing for conservation purposes. The treaty would not take effect until Russia and Japan joined Britain and the United States in another treaty to control pelagic sealing throughout the North Pacific.[56]

Canadian acceptance of the treaty depended less on the specific terms than on the recognition that pelagic sealing was no longer a vital national interest. For domestic political reasons, Canada had held out for something tangible in exchange for publicly relinquishing a right for which the Dominion had fought for almost a quarter of a century. But in the end, Laurier and Pope discovered that 20 percent of the herd and the intangible benefits of having negotiated a treaty with the United States were worth far more than the minimal returns of the few remaining sealing vessels and the honor in having stood up for a wasteful, if legal, practice.

For the United States, the Anglo-American treaty was not so much a victory as it was a means of attaining a four-power sealing agreement. For several years, Americans had recognized that Japanese sealers were the real threat to the Pribilof seals, but Japan would not accept restrictions that did not also apply to Canada. With pressure mounting to save the species, the United States was willing to compromise in order to pave the way for a deal with the true threat to the seal, the pelagic sealers of Japan. With Canada now among the nations with an interest in opposing pelagic sealing, Americans hoped for a quick resolution with Japan.

SEALING THE DEAL

With the conclusion of the Anglo-American sealing convention in February 1911, Nagel, Anderson, and American scientists all had reason to anticipate an imminent solution to the long-running sealing controversy. The Canadians were finally in the fold, and Japanese diplomats had made it clear that they too would consider ending pelagic sealing. As the long-awaited four-power conference opened in Washington in May, Americans believed that the conferees were coming from roughly equal positions, because each had an interest in promoting land sealing and all could agree that pelagic sealing was indefensible. But the Canadian and Japanese representatives soon indicated that they saw the conference as a meeting between two pelagic sealing powers and two rookery-owning powers. American efforts to resolve this difference of opinion took several weeks of hard bargaining that relied on science, economics, and appeals to morality.

Each nation sent diplomats and scientists to the conference, which convened on 11 May 1911. In addition to Nagel, the American delegation consisted of Anderson and a fisheries official, Dr. Hugh Smith. The British delegation included Bryce, Pope, and a Canadian scientist, James Macoun, a staunch defender of pelagic sealing. The Russian and Japanese entourages included career diplomats as well as scientific advisors. The combination of scientists and sympathetic statesmen, such as Nagel and Bryce, ensured that conservation of the herd would remain a top priority. At separate meetings, the scientists discussed ways to protect whales, sea otters, walruses, sea birds, and other sea creatures.

In reality, the scientists were as much nationalists as impartial researchers. Macoun tried to use his acquaintance with American scientists to find a weak link in the American diplomatic position. Using a pantomime to illustrate shooting at seals, the Japanese delegate Hitoshi Duaké indicated to Macoun that he relished the opportunity to resume high seas sealing against the Russian herd.[57] Likewise, Smith, as a government employee, was not about to contradict the official American line. Still, their presence at the conference proved that each power recognized that scientific knowledge would play a key role in the ensuing negotiations.

The conference opened with an American proposal to end all pelagic sealing in the Pacific north of the 35th parallel. Then Anderson officially informed the Russian and Japanese delegations of the terms of the February treaty. He declared that the United States and Canada had agreed to the distribution of the skins in order to create a partnership between them. Without offering compensation he called for Japan and Russia to join in the agreement because all four nations now had an interest in protecting their seal herds from pelagic sealing. The Russian delegate, Minister to Morocco Pierre Botkine, endorsed the American plan, as did Ambassador Bryce.[58]

If the American representatives had hoped for quick negotiations, they were disappointed. The Japanese diplomat Baron Yasuya Uchida, in a statement that Bryce termed "inacceptable to the point of ineptitude," challenged the American assertion that the four conferees came from equal positions. He saw no communion of interests between Japan and either Russia or the United States. Considering Japan's large and modern sealing fleet, he demanded concessions similar to those that the United States had granted to Canada. Above all, Uchida argued, resolution of the sealing crisis would require "cooperation between the countries possessing breeding grounds and the countries engaged in pelagic sealing."[59]

Uchida's counterproposal allowed the Canadians to express their own disenchantment with the American plan. In particular, Pope took the opportunity to distance Canada from Anderson's "fantastic interpretation of our recent treaty." To Bryce's dismay, Pope argued that Canada's 20 percent was compensation for ending pelagic sealing against the Pribilof herd; if partnership had been the goal, then Canada would have gained some say in the management of the herd. In addition, Canada had agreed to stop pelagic sealing only in the eastern half of the Bering Sea. Therefore, the Dominion was free to strike similar deals with Japan and Russia for the western Pacific and had an obligation to do so to protect its rights on the high seas.[60]

Anderson and Nagel struggled to support the contention that all four nations now had a stake in land sealing, and, therefore, each had reason to end pelagic sealing. Anderson argued that, as owner of Robben Island and the Kuriles, Japan could expect a profitable return on land sealing if pelagic depredations ended. Along these lines, the United States had given Canada 20 percent of the Pribilof herd as a gift in order to make Canada an equal partner in efforts to control pelagic sealing. In response, Uchida noted that Japan's rookeries were unproductive rocks compared to the Pribilofs. Japan and Canada had similar interests in that they had long defended freedom of the seas and because their share of land sealing was going to be tiny. In his opinion, the February treaty had been a case of direct compensation, and Japan deserved analogous treatment. Pope's similar interpretation undermined the American stance.[61]

With the temperature and tempers hovering around 100°F, Anderson's first instinct was to return to the confrontational diplomacy that had done so poorly in the past. Angrily, he reminded the conference that in 1896 and 1905 the American government had considered wiping out the majority of the seals in order to save money and reduce the likelihood of an international incident. If the conferees could not come to some sort of solution, he observed, "there is certainly no reason why the United States should continue to protect . . . its fur seals without profit and at considerable expense and annoyance to itself for the sole benefit of those engaged in the business of pelagic sealing." [62] In his opinion, the United States had no obligation to pay foreign governments not to kill American seals. If need be, he threatened, the United States would unilaterally destroy the Pribilof herd and be done with it. The obvious problem with this threat was its opposition to the standard American position that killing female seals violated both civilized morality and scientific management.

Pope may have been new at his job, but he knew a bluff when he saw one and countered with a more subtle one of his own. Instead of backing down and leaving Japan to fend for itself, he too returned to the basic Canadian position of years past. He asked his superiors for instructions indicating "that it is by no means certain that the Government would consent to sacrifice its consistency for the sake of securing a treaty which after all does not affect two hundred persons in Canada, most of whom are Indians." [63] If the Americans really wanted a treaty, then they would have to support Canadian claims to compensation from the Asian powers, even if that meant acknowledging Uchida's demand for the same.

Pope aimed his bluff as much at Bryce as at Anderson. He hoped that his ploy would scare Bryce, whose leading desire was to secure a treaty, into supporting the Canadian position. Bryce thought that he, Anderson, and Botkine would form a coalition to bring Uchida to a settlement. He had not anticipated that Uchida would find an ally in the Canadian delegate. Bryce would not be outfoxed by a rookie, however, and he maneuvered Pope into a compromise. The savvy ambassador impressed upon Pope that Canadian intransigence would cost the Dominion the excellent settlement it had won in February and threaten the London fur industry.

On 1 June, with Pope chewing on Bryce's advice and the fate of the seals hanging in the balance, Bryce and Nagel agreed to offer Japan a portion of the skins. From Bryce's standpoint, it was a necessary concession to keep

Uchida at the table. Nagel, however, saw the offer as a means of punishing Pope. The Canadian's tactics had incensed the American delegates, and in retaliation they proposed that Canada should surrender to Japan part of its 20 percent of the Pribilof herd. Now it was Pope's turn to squirm, as he handled "the disagreeable duty" of dealing with the intransigent Japanese.[64] The American offer had turned the proceedings into a scramble to devise an equitable method of dividing the skins.

Pope's lone ally was now his main competitor. The Russians and Americans put 25 percent of their sealskins on the table for the Canadians and Japanese to divide and got out of the way, much as one might toss raw meat to two wild dogs. But Uchida and Pope started out from radically different positions. Uchida wanted 35 percent of both the Russian and American herds, while Pope offered Japan 20 percent of the Russian herd and 5 percent of the American herd in exchange for 5 percent of the Russian herd and 15 percent of any Japanese skins. The chasm between the two positions was so great that Pope confided to his superiors that the Japanese position "savours of extortion." [65] The change in the Russo-American position had succeeded in bringing Canada into line against Japan.

In part, Japan and Canada were so distant because of a disagreement between Macoun and Duaké over Japan's interests in land sealing. Based on his years of experience, Macoun suggested that the Japanese would find Robben Island to be productive, and even the Kuriles might yield a few hundred skins each year. Therefore, Japan deserved less compensation than did the Canadians. Duaké countered that, because of its size and geography, Robben Island would never yield more than 750 skins, and the Kuriles were not viable rookeries. In contrast, the Japanese anticipated that the Pribilofs would yield almost 60,000 skins by 1926. In other words, in year fifteen of the treaty, Canada would receive 12,000 seals from the American herd, while in the entire fifteen years Japan would have received fewer than 10,000 skins from its own herds. Under such circumstances, Uchida demanded that the United States and Russia each put 35 percent of their herds on the table, of which the majority would go to Japan.[66]

In an attempt to find a compromise, Pope found himself in the unlikely position of listing the ills of pelagic sealing from moral and scientific perspectives. He called pelagic sealing "improvident and wasteful," and he admitted that "it is in the interest of all the countries concerned that it should cease." He urged the baron to consider lowering his demands, because the time had come to resolve the sealing crisis in order to save the species. If Japan and Canada could find a way to split 30 percent of the Russian and American herds, then all sides would win.[67]

Uchida, however, thought as Pope had a few years before; while he understood the flaws of pelagic sealing, he would not easily surrender the right to pursue it. In Uchida's mind, Japan wanted only "reasonable concessions" from the Russians and Americans. Japanese sealers caught far more animals than did the Canadians, yet the rookery powers refused to offer similar compensation. Japan, he claimed, had fifty-one active sealing schooners—fifty more than the Canadians—and the crews and investors deserved some reward for ending their lawful pursuit. Finally, Uchida did not have the authority to accept less than his demands. Therefore, he concluded, it was time to go home.[68]

With the Japanese delegation threatening to leave, Bryce and Nagel called upon public opinion to break the deadlock. When the delegates reconvened on 12 June, the Japanese refused to make a counterproposal and insisted that unless the Americans had a new offer they would go home. With no alternative in sight, Nagel persuaded President Taft to ask the Japanese emperor to intercede. In his message, Taft first laid out the potential benefits of concluding a treaty, but he also warned that "a failure to reach an agreement in this case will inevitably result in the extermination of the fur seals, and owing to the deep interest taken by the people of the United States in this question, such failure would have a most unfavorable effect both upon official and public opinion here." He then suggested that Japan and Canada should each get 15 percent of the Pribilof herd as the basis for a settlement. At the next session, Ambassador Bryce told Uchida that the world would hold Japan responsible if the conference collapsed and the seals became extinct. Simultaneously, the *New York Daily Tribune,* in an editorial that noted the "reasonableness" of Japanese demands, condemned pelagic sealing as "not only an economic blunder of serious proportions, but a discredit to humanity as well."[69]

Taft's message apparently tipped the balance of power in Tokyo regarding the sealing question. The Japanese Department of Agriculture and Commerce, which supplied Uchida's scientific advisors, had concluded that pelagic sealing had reached a point of equilibrium. They expected Japanese sealers to continue to bring in about 9,000 skins each year. Unless the United States and Russia were prepared to offer more than that, the ministry saw no reason to surrender the right to catch seals. The Foreign Ministry, on the other hand, saw sealing as a minor industry, with its main product being ill will. The prevailing mood in the ministry suggested that, while the empire should not accept a bad deal, it would be a mistake to stain Japan's reputation for the sake of a few furs, especially at a time when Japan and the United States were working on a trade agreement.[70] Taft's warning helped persuade the emperor that the diplomats' fears were warranted, and he agreed to the president's proposal.

Although there were still some minor points to be settled, Taft's appeal had cleared the way for a final agreement on 7 July 1911. In exchange for outlawing pelagic sealing, Canadians received the $200,000 advance, 15 percent of the American and Russian herds, and 10 percent of the Japanese herd. For its sacrifice, Japan also received the advance and 15 percent of the two herds. Russia received 10 percent of any Japanese skins, and the conferees granted the United States the same plus 10 percent of any herd that might settle in Canadian territory. Both the United States and Russia also guaranteed a minimum payment to Japan and Canada if land sealing were to be suspended. In addition, the United States and Russia retained the right to determine the number of seals killed each year.[71]

The final round of negotiations succeeded because each of the four countries accepted, sometimes grudgingly, the scientific and moral evidence that pelagic sealing had to end, even though it was a legal practice. American scientists had proven that, unlike managed land sealing, pelagic sealing was unsustainable because it depended on harvesting breeding females. Scientists, conservationists, and statesmen had then turned the image of dying pups into a symbol of the immorality of pelagic sealing. When the United States and Russia added pecuniary considerations into the mix of scientific evidence and moral qualms, the basis for a cooperative settlement had been reached.

CONCLUSION

Before seal conservation could be completed, the treaty's enabling legislation had to make its way through the U.S. Congress. As with the fisheries treaty, the Taft administration's scientific advisors found themselves fighting for respect on Capitol Hill. In this case, though, the issue was not the economic impact of the treaty but rather scientific expertise. For several months, Hornaday and Elliott battled the administration and its supporters for influence in Congress. In the end, as one British diplomat commented,

Elliott won because he "gave the impression that he knew more about the seals than the other witnesses."[72]

It so happened that Congress was already investigating allegations of corruption in the administration of the Pribilof Islands. Elliott and Hornaday had decided that Nagel's different interpretation of the sealing act of 1910 deserved punishment. Under Elliott's spur, the House Committee on Expenditures in the Department of Commerce and Labor had been scrutinizing government agents and their policies on the Pribilofs, looking for evidence that Nagel and his subordinates had violated the act. In particular, Elliott charged that Lembkey had knowingly encouraged the killing of females and yearling males to fulfill his quotas over several years.[73]

The hearings were so meanspirited that they succeeded only in widening the chasm between Elliott's friends and foes. Outraged by Elliott's power over the committee, Fisheries Commissioner George Bowers accused Elliott of championing "nearly every improper, vicious and pernicious practice possible in the conduct of the fur seal industry." Elliott struck back in typical fashion with wild charges of perjury and corruption. The hearings reached new depths when the chairman brought in a trained seal from a very popular exhibit in the Fisheries Commission building. Appropriately, "George" performed the usual routine of circus tricks, and he also responded to certain names. When he heard "Professor Elliott," he barked and waved his flippers. Upon hearing "Commissioner Bowers," he hid under a chair.[74] It must have seemed that Elliott had the endorsement of the animal kingdom.

Into this circus atmosphere, Representative William Sulzer of New York introduced the treaty's enabling legislation on 7 February 1912. The bill authorized the advance payments to Canada and Japan and the method of dividing up the skins agreed to in the treaty. The House passed the bill unscathed after a bruising battle, but in the Senate Hornaday and Elliott were waiting in ambush. Their agent, Senator Gilbert Hitchcock of Nebraska, attached an amendment to the bill that placed a ten-year closed season on land sealing operations.[75] The final outcome would be determined in a conference committee.

As Congress considered the Hitchcock amendment, administration scientists struggled to present their own rationale for killing seals. The members of the Fur Seal Advisory Board argued that male seals had to be harvested for the long-term health of the herd. If left alone, the thousands of young males that survived 1912 would be bulls by 1918. The scientists feared that several thousand extra males would lead to havoc and trampled pups on the breeding beaches. Hornaday demolished their credibility in one sound bite: "As if a wild species does not know how to breed and multiply successfully without the help of man!"[76]

The government scientists also tried to undermine Elliott's credibility. His detractors complained that Elliott was using the franking privileges of several senators and representatives to spread his propaganda. George Clark and Jordan accused him of working to kill the treaty in order to encourage the resumption of pelagic sealing, although they offered no reason why Elliott would want such a result. Jordan asked Hitchcock why Congress insisted on listening to "a discredited adventurer, a man without scientific training" when there were so many smart men in the Smithsonian Institution and the Bureau of Fisheries. The Boone and Crockett Club, an organization of prominent, conservation-minded hunters, urged the Senate to accept the Fur Seal Advisory Board's advice.[77] But to many congressmen, Jordan and his associates had been discredited. The suggestion that killing seals was somehow consistent with conservation seemed counterintuitive and somewhat risky.

The administration also tried to block the Hitchcock amendment, citing the harm it might cause to the treaty. Nagel argued that the amendment violated the spirit of the agreement, because the other powers expected seal harvesting to continue as long as the species was in no danger of extinction. Worse yet, Congress's action undermined the longstanding American position that land sealing caused no harm to the health of the herd. Russian and Japanese newspapers had expressed reservations about the convention, and American diplomats remembered that Botkine and Uchida had left Washington in foul moods. Nagel warned Congress that any of the other signatory powers could use the Hitchcock amendment as a reasonable pretext for renouncing the treaty.[78]

Unbeknownst to Nagel and Anderson, none of the other powers was prepared to withdraw from the convention. Russia had halted its land-sealing operations for five years for the same reasons Congress considered. Japanese diplomats protested, but all they asked was that Taft try to repeal the closed season if it passed. Assessing the treaty from Canada's standpoint, Pope commented, "I hope our Press will not crow too loudly," although some government officials were concerned that the Americans would not uphold the agreement. Finally, Ambassador Bryce observed that all negotiators had understood that Congress had the right to shut down sealing and had written the treaty accordingly.[79] The feared diplomatic backlash was nowhere to be found.

The struggle in Congress over whether to allow land sealing to continue reflected the divisions between the scientists. The FSAB's supporters emphasized the expertise and training of the government's advisors, while those who favored a ban relied on brash criticism of Jordan and his colleagues. At the heart of the debate were the differing views of nature that split the conservation movement. Those who wanted to halt land sealing agreed with Hitchcock when he commented, "A whole army of experts could not convince me that Mother Nature can be improved upon." [80] Those who supported sustained harvesting of the seals compared killing seals to managing a herd of cattle; man had so altered their existence that they were no longer wholly wild.

Either perception of nature was open to criticism as being inconsistent. Many of those who trumpeted the innate superiority of unaltered nature had well-manicured lawns, kept domesticated pets, and ate grains and livestock bred for certain qualities. Senator Hitchcock might have had difficulty convincing his Cornhusker constituents that they should harvest only what perfect Mother Nature pushed forth from Nebraska's prairies. On the other hand, seals were not domesticated, nor could scientists hope to manage them like cattle. To argue that their survival required human intervention was to ignore the seal's successful evolutionary path. In addition, that argument stripped the species of its wildness in a manner inconsistent with the preservationist impulse.

In the end, Hornaday and Elliott won a partial victory when Congress agreed to a five-year suspension of land sealing. Secretary Nagel was unhappy, but he could only recommend to Taft that a veto would further delay conservation of the fur seal. As Hornaday promised, when sealing resumed in 1917, it was highly profitable. By 1920, the harvest was generating more than three million dollars annually, and the herd was growing rapidly. In a sense, both sides had been vindicated. The suspension had not harmed the herd, and land sealing was compatible with preserving the species from extinction. All agreed on one point: the end of pelagic sealing had given the fur seal a new life.

Diplomatically, the treaty satisfied all the participants. The United States finally settled a longstanding dispute with Great Britain and Canada. British diplomats succeeded in solidifying their ties with the United States. Canadian leaders, especially Joseph Pope, earned praise for their staunch defense of the Dominion's interests and the lucrative settlement they attained.[81] In conjunction with the arbitration settlement of the Newfoundland fisheries dispute, the resolution of the fur seal issue cleared the way for increased cooperation among the United States, Canada, and Britain. Likewise, the Japanese and Russian governments were pleased to be rid of a thorny diplomatic issue, and the Japanese in particular had strengthened their ties with the United States.

Economically, the treaty received a mixed evaluation. The Russian press criticized Botkine and American diplomats for giving away too much of the herd, but some Japanese editorials expressed the sentiment that Japan had received too little.[82] On the other side of the Pacific, though, opinion was in favor of the terms. A few Canadians worried that the Dominion had abandoned its principles, but most realized that "it would net us between a quarter and a half million of dollars annually, in return for nothing."[83] Likewise, most concerned Americans recognized that ending pelagic sealing guaranteed the return to long-term profitability of the sealing business on the Pribilofs. Giving away one-third of the proceeds was better business than paying for four revenue cutters that were incapable of actually guarding the islands.

According to the conservationists, the treaty also produced mixed results. On one hand, conservationists and scientists found themselves in the rare position of having influence over the course of American diplomacy. As a result, the convention snatched the northern fur seal from the jaws of extinction and allowed the herd to rebound to approximately two million individuals. On the other hand, those same people had squandered much of their energy fighting among themselves. Their differences not only caused wounds in the movement that never healed, but they also revealed a fundamental disagreement about attitudes toward nature in the larger conservation movement. The split between Jordan and Hornaday on the issue of managing seals was emblematic of feuds that hindered the movement's effectiveness for years.

The moral and scientific arguments against sealing took a while to sink in, but they were eventually widely accepted. At the conference in 1911, even the statesmen from Japan and Canada freely acknowledged the wastefulness of pelagic sealing and, at times, agreed that it was immoral. Few people had ever seen a seal in the wild, but thanks to Elliott, Hornaday, and Jordan the seals were more popular than most diplomats. Science and sentiment knew no boundaries and could bring people together under the right circumstances.

The diplomats had taken twenty-five years, but they had finally found an equitable solution to the sealing crisis. The depletion of the herd was so great that they could not have delayed any longer. In some ways, the animal's decline had been the catalyst for both the diplomatic crisis and its resolution. When the herds became so thin that pelagic sealing lost its appeal and public opinion recoiled at the accounts of starving pups, even the most committed pelagic sealer could see the end of the road. Once the weight of American scientific evidence proved the damage done by pelagic sealing, the only question became whether the various nations could come to some sort of cooperative agreement before the species disappeared. In 1911, they finally did.

PART III

THE MIGRATORY

BIRD TREATY

Like the fish and fur seal treaties, the Migratory Bird Treaty was a response to a distressing decline in valuable wildlife that migrated across international boundaries. Migratory birds faced increasing hunting pressure and damage to their ecosystems, and by the 1880s many knowledgeable observers believed that wild birds were declining to the point that irreversible damage would soon occur. That conviction grew stronger as the passenger pigeon disappeared from the wild and several other species neared extinction. The movement that sprang up in the 1880s to protect birds started with the belief that people had a moral obligation to save interesting species from possible extinction. Thus, unlike the previous two treaties, the Migratory Bird Treaty of 1916 (MBT) was a child of sentiment, in that it grew out of the desire to save birds. It was not a response to an international economic disagreement, as the other two treaties had been.

The unusual diplomatic milieu helped to produce a good treaty. The maturing of the Anglo-American rapprochement ensured that the two sides would approach each other in an atmosphere of trust, even after the untimely demise of the fisheries treaty. More important, the late arrival of diplomats to the issue of bird protection prevented many unnecessary entanglements. First, conservationists in the two countries were able to build a consensus on their own, without the air of international rivalry that even friendly diplomats can foster. Second, because diplomats had not created this crisis, they felt no particular pressure to resolve it; their general indifference allowed bird preservationists to shape the treaty with only minimal outside interference. At times the conservationists had to yield to the diplomats, but usually not on issues of substance.

Those who emerged as the leaders of the bird protection elements in

American society always had a love of birds close to their hearts, but at times they set that sentiment aside for the realism of science and economics. Some of the leaders thought of themselves as gentleman hunters, for whom game bird preservation also meant the preservation of their lifestyle. Thus they were sentimental about birds and about the simpler times, as they perceived them, when hunters followed a code of ethics. Largely on such sentiment and a small dose of scientific curiosity, early conservationists built the skeleton of a system of bird protection.

As with fish and seal conservation, though, eventually bird protection came down to science and economics. Appeals to aesthetics could not overcome all of the economically driven despoilers of the continent's bird populations, nor would those who clung fiercely to states' rights ideology yield because of the plight of migratory birds. Their opposition had to be broken, and in the Progressive era hard science and cold economics could apply the necessary pressure. In their efforts to win battles on the national stage, then, treaty advocates turned away from sentimental arguments, perhaps fearing that they would not be taken seriously. Knowing that the bird lovers would be with them in any case, they concentrated on the scientific and economic justifications for federal control that would sway the skeptical and the apathetic.

The road to the successful conclusion of the MBT traveled through three stages. In the first, the number of Americans who responded to the natural appeal of birds began to grow in the late nineteenth century. Spurred by hunters and nature writers, by the early twentieth century enthusiasts were organizing to agitate for bird protection laws. In the second stage, with their bird laws under attack as unconstitutional, they turned to diplomacy and concentrated on a rational approach that would win recognition of their principle, even if it meant accepting an imperfect arrangement. In the final stage, they returned to the domestic forum and a final showdown with their opponents. Casting aside sentiment, except in their appeal to patriotism in time of war, they won their fight largely on the basis of rational arguments, although congressmen no doubt knew that conservationists had the backing of thousands of people who thought of birds mainly in aesthetic terms. When the Supreme Court upheld the treaty on the basis of the national interest in protecting birds, while ignoring the government's legal case, it demonstrated that the conservationists had won because of their ability to convince people throughout society that bird protection was important enough that it had to be done well.

6

Of Mallards and Men,
1883–1913

Long before anyone thought of using treaty power to protect migrants, conservationists were at work combating those forces in society that threatened bird life. Writers and scientists, hunters and nature enthusiasts found in birds a noneconomic value that was unique among wildlife. They feared that Americans would drive many species of birds to extinction, and they slowly gathered the political strength to fight that trend. By 1913, they had achieved a great victory through the passage of the Migratory Bird Act, or Weeks-McLean Law, which set the stage for the conclusion of a treaty.

While the bird protection movement had its roots set firmly in sentiment, in the years leading up to 1913 conservationists discovered the necessity for scientific evidence and an economic rationale to justify government intervention. Gentlemen hunters who thought of themselves as pursuing a way of life and birdwatchers awed by avian accomplishments started the movement with the simple goal of providing legal and popular support for birds. But they gradually came to understand that they needed more than their own view of birds to make their cause truly popular and politically viable. They needed to sell bird protection to the vast majority of citizens who did not share their attitudes.

Thus the years up to 1913 became a time of experimentation, as bird protectionists tried out scientific and economic explanations of the need for bird protection and simultaneously sought the proper role of government in their endeavors. They discovered which lines of reasoning appealed to people, and they generated public support for private and government efforts to conserve wildlife. At the same time, they worked to break the political and economic power of those who hunted birds for the market. Slowly, they succeeded in reducing bird harvesting from a moderately legitimate enterprise to a scorned, largely illegal occupation. By both building support and crippling the opposition, those who fought for real protection of birds helped to make the Migratory Bird Treaty possible.

BIRD LOVERS AND GAME HOGS

The natural human affinity for birds played a crucial role in the success of the Migratory Bird Treaty. Birds have always delighted and fascinated humans. But just as they have been a source of inspiration, birds have also been targets for hunters in search of food, sport, and ornament. In the Progressive era, bird lovers fought to stop the unethical use — which they usually defined as commercial — of birds, although they were not completely opposed to hunting. Before they could unite on a plan of action to attain bird protection, conservationists had to hammer out their code of ethics about killing birds.

People like birds because, of all the common wild animals, they are somehow the most like humans. They are warm-blooded, bipedal, social, diurnal, visually oriented, vocal, and terrestrial. They form apparently monogamous bonds, build homes, raise young, and then head south to avoid the cold weather. Some birds stake out territories as well as any fence-loving suburbanite, but others will form huge garrulous flocks. Because they are visually and aurally oriented, like humans, they make their presence known to us. Finally, birds are the most common vertebrates that a person might normally encounter, barring a serious rodent problem.

At the same time, birds can seem to be almost extraterrestrial in their behavior and appearance. There is nothing so striking among fish or mammals as a singing male scarlet tanager in full breeding plumage. Other species, such as the woodcock and the prairie chicken, engage in startling mating displays. The ability to fly, especially on long migration flights, inspires awe among earthbound observers. The hawk effortlessly soaring on a thermal, the hummingbird maneuvering like a helicopter, or the swallow twisting and turning after a nearly invisible insect — these are the sights that can convert an otherwise normal person into a diehard birdwatcher. Birds are like humans in some ways, and yet they are still wild animals with remarkable skills.[1]

Migration may be the most wondrous of all the mysteries of bird life. For centuries, migration has perplexed humans, giving rise to all sorts of theories. One suggested that some species hibernated in muddy pond bottoms, while another had birds heading to the moon. In fact, the real answer to where birds migrated was only a little less amazing than the lunar landing hypothesis. In the nineteenth century, scientists began to understand that birds weighing as little as a few ounces flew thousands of miles in a few days to move between their breeding grounds and winter ranges. Even more astounding, they learned that individual birds returned to the same location year after year. In 1915, the *New York Times* carried a long article on the latest discoveries about bird migration that reported that the Biological Survey had accumulated "500,000 facts" that led to a greater understanding of the subject. Still, scientists could only speculate as to why birds migrated, and even today how birds navigate on these trips is poorly understood.[2]

The species undertaking migration follow many different strategies. Smaller species, such as hummingbirds, warblers, and most of the shorebirds, might travel thousands of miles between Latin America and the northern United States and Canada. Hardier songbirds and many of the larger game birds make shorter migrations between their winter territory in the southern United States and their northern breeding grounds. Some species make their moves in one huge push when the weather allows, while others travel slowly on the front edge of the new season. Some migrate at night, while others move during the day. Finally, a surprisingly large number of species follow one path in the spring and another in the fall. The only consistent rule for North American migrants is that they head north in the spring and south in the fall.

From a management standpoint, the effect of migration is to move many species of birds through a large number of states in a staggered fashion. A particular species may appear all along a flyway, or it may bypass some states altogether. Species that arrive simultaneously in one state may be days apart in the next. Migration patterns change from year to year, and weather conditions can affect the number of migrants and their length of stay at particular locations. Hunters can never be certain of their future opportunities, nor can regulators predict with certainty what each new migration season will bring. As a consequence, crafting fair and reasonable regulations for the hunting of migratory birds can be almost impossible.

The fly-by-night quality of migration encourages gunners to take what they can in the short time that migrants are in their neighborhood. Naturally, many hunters think of ducks as immediate targets, opportunities not to be wasted, even if that reduces the chances for other hunters. Especially when the birds come in great numbers, it is hard to see that a particular species has limits and cannot be hunted forever. As Garrett Hardin explained succinctly in his essay "Tragedy of the Commons," it takes only a few users of a common property resource with selfish motives to make a disaster. If the unscrupulous members of the hunting community take more than their fair share, there can be no equilibrium. Some of those hunters who do think in the longer term might conclude that restraint is futile and join in the destructive behavior. In such a situation, some authority must step in to regulate the behavior of all the users of a particular resource.[3]

Protective regulations for these winged wanderers were few and weak near the turn of the century. Not surprisingly, the individual states often took a competitive approach to game bird management. Instead of planning for the future, most states in the 1800s acted as if any bird that left the state was a wasted resource. State legislatures rarely had the courage or foresight to restrict their constituents when hunters in other states had free reign. For instance, if Missourians had the right to kill ducks on their northward migration, then hunters in every other state along the Mississippi would demand the same privilege. The only way to break the standoff among the states was to impose some sort of national system of regulations, but such rules were not even conceivable given the generally accepted standards of states' rights in the United States in the late nineteenth century. Bird protectors, then, had to find a way to work around the twin problems of reluctant legislators and constitutional restrictions.[4]

In the eyes of bird lovers, the main enemies were the "game hogs," who found more reward in killing than in stalking. A leading conservationist, John Burnham, believed that prosperity allowed more people to own hunting equipment, but it had not given them the necessary ethics. "We have been throwing pearls to swine!" he complained. For game hogs, hunting was not so much the challenge of outwitting the elements of nature as it was target practice. Such a hunter simply took great pleasure in each goose downed. The editor of two anthologies about duck hunting told his readers about one thirty-minute span on the Des Plaines River, during which he killed thirty-two blue winged teal. Although the tone of the story did not reveal it, he admitted to "feeling somewhat guilty and thinking that I had depopulated the duck family enough for one day."[5]

While hunting magazines took editorial stances against hoggish behavior, they still carried some articles glorifying unrestrained slaughter. For instance, one author recounted his four-day expedition in British Columbia, during which he and his friend shot about eighty ducks. He reported that his favorite tactic was to shoot at a distant flock in order to scare the ducks in the direction of his companion, who would then knock them out of the sky. With the glee of a small child recounting some grand adventure, he wrote, "Undoubtedly this was the best day's sport my companion and myself ever experienced and if we had a larger supply of ammunition we might have done better still."[6]

The worst subspecies of game hog was the market hunter, whose financial motivations put him completely beyond reform. As T. Gilbert Pearson of the National Association of Audubon Societies observed, "It is chiefly the birds that could be commercialized, either for their flesh, or their feathers, that have suffered great diminution in numbers."[7] Whereas the average game hog simply shot more than he could eat, the market hunter resorted to many unscrupulous practices to increase his inventory. One unsporting tactic that infuriated conservationists involved approaching a flock of sleeping ducks at night on the water. When the hunter got within a few feet, he would fire a huge gun filled with buckshot, nails, or any other handy projectiles, often killing dozens of ducks at a time. For such game birds, a large market existed in eastern cities. In fact, in many cities one could buy almost any winged creature for the pot. The passenger pigeon, once the most numerous bird in history, fell victim by the millions from the 1830s to the 1880s to market hunters, who filled railroad cars with dead pigeons. But food was not the sole goal of the market hunters — they also pursued beautiful birds in order to sell plumage to milliners.

Unlike fishermen, market hunters were not a powerful or easily defined group. Because most valuable birds were migratory, market hunting was usually a part-time occupation, and there were no hunting communities in the same way that there were fishing towns. If the conservationist accounts were accurate, most market hunters came from the lower rungs of the economic ladder. William T. Hornaday expressed the view of many leading conservationists that recent southern European immigrants and poor African Americans caused the most damage, although they all seemed to single out Italians as the worst offenders. In response, many conservationists supported laws that restricted gun ownership to citizens of the United States. No matter who the market hunters were ethnically, they were people who worked alone, part-time, for very little money. They were no match for the politically powerful and wealthy people who supported conservationism.[8]

As a weak group, market hunters presented an easy target for critics. Most bird lovers would have agreed with the *New York Times* assessment that "the market hunter is an utterly ruthless person, with no thought whatever for the morrow." Hornaday, always looking to coin a phrase, called them "the Army of Destruction" and urged conservationists to marshal a counterforce. Skillfully combining both class and ethnic bias, William B. Mershon, a sportsman from Michigan, complained that while he tried to build a productive business "the labor union dynamiters and the market hunters, shooting illegally and out of season, get off Scot free." [9]

Because the trade in birds was unregulated and haphazard, conservationists had to resort to anecdotal evidence to prove how destructive it was. An observant person who walked through the city markets could see that any bird with even a little meat was available for sale. *Rod and Gun in Canada* reported that Tennesseeans had killed 150,000 robins in the winter of 1909 and sold them for ten cents per dozen. Another author wrote of the use of gill nets by market hunters to catch diving ducks underwater. Hunting magazines also liked to show pictures of single hunters with dozens of dead ducks, thereby convicting the subject of the crime of game hoggery. Conservationists were usually masters of public relations, and they used their ties to papers and magazines with skill. [10]

No matter what the motives of the hunter, the expanding American economy multiplied the threat to wild birds. The increasing accessibility of the countryside severely reduced the undisturbed habitat where animals could hide, and better transportation allowed hunters to get to even the most remote area. Automatic and pump shotguns enabled hunters to fire more quickly and more often. On the increasing demand for such weapons, Hornaday wrote, "Undoubtedly, the owners of automatic and pump guns would use Gatling guns on American game if they could." [11] Improved cold storage techniques made possible the shipment of game from distant points into the major cities. The only thing missing was a better dog, perhaps because the retriever had already been perfected.

Unlike the ill-fated fish, birds had a number of human supporters who battled the game hogs and market hunters. As with the fishermen, those who hunted for sport usually found themselves in conflict with those who hunted to earn money. Sport hunters, though, had more influence than did anglers. Bird conservationists also included birdwatchers, farmers, and the average citizens who enjoyed having birds in their neighborhoods. The groups overlapped to such an extent that many individuals fit into all four categories, and they rarely worked at cross-purposes. Also in contrast to the fisheries case, politically powerful people, such as Henry Ford, fought for the bird protectors. Generally, the people who led the fight for federal intervention into migratory bird protection enjoyed recreational hunting, voted Republican, could identify nongame birds, and liked political scraps.[12]

While sport hunters have recently fallen out of favor with modern environmentalists, in the Progressive era they provided much of the leadership for the wildlife protection movement. Led first by G. O. Shields of the League of American Sportsmen and William T. Hornaday of the New York Zoological Society, gentlemen hunters tried to establish restraint as the key to appropriate hunting behavior. To that end, they launched a campaign against the game hog and the market hunter. Although they occasionally broke into bitter debates about the use of automatic shotguns and bird dogs, for instance, they all agreed on the basic need for discipline. One Canadian writer summed up the situation: "A hog is a hog, no matter how equipped, and a gentleman is no less a gentleman because he uses an effective weapon and loves one of God's noblest creatures." [13]

The sport hunters saw no contradiction between their efforts to shoot animals in moderate numbers and their work to conserve wildlife. They believed that they could take the surplus of game that nature produced annually without harming the environment. As conservationists, they tried not to waste what they shot, nor did they have commercial motives. They sought to prevent a decline of the bird population and thus of their opportunities for recreation. If anything, they argued, their contact with nature made them especially knowledgeable and sympathetic to the plight of wildlife in America. The avid hunter John Bird Burnham commented late in life that he had finally laid down his gun and taken to full-time observation because he was "uncertain about the game laws of the Kingdom Come." [14]

Discounting the game hogs among them, many sportsmen were in fact birdwatchers and nature lovers. Those species that were not game were still interesting to them from a natural history standpoint. Hunting magazines and anthologies often incorporated descriptions of natural beauty, and hunters liked to embellish their stories with accounts of the other wildlife they encountered. Recounting a two-day excursion in Manitoba during which he used both shotgun and camera, one sportsman wrote: "Silently we slipped along, thrilled as sportsmen could not fail to be, and almost questioning our right to be there, as awed by the vast wild spirit of the marsh, we felt ourselves small fragments in the vast schemes of Nature." [15]

The man who most embodied this combination of hunter and observer was President Theodore Roosevelt. The boy who filled his own "Roosevelt Museum of Natural History" with his desire to collect dead animals grew into a keen student of bird behavior who still knew how to shoot things. He advocated a serious approach to ornithology, lest the science slip into the control of dilettantes "with opera-glasses." Still, he understood how birds appealed to the human spirit:

> Birds should be saved because of utilitarian reasons; and, moreover, they should be saved because of reasons unconnected with any return in dollars and cents. . . . To lose the chance to see frigate-birds soaring in circles above the storm, or a file of pelicans winging their way homeward across the crimson afterglow of the sunset, or a myriad terns flashing in the light of midday as they hover in a shifting maze above the beach—why, the loss is like the loss of a gallery of the masterpieces of the artists of old time.

The only recourse, he believed, was to enact protective laws and establish refuges for interesting species. But TR was no sappy sentimentalist, for on the same trip where he caught sight of these wondrous birds he dug up a nest of turtle eggs to make "delicious pancakes."[16]

Despite their considerable labor on behalf of wildlife, sport hunters often had a hard time convincing others of their commitment to broad conservation. There were enough troublemakers among them to make some people skeptical about the bona fides of anyone with a shotgun. Many people wondered how someone could appreciate the beauty of a wild bird and subsequently shoot it. In 1901, the nature writer Ernest Thompson Seton summed up the suspicion: "This is the mind of the head-hunting sportsman. The nobler the thing that he destroys, . . . the greater his pleasure."[17] While Seton's charge had some truth to it, he failed to acknowledge that those sportsmen were also involved in very productive conservationist work.

At the same time, the rules of when and how to hunt opened the sport hunters to charges of elitism and inconsistency. Despite the bounty of the continent, Americans had not traditionally been picky when it came to eating wildlife. Now a wealthy group of hunters wanted to restrict hunting to certain species and times of year. To many people, the rules about what was game must have seemed arbitrary. Some songbirds were certainly edible, but gentlemen hunters deemed shooting them to be unsporting and incompatible with conservation. Likewise, rules about certain types of equipment or methods that sportsmen condemned were based on a code of conduct to which many hunters did not subscribe. Because of their hold on the conservationist movement, however, hunters were able to formulate bird protection laws to match their concepts of sport.

Roosevelt and the sportsmen's war against game hogs reflected a growing American affinity for birds. In 1886, the Yale graduate and editor of *Forest and Stream* George Bird Grinnell decided that the time was ripe to tap into this latent feeling. He called on readers to join a new organization, the Audubon Society. The terms were easy; he charged no dues, and members had only to agree to limit their hunting to game birds for their own food. In particular, Grinnell assailed those who shot birds for profit, whether game birds for the market or plumage birds for the millinery trade. There were no local chapters, and the society did not attempt any political action. All it really had was a thin bimonthly magazine.[18]

Although this first attempt at popular bird protection failed in just a few years because of organizational deficiencies, it revealed that thousands of Americans recognized the problem. Without expending much effort, Grinnell had found 39,000 people who favored bird protection. Granted, they had not been required to put money on the table, but they had taken the initiative to respond to Grinnell's invitation. They were the first to band together to protect all birds, and they were a harbinger of those to come.

Although Grinnell's effort to motivate the amateur birders was going awry, he did help start the scientific movement to protect birds. In 1883, twenty-one men came together in New York to form the American Ornithologists' Union (AOU) to promote the scientific study of birds. The founders included names familiar to the modern birdwatcher—William Brewster, C. E. Bendire, and J. A. Allen—as well as important government scientists such as H. W. Henshaw and C. Hart Merriam. Although not present at the creation, Grinnell quickly became involved in the AOU's Bird Protection Committee. In 1886 this committee drew up the AOU's model bird law, which it recommended to every state legislature. Under the influence of the sport hunters' code, the AOU advocated protection for most nongame birds and restricted hunting of most game species.[19]

In addition to promoting the model law, in 1883 the AOU began scientific work that led to the formation of the United States Biological Survey, the most important wildlife conservation agency in the federal government. The union was particularly interested in studying bird migration and distribution, and its calls for information yielded 1,400 volunteers who swamped the AOU with data. Unable to process so much information, the ornithologists resolved to seek federal assistance, preferably financial. Through a series of events, in 1886 C. Hart Merriam found himself chief of the new Division of Economic Ornithology and Mammalogy, which would later be renamed the Bureau of Biological Survey, and then the Fish and Wildlife Service. At congressional behest, the division focused on the economic importance of birds to agriculture, but the volunteers kept filing reports on migration and distribution.[20] The efforts on both fronts would later provide the bird protectionists the information they needed to justify federal bird laws.

Coinciding with the growing interest of the scientific community, a number of writers had been entertaining the public with their roughly factual nature stories. Although they were known to exaggerate their tales on occasion—such as the one in which a woodcock made a cast for its broken leg—most of these writers found sufficient adventure in animals' daily struggle for existence. By tapping into basic human compassion, writers were able to stir up sympathy for the plight of wild animals. Their books took the same message to millions of readers: wild animals were interesting, valuable, and in need of protection.[21]

John Burroughs reigned as the king of the nature writers, selling hundreds of thousands of books. His first, in 1871, included a chapter titled "The Invitation," in which Burroughs encouraged his readers to undertake the study of birds. He wrote more than a dozen books from his own experience, and while he often assigned thoughts and feelings to his protagonists, his stories were based on fact. In addition, his crisp writing style kept the reader's attention. Describing a bluebird defending its nesting site from an aggressive wren, he painted a vivid image: "The bluebird, with his bright coat, looked like an officer in uniform in pursuit of some wicked, rusty little street gamin."[22]

Even with the popularity of writers such as Burroughs, into the 1890s the bird protection movement was still a disorganized force with only a rough plan of action. But the seeds had been sown for future success. Amateur and professional ornithologists were piling up data to prove that birds had economic value; more people were expressing their opinion that birds had aesthetic value; and writers were spreading the idea that birds were fascinating creatures worthy of closer study. In 1896, when the first important breaks would occur, the movement was ready to begin challenging those forces responsible for the decline in bird populations. The Migratory Bird Treaty was still decades away, but scientists and conservationists had already

(Top) California Audubon meeting, 1904.
From *Bird-Lore,* vol. 6

(Bottom) Junior Audubon Society in New Jersey, 1912.
From *Bird-Lore,* vol. 14

(Top) Theodore Roosevelt camping with the naturalist John Burroughs.
Theodore Roosevelt Collection, Harvard University Library

(Bottom) Hunters in Kansas City, about 1912.
From Hornaday, *Our Vanishing Wild Life*

Birds thought to be extinct in 1912; clockwise from top left:
great auk, labrador duck, Pallas cormorant,
Carolina parakeet, passenger pigeon, Eskimo curlew.
From Hornaday, *Our Vanishing Wild Life*

T. Gilbert Pearson at an Audubon Sanctuary.
National Audubon Society Records, Manuscripts and Archives Division,
New York Public Library Astor, Lenox and Tilden Foundations

Two powerful images of doomed snowy egrets *(Egretta thula)*.
From Hornaday, *Our Vanishing Wild Life*

HIS PLATFORM—CONNECTICUT FIRST
GEORGE P. McLEAN
UNITED STATES SENATOR

(Top) Author Mabel Osgood Wright, 1915.
From *Bird-Lore,* vol. 15

(Bottom) Senator George McLean's 1912 campaign flyer.
Simsbury Historical Society Archives

John Bird Burnham, 1936.
American Heritage Center, University of Wyoming

(Top) The Dominion entomologist, Dr. C. Gordon Hewitt.
National Archives of Canada PA 143057

(Bottom) Senator James Reed of Missouri.
Senate Historical Office 5480-19

had more success protecting birds than they would have protecting boundary waters fish.

THE BREAKTHROUGH YEAR, 1896

All of the work leading to bird protection was inadequate until the movement created a structure for political action and set a specific goal. In 1896, bird protectionists produced the former and established the latter. The founding of the Massachusetts Audubon Society was the first step toward creating a national network of bird protection, and the Supreme Court case *Geer v. Connecticut* provided the movement with a common goal, the establishment of state bird laws.[23] These two developments did not immediately lead to thorough bird protection, but they did help to build momentum toward the eventual creation of the Migratory Bird Treaty.

Geer v. Connecticut was the inevitable product of the passage of the AOU law by a handful of state legislatures in the 1880s. In October 1889, Edgar Geer of New London, Connecticut, was caught shipping grouse and quail to other states. The birds had been killed legally, but, in an effort to reduce market hunting, the state had outlawed the export of certain game birds. A jury had found him guilty, as he did not contest the facts. Instead his lawyer argued that the law was not valid. Geer's misfortune at being caught and convicted was probably rare, and he had reason to believe that he would win his appeal.

After Connecticut's highest court upheld the law, Geer appealed to the United States Supreme Court late in 1895. Geer's lawyer argued first that the law was unconstitutional, because the state was attempting to regulate interstate commerce by restricting export of a legally obtained commodity. Only Congress, he claimed, could take such action. Geer also used as a defense the long history of common law regarding wild animals. In the United States, where there were no royal forest reserves, live wild animals were free for the taking to all citizens. Only when reduced to the actual possession of an individual did wildlife become property. In order to regulate hunting, some states had created laws restricting seasons and bag limits, but none had interfered with the right of an individual to use the fruit of the hunt. Therefore, Geer argued, the birds were his to dispose of as he wished.[24]

On 2 March 1896, the court disagreed with Geer's analysis on both points. Justice Edward White expressed the majority opinion that the law only "remotely and indirectly" affected interstate commerce and that such imposition was minor compared to the state's duty to preserve game animals as a food source. He cited both a long history of common law and recent rulings by state supreme courts as precedents for his ruling that "indeed, the source of the police power as to game birds flows from the duty of the state to preserve for its people a valuable food supply. . . . hence by implication it is the duty of the legislature to enact such laws." [25]

The *Geer* decision helped to give the bird protection movement the focus that it badly needed. The court had established an important precedent that, in fact, someone did have a responsibility to protect birds. The fledgling bird protectionists could now focus their energy on persuading state legislatures to pass the AOU model bird law. Conservationists hailed the decision and urged swift action to exploit the opportunity, but doing so required organization. The AOU Bird Protection Committee, which had accumulated a thick layer of dust over the last decade, began to stir again, but it was not a large, grass-roots organization. The opportunity was there, but exploiting it would not be easy.

Coincidentally, in the winter of 1896 a group of Bostonians gathered to form an organization to protect birds. Bringing together both respected society women and well-known scientists, this new Massachusetts Audubon Society had both social influence and scientific credibility. The society had two basic goals. First, the members wanted to "further the protection of native birds," especially through the reduction of the plumage trade. Second, they targeted children for a thorough educational campaign about the value of birds.[26] The spark in Massachusetts created flames throughout the northeastern quarter of the United States. Later in the year, New York had an Audubon Society, with Pennsylvania and Ohio close behind. By 1898, societies had formed in the District of Columbia and fourteen states. In a few years branches had formed in most states.[27]

The source of the spark was the growing outrage over the slaughter of birds for the millinery industry. In the 1880s, a fashion trend emerged in which women wore various bird parts on their hats. The most controversial ornament was the aigrette, or plume, from breeding egrets and herons. In the survival-of-the-fittest world of fashion, though, milliners kept trying to outdo each other. In addition to the plumes, they moved to wings, heads, and even whole bodies of songbirds, hummingbirds, woodpeckers, terns, and anything else that caught fashion's fancy. Because birds were trendy items, many people became specialists in hunting them for the milliners.

Naturally, the demand for some species outstripped their ability to reproduce, and soon prices for various bird parts exploded. For instance, around
1910, an aigrette was worth more than its weight in gold. In turn, the higher
prices encouraged gunners to pursue rare species with increased intensity.
It was a cycle headed straight for extinction.

For conservationists, the use of birds in the millinery trade was the most
egregious example of the American war on birds. While there were many
causes for the general decline of birds in North America, no other was so
wasteful. Even market hunters and those reviled gunners who killed songbirds were at least feeding people. Likewise, those who destroyed bird habitat usually did so under the cover of economic growth, which few conservationists opposed. But millinery was fickle fashion, apt to change overnight,
and basically self-indulgent. Dr. Frank Chapman, an ornithologist with the
American Museum of Natural History, vilified the use of birds on hats: "The
woman who places its always disgustingly mutilated body on her bonnet,
does so in deliberate defiance of the laws of humanity and good taste."[28]

Audubon societies gained strength as people learned about the methods
of gathering the plumes from snowy egrets and common egrets. One industry representative actually testified to Congress that egret plumes came from
farms in Venezuela where happy workers collected the shed feathers. But
Audubon agents had films to prove the gruesome truth. Egrets nested in
large rookeries throughout the Caribbean basin, and their breeding plumes
were at their most beautiful just as the young hatched. The demand for
plumes was so great that hunters found almost every rookery and knew
when the plumes were most valuable. The results were sickening. Hunters
would shoot every adult in the rookery in order to rip the plumes off the
birds' heads. Pearson shocked readers with his account of one shot-out
rookery in which a fatally wounded adult egret was eaten alive by insects
while its starving young squawked piteously in the nest above.[29]

In order to combat the feather trade and other depredations against
birds, Audubon members lobbied for state legislation to restrict hunting
and the sale of wild animals. They focused on the AOU model law in an
effort to bring some uniformity to bird laws throughout the United States,
but they soon found that the rewards for such work were minimal. Passage
of the bill was never easy, and most states were unwilling to spend much on
enforcement. In other words, it was impossible to get every state to protect
birds, much less to ensure uniformity of bird protection laws.

Even when the states passed the AOU law or a tough equivalent, they faced a constant struggle to enforce it. For instance, in New York, which had one of the best conservation programs in the Union, the chief game protector John Burnham and his wardens faced frequent threats. In September 1908, the warden E. T. Couterman got a report of Italians hunting robins and meadowlarks near Brewerton. After an all-day search, he and his two assistants caught up with the offenders, who then turned and fired on his party. They wounded a bystander and escaped into the woods, only to be tracked down several miles away. Another warden reported that he had had to wrestle a man to the ground after arresting him twice in one day for hunting robins and woodpeckers. If the *Geer* decision required this much effort even in progressive New York, then it was not much of a victory after all.[30]

Bird protectionists did have some success when they could target specific locations in their battle against the commercialization of wild birds. For instance, it was easier to outlaw the sale of game in New York than to restrict hunting in every state that fed New York City's market for game. Part of the convenience came from the physical proximity of most leading conservationists to New York, which allowed them unusual influence in Albany. When conservationists succeeded in shutting down New York's game markets in 1913, one result was a rebound in duck populations in Currituck Sound, North Carolina, a major waterfowl wintering ground that had been a favorite site for market hunters.

The recognition that state governments could not and would not protect most migratory birds forced bird protectionists to look to the federal government for assistance. But because the *Geer* decision declared the regulation of wild animals to be a state prerogative, they knew that the federal government would not willingly take a leading role in wildlife protection. The Bureau of Biological Survey was conducting serious research, but the bureau's scientists were not in the business of providing policy recommendations. While there were sympathizers in other places in the federal government, there was no mandate for federal action. If the bird protectionists were to get anywhere, they would have to force the federal government to take the lead.

The first step toward federal intervention came in 1900 with passage of the Lacey Act. Sponsored by Representative John Lacey of Iowa, the law was actually a composite of three bills that had stalled in 1899. The core idea was that the federal government use its power to regulate interstate commerce to reduce trade in birds. The law required that all packages containing birds or bird parts be clearly labeled as to contents and point of origin. In addition, the act stipulated that both in the state of origin and the state of arrival the contents had to be legally obtainable under state law.[31]

In today's atmosphere of pervasive federal environmental laws, the Lacey Act seems frightfully weak, but it was a major first step. The law was, certainly, a roundabout way to get at a problem, and it did not guarantee any success. But by passing it, Congress had agreed that the depredation of America's wildlife was not sustainable or acceptable.[32] Beyond this moral victory, the law brought the authority of the federal government, albeit in an oblique manner, into the campaign against the market hunters. Finally, for the first time, bird protectionists throughout the country knew that they had a common legal basis for action. With this tool in hand, conservationists began to clear the markets of dealers in birds.

In the aftermath of the Lacey Act, the bird protection movement began to accumulate victories. Theodore Roosevelt ascended to the presidency in 1901, bringing a dedicated conservationist to the White House for the first time. In 1903, by setting aside Pelican Island in Florida, he opened a campaign to establish bird refuges around the country. Simultaneously, the Audubon leaders increased their efforts at creating refuges and providing wardens to protect rookeries, especially for egrets. Under pressure from the growing Audubon societies — which had incorporated as the National Association of Audubon Societies (NAAS) in 1905 — more states adopted strict bird protection laws. Based in New York, the new Audubon command post kept a close eye on the milliners and game dealers and members even took turns enforcing the law.[33]

While bird lovers continued to pursue political victories, they did not lose sight of the need for a broad-based educational program to turn American opinion in favor of bird protection. The first step was the Audubon association's efforts to reach schoolchildren. The association produced educational leaflets complete with paintings of a particular bird and a description of its behavior and value. Through the Junior Audubon program, the society reached hundreds of thousands of children in all corners of the United States and into Canada. The leaflets encouraged children to build birdhouses and take other steps to protect birds. Perhaps most important, Audubon was instilling in future leaders and voters a positive attitude towards birds.[34]

The energy behind this movement came largely from a quiet southerner, Thomas Gilbert Pearson, who was moving up the pecking order in the Audubon association. A former professor at a teacher's college in North Carolina, Pearson brought vital experience and communication skills to the association's educational efforts. His love of birds and fear for their future linked with his mastery of organization to provide strong leadership for the bird protection movement. He loved raising funds, and he was financially and politically conservative. Although he tried his hand at hunting, he focused on the need to protect nongame birds, especially the egrets and songbirds. But the hunters rarely begrudged Pearson's leadership; in later years John Burnham would call Pearson "the big brother of the birds." [35]

Beyond the official Audubon publications, there was a growing literature devoted to promoting the protection of birds in North America. Children's books took one of two paths. The first, followed by writers such as the formidable columnist for *Bird-Lore,* Mabel Osgood Wright, consisted of propaganda pieces thinly disguised as stories. In *Citizen Bird: Scenes from Bird-Life in Plain English for Beginners,* two children visit their uncle, Dr. Roy Hunter, on his farm. While there, they learn the conservationist ethic, as Hunter teaches them the economic and aesthetic value of the various birds in the region. The second approach, pursued by scientists like Dr. Frank Chapman — whom one publisher called "the birds' historian" — targeted natural childhood curiosity. In his book *The Travels of Birds,* Chapman tried to explain bird migration in an accurate, yet simplified, manner. He closed each chapter with study questions that challenged his readers to spend more time observing the world. [36]

Not all of the writers wrote for a younger audience. Wright wrote a more straightforward book for adults who were interested in learning about birds; Chapman was just one of several who wrote to encourage people to hunt birds with the camera instead of the gun. Other authors advised people how to attract birds to their yards and how to protect them from stray cats and mischievous boys. Field guides, including one to help observers identify and understand birdsongs, made their first appearance and sold thousands of copies. Birds were increasingly the subject of literary works and poetry. In all of these books, the message was clear, if not always explicit — birds were beautiful and useful creatures that deserved protection. [37]

Despite the forward momentum of the bird protection movement, by 1910 American birds were still not safe from human predation. The massive educational effort undertaken by the NAAS and the Biological Survey had reached only a fraction of the public. Consequently, some states still had little in the way of bird protection laws, and others could not enforce their laws. The murder of an Audubon warden in Florida by plume hunters — and their subsequent acquittal — proved to the stunned leaders in New York that their influence was not as great as they had hoped.[38] Unless they found a new way to spread and enforce the law, their cause would be lost.

THE WEEKS-MCLEAN ACT

In response to the difficulty of generating a collection of uniform, effective state laws to protect birds, conservationists decided that they had to push the federal government into the business of protecting birds. For its part, the government fought this move every step of the way. The educational campaign had reached many powerful and influential people in Washington. But their acknowledgment that birds were valuable did not necessarily change their opinion that wildlife was a state concern. Therefore, the next move for the conservationists had to be one of political lobbying in the nation's capital.

The first serious proposal that the federal government take charge of migratory game protection was dead on arrival in Congress. Authored by Congressman George Shiras III of Pennsylvania in 1904, the bill would have required the federal government to protect migratory game birds. Shiras, a well-known photographer who chose to serve only one term in Congress, observed that the federal government took the lead in combating the spread of bacterial diseases on interstate rail transportation. Extending that logic, he concluded that a bird that migrated beyond the boundaries of a particular state could not be the ward of any state. Only the federal government, under the interstate commerce clause of the Constitution, could have authority over such birds. This important insight was, according to Grinnell, "the greatest single accomplishment ever made in wild life protection." Shiras undermined his own cause though with both his refusal to stand for a second term and his statement that the bill was meant mainly to stimulate discussion. Many people, including President Roosevelt, liked the bill, but few advocated concerted action.[39]

The Shiras bill floated around Washington for several years, gaining little support until bird lovers broadened its appeal. Its focus on game birds limited its appeal to sport hunters and the leaders of the conservationist movement. Pearson provided the first strategic breakthrough in the summer of 1912 when he suggested that the bill would be more complete if it included protection for all migratory birds. Because much of the Audubon educational effort had gone into teaching people the value of songbirds and other nongame birds, he correctly reasoned that many Americans would be willing to support a more broadly based bill. In particular, he predicted that congressmen from farm states would support the bill if they learned that bird protection was good for agriculture.[40]

As so often happened, William Hornaday commandeered the idea and took credit for engineering its success. In September 1912, Hornaday called about a dozen leading conservationists to a club in New York for dinner in order to discuss the stranded migratory game bird bill. With little dissent, they agreed to add migratory nongame birds to the list of protected species in order to revive the bill. With the Fourth National Conservation Congress coming up in Indianapolis in October, Hornaday and Pearson prepared rousing speeches on the need to protect nongame birds. Hornaday printed 10,000 pamphlets entitled "Slaughter of Useful Birds: A Grave National Emergency," which he distributed at the gathering. The tract was so effective that the leaders of the congress sent 1,850 to newspapers around the country as representing their position.[41]

According to Hornaday, their success at the Conservation Congress helped to generate pressure on the U.S. Congress for federal bird protection legislation. When Henry Ford heard of the measure, he dispatched the advertising agent Glenn Buck, reportedly with the command to "go to New York and Washington and don't return until that bill has been passed." Buck and Hornaday supplied 1,000 newspapers with articles and letters supporting federal action, and in turn those published items generated thousands of letters to Congress. Whatever else he was, Hornaday was the conservationists' master of public relations.[42]

In the U.S. Congress, this new approach came together under the leadership of Senator George McLean of Connecticut and Congressman John Weeks of Massachusetts. A future Secretary of War, Weeks had kept the Shiras bill alive by occasionally reintroducing it in the House, but he had not had any more success than Shiras. McLean, who became known as "the bird man of the Senate," had worked with Weeks on the game bird bill, but now he took the lead in extending the bill to nongame species. He befriended Pearson, Hornaday, and other conservationists, and he relied on their advice. In 1912, he teamed with Weeks to write a broad bird conservation bill, based on Pearson's idea, known both as the Federal Migratory Bird bill and the Weeks-McLean bill.

In its new format, the bill was all of one page long, but it contained some revolutionary ideas. Basically, its proponents believed that birds were common property in need of cooperative protection. In line with the various state laws, the bill made it illegal to shoot most nongame birds. Another important feature was the clause outlawing hunting of game birds during the spring migration. While the bill specified only a few of the precise steps that the government should take to protect birds, it did establish that most Progressive institution — the committee of experts. This new federal migratory bird committee would consist of well-known scientists and conservationists whose job it would be to create specific regulations within the general framework of the bill. McLean, then, had proposed to transfer control over migratory birds from the lethargic state authorities to a gung-ho group of activists with federal backing.

McLean's bill got a boost from a new hunters' organization, the American Game Protective and Propagation Association (AGPPA). The AGPPA was the brainchild of the shotgun and ammunition makers, who deduced that they would all be out of business unless someone halted the decline of game birds. Initially, they approached Pearson, believing that their money would go farther if it did not have to pay for the infrastructure of a new organization. After a bitter internal fight about accepting what some saw as blood money, the NAAS turned down the annual gift of $25,000 in 1911. The manufacturers then accepted Grinnell's recommendation and hired John Burnham to run their organization. Burnham made his goals clear: "My work is . . . to preserve the game of the country so as to insure the continuance of field sport." [43]

The strengths of the AGPPA complemented those of the Audubon association. Because the gunmakers bankrolled the organization, Burnham and his assistants did not have to worry about developing and maintaining a large membership; therefore, they spent most of their time and energy lobbying legislative bodies and traveling to trouble spots. The connection with hunting also helped to provide a bridge to people, such as Dr. E. W. Nelson, Chief of the Biological Survey from 1916 to 1927, who believed that the Auduboners could be "unreasonably stringent." From New York, Theodore Roosevelt commented, "The manufacturers are showing sound public spirit as well as farsighted recognition of their own interests. . . . They should be backed up by every sportsman worthy of the name, and by every lover of nature." [44]

Burnham's blunt personality contrasted well with Pearson's reticence. Whereas Pearson fit in with the NAAS's committee-style leadership, Burnham wrote, "The more I see of the other fellows' ideas the better I like my own." He was an adventurer who tried his luck in the Klondike gold rush, during which he actually made money by transporting men and equipment through dangerous whitewater canyons. In 1912, he ran for Congress on the Bull Moose ticket and did tolerably well. When the United States entered the World War, he offered to serve in TR's proposed volunteer division, citing his leadership abilities as his qualifications. According to one admirer, "The world is full of men who can *talk* about doing things but there are d— few men who *can put things across.* You are one of the few."[45]

In conjunction with Pearson and Burnham, William Hornaday brought his unstoppable zeal into the fight for the bill. Like nuclear power, Hornaday had unlimited energy that could be harnessed, but he was volatile and left behind a toxic legacy. With "a magician's power when it comes to raising money," the prolific writer enjoyed legislative combat for wildlife, and he rarely tolerated his opponents or experienced defeat. In December 1912, he published *Our Vanishing Wild Life* with funds from his own Permanent Wild Life Protection Fund and sent a copy to every member of Congress. In his quirky, combative style, he hammered home his points: Americans were killing wildlife faster than ever before, and, unless conservationists got the necessary laws soon, major extinctions were imminent. In the military terms that Hornaday loved, Senator McLean praised the timing and force of the zoologist's writing: "Your book . . . came in just the nick of time and put a thirteen-inch hole clear through the hull of the enemy."[46]

In the Senate, McLean built upon the intense lobbying of the conservationists. He contended that "the strong temptation pressing upon every State to secure its full share of edible game birds during the spring and fall migrations has rendered harmonious and effective State supervision impossible." Citing the seal and fish agreements, McLean concluded that the federal government had a "dormant and unused power" to regulate birds. To support his cause, he provided a list of examples of overhunting under the lax state laws, such as a case from 1864 in which one New York city dealer sold over twenty tons of prairie chickens.[47]

To justify federal intervention to skeptics, McLean invoked the utilitarian mantra of insect damage to American agriculture. The state ornithologist of Massachusetts, E. H. Forbush, had estimated that insects caused $800,000,000 worth of damage annually throughout the nation, a number that quickly gained widespread acceptance among conservationists. In the best tradition of Congressional demagoguery, McLean called this figure the "insect tax," and he asked his colleagues to consider how far that money could go toward educating children. He then invoked horror stories of insects reproducing unchecked, spreading billions and billions of plant-munching invertebrates through the forests and fields of America. In McLean's world, "The birds have been, are, and will be without question one of the most important agencies in staying the inroads of insect devastation."[48] While this argument made bird protection more appealing, it was based more on optimism than on fact. Although the Biological Survey could prove that a wide variety of species ate crop-destroying insects at some time, it had no certain method for determining how many insect pests died because of birds, other insects, disease, or weather.

The bill was charming in its brevity, but it did have many shortcomings. The most glaring omission was any sort of enforcement mechanism or appropriation. There was no system for obtaining arrest or search warrants, nor did the bill allow for the appointment of special wardens to enforce the law. The bill did not extend protection to birds of prey, even though hawks and owls were as valuable to farmers as any insectivores. Likewise, protected species were listed in general terms, instead of by scientific name, which caused confusion. In a surprising oversight, the authors did not provide an exemption for scientists who needed to collect study specimens. In general, though, the bill accomplished a great deal in a small space.

The need for stricter protection of birds was widely accepted, but not everyone agreed that McLean's bill was constitutional. Senators Elihu Root and Henry Cabot Lodge did not hide their feeling that the Weeks-McLean bill would not stand up to a review by the Supreme Court. As a favor to conservationists, Root did not oppose the bill on the floor, but he did encourage them to seek an alternate route.[49] Likewise, C. D. Clark of Michigan, chairman of the Senate Judiciary Committee, originally opposed Weeks-McLean as unconstitutional. Later, though, he wrote to a constituent: "Since listening to Senator McLean's speech of yesterday on the evident necessity of preservation of the migratory birds, I shall vote for the bill . . . and let the question of the power of Congress to act take care of itself."[50] Between McLean's orations and the testimony of scientists and conservationists, bird protection had gained respect in Congress, just as it had among the general public.

Despite the progress in Congress, McLean's allies knew that President William Howard Taft would not sign the bill. As a conservative legal scholar, Taft opposed the extension of federal power that the bill mandated. In response, Burnham advocated the risky tactic of adding the bird bill as a rider to the Agriculture Department appropriations bill heading through Congress in January 1913. The president had publicly promised to use his veto power to halt such tactics, but conservationists saw no alternative. Seeking allies, Burnham went to see the chairman of the Senate Committee on Agriculture and Forestry, Senator Henry Burnham of Vermont, and discovered that they were very distant cousins, tracing their lineage back to a shipwreck off New England in 1638. Perhaps inspired by the fates, Senator Burnham chose to endorse the conservationists' strategy; the Senate then passed the amended bill.[51]

Although he refrained from public comment, Elihu Root must have been unhappy with this sly maneuver. In effect, it was an admission that conservationists could not win a fair fight in Washington. Root wanted protection for migratory birds, but not through parliamentary trickery. His solution was to offer a resolution in the Senate that urged the president to negotiate treaties with other North American countries with the purpose of protecting birds. Root made his proposal in January 1913, but with Taft on his way out of office there was no real point to pursuing it. Although Root's resolution did not lead to immediate action, it did introduce the idea of a migratory bird treaty to both conservationists and diplomats.[52]

With little fanfare, the House also passed the appropriations bill and sent it, with its rider, to the White House. It arrived in the waning hours of 4 March 1913, the last day of Taft's presidency. While conservationists fretted that the veto was coming, Taft was frantically packing his bags. Believing that Congress had heeded his threat, the president did not read the bill before he signed it. Ironically, then, one of the last acts of Taft's lame-duck presidency was to put the federal government on the front line in the fight to protect migratory birds. In later years, Taft insisted that the federal migratory bird bill had not passed during his administration: "If it had come before me," he said, "I am inclined to think that I would have given it my veto."[53]

When the federal migratory bird bill became law, bird protectionists celebrated. Hornaday called the law "the most important single measure ever enacted into law in this country for the protection of birds." Pearson and McLean also placed the law among the greatest conservation coups of history. In Washington, Dr. T. S. Palmer, chief of the Biological Survey, began to organize the new migratory bird commission, and he filled it with familiar faces: Burnham (as chairman), Hornaday, Pearson, Lacey, Forbush, and Shiras, among others.[54]

In Ottawa, Canadian conservationists saw the passage of Weeks-McLean as an opportunity to work with Americans to create a mutual scheme to protect birds. The first Canadian to advocate such action was Maxwell

Graham, a biologist in the Animal Division of the Dominion Parks Branch. On 18 March 1913, he informed his superior, J. B. Harkin, that "the knowledge we already possess is sufficient to justify this Branch in bringing before the Dominion Government the expediency of its administering the protection of migratory birds, and thus cooperating with the United States Government." [55] He encouraged Harkin to canvass other experts in government service to determine the best possible course of action, and he undertook his own campaign to contact those same people. At the time, bird protection was the responsibility of the provinces. The laws were generally good, but enforcement was rare. [56]

Like many Americans, Graham argued that the government had to step in because of the economic interests at stake. He claimed that there were 154 species of insectivorous game birds being hunted legally in Canada, although he did not cite a source for this suspect figure. He also estimated that insects caused over $80,000,000 in damage to agriculture annually in Canada. He based this assumption on a belief that Canada's agricultural base was roughly one-tenth that of the United States, and then he worked backward from Forbush's figure of $800,000,000 damage to American agriculture. In a letter to the minister of interior, Graham argued, "It is a matter of dollars — a matter of vital commercial importance," and he traced the damage to the "disturbance of nature's balance." Birds were nature's insecticide, and people were only harming their own interests when they killed them. [57]

Graham's arguments, right down to the inflation of birds' power as insectivores, were right in line with those of most leading conservationists in the United States. On both sides of the border, government officials and many conservationist leaders saw cost/benefit ratios as the key to successful advocacy of bird protection. Those who loved birds for their aesthetic qualities were already squarely behind efforts to ensure preservation of species. Victory depended on bringing the average citizen into the fold, and the surest way to do that was to emphasize — or even exaggerate — the economic benefits of bird protection. One Canadian scientist recognized that "in order to secure the active support of the people of Canada in the conservation of our wildlife, it is necessary . . . to indicate . . . the economic significance of such measures." [58] To that end, even herbivorous game birds garnered the label insectivore. The arguments that opponents could use against any type of bird protection were that it was costly to administer and it would harm those people who depended on market hunting. Conservationists, then, felt pressure to demonstrate how protection benefited legitimate sectors of the economy, such as farming. For many purists, this approach was unfortunate. Birds, they believed, deserved protection not because of their ephemeral value to humans but because of their place in nature.

One scientist who challenged Graham's reasoning, although not his conclusions, was P. A. Taverner, a young ornithologist working for the Dominion Geological Survey. He agreed that "game protection in America should be done through some international agreement." In his opinion, the greatest impediment to cooperation had been the knowledge of Canadian sportsmen that their American counterparts hunted under much less stringent laws, much as Canadian fishermen resented their American competitors. With the new federal law in place, Taverner hoped that the imbalance would come to an end. But he was skeptical that there were 154 insectivorous game birds, and he criticized the idea that protection for such species should depend upon their eating habits. "There are many enough good reasons for their protection," he told Graham, "so it is not necessary to weaken the argument with strained logic." He urged cooperation with the Biological Survey, which had been doing fieldwork in Canada for fifteen years, and he encouraged Graham to contact "our leading bird men" for their opinions.[59]

The three "leading bird men" expressed different opinions about the need for cooperation with the United States. Allan Brooks, of Okanagan Landing, British Columbia, declared Canadian laws to be entirely adequate if enforced. In his opinion, the great menace to Pacific Coast bird life was the dumping of crude oil on the water: "This is wreaking havoc in a way that an army of Italians with shotguns & liberty to use them could not approach." In contrast, J. H. Fleming of Toronto thought that Weeks-McLean's passage made "concurrent legislation . . . necessary if either country is to benefit." Perhaps with an eye towards the brewing trouble in Europe, he also suggested that preserving the shooting sports was good for the "military strength of a people." Like Fleming, W. E. Saunders of London, Ontario, expressed "a very decided opinion in favor of co-operation with the United States Government in the protection of migratory birds." In particular, he wanted protection for the very large birds, "which nearly every so-called sportsman seems to think he ought to shoot at if he gets a chance."[60]

Most Canadian naturalists and hunters agreed that the decline of birds was due to lax American laws. With game birds, the main problem was spring shooting, which many American states allowed. Scientists had concluded that ducks formed mating pairs early in their migration. Many migrating females were already pregnant as they headed north to the nesting grounds. Thus, a hunter who killed a bird on its northward migration disrupted the breeding cycle at a crucial time. Females were killed before getting a chance to raise their broods, and those that lost a mate would not pair up with another male. Regarding insectivorous birds, many Canadians believed that they were frequent targets for southerners. While many Canadians recognized that their own laws were poorly enforced, they reasoned that the greater population in the United States led to greater depredations. Until Americans demonstrated a willingness to protect migrants, any Canadian protective efforts would be futile. The best approach would be to tie the two countries together by treaty.

CONCLUSION

The Weeks-McLean law represented thirty years of effort on the part of conservationists to protect the birds that were so dear to them. With a little luck and a lot of skill, they had made the nation's birds the nation's responsibility. The long road to that end had begun with small groups of self-styled ethical hunters protecting their code of behavior, bird lovers devastated by indiscriminate slaughter, and scientists worried about the loss of their objects of study. For their own reasons they worked together to bring about effective protection of birds. But they soon learned that they could not count on sentiment and scientific curiosity alone to justify their cause. In order, then, to win their fight, they had to broaden their support by putting bird protection in economic terms. Thus, scientists became especially important for their ability to translate data and hypotheses into tales of woe and wails of anguish — life without birds.

Despite its symbolic meaning and success in curbing excesses, the Weeks-McLean law was weak. In later years, one conservationist estimated that the law reduced illegal shooting by 75 percent, in part because hunters throughout the country knew that it provided uniform regulations and in part because most citizens obey the law, even if they disagree with it.[61] But supporters and detractors agreed that the long-term viability of the law depended upon consistent enforcement, which in turn depended upon firmly establishing its constitutionality. With the law's legal status in doubt, conservationists felt compelled to try their hands at diplomacy, as Root had suggested, in an effort to protect their hard won gains. Victory in their endeavor would come only if their arguments could penetrate the world of diplomacy.

7

Coordinating Science, Diplomacy, and Public Relations, 1913–1916

The constitutional problems with the Weeks-McLean Act forced conservationists to look for a means to guarantee permanent federal control of migratory birds. With few alternatives before them, they embraced Senator Root's treaty proposal. As the bird protectors entered this uncharted territory, they found that the strength of their arguments had no effect on diplomatic machinations, although at times the weight of their political power could make a difference. Their beloved dream was at the mercy of diplomats who, in a time of stress, viewed it as secondary, if not frivolous. The bird supporters did what they could to facilitate the progress of the negotiations, mainly with constant prodding and an obvious willingness to offer unsought advice.

Though the actual diplomatic processes were often beyond their control, conservationists continued to work toward the general goal of protecting birds. First and foremost, they still had influence at either end of Pennsylvania Avenue, which was useful both in launching and finishing the treaty drive. By lobbying government officials in Canada and the United States, they ensured that their aims would get a fair hearing. Of nearly equal importance, government scientists in both countries lent their expertise to shape the actual terms of the treaty when it was not in the diplomats' hands. Finally, conservationists continued their general campaign against unethical hunters, which no doubt helped fill the air in Washington with the bird protection doctrine. Along the way, though, they found that the sentiment that had started the movement and the science that had given it a boost had become secondary to simple power politics and the art of the deal.

FOCUSING ON CANADA

Conservationists' acceptance of the need to turn to diplomacy forced them and their diplomat partners to decide with which country to negotiate. The obvious choices were Canada and Mexico, although Root's resolution had not been specific on the subject. Each country presented opportunities and hazards, and treaty advocates finally settled on Canada as the best partner. That choice reflected the realities of the Anglo-American rapprochement, the necessity for a quick resolution of the issue, and recognition of a people and government with similar interests. All of those elements eased the passage of this unprecedented diplomatic effort.

In early 1913, American conservationists found common cause with their counterparts in the British empire, as both groups attacked the millinery trades. Henry Oldys, an Audubon activist from Washington, D.C., recognized in January 1913 that the upcoming tariff discussions in Congress presented an opportunity to save birds around the world. While the Audubon societies had succeeded in limiting the use of domestic birds on ladies' hats, they had been powerless to restrict the importation of bird parts. In their ceaseless search for exotic items, milliners had discovered such striking creatures as the various birds of paradise from the German colony on New Guinea. Throughout the tropics, hunters pursued unusual and brightly colored birds with the intention of shipping them to markets in the western world. Oldys correctly calculated that he could strike a blow for birds around the world through one well-considered clause in the American tariff code. As he reported to George Grinnell, he did not have to worry about states' rights, cost of enforcement, or constitutionality.[1]

Oldys's action sparked a frenzied, although poorly publicized, fight between milliners and conservationists. After the House accepted a total ban on plumage imports, the stunned milliners launched a damage-control campaign. Industry representatives expressed a willingness to use only those birds that were pests or edible; that is, only birds that would be shot anyway. On the surface, their offer seemed like an acceptable compromise. It was, after all, conservation to use the feathers of such birds rather than see them go to waste.[2]

Conservationists disagreed. T. Gilbert Pearson rallied the Audubon membership with impassioned editorials in *Bird-Lore* and testimony before Congress. William Hornaday, especially, railed against any compromise, as he had through most of his life. In the end, he sank the milliners' ship by suggesting that "edible" and "pest" were labels that applied to at least 2,300 species of birds worldwide. The number was probably a very rough estimate based on a few minutes of pondering the problem, but the message was clear. For all any American knew, the people of New Guinea loved bird-of-paradise stew, and farmers in Venezuela considered egrets to be pests.[3]

Hornaday aggressively backed up Oldys's campaign. After testifying to Congress with his usual vigor late in January, he wrote a lengthy article for the *New York Times* decrying the whole millinery trade. But for all of his efforts, the Senate initially accepted the milliners' offer. Sensing an impending defeat, Hornaday encouraged thousands of women to write to Congress, and he published a broadside titled "The Steam Roller of the Feather Trade in the U.S. Senate." Finally, in October, the Senate's Democratic caucus swung around to his position and accepted a total ban on millinery imports in the new Underwood tariff. In later years, Oldys gave credit to Pearson and to Hornaday, who "struck sledge-hammer blows (which did not always fall on the enemy.)"[4]

Simultaneous with Oldys's campaign, Lord Harcourt, the British secretary of state for the colonies, joined the fight to outlaw millinery imports throughout the British empire. Harcourt was responding to an earlier Franco-German initiative to control the plumage trade that the British government considered to be farcical. Rather than partake in a useless international agreement, Britain chose to enforce strict laws throughout the realm. Through their efforts, Harcourt and Oldys crippled avian-based millinery in London and New York especially and helped to pressure Canada into passing similar legislation. The twin victories put Canada, Great Britain, and the United States in the same position on an issue of importance to conservationists; revealed that citizens of the empire and the United States had a mutual interest in bird protection; and, most important, demonstrated that conservationists, with a little resourcefulness, could use the traditional tools of international relations.[5]

On 7 April 1913, with the tariff bill fight heating up, Senator George McLean renewed his efforts to secure effective protection of migratory birds. Following up on Root's resolution, which had stalled quietly in the previous session, McLean introduced his own, which the Senate passed: "Resolved, that the President be requested to propose to the governments of other countries the negotiation of a convention for the mutual protection and preservation of birds." Within two days, McLean, Burnham, Dr. T. S. Palmer of the Biological Survey, Colonel John Wallace of the Alabama Department of Fish and Game, and Alabama's two senators had a meeting with President Woodrow Wilson and Secretary of State William Jennings Bryan to impress upon them the need to promote international protection of birds.[6]

Wilson asked Wallace for a detailed report on the methods of international cooperation to protect birds, and the colonel responded enthusiastically. He began with the argument that migration threatened to make even the Weeks-McLean law ineffective, because birds spent so much time in Latin American countries with weak conservation laws and attitudes. He suggested that the government establish a three-member committee of game law experts to negotiate treaties to protect migratory wildlife throughout the western hemisphere. Wallace hoped that all of the nations of the hemisphere would participate, but he emphasized that the United States had to take the lead in spreading protective legislation. He closed by arguing, "Every possible safeguard should be thrown around our great resource consisting of migratory birds to the end that they may be saved from certain depletion and possible obliteration."[7]

Wallace's report and the group's visit impressed Wilson, who revealed himself to be far more sympathetic to federal bird protection than President William Howard Taft had been. On 19 April 1913, Wilson broached the subject of a treaty to Bryan, noting, "Personally, I should very much like to do this. I wonder if you feel that this is the time when it would be feasible to take the matter up." Bryan agreed that it was, as the State Department had already forwarded Wallace's ideas to the Agriculture Department for comment.[8]

In early May, the Agriculture Department responded with a list of issues that might fall under Senator McLean's resolution. At the top was, of all things, the regulation of traffic in quail with Mexico. "Agreements with Mexico, Canada, and certain South American countries looking to the mutual protection of migratory birds" ranked second. Also included were cooperation with Germany, France, and Britain to end the millinery trade and talks with Japan to protect Pacific island birds. Finally, Agriculture wanted an agreement with Canada about stopping the liberation of imported birds that might spread into the United States.[9] For the purposes of carrying out the protection of migratory birds, only the second suggestion had any relevance, and it left open the decision whether to look north or south.

The State Department, then, faced a difficult decision between opening negotiations with Mexico or with Great Britain. There were advantages to beginning with Mexico, which was in greater need of bird protection laws than Canada. A treaty would have helped to rectify that problem, at least on paper. As early as 1910, the chief of the Biological Survey had communicated with a Mexican government scientist about the possibility of cooperative conservation efforts, and the assistant chief, E. W. Nelson, had spent years conducting research in Mexico. In addition, Burnham had associates among the small group of gentlemen hunters in Mexico who had joined the AGPPA. Also, Wallace's original memorandum had clearly implied that Mexico should be the first target for such an initiative.[10]

But Mexico was politically unstable and not yet supportive of a conservation movement. After the government of Victoriano Huerta came to power in 1910 in the midst of a revolution, it became locked in a struggle with an uncompromising Wilson.[11] Even if there had been political stability in Mexico City and friendly Mexican-American relations, the Mexican government would not have invested much political capital in trying to prevent the hunting of migratory birds. The country's other problems were so great, and the conservationists so few, that the government probably could not have given a high priority to any serious conservation scheme. In fact, when Mexico finally agreed to a migratory bird treaty in 1936, American conservationists admitted that they did not anticipate a major improvement in Mexican bird protection activities.[12]

Despite these problems, the State Department initially opted for Mexico. On 22 May 1913, the solicitor asked Secretary of Agriculture David Houston for a draft of a convention with Mexico for the protection of migratory birds. As he explained to a colleague, the solicitor believed that the Mexican treaty "will likely be the most important convention" in terms of conservation. He also noted that such a treaty would set a precedent for agreements with other countries in the hemisphere. Acting Secretary of Agriculture Beverly Galloway promised to move quickly.[13]

Sometime in June 1913, conservationists and officials in the administration apparently forgot that they had been considering a treaty with Mexico. On 9 July, John Burnham wrote to both Wilson and Bryan urging them to meet with British diplomats to discuss terms for a treaty to strengthen American and Canadian bird laws. He assured them that "there is a strong sentiment throughout Canada in favor of reciprocal action by that country and the United States for better protection of birds." Meanwhile, Agriculture Department officials had drafted a treaty proposal for Canada with the help of an AGPA attorney.[14] Once the fate of the plumage clause in the tariff bill became known, they would be able to conclude their draft and send it to Secretary Bryan.[15] The idea of a treaty with Mexico had disappeared and would not resurface until 1918.

The summer shift probably resulted from a reality check in the State Department. The growing feud between Wilson and Huerta made routine negotiations between Mexico and the United States almost impossible. A treaty proposal from the United States could have been misconstrued as a conferral of recognition. In contrast, the Anglo-American rapprochement, highlighted by the conservation-oriented North Pacific Fur Seal Convention, demonstrated that the United States, Canada, and Great Britain had an ease of communication that few countries could match. While that did not imply that the diplomacy would be simply automatic, it did mean that an overture about such a treaty would not become entangled in other problems.

Conservationists accepted this change of direction because they recognized that they needed a treaty with somebody soon in order to head off a negative Supreme Court ruling. Their goal was no longer to spread the gospel of conservation into the wilds of Latin America but to consolidate their gains domestically. The great cultural similarities allowed for a sense of kinship between Canadian and American leaders. Canadians joined organizations such as the Audubon Association and the American Game Protective Association, and as a people they were as sympathetic to conservation as were Americans. Scientific understanding of the ecology and behavior of birds was much better in Canada than in Mexico, largely because of collaboration between Canadian and American scientists, which had laid the groundwork for cooperation on conservation.[16]

However, in abandoning Latin America, conservationists were surrendering their dream of extending protection for "American" migrants on their wintering grounds. Unlike Mexico, Canada had bird protection laws that were already better than most of those in the United States. Even British Columbia, which would fight the Migratory Bird Treaty, had reasonably good laws on the books. A treaty would grant the Dominion more authority, but the provinces did not have quite the reputation for laxness that so many states had. Allowing centralization was good for the long term, but there was no immediate need to reform Canada's approach to bird protection. In other words, the treaty could only marginally improve conservation in Canada.[17]

The decision in June 1913 to focus on Canada meant that the main accomplishment of the Migratory Bird Treaty would be to ward off those who challenged the constitutionality of federal intervention in migratory bird protection. When Root first offered his resolution to the Senate in January 1913, it held promise as a means to solve the constitutionality problem and shield migratory birds throughout the hemisphere. By the time the Senate actually adopted McLean's resolution in July 1913, most treaty proponents recognized the futility of trying to negotiate an agreement with any government that did not already espouse conservation. Conservationists dreamed of spreading their laws wherever American birds migrated, but imposing their ideals on other cultures would be very difficult.

NEGOTIATIONS AT HOME AND ABROAD

Negotiations between Canada and the United States would prove to be less contentious than the struggles within each country about the content and fate of the treaty. In the United States, conservationists had to overcome questions about the constitutionality of their plans and the indifference of the State Department. In Canada, they worried about provincial governments that opposed the treaty out of sheer stubbornness and on constitutional grounds. Given the unusual nature of the proposal, both sides moved fairly quickly to conclude a treaty before the Supreme Court could undermine the cause.

With the final approval of the Underwood tariff in October 1913, conservationists were prone to think that they had their opponents on the run. In less than a year, they had gained federal protection of most migratory birds, a ban on the importation of birds for the millinery trade, a ban on the sale of game in New York, and a Senate resolution calling for treaties with other countries to protect birds. In addition, leaders such as Pearson and Burnham knew that treaty negotiations were progressing. But George Bird Grinnell understood that some of the hardest battles were still ahead, and he admonished followers not to be overconfident. "This, of course, is a dangerous mental attitude," he warned. "Some day before we know it the pendulum will begin to swing back again, and we may lose much of what has been gained." [18]

Soon enough, the pendulum did begin to swing back, as the Weeks-McLean Act turned out to be less of a victory than conservationists had anticipated. Congress would appropriate only a miserly $10,000 — the same amount that Audubon spent on egret protection — for the USDA to enforce the law.[19] The Biological Survey wanted $200,000 to hire additional wardens and prosecute violators, but conservationists could not pry that out of Congress. With so little money, the survey was forced to rely upon local enforcement efforts and an uneven collection of wardens. For instance, in Missouri—the center of opposition to the federal bird law—the federal game officer used his position to develop a business partnership with some of the most notorious poachers in the St. Louis area. When the government finally removed him, the editor of the *St. Louis Globe-Democrat* sarcastically announced that the warden was the first person convicted under the law in the state. In Florida, at least two Audubon wardens were caught selling egret plumes from the rookeries they were supposed to protect.[20]

Beyond the financial difficulties, proponents of the bird law continued to worry about the uncertain constitutionality of the law. In November 1913, the attorney general of New York, Frank Carmody, declared the law to be unconstitutional. Hornaday expressed the feelings of many when he wrote, "Carmody has been acting very badly, and I have been trying to trim him to make him fit the spirit of the times in New York State."[21] USDA lawyers, however, believed that Carmody's views were widely shared in the legal community, and they persuaded the Biological Survey to enforce the law selectively. In January 1914, the chief of the Biological Survey, T. S. Palmer, admitted, "If any test is to be made on the law we should much prefer to have a straight spring shooting case in a district where all the conditions are favorable."[22]

Opponents of the federal law and the proposed treaty began to organize in the heart of the country. In February 1914, hunters in Missouri formed the Interstate Sportsmen's Protective Association (ISPA), which had as its goal the repeal of the Weeks-McLean Law. One hunter summed up the feeling of many along the Mississippi River that the law was "unjust and unnecessary and UNCONSTITUTIONAL." Senator James A. Reed of Missouri gave them legislative leadership, as he never missed an opportunity to criticize federal bird protection action. There were opponents in every state, but Missourians and their neighbors formed the core of the opposition right up to the court case that decided the fate of the Migratory Bird Treaty, *Missouri v. Holland.*[23]

The source of the Missourians' discontent was the ban on spring shooting. Many hunters argued that their only opportunity for ducks came in the spring, because the birds did not stop in the Midwest on their way south in the fall. Generally, these hunters had purchased memberships in duck clubs that held exclusive hunting rights to certain ponds and small lakes. These ponds, however, were filled by spring rains; they were usually dry by the time the fall duck migration occurred. Contrary to the claims of Missouri's hunters, then, duck hunting was possible in the fall but only on natural waterways that were open to all. The Weeks-McLean Law had made such club memberships worthless, and members were prepared to fight.[24]

They were so adamant that, for a time, they had convinced Burnham and some of the Biological Survey scientists that they were simply aggrieved gentlemen hunters looking for equal treatment. In the hope of building bridges to those hunters, Burnham's advisory committee urged the survey to send an expert to the region to show them what to plant in order to improve their fall hunting. Missourians were not alone, as the new federal regulations carved the country up into many zones, each with its own specific open seasons, and each with its own aggrieved hunters sure that they were the victims of favoritism. The government biologist George Lawyer reported that the hunters of Conneaut Lake, Pennsylvania, were furious that they did not have the same open season as did the hunters of New York and Ohio: "For over two hours they gave me my gruel but I stood it manfully." Having had his fill of gruel, Lawyer suggested that the advisory committee should look into addressing these complaints.[25]

With so many angry hunters, several court challenges to the Weeks-McLean Act arose in 1914 and 1915. State courts in Maine and Kansas joined with two federal courts in declaring the bird law unconstitutional. In the most important of these, *United States v. Shauver,* a volunteer federal game warden, Colonel Joseph Acklen, had arrested Harvey Shauver of Jonesport, Arkansas, for shooting coots out of season. Shauver was prepared to plead guilty, but Acklen decided that a conviction was less important than a test case for the Supreme Court. The warden persuaded the hunter to plead *not* guilty by offering to pay his legal expenses and by impressing upon him the nature of this patriotic duty. When a federal court declared the law unconstitutional in May 1914, Acklen had his test case and government attorneys had a challenge.[26]

Supporters of the law knew that they had at least a year to devise a strategy before the *Shauver* case reached the Supreme Court. The famed constitutional scholar E. S. Corwin of Princeton drew out an elaborate and convoluted argument that the federal government had an obligation to protect birds, which were the guardians of the national forests, which were in turn guardians of watersheds, which supplied navigable rivers and therefore were crucial for interstate commerce. If this was the best that the treaty supporters could muster, then they had cause to anticipate defeat. With good reason then, Senator McLean planned to introduce a constitutional amendment to Congress if the court found for Shauver.[27]

Even before the *Shauver* case started through the courts, the bird protectionists realized that they needed a treaty quickly. The worst thing imaginable, both for bird protection and conservation in general, would have been an adverse ruling from the Supreme Court. Because Root had assured conservationists that the federal government had the constitutional authority to negotiate a treaty to protect migratory birds, they decided that their only hope was to push for a quick settlement with Canada. Success would come only if they got their treaty before the Supreme Court decided the *Shauver* case; the race was on.

On 3 January 1914, Agriculture Department officials finally got around to delivering a draft treaty to the State Department. They gave no reason for the delay, but there may have been internal disagreements that had to be reconciled. The first draft within the department had come from William Haskell, the attorney for the AGPA, who based the provisions on those in the Weeks-McLean law. His proposal was far too complex. Instead of providing a broad framework for action, it established specific rules and zones for all of North America. Some American officials recognized that the proposal would have to be simplified or else Canadians would see in it an attempt by Americans to control Canadian conservation efforts.[28]

The document that came to the State Department reflected both the political wariness and accepted scientific knowledge of the government's biologists. This initial draft sustained the Weeks-McLean law's distinction among game, insectivorous, and nongame birds, and it prohibited the hunting of the latter two groups. With game birds, however, the department sought a middle ground between those friends of birds who wanted to end the open season in January and those hunters who demanded the right to hunt into March. The draft allowed each country to establish an open season of three and a half months within the broader time frame of 1 September to 1 February. Not all of the compromises between political expedience and scientific knowledge were detrimental to conservation. Within the grouping "migratory insectivorous birds," the scientists included hummingbirds, waxwings, and grosbeaks — some of the most beautiful birds on the continent, but hardly scourges of the insect world.[29]

Meanwhile, the State Department appeared to lose interest in the treaty. In mid-January, a department attorney told Colonel Wallace that he was still waiting to hear from the Agriculture Department, even though the

State Department had had the draft for two weeks. The department's solicitor, Joseph W. Folk, who was responsible for determining the legality of the department's actions, dismissed the proposal as "going rather far in treaty making." But, he concluded, Congress had passed the resolution, and State had to pursue it. With that tepid endorsement, the diplomats kept the substance intact but polished the language into the words of diplomacy. On 16 February 1914, the State Department turned over the draft to Ambassador Sir Cecil Spring Rice with the typically roundabout hope that "it may be that His Majesty's Government would not be indisposed to extend this protection to the Dominion of Canada by a convention with the United States."[30]

Spring Rice was cautious. He thanked Secretary Bryan and expressed his hope that they could reach an accommodation. He asked the department to pass along copies of all regulations for the protection of migratory birds then in force, so that the Dominion government could study them. But he also pointed out to Bryan that the memory of the failed inland fisheries treaty was fresh. Therefore, he asked for assurances that the proposed agreement was constitutional and had the support of the states. Spring Rice then sent the document to Foreign Secretary Sir Edward Grey, noting that the federal migratory bird regulations to which the Americans referred were "the subject of considerable controversy in this country, since their constitutionality is doubtful."[31]

The United States government succeeded in convincing Spring Rice that it was sincere about the Migratory Bird Treaty. Based on a memorandum from the Department of Agriculture, the ambassador reported on 30 April 1914 that the machinery was present on both the state and national level to carry out the treaty and that the state authorities were cooperating with federal officials in enforcing the law. "Consequently," he wrote, "the proposed treaty would seem to stand on a very different basis from the Fisheries Treaty of 1908." While he admitted that conservationists feared a challenge in the courts, he mistakenly concluded that "inasmuch as there is no very strong commercial interests in opposition to it, it may be very long before such a case arises." American authorities were anxious for a quick decision, he wrote, only because they desired to expedite their preservation work.[32]

Before the draft treaty made it through the diplomatic channels to Ottawa and London, the Canadian government learned the terms of the proposal from a young government scientist, Dr. C. Gordon Hewitt. Employed in the Dominion Department of Agriculture as an entomologist in the days when that profession seemed bent on eradicating insects, Hewitt believed that birds were an underutilized resource that could aid Canadian farmers. He also believed that effective bird protection in Canada and the United States depended upon rapid completion of the treaty, and he worked tirelessly to promote cooperation. In the winter of 1914, Hewitt had been in Washington to discuss bird conservation efforts with USDA scientists, and they had kept him fully informed of the status of the proposed treaty.[33]

Despite Hewitt's effort and commitment to the cause, he was not uniformly liked. Hornaday spoke highly of him and lamented his premature death in 1920. The Royal Society for the Protection of Birds awarded him its gold medal for 1916 for his work on the treaty, and government officials in the United States and Canada praised his efforts. But Maxwell Graham, the Parks Branch employee who had first raised the issue of cooperation in 1913, complained in 1916 that Hewitt seemed to be monopolizing the issue without even consulting others. Reminiscing in the 1930s, the gruff Burnham groused, "In the presence of his official superiors Hewitt was always too oily to suit me. He was the type of man who would do anything for someone from whom he expected to receive a favor." Like him or not, people had to deal with Hewitt because he became the uncontested point man for the treaty in Canada.[34]

The winter of 1913–14 had brought an interest in strengthening bird protection statutes in Canada. The *Ottawa Journal* urged its readers, "Let's try to have more birds," and the *Montreal Star* carried an article on the need for a migratory bird treaty. Maxwell Graham reported that the Weeks-McLean law had "aroused general interest in the protection of birds" in the United States, and he called on the government to do the same thing in Canada. The Canadian Commission on Conservation adopted a resolution calling for a treaty to reinforce the efforts being made in both countries. Presumably in response to this show of support, Hewitt went to Washington and "conferred informally" with Biological Survey personnel on bird protection.[35]

Still, Canadian conservationists feared that the treaty might provoke a constitutional crisis in their own country. The Conservation Commission emphasized that the provincial governments had to take the lead by petitioning Ottawa to conclude a treaty. Provincial leaders might drag their feet on a sound agreement if they believed that the Dominion was "too domineering." In an ironic misunderstanding of the situation, Harkin complained to his superior that Americans recognized that migratory birds belonged to the nation, while Canadians squabbled over which branch of the public service had jurisdiction.[36]

When the official proposal from Washington reached Sir Joseph Pope, Canada's undersecretary of state for external affairs, in mid-March, he immediately took steps "to obtain the views of the various Provincial Governments upon this subject." [37] He apparently did so on his own volition, although he may have been aware of the attitude of Canadian conservationists regarding the proper channels for such action. While Pope's action delayed any possible reply to the United States for several months, it saved the Dominion government some grief in later years. By consulting with provincial authorities, Pope gave them participation in the treaty-making process that later diffused most of the opposition.

Most of the provincial governments quickly expressed their general support. Several lieutenant governors reported that their provinces' laws were already in line with the regulations proposed, but they also noted some small divergences. For instance, Lieutenant Governor G. W. Brown of Saskatchewan reported that his constituents would oppose protection of sandhill and little brown cranes (probably a subspecies of the sandhill crane), which had undeserved reputations as crop destroyers. He concluded, though, that "our citizens would doubtless willingly forego this privilege for the benefit of the continent as a whole, when the matter is explained to them." Other reservations came from the Atlantic provinces, where hunters wanted an earlier open season on shorebirds, and of course contentious Quebec, where the government suggested that the Dominion did not have the authority to establish such regulations in the province.[38]

The lone holdout was beautiful, bitter British Columbia, which may still have been annoyed by the outcome of the sealing convention and the fisheries treaty. The provincial secretary admitted that "the principle of the proposed treaty is an excellent one," but he objected to the proposed closed seasons on geese, swans, wood ducks, curlews, and cranes—all of which were endangered on the Pacific coast.[39] Lieutenant Governor Thomas Patterson reported to Pope that the provincial government

> feels that it cannot become a party to the Treaty as it stands at present. It is felt that the conditions in British Columbia are so different from those existing in the United States that it would not be advisable to consent to any arrangements which would interfere with the Government's own local authority.[40]

Canadian conservationists now faced a serious challenge: they could compromise, quit, or ignore the dissenting provinces.

Harkin and Pope both recommended that the Dominion government negotiate with the provincial leaders. Pope assured the minister of interior that Section 132 of the British North America Act gave Ottawa the authority to enact laws based on a treaty. Still, most of the provincial governments had some objection to the terms of the proposed treaty, and Pope urged the Interior Department to decide if they were "of sufficient importance to be made a *sine qua non* to the conclusion of a treaty which is so generally considered advantageous." Following up on Pope's suggestion, Harkin urged his superior to call a convention in Ottawa of game wardens, provincial officials, hunters, and conservationists to hammer out a response to the American proposal. At that point, though, the outbreak of the European war diverted all the energy of the Canadian government, and the treaty was dead in the water.[41]

Nevertheless, by August 1914, Canada had made much more progress toward completing the treaty than had the United States. Both the Canadian and American central governments had taken all of the appropriate steps to give the proposal legitimacy, but only Dominion officials had done anything to consolidate support beyond the capital. By consulting the provincial leaders, treaty supporters had identified the sources of opposition and could prepare a strategy. In contrast, American officials seemed willing to wait for the Canadian response while hoping that nothing too bad happened in the interim. Certainly, Burnham, Hornaday, Pearson, and their colleagues kept up a campaign to promote the treaty, but even they seemed less intense than usual.

There were, of course, differences in the two countries that made the contrasting approaches inevitable. First, as the recipient of the treaty draft, the Canadian government had an obligation to prepare a response that it could support. As the instigators, American leaders really could not do much without a Canadian response. Second, with only ten provinces to canvass, Pope and Hewitt could build a consensus in a way that Americans could not imagine. Third, and related to the second, American states were traditionally more independent than Canadian provinces. These last two factors made it possible for Canadian leaders to reach a consensus — which American leaders had been unable to do — before returning to the official diplomatic channels.

DELAYED RATIFICATION

Between the outbreak of war in August 1914 and the final ratification of the treaty in December 1916, supporters and detractors fought several battles in both countries in an attempt to shape the final outcome of the agreement. The delay caused by the war actually may have helped, in that it gave plenty of time to resolve these disagreements. Even within the conservationist movement, there were conflicts about how to handle the opposition, with some urging compromise and others fighting for principle. While treaty proponents were unable to completely resolve their internal problems, they were able to defeat their various opponents.

On 7 April 1915, the Dominion parks official J. B. Harkin resurrected official efforts to move the Migratory Bird Treaty forward. Earlier in the year, Hewitt had visited Washington to discuss the treaty with American scientists, and it is plausible that he encouraged Harkin to take action. Harkin lamented the sudden derailing of the treaty process, which "had been making very satisfactory progress up to the time of the declaration of war." Indirectly, he suggested that the treaty was a war measure because insectivorous birds protected crops, an argument that would later form the spine of conservationist reasoning. He did not pursue this idea, however.[42]

On 31 May, the Dominion Privy Council discussed the status of the American treaty proposal. Joseph Pope urged the council to accept the document with minor amendments that satisfied most of the provincial complaints, although not all of those from British Columbia. Pope's motion had the support of the Conservation Commission, the Interior Department, and the Agriculture Department. On 7 June, the governor general reported the council's support to Ambassador Spring Rice.[43] Prospects looked good for a settlement before 1916.

The arrival of the treaty in Washington should have been quite welcome to the American bird protection movement, which was beginning to unravel under the assault of the Missouri spring shooters. In March 1915, a federal judge in Kansas City, Kansas, ruled that the Weeks-McLean law was unconstitutional, giving further momentum to the *Shauver* case boulder heading for the Supreme Court. Meanwhile, Edward T. Grether, the editor of the *St. Louis Globe-Democrat,* continued his campaign to reveal mismanagement and corruption in federal intervention into bird protection. He admitted that he "used to be a crank" about the law, but he had decided to oppose it "when everything went wrong and there seemed no prospect of getting relief." [44]

The opposition from Missouri threatened to split the bird protection forces. Only the slightly crazed Hornaday and the quiet Pearson seemed unfazed by the turmoil. Some scientists in the Biological Survey were willing to compromise with the midwesterners. Dr. Edward W. Nelson, then the assistant chief, worried that "the untamed protectionists" would start "an impractical campaign." In particular, he singled out Hornaday for being ill-informed and in favor of "indigested plans." His good friends Charles Sheldon and John Burnham agreed that men such as Hornaday did not understand that the hunters of Missouri were good conservationists who just wanted a fair share of hunting.[45] Ironically, Hornaday was working on a stirring article defending the Biological Survey from hunters who, among other things, claimed it was full of protectionists who were trying to outlaw hunting. To that charge, Hornaday replied, "What arrant *nonsense!* It cannot be true that any man who can be trusted with a loaded gun is so foolish as to give serious ear to such a suggestion." [46]

Unbeknownst to all interested parties, the diplomatic machinery had failed at the time that conservationists needed it most. In the State Department, Third Assistant Secretary William Phillips, guardian angel of the treaty and brother to the Audubon activist John Phillips, waited patiently for word from Canada. American bird protectionists assumed that the strain of the war had delayed Canada's response. In Ottawa, treaty supporters waited for a reply from the United States, assuming that the U.S. government was contemplating the Canadian revisions. Meanwhile, no one realized that a clerk in the British embassy had misfiled the response from the governor general, leaving it in the diplomatic equivalent of the Bermuda triangle.

In October 1915, as the treaty gathered dust in a file cabinet, conservationists focused their worry on the outcome of the *Shauver* case, then being argued before the Supreme Court. Nelson stressed that "this is an extremely critical point in our conservation work. An adverse decision would do an enormous injury to bird life in this country." Others believed that the Justice Department was at best apathetic toward, and probably opposed to, the law. In reality, the government's lawyer, E. Marvin Underwood, was in communication with Pearson both in regard to the Weeks-McLean law and ornithology in general. Pearson gave Underwood a bird book for his young son and tips on bird feeding, and in turn Underwood expressed his great respect for the accomplishments and input of the Audubon association.[47] But Underwood's personal feelings could not alter the weakness of his case.

After the court heard the case, another lull came while all parties waited for a decision, expected in February 1916. Conservationists busied themselves preparing for either result. Senator McLean drafted a constitutional amendment to place wildlife under federal control if Shauver won. Burnham continued to seek a compromise with the Mississippi River hunters. Pearson went to Ottawa to plan strategy with Hewitt and his superiors. For his part, Hewitt urged the Agriculture and Interior Departments to join with the Conservation Commission in an effort to build public support for the treaty.[48]

But the most productive effort came from William Hornaday, who rescued the treaty from the tyranny of misfiling. With a decision from the court imminent, Hornaday became suspicious about Canada's long silence. Following a tip from Hewitt, on 12 February 1916 the insufferable, unstoppable Hornaday marched into the British Embassy and demanded satisfaction. He pointed out that the State Department was still waiting for some response from Canada, and he reported that the Supreme Court was about to hand down a defeat for the Weeks-McLean law. Thus goaded, embassy staff found the Canadian response.[49]

That very same day, Ambassador Spring Rice put the treaty back on the fast track to ratification. He sent letters explaining the error to Secretary of State Robert Lansing, the governor general, and British Foreign Secretary Sir Edward Grey. He apologized for the "unfortunate oversight due to the stress of work connected with the war" and offered to assist in any way possible to expedite the conclusion of the treaty. To Lansing, he reported that the Dominion government believed that bird protection "is important, especially in the case of insectivorous birds, on economic grounds, and harmonizes with a widely growing sentiment of the desirability of conserving the creations of nature."[50] He also suggested further negotiations to resolve the complaints put forward by the provinces, especially British Columbia.

On top of the good news from the embassy, February brought an unexpected decision from the Supreme Court. On 28 February 1916, the court called for a reargument of the *Shauver* case in October 1916. The court had only eight members and the justices apparently deadlocked. Possibly, the justices decided to give the diplomats and conservationists more time to iron out the treaty details. Conservationists were surprisingly subdued about this result, which was better than most of them had expected.[51]

March 1916 saw a flurry of activity brought on by the desire to finish the treaty as quickly as possible before anything else could go wrong. At the request of the Privy Council, Hewitt traveled to Washington to meet with Nelson to discuss treaty revisions on 9 March. Within days, a delegation from the Agriculture Department delivered a revised version of the treaty to the State Department with a demand to expedite its conclusion. Hewitt assured any who would listen that he represented the views of Canada's government in assenting to this revised convention.[52]

The meeting between Hewitt and Nelson to hammer out the flaws of the first draft was unorthodox but rational. Both sides recognized the need for some changes that were, in large measure, based more on domestic policy than diplomatic necessity. Therefore, it made sense to dispose of the diplomats and allow the experts to negotiate a settlement. While both men had some objection to the other's proposed changes, they each recognized that compromise was the best course at the time. Dr. Hewitt and Dr. Nelson, two pragmatic scientists serving their countries, had an instant basis for understanding and cooperation. Had they been free to work together beginning in 1913, they probably could have produced a treaty in less than a year.

The revised draft of the Migratory Bird Treaty contained five changes meant to quell dissent. To satisfy Canadian opponents, Hewitt and Nelson moved up the open season on shorebirds from 1 September to 15 August all along the Atlantic coast north of Chesapeake Bay. They also exempted British Columbia from the mandatory closed seasons on cranes, swans, and curlews. Based on the USDA's experience with the Weeks-McLean law, Nelson added two more changes: first, he included provisions for Native Americans in the northern reaches of the continent who relied on wild birds and their eggs for food; second, he allowed for a system of permits to kill protected birds if they became a serious threat to economic interests, especially agriculture. Finally, they pushed the limit on the open season on all game birds from 1 February to 10 March.[53]

The final change was the most difficult to agree to. Nelson pointed out that the actual open season would still be only three and a half months, so no one would have the opportunity to hunt in both the spring and fall. Burnham and the survey scientists openly admitted that the later date was meant to appease the Missourians, because Senator William J. Stone of Missouri was the chairman of the Foreign Relations Committee. They feared that he would either pigeonhole the treaty or muster the thirty-three votes necessary to stop ratification. Burnham bluntly told his colleagues that he "would rather have a too liberal law actually in force and efficiently enforced than the most ideal law which was neither."[54] Hewitt, then, agreed to the change only after USDA officials pledged to do everything in their power to persuade legislatures in Missouri, Kansas, Nebraska, Iowa, and Illinois to end spring shooting.

When Hewitt returned with the new terms, he found that he once again had to deal with stubborn provincial officials. In the effort to line up provincial support, Canadians and Americans worked together in an unusual alliance. In response to Hewitt's troubles in Quebec, Burnham used his ties to Canadian rail and steamship company executives to twist arms in the Quebec provincial government. British Columbia showed no signs of yielding, however, even after a second visit from Hewitt. British Columbians especially wanted more than three and a half months of hunting, even though by most accounts they already had the best hunting opportunities on the continent.

In early June 1916, Burnham went to Ottawa to meet with Hewitt. Friends had informed him that Hewitt was returning from the West Coast empty-handed. After missing him at the train station, Burnham found the entomologist in his office in a state of despair. When Hewitt suggested that he would tell his superior that he had failed to bring British Columbia onboard, Burnham exploded: "This is a crisis. Wake up! . . . The stake is the migratory birds of the continent. One province should not be permitted to interfere with their salvation."[55]

After this barrage, Hewitt chose to introduce Burnham to his superior, Minister of Agriculture Sir Martin Burrell. It turned out that Burrell was from British Columbia, and he had "qualms when he [thought] of running counter to public opinion in his own province." Burnham, however, convinced him that many important individuals and corporations supported the treaty and that no one province had a right to block such an important agreement. The minister relented and agreed to recommend that the Privy Council support the treaty with only minor revisions acceptable to both Canadian and American conservationists.[56] The consulting process that Pope had begun in March 1914 was paying off.

While the Canadians were reaching a consensus on their exact response, American bird protectionists were struggling with the extension of the open season into March. Nelson and the advisory board headed by Burnham had the responsibility for formulating the Weeks-McLean regulations for the 1916 hunting season. As with the treaty revisions, they felt trapped between the Interstate Sportsmen's Protective Association (ISPA) — and its fifty congressional supporters — on one side and Hornaday and the Audubon people on the other. Nelson feared that the ISPA would be able to cut off the appropriation for the Biological Survey in Congress, and he did not really acknowledge that spring shooting was an especially disruptive practice. To that end, with Burnham's support, he proposed giving midwestern states the option of including an open season between 10 February and 10 March 1917 in their three-and-a-half-month hunting season.[57]

To his surprise, Nelson found that his compromise made no one happy. The ISPA demanded a spring season from 15 February to 31 March in addition to a fall season, and it still threatened to attack the Biological Survey in the budget appropriations. On the other side, Pearson reminded Nelson that he had promised the Board of Directors of the NAAS that he would offer nothing more than the extra month of hunting. Even that pledge had not pleased the directors, who wanted no expansion of the hunting season but had reluctantly agreed to support Nelson in any decision. Pearson politely warned Nelson that, rather than criticizing the survey, "it would be a thousand times more pleasant to get into a public fight in the support of the Biological Survey."[58]

Per law, in late April Nelson called together the advisory board that had been established by the Weeks-McLean Act to help the survey devise hunting regulations. He advised the members of the changes that he thought best, especially the new open season. Hornaday and E. H. Forbush fought the proposal, but in the end the other members voted to support Nelson. They feared that the hunters in the Midwest, with the support of Senators Reed and Stone, had enough power to end the appropriation for the Biological Survey, and they thought it wise to prevent such action.[59]

Forbush was furious, especially with the leadership of the Audubon association. In a long and emotional letter to Pearson, he asked, "Why do we continue to let this thing go on and not a word or voice raised in opposition?" He wondered what the group's leaders would tell the friends of the birds when they discovered that the association had not matched the pressure that the Missourians put on the survey. He argued, "We can bring pressure to bear on the administration. We only need *to be alive*. We have a majority of the people with us if we only let them know what we want." What the association should want, he pointed out, was a continued ban on spring shooting. The NAAS had to move quickly or lose the battle.[60]

Now Pearson knew how Nelson felt, caught between political expediency and scientific evidence. After briefly trying to convince Forbush of the necessity of backing the Biological Survey, he threw his support to Forbush's plan to send an agent to "every state where the monster shows its head" while simultaneously arousing public support. The agent, Dr. G. W. Field, delivered a crushing indictment of spring shooting and its proponents. In particular, he concluded, "The great menace to the useful wild birds today is that type of political influence controlled by wealth and self-interest." At the same time, Audubon rallied its membership to protest the new regulations. Even Burnham, disgusted by the mean spirit, mendacity, and mule-headedness of the Missourians, voted to remove the late-winter hunting season. The combination of Field's report and public criticism succeeded in overturning the new set of rules in August 1916.[61]

While bird protectionists were winning their last battle for the Weeks-McLean law, the treaty was slowly finding its way through the diplomatic channels. After the Dominion Privy Council approved the revised version, on 29 June 1916 the governor general sent it to Ambassador Spring Rice. On 5 July, Spring Rice forwarded Canada's acceptance to the State Department.[62] At that point, conservationists believed that only the Senate's ratification stood between them and bird protection nirvana.

On 10 July, USDA officials called on the diplomats to urge rapid action on the treaty. Their Canadian contacts had told them that the treaty had cleared the British Embassy, and they wanted to ensure that there would be no unnecessary delay. Perhaps the anticipation of finally accomplishing their goal clouded the conservationists' judgment, because they were not especially charitable. E. H. Forbush commented that "the treaty will go to the President when it can be *rescued* from the State Department." In fact, William Phillips was keeping a close eye on the agreement, but he could not forward it to President Wilson or the Senate until Spring Rice got approval from London.[63] Once that arrived, the State Department sent it off to the Senate.

Having witnessed the fights over funding for the Weeks-McLean Act, State Department officials were very careful about how they packaged the treaty for the Senate. A member of the solicitor's office mildly concluded, "The treaty will undoubtedly arouse considerable interest in the Senate." He suggested that, when the administration submitted the treaty, it should remind senators that they had begun the process by voting for McLean's resolution. In that way, presumably, the department could avoid responsibility for any brawls that broke out involving Senator Reed. When Secretary Lansing sent the treaty to the president and the Senate on 17 August, he emphasized both the benefits of bird protection and the origins of the treaty. The Senate gave its consent to the agreement by a show of hands on 29 August, and President Wilson signed it a few days later.[64]

Senator Reed failed in his last effort to prevent the ratification of the treaty when the Senate was in executive session. According to Hornaday, when Reed started a "rough-house speech," one southern senator cut him short. "We have got to protect these birds," he told Reed, "and we are going to do it *now*, so *sit down*, Jim!" Hornaday gloated that Reed had hurt his own cause with his tiresome and virulent speeches. Displaying a bit of his own virulence, Hornaday crowed, "Praise God, from whom all blessings flow; and now the spring-shooters of Missouri can go to hell!"[65]

Even before the Senate approved the agreement, Audubon's promotional machine had kicked into gear. Bird lovers, suffrage workers, groundskeepers, and newspaper editors wrote to Wilson asking him to help stop "the terrible slaughter of these birds."[66] In a pointed effort to counter Reed's influence, a number of letters came from organizations and individuals in Missouri. One of the most telling letters came from an ammunition manufacturer who told Wilson, "You surely must realize how many people are deeply interested in this matter which is so vital not only from an economic standpoint, but also that of the sentimentalist, the bird lover."[67] All the writers agreed; Wilson should lean on Congress to force action quickly.

To their surprise, conservationists found that they had to wait for the signature of the king before the treaty could be official. Hewitt, who like many other conservationists thought that the treaty was finally locked up, wrote to Nelson, "I must confess that the necessity of the formal ratification of the treaty by the King was a surprise to *me,* but then we are not supposed to be diplomats."[68] Given the strain of wartime and the slow transportation methods, the signed treaty did not make it back to Washington until December. On the 7th of that month, the two nations formally exchanged ratifications. The Migratory Bird Treaty was finally a reality.

CONCLUSION

The Migratory Bird Treaty, from Senator McLean's resolution to final ratification, hatched after three years and eight months in the nest. Despite the long gestation period, however, the draft that conservationists created in February 1914 had changed very little by the time that King George V signed it in November 1916. This odd combination of slow progress and minimal alterations resulted from a number of factors, including the unique role of nondiplomats in the negotiations, the outbreak of war, the cautious goals of conservationists, and the weakness of the opposition in both countries.

The American decision to work with Canada reflected the diplomatic realities of the day and the revised goals for the treaty. Conservationists needed the quickest possible means to resolve the constitutionality question, and the placid Anglo-American relationship promised the path of least resistance. To all of those who agreed that the Weeks-McLean law was a valuable, but vulnerable, tool, the exact terms of the treaty were not as important as the precedent of establishing uniform regulations throughout the continent. Domestic opposition was pesky, but in the end it had less of an impact than the outbreak of war on the progress of the treaty. Therefore, the birds' protectors were not so much concerned with winning intellectual debates as they were with exercising their political power.

The scientists and conservationists had an unusual role to play in the negotiations. Officially, the treaty went through the traditional diplomatic channels, complete with the necessary rewriting in the language of diplomacy. Treaty supporters were unable to alter the pace at which this machinery worked, much to their frustration. But those scientists and conservationists did have a great deal to say about the actual contents of the agreement. They created the drafts, examined the flaws, and agreed on revisions, all without the meddling of diplomats, who seemed at least a little puzzled about the treaty. This unorthodox system worked.

With the exchange of ratifications on 7 December 1916, conservationists succeeded in their ultimate goal of heading off a challenge to the constitutionality of federal protection of migratory birds. Instead of replaying the arguments of the *Shauver* case in October 1916, the Supreme Court agreed to postpone any hearing given the impending signature of the accord by the king. In celebration, William Hornaday called the Migratory Bird Treaty "the greatest victory ever achieved for the birds of this continent, or any other continent. It will give genuine joy to all farmers and forest owners, all friends of birds, now to be numbered by millions, and all true sportsmen." [69] His words, though, were a bit premature, as opponents of the treaty had several more opportunities to fight in Congress and the courts.

8

Protecting the National Interest,
1916–1920

The final ratification of the Migratory Bird Treaty in December 1916 brought bird protectors within two steps of finally having a reliable law for their cause. First, Congress had to pass enabling legislation, and then conservationists had to win the inevitable court battle. To the surprise of treaty supporters, the opponents of federal control of migratory birds were able to put up a determined fight in Congress that combined with American entry into the world war to threaten progress on the treaty. Treaty opponents also made a determined effort to destroy the treaty in the courts.

While American entry into the war tied up Congress for months, it did give conservationists an opportunity to sell their vision of bird protection, as embodied in the treaty, to the nation and Congress. For the previous few years they had been active in the world of diplomacy; now they had to return their focus to legislative combat, which required public relations. They had long argued that bird protection made good economic policy because of birds' value in destroying crop-eating insects. Now bird protectors realized that they could present the Migratory Bird Treaty Act (MBTA) both as a food conservation measure and as a means to help an ally in wartime; they had found an argument that, because of its patriotic importance, was very hard to refute. Instead of waiting for the war to end, conservationists used it to advance their cause. Inevitably, a challenge arose in the courts—from Missouri naturally—and the ruling demonstrated how well the conservationists had embedded their message in the American mindset.

The struggle to turn the treaty into a valid law in the United States revealed that the conservationists had mastered the tactics of mobilizing public support and lobbying Congress. From around the country citizens petitioned their leaders to support the treaty, and bird lovers flocked to Washington to have their say. Conservationists employed public relations professionals to spread their message through the country, and they utilized their own scientific expertise in persuading congressmen of the merits of their cause. Finally, they appealed to the ultimate sentiment in politics, patriotism, as they made bird protection a war measure. The final success of the Migratory Bird Treaty, then, depended on the ability of the treaty's supporters to sell their ideas at all levels of society.

HARD-NOSED REALISM ON CAPITOL HILL

From the day that the United States and Great Britain exchanged ratifications of the Migratory Bird Treaty, 7 December 1916, conservationists moved quickly to ram the enabling legislation through Congress. Three factors motivated them: the memory of the failed Inland Fisheries Treaty, their years of anticipation about this moment, and the realization that they had momentum at the end of 1916. With joy they returned to the halls of Congress to lobby and got back to the work of convincing people of the value of birds. But they also realized that sentiment, while a useful tool for motivating some people, would not be enough to win legislative debates. Thus they turned their attention more and more to diplomacy and economics to justify the treaty.

Fortunately, the sentimental friends of birds knew how to launch a public relations campaign. For instance, the National Association of Audubon Societies (NAAS) used a sly arrangement with Thomas R. Shipp and Company, a New York public relations firm, to spread the association's beliefs. T. Gilbert Pearson wrote reports and sent them to Shipp. The company modified the pieces and sent them out to hundreds of newspapers over a company byline. The newspapers then printed the articles as if they were objective news of the latest controversy about birds in Washington. Pearson was not entirely comfortable with this method and believed that he had to cover his tracks in this publicity campaign, lest he create a public backlash.[1]

The Pearson-Shipp collaboration jumped out of the starting gate with an article sent out on 8 December 1916, just one day after the exchange of ratifications. Pearson had written the piece in late October in anticipation of the completion of the diplomatic formalities, although he was not on the byline. The article included pictures of Senator George McLean, Pearson, and the recently retired chief of the Biological Survey, Henry Henshaw — an interesting collection of legislator, activist, and scientist. It described the treaty as "a coup on the part of the bird protectionists" and praised the three men for their aggressive efforts on behalf of the birds. The end of the piece quoted Pearson calling on "all friends of birds" to lobby Congress for rapid passage of the enabling legislation.[2]

To pay for the lobbying effort, Pearson undertook an aggressive fund-raising campaign. If birds were Pearson's first love, fund-raising came in a close second. In mid-December, he had $1,000 earmarked to finance the lobbying effort for the MBTA. He estimated, however, that he would need at least $2,500 — the amount that he had spent on the tariff bill fight in 1913. In a letter to a benefactor, he spelled out the need for action: "This is by all odds the most important legislative measure that has ever come up for the attention of any legislative body in the world." Given his track record of pulling the NAAS out of budgetary difficulties, Pearson probably raised far more than he thought he would need.[3]

Pearson's call for lobbying may have been premature because Congress did not yet have any bill to consider. Dr. E. W. Nelson, now chief of the Biological Survey, was working on legislation that included all of the provisions specified in the treaty, plus some interesting additions. Among them were an appropriation of $275,000 to pay for wardens, rules for prosecution of violators, and steps necessary to protect the endangered species mentioned in the treaty. The bill also updated the provisions of the Lacey Act of 1900, set maximum punishment at $500 or six months in jail for each offense, and continued the advisory committee that had the task of drawing up specific hunting regulations. In addition to crafting the bill, Nelson also made an important political decision. Instead of putting Senator McLean, a Republican, in charge of the bill, Nelson yielded to pressure from the Wilson administration and chose Senator Marcus Aurelius Smith, a Democrat from Arizona.[4]

While conservationists were generally happy with the bill, Pearson spoke for most when he complained about Nelson's choice of Smith. The Democrats respected McLean as the Senate's leading expert on bird protection, and no one had done more to make the treaty a reality. McLean, however, understood Nelson's problem. He told Pearson that "our opposition in the past has come from Democratic sources, and as my sole object has been to secure able and effective legislation, I am always willing to submerge myself in the interest of the cause." As it turned out, McLean spent more time than any other senator fighting for the bill.[5]

Congress took up the issue on 13 January 1917, when Senator Gilbert Hitchcock of Nebraska and Congressman Henry Flood of Virginia simultaneously introduced Nelson's bill.[6] The bills were dispatched to the House

Committee on Foreign Affairs and the Senate Committee on Agriculture and Forestry, but they soon were lost in the swirl of business in Congress, especially the debate over America's role in the European war. Realistically, the bills needed close coordination and the removal of obstacles, such as Senator Reed, to have even a slim chance of getting through Congress by the March adjournment. Even though such coordination was unlikely, conservationists hoped for rapid action and tried to expedite the bills' progress.

The Audubon association turned up its publicity campaign another notch in conjunction with the introduction of the legislation. Using Shipp's agency, Pearson once again called on bird lovers to lobby Congress about the Flood and Hitchcock bills. Newspapers in Brooklyn, Chicago, Richmond, Columbus, Boston, Buffalo, and other cities produced favorable editorials based on the Shipp article and urged their readers to write their congressmen. The *New York Herald* got into the spirit the best when its editor suggested, "When this treaty becomes a law the protection of migratory birds will be an international duty and then all our feathered friends from the Arctic Circle to the Gulf of Mexico will be safe."[7]

Pearson supplemented his furtive newspaper campaign with heavy personal lobbying in Washington, spending most of January and February in the capital meeting congressmen. Whenever he came upon an opponent, he rallied the local Audubon society to send at least forty telegrams expressing support for the bill. He also contacted local politicians known to be sympathetic to birds to express that sentiment to the waffler, and he mailed Audubon pamphlets to influential people in the district. Based on his personal contact, Pearson was certain that the enabling legislation would have sufficient support in Congress if it came to a vote.[8]

The sport hunters worked to complement Pearson's quiet determination. The Camp Fire Club of America (CFC) and the Boone and Crockett Club were organizations of influential men who liked to think of themselves as cut from pioneer cloth, able to survive in the wilderness and kill large, ferocious animals with ease. They endorsed the enabling legislation and helped to expand on the sentimentalists' arguments. In a strong editorial in *Forest and Stream,* which billed itself as the official organ of the CFC, John Burnham demanded that duck hunters give their support to the bill not only because it would preserve game, but also because it was an important conservation measure. The Camp Fire Club called on President Wilson to use his influence to pass the bill, especially in light of the dishonor brought about by the failure of the Inland Fisheries Treaty. The Boone and Crockett Club went further by pointing out that the United States now had a legal and moral obligation to Canada to carry out the terms of the agreement quickly.[9]

Simultaneously, conservationists mobilized their business allies to emphasize the importance of the enabling bill. E. H. Forbush wrote to Henry Ford urging the automaker to pressure Wilson to expedite the legislation. Ford obliged, telling Wilson that if Forbush thought that the bill was important then it deserved Wilson's attention.[10] In Alabama, John Wallace encouraged his friends in Birmingham's business community to write to their congressmen. In response to one letter, Congressman George Huddleston wrote, "The fact that you wish me to support it will cause me to give it favorable consideration." The overall strategy seemed to be working when Secretary of State Robert Lansing took the unusual step of expressing the administration's interest in the bill to Flood and Senator Thomas Gore of Tennessee, chairman of the Committee on Agriculture and Forestry.[11]

On 6 February 1917, the House Committee on Foreign Affairs reported out Flood's bill favorably. In fact, the committee strengthened the bill by including a clause that repealed any act inconsistent with the MBTA. Charles Stedman of North Carolina, reporting for the committee, emphasized that state game officials and bird preservation groups strongly supported the bill. In addition, he reminded the House "that demands of international courtesy" made rapid passage of the law imperative.[12] While the committee's report was an important step, proponents of the law knew that they had less than one month before Congress adjourned. In that time, they had to get the bill out of the Senate committee, through both houses and a conference committee, and onto the president's desk.

Conservationists continued to apply pressure on the administration, much as Forbush had challenged them to do in the spring of 1916. The Biological Survey and Wallace would not let Secretary of Agriculture D. F. Houston forget about the treaty. They kept him abreast of developments in Canada and gave him unsolicited advice as to the best way to expedite the enabling legislation. Wallace, in particular, urged the administration to call in Flood, Hitchcock, and several other congressmen and chew them out for not doing more to move the bill. He warned Houston that people were not obeying the Weeks-McLean law anymore and therefore the USDA was the subject of ridicule throughout the country, all because Congress was dallying.[13]

Not wanting to look the fool, Houston leaned on Lansing to get results. Instead of focusing on the benefits of bird protection, Houston concentrated on Canada's efforts to secure and enforce the treaty. After briefly recounting Hewitt's efforts in lining up the provinces and ministers, he told Lansing:

> I wish to call your attention to the fact that this treaty was negotiated with Great Britain at the request of the United States and despite the preoccupation of that country and Canada in the war, they . . . have shown a friendly desire . . . to carry out the obligations of the treaty with complete good faith.[14]

In addition, Lansing heard from his own assistant secretary, William Phillips, on the matter. Listing the same congressmen that Wallace had, Phillips urged Lansing to impress upon them the need for the United States to demonstrate its good faith by passing the bill.[15]

On the same day that Houston was dumping this problem on Lansing's desk, 20 February 1917, the Senate Committee on Agriculture and Forestry finally reported out the Hitchcock bill. Ellison "Hoke" Smith of South Carolina, filling in for Gore as chairman of the committee, announced a series of amendments "to restrict the operation of the bill to the terms of . . . such State laws as are now in force." In effect, Hoke Smith was doing to the Migratory Bird Treaty what Senator William Smith of Michigan had done to the Inland Fisheries Treaty. In the words of William Hornaday, he "*cut the vital organs out of the bill!*" With only twelve days until adjournment, Congress had two very different enabling bills still awaiting passage.[16]

Lansing was no more willing to suffer indignity than Houston, and he turned to both the White House and Capitol Hill. On 23 February, he asked Wilson to call in the usual suspects from Congress, and at the same time he wrote to Flood and Smith. Lansing believed that the failure of the fisheries treaty had damaged "the good faith" of the United States, but he trusted "that the feeling aroused in Canada by that incident will be overcome" if Congress acted quickly on the bird treaty. At that late date, Lansing was clutching at straws. Wilson told him, "Of course, I am willing to get behind it," but he realized that it was too late for the 64th Congress to act.[17]

In Canada, the government was not making much more progress in putting the treaty into force, but at least Parliament had an excuse. Unlike the Americans, Canadian conservationists did not have a law such as Weeks-McLean on which to base their enabling legislation. In January the cabinet appointed Hewitt to form an advisory council to draw up the law, which he submitted promptly. The bill was not a matter of much contention, although some of the members from Quebec and British Columbia protested that the United States would leave Canada hanging as it had with the fisheries treaty. Hewitt and his allies countered that the situation was very much different and seemed to have the situation in hand. But in early February Parliament adjourned for three months while Prime Minister Sir Robert Borden and some of his cabinet attended the Imperial War Conference in London. No progress could be made until Canadian leadership returned in May.[18]

Although the Hitchcock and Flood bills had not become law, conservationists had won some victories. First, they had mobilized enough public support and newspaper coverage to demonstrate that the treaty was not just an issue for "bird cranks" and wealthy duck hunters. Second, they had shown an ability to press the right buttons in the administration to get concerted action, as they had used different but effective arguments with both Houston and Lansing. Finally, they learned that their main enemy in Congress would not be Reed but the system of doing business. They looked forward to passing the bill in the new session of Congress that would open in April 1917.

THE WARBIRDS

When Congress reconvened on 2 April 1917, it faced the monumental task of responding to President Wilson's request for a declaration of war against Germany and Austria-Hungary. Although Congress quickly accepted Wilson's call to arms, the steps necessary to prepare the nation for warfare took months of congressional wrangling. Conservationists understood that the migratory bird treaty bill would have to wait while Congress laid the groundwork for war, but they also discovered that they could use the war to their benefit by building upon accumulated scientific evidence. By concentrating both on the value of birds as insectivores and the need to uphold an agreement with a partner in the war against Germany, friends of birds demonstrated that the enabling legislation was an important war measure. In the process, they tied together sentiment, science, and economics, sometimes in ways that had not occurred to them before.

Once again, conservationists stepped up their campaign to inundate Wilson and Congress with letters. Well into 1918, Congress was still receiving fifty letters per day from around the country supporting the bill.[19] Mail came from traditional leaders such as Pearson and Burnham, but some of the most persuasive tracts came from local officials and average citizens.

Of those that have been preserved, there were three basic types. The first came from game and fish commissioners from nearly every state who were especially interested in the provisions to halt the decline of game birds. The second were those letters from ordinary citizens who had some affiliation with a local bird club that was undertaking a letter-writing campaign. The third group included an odd mix of scientists, businessmen, and conservation organizations who wanted to express some particular theory about the bill.[20] Most of the letters shared some basic similarities. The writers acknowledged that Wilson was very busy with the war, but they urged him not to forget about the birds. Many emphasized that the United States had an obligation to Canada to expedite passage of the bill, especially now that the two countries were partners in the war against Germany. Almost all agreed that bird protection should be a part of the war effort, either because birds ate insects that destroyed crops or were themselves food.

Hunters and state game officials were some of the most prolific and committed supporters of the bill, probably after prodding from Burnham. They had an obvious desire to see increased numbers of game birds, but game commissioners also took a broad approach to the issue. The National Association of Game and Fish Commissioners unanimously passed a resolution stating that "protection of the migratory insectivorous birds is so closely related to the conservation of the food, cotton and timber resources [that] the said bill is and should be considered an important war measure." Similar letters came from commissions in California, Wisconsin, Virginia, New York, and other states.[21] In addition, *Forest and Stream* editorialized that the bill's passage "will be a contribution to the public welfare whose importance it would be hard to overestimate."[22]

Wilson also received a number of letters from bird watchers, especially in Missouri. The St. Louis Bird Club and the Audubon Society of Missouri both organized letter-writing campaigns, probably with the intention of counteracting Senator Reed's stubbornness. Their letters were usually handwritten and often came from women. Oddly, the writers cited the American obligation to Canada and the economic value of birds as the major reasons to pass the bill, even though their club membership indicated that they appreciated birds mainly for their aesthetic value. Although their letters were not especially original or eloquent — one writer spelled Wilson's first name "Woodroe" — these writers proved that leaders like Pearson did have a large following.[23]

The writers who probably carried the most influence, though, were those citizens who laid out reasoned arguments for the bill's passage. As usual, scientists were among the first to write on behalf of the bill. On 24 April, E. H. Forbush informed Wilson that Great Britain had "recently passed as a war measure an act prohibiting the importation of the plumage of birds" on the grounds that birds protected crops in countries that exported food to the island nation. Forbush believed that the United States should use the same reasoning to pass the enabling legislation. He also pointed out that the United States now had a "solemn obligation to a friendly power" to act on the treaty. An entomologist from the University of Missouri told Wilson how farmers rued the loss of the common quail, which had combated many of the worst crop destroyers. Other scientists agreed that the evidence demonstrated that bird protection led to increased crop production. These writers were the first to link bird protection with the war effort.[24]

From the Mississippi and Missouri valleys came support from a number of business and civic leaders hoping to counteract the Interstate Sportsmen's Protective Association. Edmund James, the president of the University of Illinois, told Wilson that the "friendly assistance" of birds made agriculture possible. A grain farmer from St. Louis argued that "plenty of birds means no insects. Insects destroy millions of bushels of grain every year." The president of the Missouri Pacific Railroad begged Wilson to consider "my small share of influence and conviction" when he approached the issue.[25] But the most unusual spin on the war measure idea came from W. S. McCrea of the People's Gas, Light and Coke Company of Chicago. He suggested that, because the federal bird law was in limbo, the lack of enforcement was leading to a general contempt for "Uncle Sam's laws in sections that would produce some of our ablest fighting material should the spirit of patriotism once prevail." In a second letter to Wilson, he focused on the enabling bill as the means to attack the conglomerate of draft-dodging, law-breaking, moonshining, pro-German market hunters, bootleggers, and Wobblies that thrived in the Mississippi valley. "The combination is always bad," he wrote, "and can be broken up by the proposed law and a quick and rigid enforcement of it."[26] McCrea also got two of his friends, the sheriff and the coroner of Cook County, Illinois, to send letters on official stationery to their congressman on behalf of the treaty.[27]

Conservation organizations also poured letters into Washington to support the bill in the new Congress. The Camp Fire Club and the Boone and Crockett Club reiterated their position that the bill's passage was necessary both to uphold American honor and to increase the food supply. New

York Conservation Commissioner George Pratt wrote, "In this time of war, especially, all kinds of food supplies must be conserved and the birds, as co-workers with the farmers, should be protected." William Frederic Badé of the California Associated Societies for the Conservation of Wild Life opined that the bill's passage would be "a gracious act towards Canada" and a "war measure in the interest of a higher agricultural efficiency." [28]

The lobbying campaign that linked bird protection with the war effort was a natural outgrowth of the educational efforts that conservationists had made for years. Bird protectionists had known for some time that they could not expect to win congressional votes with aesthetic or sentimental arguments alone. Even back to Senator McLean's "insect tax" speech in 1912, before the war made food conservation a vital activity, they had concentrated on the economic benefits of bird protection in the form of increased agricultural production. No one knew exactly how much damage insects caused each year in the United States, although conservationists liked Forbush's estimate of $800,000,000. [29] In wartime, it was very easy to convert that damage figure into the stark terms of starvation. For instance, in the July 1917 Bird-Lore, Dr. Frank Chapman argued, "The food now destroyed in America by insect and rodent pests would feed the people of Belgium. Can we spare a single insect-eating bird?" [30] With food administrator Herbert Hoover's wheatless Mondays and meatless Tuesdays emphasizing to Americans the importance of using food wisely, especially at a time of poor grain crops, conservationists had a golden opportunity to link bird protection with wartime patriotism. [31]

Not only did the war provide conservationists an important opportunity to advocate this cause, but it also made people more open to the idea of federal control of resources. In the interest of increasing efficiency in prosecuting the war, the federal government undertook the greatest centralization of power in American history up to that time. Compared to federal control of the railroads, for instance, the Migratory Bird Treaty was barely an extension of federal power. Opponents of the bill could not base their opposition on its supposed unconstitutionality while agreeing to the massive federal power grab, but they could challenge the conservationists' claim that the bill encouraged food conservation. [32]

On 20 April 1917, conservationists launched their second congressional offensive for the treaty's enabling legislation. In the Senate, Marcus Smith finally showed some inclination to work for the bill that Nelson had handed to him in December. Bird preservationists—including the head of the Arizona Audubon Society—doubted his commitment to bird protection, but Smith did his part on this occasion. Quoting heavily from Congressman Stedman's House committee report of 6 February, Smith reported out the bill from the Senate Committee on Agriculture and Forestry. This time, the bill left the committee intact.[33] The pressure of the war, however, delayed debate on the floor of the Senate until late June.

When the bill did reach the whole Senate on 28 June, it ran into stiff opposition. James Reed objected immediately to even considering the bill while the nation was at war, but he then opened debate on the bill's provision that wardens did not need a warrant to make an arrest. William Borah of Idaho joined Reed in questioning the constitutionality of the warrant provision, giving the Missourian more credibility than he deserved. In response, McLean and Hitchcock countered that Canadians were losing their faith in the United States because of Congress's delay, and they pointed out that state game wardens were not forced to get warrants. Sensing an imminent defeat, Smith agreed to withdraw the bill so that the Senate could consider more urgent measures.[34]

On 9 July, Smith was back, but this time he was prepared. Finally responding to conservationist logic, he declared that the bill deserved attention as a war measure, thereby undercutting Reed before he could object. He also announced that the bill's supporters had agreed to add a provision requiring wardens to get warrants as any federal officer would. Desperate for a new bogeyman, Reed objected to the concept of the advisory board, which he predicted would be as "impudent" as the various war boards that the administration had assembled. He then suggested that Congress needed a ruling from the Supreme Court on the constitutionality of the Weeks-McLean Act, which the court had no intention of making.[35]

In response to the latest chapter in Reed's tireless effort to stop federal bird protection, Smith demonstrated that he had finally assimilated the conservationist line of reasoning. He cited a number of somewhat scientific reports as evidence that insects held the potential to defoliate the planet if not held in check, and he suggested that insectivorous birds were in fact "winged squads of workmen" laboring to save crops. As to game birds, he noted that those "interested in our wild life have long realized the impossibility of saving what was left of this great national asset by state action." By taking action in 1913, the federal government had saved some species from extinction and had encouraged the remarkable recovery of more than a few others. Lest any believe that extinction was not a real possibility, he recounted the sad tale of the passenger pigeon, an example that was always in the back of conservationists' minds. With his eloquent and persuasive speech, Smith had given the bill an important boost.[36]

Three weeks later, on 30 July, the treaty's enabling bill came up for its third reading in the Senate, and Smith and Reed were ready for one last confrontation. In introducing the bill, Smith praised the Canadian Parliament for passing its enabling legislation without amendment just days earlier. Reed pounced, moving that the senators should postpone action until the Foreign Relations Committee could study the Canadian law. Henry Cabot Lodge of Massachusetts, Smith, and William Stone of Missouri — the chairman of said committee and a man that conservationists feared — shot down Reed's motion, leaving him with one last chance to argue against the bill. In a bitter speech, the Missourian lashed out at the "incompetents" in the USDA and the gunmakers who were conspiring to reserve hunting for the wealthy few. Finally, he warned that a vote for the bill was equivalent to tearing the Constitution to shreds. In the end, Reed's vicious attack probably helped the bill, which passed on a show of hands.[37]

But on the other side of Capitol Hill, conservationists were unable to get the bill out of committee. The Democratic caucus had agreed to consider only war bills or those with the explicit endorsement of the president. Burnham concluded that Flood "won't take a particle of interest in this bill until the Secretary of Agriculture tells him to put it through." In May, he appealed to his fellow New Yorker Bernard Baruch "to get the matter to the President's attention" in order to bring pressure on Flood, but Wilson did not move and neither did Flood. Without pressure from the White House, Congress allowed the bill to remain in committee when it recessed in early October.[38]

The gridlock in the House scared conservationists, who were witnessing the beginning of a backlash against their regulations. Pearson warned Herbert Hoover that pressure to open up hunting laws was building from "many persons in all parts of the country [who] would prefer to shoot birds rather than do more constructive work." On behalf of the association's 300,000 members, he urged Hoover to block their efforts.[39] He also reported to Hewitt that "you would think that the United States is on the verge of starvation" from the hysteria mounting to break up the game laws. In a *Bird-Lore* editorial, Frank Chapman argued, "Never since this Association began its organized work . . . have there been so many indications of concerted effort to break down bird- and game-restrictive measures as right now."[40] The heart of the opposition was still fair Missouri, where Senator Reed, the state government, and the newspaper editor Edward Grether formed the core of a powerful force of angry hunters.

The repeal movement impelled bird preservationists to renew their pressure on Flood when Congress reconvened in December. Burnham met with the Virginian, but he left the meeting feeling pessimistic. Secretary Lansing reminded Flood of "the bad impression made in Great Britain and Canada" by the failure of the fisheries convention, and he expressed the hope that a similar situation could be averted. McLean, too, was upset by Flood's attitude. He complained that "it is a treaty obligation, and we are treating it as a scrap of paper . . . our Canadian friends are suspecting our good faith." Even William T. Hornaday, who had spent the last several months working for military mobilization, petitioned Colonel Edward House, an advisor to Wilson, to make the bill a priority for the administration. He blamed "the irreconcilable spring-shooting game-hogs of Western Missouri, who, by the way, are a disgrace to that state" for creating "a state of deadlock" that only Wilson could break.[41]

The pressure paid off in January 1918, when the Foreign Affairs Committee finally reported the bill favorably. In a brief but stirring report, Stedman wrapped Old Glory around the nation's birds:

> Its passage is demanded by a sense of patriotic duty. . . . By preventing the indiscriminate slaughter of birds which destroy insects which feed upon our crops . . . it will thus contribute immensely to enlarging and making more secure the crop, so necessary to the support and maintenance of the brave men sent to the battlefield by this Republic, to preserve the honor of its flag.[42]

Stedman did not mention sentiment or aesthetics; it was purely a matter of applied science helping to make the world safe for democracy. With that important hurdle cleared, Pearson and Burnham called on their supporters to lobby their congressmen.[43] Victory finally seemed imminent.

After leaving the committee, however, the bill stalled once again in procedural entanglements. On 30 April 1918, Senator McLean complained angrily to Lansing and Wilson that

> for some unaccountable reason, the Enabling Act . . . is allowed to remain on the calendar in the House without any effort to secure a vote and it begins to look as though the subterranean forces that have succeeded in

preventing action on this matter in the past would succeed in carrying it by the present Session.

He reminded them of the "impropriety and manifest discourtesy" of Congress's delay and demanded that they do something to get the bill to a vote in the House of Representatives. Wilson told Lansing, "I entirely sympathize with the suggestion . . . from Senator McLean," and a few days later Flood received a sharp letter from the State Department.[44]

Debate began in the House less than three weeks after the exchange of letters. It opened on 24 May with a brief spat between Edward Pou of North Carolina and Frank Mondell of Wyoming over the bill's support. In demonstrating the importance and popularity of the bill, Pou cited the volume of letters coming in from around the country, which were in part a response to a form letter that Burnham had circulated asking AGPA members to write to Pou and Flood. In response, Mondell called the letters propaganda of "well-meaning but uninformed folks." Like Reed, Mondell bitterly opposed the extension of federal power and had compared a vote for the Weeks-McLean bill to a vote for imperial rule from Washington.[45]

On 4 and 6 June, the House debated the bill fully, and some supporters demonstrated a scary lack of understanding of the issues at hand. Flood, for instance, thought that the law would protect "the game which kills the insects," even though the treaty and bill explicitly separated game birds and insectivorous birds. Another supporter of the bill claimed that insects caused $1,500,000,000 worth of damage each year, which was double the standard estimate used by conservationists, although one that Hornaday at times liked. Other proponents of the legislation could not agree on whether there were five hundred thousand or five million hunters with an interest in the bill.[46] Despite the lowbrow beginning, the debates provided a vital insight into how people saw the pitfalls and advantages of federal and international efforts at migratory bird protection.

Fortunately, the debate improved in quality as the two sides squared off on four important issues, beginning with the charge of elitism. Charles Bland of Indiana accused the bill's supporters of being "bird cranks and resort-visiting fellows," whom he distinguished from "the ordinary man." He argued that the former just wanted to preserve game for wealthy hunters who could travel to Florida each winter while his constituents got no hunting at all. In rebuttal, Daniel Anthony of Kansas claimed that the opposition consisted solely of unscrupulous market hunters who were afraid of the impending restrictions. Flood was also quick to list important politicians—including the governor of Missouri—and organizations that had publicly supported the bill.[47] Conservationists were open to charges of elitism in regard to the game birds, but they certainly tried to argue that bird lovers came from all places in society.

The role of the USDA in making the regulations became the second point of debate. John Tillman of Arkansas argued that, as written, the bill would allow the secretary of agriculture to stop all bird hunting, because he was not required to set an open season. Opponents did not approve of yielding congressional authority to, as Bland put it, "some whippersnapper . . . with a deferred classification." But one supporter pointed out that Congress commonly delegated "to an officer of the Government the power to enforce a law that is general in its terms." Edmund Platt of New York reminded Congress that the regulations had to be based on Biological Survey data, which could change from year to year; therefore, Congress was in no position to make specific rules.[48] The committee of experts was a standard Progressive era tool to solve problems, but men like Bland obviously did not trust the concept.

The third target for the attackers was the constitutional validity of the bill. George Graham of Pennsylvania summed up much of the opposition when he asked, "How can we make a treaty and do an unconstitutional thing by it?" Like some of his colleagues, he believed that the states could and should make the necessary regulations; the treaty was no more than a trick to evade the Constitution. Conservationists responded that migration gave these species multinational ranges, which in turn made them a common possession of humanity. The states could not but fail to protect these species, especially so long as they claimed ownership of the birds. As Platt said, "It is futile to claim that birds flying over a specified territory or resting for a day or two are anybody's property." [49]

Finally, opponents of federal intervention objected to the basic idea of bird protection, especially at a time of war. Tillman, the former president of the University of Arkansas, denounced conservationists for wasting "two days passing a measure protecting meadowlarks and woodpeckers [while] the U-boats are . . . barking and biting at our doors." He then asserted that the bill would "make our boys sissies." "God made woodpeckers, meadow larks, wild ducks, and bobolinks for boys to shoot," he continued.[50] Stedman, though, summed up the reason for the broad-based support in a speech interrupted many times by applause: "The indiscriminate and wholesale slaughter of birds for many years past has been not only a blot upon our civilization, but also a serious blow to our agricultural resources."[51]

When the dust finally settled on 6 June, the bill had escaped basically unscathed. The fifty members of the House who had signed on with the Interstate Sportsmen's Protective Association had been too few to alter more than the warrant provision. That small change, however, did not mesh with the Senate's version, and the two houses wasted a few weeks with the typical conference committees. Finally, they resolved their differences and sent the law to President Wilson, who signed it on 3 July 1918.

Conservationists finally had reason to celebrate, and they did. "We are told that all things come to him who waits," wrote George Bird Grinnell, "but then, on the other hand, I have waited a long time." A doctor from Des Moines congratulated Burnham on finishing "the greatest piece of work ever done in this or any other country for the protection of game." Burnham himself was so happy that he praised Flood's masterful handling of "this epoch-making legislation."[52]

In contrast to the fierce struggle in Congress, the Canadian Parliament had earlier passed its enabling legislation with little trouble. The interior minister, W. J. Roche, introduced the bill on 21 June 1917 with a Hewitt-inspired plea to pass it in order to halt the collapse of bird life throughout the continent. There was no real opposition, although Sir Wilfrid Laurier, in support, revealed some confusion about the details. Given the nature of the parliamentary system and the general lack of controversy regarding the measure, there had been no real chance that the bill would fail. On 21 July 1917, after the third reading of the bill, Parliament had passed the Migratory Birds Convention Act. The Dominion had fulfilled its obligation almost a year earlier than the United States.[53]

In the end, then, the war had a mixed impact on the outcome of the treaty and its enabling legislation. Conservationists used the war to broaden the appeal of bird protection both among the general public and in the federal government. In Washington, the wartime demands for efficiency and the increased acceptance of centralized authority made it easier to accept the implications of federal control of migratory birds. American entry into the war also made the treaty more important to the State Department, which did not want to appear to be shortchanging Britain or Canada. On the other hand, the crush of war-related business forced conservationists to delay action on their bill and then allowed opponents a convenient excuse for further delay. In sum, the war slowed progress on bird conservation, but it broadened the base of support.

The legislative battles that conservationists fought in Congress revealed a great deal about the success that they had in selling their message. In the United States, the conservationists had mastered the art of reaching out to the public in order to put pressure on the government. In part, this success was based on the natural appeal of birds, but it also stemmed from good organization, well-considered arguments, and wisely cultivated political connections. They were also blessed with a weak, disorganized opposition that was willing to put its local interests before the national and international good.

These same legislative battles also revealed the benefits of the parliamentary system. Despite the favorable omens listed above, the bird protection forces could not change congressional procedure, which allowed a few opponents and one uninterested committee chairman to hold down the appropriate legislation for months. In contrast, the Canadian Parliament had no problem passing the bill. Since 1913, C. Gordon Hewitt and Maxwell Graham had been working to ensure that the ministers of agriculture and interior supported the legislation, and the parliamentary system assured that a noncontentious government bill cruised through unscathed.

THE MIGRATORY BIRDS COME HOME TO ROOST

Final passage of the American enabling legislation brought the long process to attain a migratory bird treaty to its final stage, in which each side tried to control how well the law worked. In both countries, conservationists celebrated their victory, but they also recognized that there was more work to do. Advisory boards put together regulations that fulfilled treaty obligations, but conservationists also worked to bring the states and provinces into line to reduce the possibility of confusion and poor enforcement. Meanwhile, the laws' opponents still mounted stiff legal challenges that reached both the Canadian and American Supreme Courts, where the decisions demonstrated that the rationale for bird protection was more powerful than its legal justification.

In Canada, the process of selling the law to the public began almost immediately after passage of the Migratory Birds Convention Act (MBCA) on 21 July 1917. The Dominion had to take such action because there had been no need to arouse public support earlier in the process. Also, Canada's lack of a large, vocal organization equivalent to the NAAS put much of the burden of public awareness on the provincial and national governments. One of the first steps, then, was to bring the provincial laws into line with the Dominion's. This task was not too difficult because most of the provincial laws were already quite close to the MBCA.[54]

As part of the campaign to spread the regulations to the public, Hewitt focused on quarrelsome Quebec, where he got his message into two newspapers in early August. The *Montreal Gazette* carried a Hewitt-inspired editorial that cited the twin problems of habitat loss and uneven provincial enforcement as the main culprits leading to the loss of birdlife in Canada. The editorial asserted that the convention was "a sign of the advancing knowledge of the values of all created things to man and his interests." For the *Montreal Herald,* Hewitt produced a long article recounting the need for and origins of the treaty. He concluded, "This convention constitutes the most important and far-reaching measure ever taken in the history of bird protection."[55]

J. B. Harkin relied heavily on Hewitt in putting together the official statement on the need for the treaty and subsequent regulations. He cited birds for their valuable work as insectivores, and like Hewitt he referred only in passing to their aesthetic value. Canada, Harkin reported, had faced a situation in which valuable birds that migrated to the United States often got eaten by southerners. This outcome was not only detrimental for the birds, but it had threatened to undermine any Canadian progress in bird protection. The treaty, he emphasized, meant that each nation had a responsibility to the other to protect migrants. "Canada," he wrote, "does not make promises lightly—this treaty is not a scrap of paper and the co-operation of all is sought in its enforcement."[56]

Unfortunately, passage of the act was not a panacea. Quebec, Manitoba, Alberta, and Saskatchewan brought their laws into the general framework of the MBCA quickly, but throughout the Dominion it became clear that enforcement would be difficult. One game warden from Hamilton, Ontario, reported that small birds were still in decline, because "the Foreign Element here is hard to control, also the Boy Element." In the Maritimes, the provincial governments took advantage of the vague nature of the MBCA to reduce their enforcement efforts. Nova Scotia had too few wardens and did not enforce the duck hunting regulations. Prince Edward Island had no bird wardens, and New Brunswick had repealed all of its bird protection laws, reasoning that such laws were now the responsibility of the Dominion.[57]

Enforcement of the law did lead to a court case, *The King v. Russell C. Clarke,* that determined the legality of the MBCA. Clarke had been caught hunting geese illegally on Prince Edward Island in 1919. He fought the prosecution on the grounds that the law was not constitutional, because the British North America Act had given the provinces control over wildlife policy. A local magistrate initially acquitted him, but the Prince Edward Island Supreme Court overturned his acquittal in 1920, based on the reasoning that the Dominion had broad authority to execute and fulfill treaties. The Canadian Supreme Court refused to hear Clarke's appeal, and the MBCA stood.[58]

In the United States, enforcement of the Migratory Bird Treaty Act was basically an extension of the efforts under Weeks-McLean, which had been pitiful. The Biological Survey increased its warden force to twenty-five, and federal prosecutors became more aggressive in their pursuit of lawbreakers. In addition, state wardens usually cooperated with their overworked federal counterparts, especially as more states brought their laws into line with the federal law. The vast majority of the cases involved waterfowl hunting in the South and Midwest.[59] Still, though, the scarcity of resources made publicity the most important tool in fighting depredations against protected birds.

One warden who had his hands full was Ray Holland, who had the challenging task of patrolling Missouri and several of the neighboring states by himself. Holland dedicated his life to working for game conservation, and in later years he served as the editor of *Field and Stream.* Along the lines of bad drama, Missouri's attorney general, Frank McAllister, was Holland's archnemesis. McAllister's motives seemed to be a combination of concern about the expanding role of the federal government and a belief in a God-given right to hunt ducks whenever they wandered into his sights. Holland was equally committed to ending the destructive practice of spring shooting, and he no doubt believed that only the federal government could provide the necessary protection. Despite their mutual interest in hunting, the two men had no grounds for compromise.

In March 1919, the feud between McAllister and Holland came to a head. The warden heard rumors that McAllister was actively encouraging friends to violate the law, especially the ban on spring shooting. The attorney general and four friends were duck hunting at a club near Nevada, Missouri, when, acting on a tip, Holland arrested them for hunting out of season. According to one conservationist, McAllister gave a false name when caught with the bag of seventy-six ducks.[60] Given Holland's evidence, the local magistrate had no choice but to convict the attorney general and fine him an undisclosed amount. When the federal district court upheld the conviction, McAllister struck back. He arranged to have Senator Reed's law partner defend those whom Holland arrested, and, at the same time, he tried to get a restraining order to stop the warden from enforcing the law. This last effort put the Migratory Bird Treaty Act on a path for review by the Supreme Court.

On 2 March 1920, McAllister and United States Solicitor General Alexander C. King argued the case *Missouri v. Holland* before the U.S. Supreme Court. The Missourian began by asserting that the MBTA was unconstitutional. English common law had given power over wild game to the several colonies, he argued, and those governments would not have ratified the Constitution if the "long arm of the federal government could reach into the states and take food from the tables of their people." In addition, the *Geer* decision had demonstrated that the Supreme Court believed that wild animals were the responsibility of the state.[61]

McAllister then shifted slightly to the argument that a treaty cannot be "the law of the land" if it violates the Constitution. Because the treaty required the government to do an unconstitutional thing, he continued, Congress was not bound to pass the appropriate enabling legislation. If the court did not heed his warning, then the "Tenth Amendment . . . is a delusion . . . and our government a very different government from that presupposed and intended by the people who ratified the Constitution." In closing, he claimed that the Migratory Bird Treaty opened the way for many potential horrors, including the possibility that the president and the Senate could conspire to give away whole states or pieces of the federal government to foreign powers.[62]

For his part, King took a conservative approach. He suggested that the treaty fell under the federal power to regulate both its property and interstate commerce, although he did not pursue that line of reasoning. Instead, he focused on the federal monopoly of the treaty power. The framers of the Constitution had given the federal government the states' treaty power, and they had not intended to give the federal government less treaty-making power than any other sovereign state had. The Tenth Amendment, King argued, did not apply because the framers had already explicitly given the federal government treaty authority in Article 6. In conclusion, King said that "the peculiar nature of its property in wild game, which is in one country during a part of the year and in another during the remainder of the year, makes it impossible for the laws of one State or one country to give ample protection." [63] King's argument revealed the conservationists' major weakness: they had not been able to develop a strong line of legal reasoning to support the treaty. More than anything, they had to hope that the court did not see the case as a states' rights issue.

In writing for the seven-member majority, Justice Oliver Wendell Holmes demonstrated that he had assimilated the conservationist position on behalf of bird protection, even if he did not think much of either King's or McAllister's arguments. Holmes believed that at times the federal government had to respond to a crisis by taking some extraordinary action. "The only question," in such a case, "is whether it is forbidden by some invisible radiation from the general terms of the Tenth Amendment." In search of such an emission, Holmes chose to examine the heart of Missouri's argument: that it owned wild game. Noting that migrants can easily traverse one thousand miles in a week, he opined, "To put the claim of the State upon title is to lean upon a slender reed. Wild birds are not in the possession of anyone; and possession is the beginning of ownership."

Holmes then went beyond the legal debate in order to establish that this was a case in which the federal government had to take extraordinary action. "Here a national interest of very nearly the first magnitude is involved," he wrote. The only way to protect that interest was through national action and cooperation with the other nations that hosted the birds. Otherwise, extinction might be imminent, and the harm would be immense:

> But for the treaty and the statute there soon might be no birds for any powers to deal with. We see nothing in the Constitution that compels the Government to sit by while a food supply is cut off and the protectors of our forests and our crops are destroyed. [64]

The conservationists' massive investment in educating the general public and leading citizens about the need for bird protection had paid off at a critical time.

The victory at the Supreme Court assured that the Migratory Bird Treaty and the whole concept of federal bird protection in the United States would be safe permanently. Holmes's opinion had not only defended the constitutionality of the treaty, but it had also emphasized the necessity for national action and international cooperation to solve this new kind of problem. In succeeding years, conservationists would build upon the foundation of the treaty and the enabling legislation to broaden bird protection.

CONCLUSION

The creators of the Migratory Bird Treaty had every right to be proud. Between 1883 and 1920 they had won numerous political victories, turned around the general American attitude toward birds, and halted the decline of bird life in North America. They had beaten strong opponents in Congress and in the millinery trade, and then they had successfully manipulated the federal government into accepting their agenda. When they found their course blocked — whether by obstinate state governments, William Howard Taft, or the standards of states' rights — they always found a new path. In short, they would not be denied the uniform regulations that they knew were necessary to save birds.

Their victory was the result of a steadily evolving strategy that took them from the simple goal of organization in the 1880s to the complex goal of international cooperation by 1913. Bird lovers began with the fear that the objects of their affection were not long for this world, as various economic forces exploited birds for their cash value rather than their aesthetic appeal. With nothing but sentiment, which was always first in the hearts of their leaders, from T. Gilbert Pearson to William T. Hornaday, they built organizations and tried to convert people to the cause of bird protection. Those who came to the cause from the ranks of the hunters had their own brand of sentiment, in which game birds were a connection to a gentlemanly way of life. At times, these bird lovers clashed, although they could always agree on the common enemy, the ruthless hunter.

But conservationists quickly discovered that sentiment alone could not bring them the protection they sought. They had to overcome the economic interests that were destroying birds and the concerns about jurisdiction that often served as an excuse for inertia. Fortunately, ornithologists had been accumulating evidence that helped when the debate moved to rational economics and politics. Their studies of migration reinforced the idea that protective regulations had to be uniform among the states to be effective, and their examination of what it meant to eat like a bird provided data that birds ate insects that destroyed agriculture. In the Progressive era, hard science counted for a lot, and this evidence helped bird lovers overcome their opponents in the struggle for national bird protection laws.

Unfortunately, as the bird protectors found themselves fighting on the national stage they tended to turn away from the sentiment that had first fueled their movement. Instead, they relied more and more on rational economic arguments that they thought would give them more credibility. This very utilitarian approach certainly worked, but it did lead to the sacrifice of some species. If the value of birds depended on their usefulness, then certainly some species would earn the tag useless, or even harmful. Thus the treaty left off many seed-eaters, such as sparrows, that did not have reputations as insectivores, and it ignored all birds of prey on the theory popular among conservationists that raptors ate useful birds and were therefore harmful.

But it would be unfair to dwell on the shortcomings of a group of far-sighted leaders who had to blaze a new trail in their search for adequate protection for their beloved birds, for sentiment alone could not have given them such success. They began with the reasonable belief that the state governments held the answer. When that proved to be untrue, they did not fold, but instead they maneuvered the federal government into a job that it definitely did not want. When that chance of victory began to melt into defeat, they pushed on into the realm of international relations, where conservation had not done especially well in the past. Yet they persevered and used their scientific knowledge, economic calculations, and a convenient appeal to patriotism to extract a remarkably useful treaty that still forms the basis of much bird protection action in the United States.

The Migratory Bird Treaty of 1916 became the first broadly effective wildlife conservation treaty. It protected hundreds of species of birds throughout two of the largest countries on earth, and it established a crucial precedent for both national and international efforts to save the environment. For the first time, the United States federal government held responsibility for a nationwide environmental problem. Unlike the fisheries treaty, the bird treaty actually worked; unlike the seal treaty, there was no strong whiff of direct pecuniary advantage to spoil the altruistic atmosphere. The treaty was not perfect, but its framers succeeded in addressing the problems of the time without alienating powerful political and economic forces.

Implications of
the Progressive Treaties

In July of 1995, while driving to Mount Rainier to search for the dipper, a nonmigratory bird of western mountain streams, I scanned across the radio spectrum just in time to hear Paul Harvey criticize the Migratory Bird Treaty Act of 1918. Law-abiding citizens, he complained, could be subject to arrest simply for picking up an eagle feather from the ground; this law was simply another example of the grasping power of the federal government in the lives of good citizens. I was surprised. What were the odds of catching that one broadcast? Had a national debate broken out over migratory bird protection? And why would anybody want to attack such an innocuous law? But mainly I was pleased: if Paul Harvey was trying to kill the Migratory Bird Treaty, then it must still be alive.

Indeed the treaty lives on in the enforcement sense. Occasionally the newspapers will carry stories about hunters prosecuted for shooting out of season or killing federally protected species. In addition, the courts have expanded the law's aegis so that polluters and despoilers of wildlife refuges can be legally responsible for damage. In the spring of 1989, the Fish and Wildlife Service used the law in a rather unusual way. A mallard hen had built her nest on the plaza of a Chicago office building, causing much media consternation about the fate of the impending hatchlings. When a concerned citizen offered to collect the ducklings and mother and release them on a pond north of the city, the FWS intervened, citing the Migratory Bird Treaty Act of 1918. In this modern version of *Make Way for Ducklings,* government biologists took the ducks and released them on a different pond north of the city.

But just as important, these Progressive-era agreements live on as precedents. They serve as building blocks in content and in spirit. As big and complex as modern environmental treaties get, they still go back to John

Foster's insight in 1892 that the United States and Canada had to cooperate in conserving the fisheries or face economic, diplomatic, and environmental ramifications. The aura of cooperation and the mixture of science and sentiment that marked the high points of Progressive conservation diplomacy also form the basis for successful modern environmental diplomacy.

A list of modern environmental challenges would not be at all strange to Jordan, Hornaday, Burnham, or Pearson. Natural diversity, which humans value for economic and aesthetic reasons, is vanishing under the onslaught of commercial development. Governments can do some things on their own, but many problems defy political boundaries, and few rush to sacrifice their interests for the future collective good. Science holds some answers, but its influence depends on grass-roots support. Such public support often has more to do with visceral appeal than with reason or logic. Some countries have a basis for cooperation with each other, and some do not. In short, some problems are easy to solve, some take extra leadership, and some must wait for the future.

One could dismiss these early treaties as unimaginative or even narrow-minded approaches to relatively simple problems, but I prefer to think of them as creative and instructive solutions to previously unimagined problems. In a time when states often failed at the most basic conservation tasks and the federal government's interest was erratic, conservationists saw an opportunity and seized it. They could have surrendered or they could have been stubborn, but instead they took advantage of the Anglo-American rapprochement to put their issues on the diplomatic agenda. Then they used science, economics, and their own love of nature to advance their cause. The essentially conservative American conservationists went so far as to challenge accepted constitutional limits on federal power.

These treaties, then, were the product of the intersection of quantifiable evidence in the form of science and economics, cultural ideas about science and nature, and shifts in the diplomatic landscape. Between the 1880s and 1920, conservationists and scientists exercised an unprecedented amount of influence in American and Canadian society. They expanded national power over migratory wildlife and other natural resources through domestic political agitation. When they reached the limits of domestic action, they found that the diplomatic climate lent itself to U.S.-Canadian cooperation, leading to the Inland Fisheries Treaty, the North Pacific Fur Seal Convention, and the Migratory Bird Treaty. In the long run, the treaties provided excellent examples of the need for and methods of cooperation among diplomats, scientists, and conservationists. But they also showed that economic pressures and public apathy could derail the most practical plans.

The Inland Fisheries Treaty failed because fisheries conservation had few friends and many enemies. Fishermen, especially in the United States, struggled against almost every regulation suggested to them, because they had difficulty seeing any economic benefit to such rules. These fishermen and the packers that worked with them were the only people to pressure the government intensely. Neither preservationists nor utilitarians saw fisheries conservation as their fight. A few scientists and diplomats put up a struggle, even though they themselves did not agree on their goals, but in the end they simply had too little influence.

The border fisheries have not fared well since then. The whitefish, trout, herring, and sturgeon of the Great Lakes have given way to lamprey, carp, alewives, and smelt, as well as salmon introduced for anglers. There is little in the way of commercial fishing on the lakes anymore. The successful completion of the Inland Fisheries Treaty probably could not have altered the patterns of pollution and habitat destruction that have done so much to destroy the lake fisheries, but it might have halted the overfishing that made the native species so vulnerable to other threats. The sockeye in the Fraser River have rebounded surprisingly well, enough to sustain both an industry and bitter fights among governments and fishermen in the region. Since the formation of the International Pacific Salmon Fisheries Commission in 1937, Canada and the United States have managed to work together in the hope of promoting sustainable use of salmon throughout the Pacific Northwest, from Alaska through Washington.[1] The signing of the Pacific Salmon Treaty of 1985 reinforced this notion.

Events in 1997, however, proved that the nature of salmon diplomacy had not changed much since 1908. In May, after three years of fruitless efforts to extend and modify the Pacific Salmon Treaty, Canadian and American diplomats broke off talks. Each side accused the other of taking too many fish, although in reality a number of intranational issues, such as the rivalry between Canadian gill-netters and Canadian trollers, had been the source of some of the trouble. For three days in July, focusing all of their anger at Americans, especially Alaskans, a few hundred Canadian fishermen used their boats to prevent a ferry from completing its run from Washington to Alaska. Some of the protestors even burned an American flag, a sure way to draw attention and provoke a response. Underlying the stress was a very real fear that just a few years of alleged American rapaciousness would be sufficient to deplete the remaining salmon runs. Jordan and Prince would have recognized the fear, and they probably would have sympathized with it.

The North Pacific Fur Seal Convention worked because seal conservation became popular, necessary, and fiscally prudent. After years of trying to intimidate each other into surrendering, the United States and Canada finally made real progress when they each admitted the strengths of the other's case. Both sides feared setting dangerous precedents, but they eventually set aside their diplomatic shields to concentrate on the implications of fur seal extinction. In the end, they did set precedents for conservation of other mammals, such as whales, polar bears, and other seals. Some of the derivative treaties worked better than others, but they all grew out of the same principle, that these wide-ranging international mammals needed a scheme that spread the costs and benefits of protection. And of course some garnered popular support easily.

The seal convention remained in effect until 1941, when the Japanese government withdrew, citing the damage that the seals did to salmon fishing. By then the seals had returned to something close to their probable carrying capacity of 2,500,000. After the Second World War, the United States, Canada, and Japan renewed the sealing regulations under the control of scientists. For political reasons, they did not allow the USSR into the consortium. In the 1950s, the decline began again, until the herd stabilized around 800,000. Although scientists were not certain, they believed that seals were suffering from both pollution and a decline in their food base brought on by overfishing. The principles of the 1911 treaty had been effective for almost fifty years, but they were insufficient to protect the seals from problems other than overharvesting. The seal hunt ended in 1984 under pressure against the fur industry.

The Migratory Bird Treaty combined all of the necessary elements for successful conservation diplomacy. Its success in saving birds and providing a basis for future action is still impressive. Unlike the other two, it is still in force, and environmentalists and government agencies still use the enabling legislation as the basis for action, as Paul Harvey well knows. Internationally, conservationists used the MBT as the starting point for the 1936 Migratory Bird Treaty with Mexico, the 1940 agreement with Latin American states on nature protection, a 1971 world convention on wetlands protection, and migratory bird treaties in the 1970s with Japan and the USSR. Conservationists had reason to crow.

Although the treaty was the most successful of the three, like the seal convention it did not provide the blanket protection that conservationists sought. The decline of hunting pressures coincided with a rising tide of habitat destruction in both temperate and tropical America. Extinctions continued, most notably the ivory-billed woodpecker, pushed over the edge by unscrupulous trophy hunters and destruction of southern swamp-forests. The bird treaty could not prevent people from draining and polluting wetlands, so that by the 1980s biologists saw "our last chance" to maintain many species of waterfowl.[2] Likewise, the treaty could not stop the destruction of tropical forests, where many of our most colorful birds spend the winter, or the fragmentation of temperate forests, which opens some species to increased predation, contributing to a crash in some songbird populations.

The success or failure of these treaties, then, came down to the interaction of science, sentiment, and economics, which in turn all affected politics and diplomacy. Bird protection had scientific support, economic viability, deep public sympathy, and diplomatic acquiescence. The seal treaty had less public sympathy but more diplomatic support, in addition to strong economic and scientific justification. Both succeeded. The fisheries treaty had no public support, diplomatic indifference, and economic enemies. Jordan almost pushed it through, but he failed in the end.

For three basic reasons, the flurry of conservation agreements in the Progressive era did not develop into a new trend in international relations. First, as did the whole Progressive movement, conservationism lost steam in the 1920s, and the diminution of conservationists' prestige certainly undermined their ability to influence diplomacy. Second, American conservationists, perhaps reflecting the mood of the country, turned inward to deal with purely domestic problems, such as game refuges. Third, conservationists and scientists had tackled the easiest issues, and nothing on the horizon had the same prospects as the sealing or migratory bird agreements. There were a few such agreements in the succeeding decades, but the next wave of environmental protection treaties had to wait until the 1970s, when the growing strength of the environmentalist movement made them possible.

In the 1990s a second and larger wave of environmental diplomacy is rising. In so many ways, the world in general and conservationists in particular have changed, even if diplomats have not. Where great powers once dominated international relations, decolonization has led to the creation of scores of weak, nonindustrial states, which often hold the keys to particular environmental issues. Even though military and economic might still prevail, the world now swarms with international organizations that facilitate cooperation, from the United Nations to the Organization of American States. Nongovernmental organizations follow in Audubon's footsteps, but there are many more and they are often multinational. Habitat destruction and pollution take a greater toll, while hunters take less. Conservation of natural resources for utilitarian purposes has given way to modern environmentalism and its emphasis on aesthetics. More than ever, the public perceives a need for stringent environmental protection. When added together, these ingredients encourage huge multilateral conferences, such as the Stockholm meeting in 1972 and the Earth Summit in Rio in 1992, where delegates tackle global issues far removed from the negotiation of the Migratory Bird Treaty. Despite the changed conditions, these Progressive era wildlife treaties hold lessons for today.[3]

First, in order to create a successful environmental protection treaty, diplomats, scientists, and environmentalists must combine their specific skills. Diplomats obviously bring indispensable experience to the formulation of such a treaty, even if they do not necessarily see its importance. American diplomats contributed nearly as much to the Migratory Bird Treaty, which they felt was a bit extravagant, as they did to the North Pacific Fur Seal Convention, which they worked on frantically for twenty-five years. Likewise, scientists must provide the basic knowledge for diplomats to work with if the treaties are to be effective. Each of the Progressive era treaties depended on scientific evidence of decline and scientific expertise to craft a solution. Finally, environmentalists play a crucial role in generating public support for environmental protection treaties. In the United States, all treaties must garner a two-thirds vote of consent in the Senate and have appropriate enabling legislation; public opinion is crucial in determining the outcome of such votes.

Second, the public reaction towards environmental problems depends more on visceral appeal than rational analysis. The fur seal was peripherally important to the American economy and only one part of the North Pacific ecosystem. The food fish along the border fed millions of people and represented an important part of the North American freshwater ecosystem. But, for a myriad of reasons, people like seals more than fish. The pattern repeated itself in the 1970s. Americans and Canadians protested vigorously against the clubbing of baby harp seals by a few hardened souls living in Canada's maritime provinces. Meanwhile, a few hundred miles south, American and Canadian fishermen faced no opposition to continuing their relentless assault on the once grand fishing banks off Newfoundland and

New England. Most people agreed that killing baby seals was cruel, but few cared that fishermen were killing their industry, an important source of food, and many species of wild animals.

As John Burnham suggested, the public's reliance on a sentimental compass is a mixed blessing. On one hand, it is the aesthetic impulse that usually provides the muscle for political victories; 300,000 bird lovers joined the NAAS, not the more scholarly American Ornithologists' Union or American Fisheries Society. Salmon and sturgeon certainly would have been better off had Jordan been able to create some emotional call for their protection. But on the other hand, a reliance on sentiment can undermine a rational, scientific approach. Scientific evidence is never perfect, but it does give a quantifiable way of assessing what should be important, both for humans and the planet. Environmental diplomacy works best when it is based on both sentiment and science.

Third, environmental protection treaties are almost unattainable unless the negotiating countries trust each other and have a mutual interest in conservation. Resource control has long been a domestic policy matter, even with resources that cross international borders. Despite the increase in modern environmental awareness, nations have a hard time surrendering their authority over traditional domestic issues. Governments are, of course, zealous in the defense of their sovereignty; they do not lightly yield control over domestic policy to a foreign government, even in the form of a joint commission. Only when all governments have an unusual level of trust and agree that cooperation is in their interest will they relinquish some sovereignty.

Despite the problems that Canada and the United States had with each other at the turn of the century, their common cultural, political, and economic background built the necessary trust. Many Canadians were suspicious of American motives regarding reciprocity and the Alaska boundary dispute, and many Americans distrusted the British empire, but they could not deny the great similarities in Canadian and American society. American and Canadian statesmen recognized that those basic similarities made conflict impossible. In short, shared U.S.-Canadian interests removed a number of potential headaches that exist in almost every other bilateral relationship.

That trust, however, has not been common in international relations, in part because of a lack of mutual interests. The proposal to negotiate a bird protection treaty with Mexico in 1913 failed because of the great gap between the two societies. Not only did the two governments distrust each other, but there was almost no common ground for cooperation. There was no Mexican conservation movement, and not much of a scientific community, with which Americans could work. At the same time, though, Mexicans were not damaging habitat or shooting birds in the same way that Americans were. The problems in the U.S.-Mexican relationship were a harbinger of the challenges of coordinating the environmental interests of industrialized and developing nations after decolonization. Relatively speaking, hammering out a conservation treaty between Canada and the United States was an easy task.

Fourth, the Progressive era treaties suggested that bilateral agreements are easier to attain than multilateral conventions, although they are rarely as effective. The presence of Japan and Russia in the fur seal controversy complicated Canadian-American efforts to resolve their differences. The incompatibility of the nations' opening positions nearly derailed the negotiations, but in the end a strong treaty emerged because all four of the sealing countries worked together. Similarly, the cause of migratory bird protection in the 1910s would have been strengthened if the United States and Canada had been able to cooperate with Latin American countries to ensure the protection of migrants that wintered south of the Rio Grande. It was far easier, though, to settle for the Canadian-American agreement.

Most of today's big problems, such as deforestation, oceanic resource depletion, pollution of the atmosphere, and destruction of diversity, demand multilateral negotiations, which can seem hopelessly cumbersome. As more countries get involved, diplomats and conservationists have a harder time overriding their traditional and understandable distrust of each other in a timely manner. The Earth Summit of 1992 in Rio de Janeiro demonstrated the great difficulty of modern environmental diplomacy, when each nation or bloc has an agenda. Often, these agendas are at cross-purposes, and the situation has to become desperate before someone will begin to compromise. Unfortunately, by then it may be too late to rectify the situation.

Finally, and most important, a successful natural resource treaty must achieve a positive ratio of environmental protection to economic restrictions in all countries involved. Most governments are willing to accept some economic restraints in order to protect the environment, especially if the quantifiable benefits outweigh the costs. Few governments are willing to help other nations' economies in the process. A good treaty, then, equalizes the costs and benefits for each nation. It may be easier for nations to balance those factors if, as with Canada and the United States, they have similar economic bases.

The two successful treaties had such ratios. The Migratory Bird Treaty best fit this requirement because it did not place much of a cost on either nation, but it provided clear benefits. Professional bird hunters did not supply a pressing need, so driving them out of business was not much of a sacrifice. And conservationists and scientists could provide both economic and aesthetic justification for protecting birds. The sealing convention achieved a good cost/benefit ratio for each country after years of negotiations. By combining the banning of pelagic sealing with a system of dividing the pelts, the negotiators devised a system that rewarded all parties. Thus, there were no strong economic arguments made against either treaty. In contrast, the Inland Fisheries Treaty had financial costs for fishermen in each country, but the benefits were not obvious to most observers. In addition, American fishermen perceived that they would bear the brunt of the crackdown. Despite the reality that they were in fact responsible for the worst excesses, American fishermen were not willing to accept even the appearance of imbalance.

The search for a balanced cost/benefit ratio can be a problem if, as with the fisheries, one country is clearly violating the rights of another. In such a case, the aggrieved nation is left to appeal to morality or surrender on some other issue — neither of which is a palatable choice. The clearest example may be the ongoing search for a solution to the acid rain problem. In the East, wind currents push American air pollution into Canada, where it comes down as acid rain, but Canadian air pollution rarely comes to the United States. Canada appeals regularly to its neighbor to do more to curb acid rain, and the United States has responded, albeit slowly, only because of the close Canadian-American relationship. Any agreement to curb acid rain will cost the United States and benefit Canada, which has no doubt encouraged the Americans to drag their feet.

Modern environmentalists, as they tackle complex international controversies, would do well to study the actions of their Progressive-era forebears. Foster, Root, Jordan, Hornaday, Burnham, Pearson, and others deserve praise for pushing conservation beyond national borders and for expanding the boundaries of diplomacy. They recognized that wildlife was more than just the property of any one government, that it was an immeasurable asset for the planet. In their efforts to save these invaluable resources, they blended together science, sentiment, economics, and diplomacy, although not always in equal measures. At times they failed, as any pioneers will. But on balance, their record stands as one to be praised and emulated.

Notes

1. In 1902, several European states tentatively agreed to protect songbirds, but they never finalized or enforced the agreement. For an excellent account of the issues that confront recent environmental protection diplomacy, see Richard Benedick, *Ozone Diplomacy: New Directions in Safeguarding the Planet* (Cambridge, Mass., 1991); other important books include Sherman Hayden, *The International Protection of Wildlife* (New York, 1942); John E. Carroll, *Environmental Diplomacy: An Examination and a Prospective of Canadian-U.S. Transboundary Environmental Relations* (Ann Arbor, Mich., 1983), which explicitly avoids wildlife issues; Lynton Keith Caldwell, *International Environmental Policy: Emergence and Dimensions* (Durham, N.C., 1984), which focuses primarily on the 1970s and 1980s; Peter H. Sand, ed., *The Effectiveness of International Environmental Agreements: A Survey of Existing Legal Instruments* (Cambridge, Eng., 1992); and Simon Lyster, *International Wildlife Law: An Analysis of International Treaties Concerned with the Conservation of Wildlife* (Cambridge, Eng., 1985).

2. Theodore Roosevelt to Governor General Lord Earl Grey, 24 December 1908, File 342, Vol. 224, Records of the Governor General's Office, Record Group 7 G21, National Archives of Canada, Ottawa. At this time, most conservationists included wild animals as a resource.

3. Two good sources on this period are Paul Kennedy, *The Rise and Fall of the Great Powers* (New York, 1987), chapter 5; and Eric Hobsbawm, *The Age of Empire, 1875–1914* (New York, 1989).

4. Howard Beale, *Theodore Roosevelt and the Rise of America to World Power* (Baltimore, 1956), 83; two good sources on Anglo-American relations are Bradford Perkins, *The Great Rapprochement: England and the United States, 1895–1914* (New York, 1968), and Charles S. Campbell, Jr., *Anglo-American Understanding, 1898–1903* (Baltimore, Md., 1957).

5. One exception to this trend was the Webster-Ashburton Treaty of 1842, which resolved border disputes in the eastern half of North America. For personal reasons, both negotiators desired to reach a quick compromise, and they put aside national differences; see Walter LaFeber, *The American Age: United States Foreign Policy at Home and Abroad since 1750* (New York, 1989), 106–107.

6. John Hilliker, *Canada's Department of External Affairs*, Vol. 1: *The Early Years, 1909–1946* (Montreal, 1990), 27–42.

7. Oscar Skelton, ed., *The Life and Letters of Sir Wilfrid Laurier* (New York, 1922), 2:50; Hilliker, 32.

8. For a hair-raising account of one prospector's trek, see Maitland DeSormo, *John Bird Burnham: Klondiker, Adirondacker, and Eminent Conservationist* (Saranac Lake, N.Y., 1978). Despite showing incredible fortitude and business sense, Burnham returned from the Klondike with only $700. He later was one of the leading fighters for the Migratory Bird Treaty.

9. The two best sources on the dispute are Charles Tansill, *Canadian-American Relations, 1875–1911* (New Haven, 1943), and Norman Penlington, *The Alaska Boundary Dispute: A Critical Reappraisal* (Toronto, 1972).

10. Skelton, 2:56–58; Joseph Pope, *Public Servant* (Toronto, 1960), 118; Samuel Flagg Bemis, *A Diplomatic History of the United States* (New York, 1955), 425.

11. Tansill, 224–35.

12. Ibid., 230; Penlington, 91–102.

13. See, for instance, Robert Falconer, *The United States as a Neighbor, from a Canadian Point of View* (New York, 1926), 155. For an alternative view of American aspirations, see Robert E. Hannigan, "Reciprocity 1911: Continentalism and American Weltpolitik," *Diplomatic History*, Vol. 4, No. 1 (1980), 1–18. Hannigan argues that the reciprocity offer was the opening shot in a renewed campaign to take away Canada's freedom of action.

14. Cited in Penlington, 112.

15. Lord Grey to Sir James Bryce, 23 February 1910, Series F-4, Vol. 1002, Records of the Department of External Affairs, Record Group 25, National Archives of Canada.

16. Penlington, 103–104; Hilliker, 26.

17. Grey, quoted in Hilliker, 25–33.

18. Peter Neary, "Grey, Bryce, and the Settlement of Canadian-American Differences, 1905–1911," *Canadian Historical Review*, Vol. 49, No. 4 (1968), 357–80.

19. The only historical study of the IJC is Chirakaikaran J. Chacko, *The International Joint Commission* (1932; rpt., New York, 1968).

20. The most thorough study of the fishery is Harold Innis, *The Cod Fisheries: The History of an International Economy* (New Haven, 1940); Tansill, 117–20.

21. L. Ethan Ellis, *Reciprocity 1911: A Study in Canadian-American Relations* (New Haven, 1939), is still the standard book on the subject, but Hannigan has a much different view.

22. Samuel Moffett, *The Americanization of Canada* (New York, 1907), 61–63, 88, 96, 103, 114.

23. The starting point for any study of the priorities of Progressive era conservationism is Samuel Hays's *Conservation and the Gospel of Efficiency* (Cambridge,

Mass., 1959). Other important books on the conservation movement are Stephen Fox, *John Muir and His Legacy* (Boston, 1981); (on Canadian issues) Janet Foster, *Working for Wildlife* (Toronto, 1978); Roderick Nash, *Wilderness and the American Mind*, 3d. ed. (New Haven, Conn., 1982); Thomas Dunlap, *Saving America's Wildlife* (Princeton, N.J., 1988); Lisa Mighetto, *Wild Animals and American Environmental Ethics* (Tucson, 1991); and John Reiger, *American Sportsmen and the Origins of Conservation* (New York, 1975).

24. Robert Underwood Johnson, "The Neglect of Beauty in the Conservation Movement," *Century*, Vol. 79 (1910), cited in Roderick Nash, ed., *American Environmentalism: Readings in Conservation History*, 3d ed. (New York, 1990), 90–91; Paul Schullery, ed., *Theodore Roosevelt: Wilderness Writings* (Salt Lake City, 1986), 16.

25. The best source on Roosevelt's evolution as a conservationist is Paul Cutright, *Theodore Roosevelt: The Making of a Conservationist* (Urbana, Ill., 1985).

26. Burnham to George Grinnell, 28 January 1919, Series 2, Folder 61, George Bird Grinnell Papers, Manuscripts and Archives, Yale University Library, New Haven, Conn.

27. Aldo Leopold, "Wildlife in American Culture," in James A. Bailey, ed., *Readings in Wildlife Conservation* (Washington, 1974), 3.

28. Arthur McEvoy, *The Fisherman's Problem: Ecology and Law in the California Fisheries, 1850–1980* (New York, 1986), 9–10.

29. *California Fish and Game*, Vol. 1, No. 2 (1915), 67.

30. For more on the passenger pigeon, see A. W. Schorger, *The Passenger Pigeon: Its Natural History and Extinction* (Norman, Okla., 1973); see also T. R. Halliday, "The Extermination of the Passenger Pigeon *Ectopistes migratorius* and Its Relevance to Contemporary Conservation," *Biological Conservation*, Vol. 17, No. 2 (February 1980), 157–61. More on the demise of the bison can be found in Dan Flores, "Bison Ecology and Bison Diplomacy: The Southern Plains from 1800 to 1850," *Journal of American History*, Vol. 78, No. 2 (1980), 465–85; and Andrew C. Isenberg, "Indians, Whites, and the Buffalo: An Ecological History of the Great Plains, 1750–1900," Ph.D. diss., Northwestern University, 1992.

31. John Burnham, undated speech, "False Prophets," Box 37, Speeches File, John Burnham Papers, American Heritage Center, University of Wyoming, Laramie.

32. There were exceptions to these trends. For instance, the demand for those species used for fashion — such as furs or birds — often depended on the whims of the industry. Also, there were cases when hunters did pursue extermination of species, usually predators.

33. Hays, 3.

34. Bean, 20–22; also see Jenks Cameron, *The Bureau of Biological Survey: Its History, Activities and Organization* (Baltimore, 1929), 70–83.

35. John Burnham, undated speech, probably 1913, to the National Game Conference, Box 37, Speeches File, Burnham Papers.

36. David Starr Jordan to G. O. Shields, 3 February 1909, Box 53, Folder 1909, January–February, William T. Hornaday Papers, Library of Congress, Washington, D.C.

1 / A PROBLEM OF SCALE

1. Richard Rathbun and William Wakeham, "Report of the Joint Commission Relative to the Preservation of the Fisheries in Waters Contiguous to Canada and the United States," 54th Cong., 2d sess., House Document 315, pp. 16–24, 36–37.

2. "Report of the Joint Commission," 40–43.

3. Phil Weller, *Fresh Water Seas: Saving the Great Lakes* (Toronto, 1990), 21–26, 47.

4. Henry Schoolcraft, quoted in Harlan Hatcher, *The Great Lakes* (London, 1944), 285.

5. "Report of the Joint Commission," 147, 154.

6. Ibid., 147.

7. William Ashworth, *The Late, Great Lakes: An Environmental History* (New York, 1986), 4. Before fishermen found a market for sturgeon, they would pile them on shore and burn them.

8. Weller, 50; "Report of the Joint Commission," 105.

9. "Report of the Joint Commission," 49–50.

10. Ibid., 99.

11. "Report of the Joint Commission," 63–65; Weller, 21; David Starr Jordan, *The Days of a Man* (Yonkers-on-Hudson, N.Y., 1922), 2:260.

12. "Report of the Joint Commission," 64, 71–73.

13. Ibid., 117–20, 133, 138–39.

14. Ibid., 146; Jordan, 2:260; Weller, 19–20.

15. "Report of the Joint Commission," 158.

16. Ibid., 156–60.

17. David Starr Jordan and Edwin C. Starks, *The Fishes of Puget Sound* (Palo Alto, 1895), 791–92; Diane Newell, *The Development of the Pacific Salmon-Canning Industry: A Grown Man's Game* (Montreal, 1989), 7. For a description of "the greater Puget Sound region," see Eugene Kozloff, *Seashore Life of the Northern Pacific Coast* (Seattle, 1983), 5.

18. "Report of the Joint Commission," 165–67, 174.

19. Grace Lee Nute, *Lake Superior* (Indianapolis, 1945), 172–73; Harlan Hatcher, *Lake Erie* (Indianapolis, 1945), 280.

20. Hatcher, *The Great Lakes,* 283, 287; Ashworth, 116.

21. Seines are the most basic fishing nets, acting basically as large scoops. Fishermen throw them into the water and then haul in the ends to trap anything caught in between. They are only useful when fishermen can actually see the schools that they want to catch, and there is no value to leaving them in the water.

22. Ashworth, 116; Hatcher, *Lake Erie,* 281.

23. Fred Landon, *Lake Huron* (Indianapolis, 1944), 133–34.

24. Nute, 173–79; Margaret Beattie Bogue and Virginia A. Palmer, *Around the Shores of Lake Superior: A Guide to Historic Sites* (Madison, Wis., 1979), 150.

25. Richard White, *Land Use, Environment, and Social Change: The Shaping of Island County, Washington* (Seattle, 1980), 15; Mary Avery, *Washington: A History of the Evergreen State* (Seattle, 1961), 32, 41–43.

26. Frederick Merck, ed., *Fur Trade and Empire: George Simpson's Journal* (Cambridge, Mass., 1931), 121.

27. "Report of the Joint Commission," 16–24.

28. Ibid., 28–32.

29. For instance, Landon described Lake Huron as "teeming with fish," which it most certainly was not (p. 133).

30. W. Harry Everhart and William D. Youngs, *Principles of Fishery Science,* 2d ed. (Ithaca, 1981), 43–45.

31. "Report of the Joint Commission," 88–92; Nute, 180.

32. Weller, 49; "Report of the Joint Commission," 88–89.

33. "Report of the Joint Commission," 88–89, 149.

34. Ibid., 82–84, 154–55.

35. Everhart and Youngs, 39–41.

36. Field notebook, April 1895, Lake of the Woods, Box 2, Richard Rathbun Papers, Record Group 3138, Cornell University Manuscripts and Archives, Ithaca, New York.

37. Professor E. E. Prince, "Report of the Commission Appointed by the Dominion Government to Investigate the Fisheries of Lake Erie and Adjacent Waters," 16 February 1909, David Starr Jordan Papers, microfilm edition, Stanford University Libraries, Stanford, California.

38. Hatcher, *Lake Erie,* 288–90; Ashworth, 117.

39. James A. Tober, *Who Owns the Wildlife? The Political Economy of Conservation in Nineteenth-Century America* (Westport, Conn., 1981), 59.

40. "Report of the Joint Commission," 159–60.

41. For a general history of the fishery, see John Roos, *Restoring Fraser River Salmon* (Vancouver, B.C., 1991). Newell, 12–24, 78–81.

42. Newell, 74–81; Daniel Jack Chasan, *The Water Link: A History of Puget Sound as a Resource* (Seattle, 1981), 41–43.

43. "Report of the Joint Commission," 169.

44. Ibid., 173.

45. Ibid., 169–170, 175; Newell, 88.

46. Everhart (p. 26) describes this phenomenon as one of the most basic perils of fishing. Weller (p. 49) also notes that yield held steady as fishermen switched species.

47. Secretary John Foster to Michael Herbert, 4 October 1892, United States, 54th

Cong., 2d sess., House Document 315 (hereafter, H. Doc. 315); the most recent study of Foster's diplomacy is Michael Devine, *John W. Foster: Politics and Diplomacy in the Imperial Era, 1873–1917* (Athens, Ohio, 1981).

48. Foster to Herbert, 4 October 1892, and Foster to Pauncefote, 6 December 1892, H. Doc. 315.

49. Richard Rathbun, "1892–1893, Investigation of Fisheries in Waters Contiguous to Canada and the United States," undated memorandum, Box 1, Rathbun Papers.

50. A good account of the origins and work of the commission on the Great Lakes is in Margaret Beattie Bogue, "To Save the Fish: Canada, the United States, the Great Lakes, and the Joint Commission of 1892," *Journal of American History*, Vol. 79, No. 4 (1993), 1429–54.

51. Rathbun, "1892–1893, Investigation of Fisheries."

52. Rathbun to Gresham, 22 December 1894, H. Doc. 315.

53. Richard Olney to President Grover Cleveland, 23 February 1897, H. Doc. 315.

54. "Report of the Joint Commission," 15.

55. Ibid., 65, 70, 106–107.

56. Ibid., 101–103.

57. Rathbun and Wakeham did not emphasize hatchery work because the mortality rate for fry was so high, but hatcheries were politically more popular than restricting fishermen's rights; ibid., 106–15.

58. Note that they failed to consider Canada and the United States as governments with jurisdiction, which would have pushed the total to seven.

59. "Report of the Joint Commission," 98.

60. Ibid., 15.

61. Ibid., 64, 71–73.

62. Hatcher, *Lake Erie*, 287; "Report of the Joint Commission," 113.

63. "Tanneries—Lake Huron," Box 1, Rathbun Papers.

64. For instance, the aptly named Mr. Gill, a fish dealer in Cheboygan, complained that the mesh of both pound and gill nets was one to two inches too small. Also, in 1892, Wisconsin fish dealers refused to take undersized whitefish from the seiners. "Regulate Mesh or Release Small Fish—Lake Huron," Box 1; Field Notebook, August, 1894, Box 2; and "Seines; Destruction of Small Fish—Lake Superior," Box 1, all in Rathbun Papers.

65. Field Notebook, Lake of the Woods, August 1894, and Field Notebook, April 1895, Box 1, Rathbun Papers.

66. Bogue, 1444–45.

67. "Report of the Joint Commission," 141.

68. Field Notebook, April 1895, Box 1, and Field Notebook, 1893, Box 2, Rathbun Papers.

69. Bogue, 1435, 1448–49.

70. "Regulate Mesh or Release Small Fish—Lake Huron," Box 1, Rathbun Papers.

71. "Close Season—Lake Huron," Box 1; Field Notebook, 1893, Box 2, Rathbun Papers.

72. "Report of the Joint Commission," 126, 147–48.

73. "Lake Superior—Canadian Side," Box 2, Rathbun Papers; "Report of the Joint Commission," 56, 61.

2 / THE JORDAN RULES

1. There is no single work dedicated to the Joint High Commission, despite its importance to U.S.-Canadian relations. This deficiency probably results from the general cloak of secrecy that existed at the time and the overall failure of the conference. The best source is still C. C. Tansill, *Canadian-American Relations, 1875–1911* (New Haven, Conn., 1943).

2. Samuel Flagg Bemis, *A Diplomatic History of the United States* (New York, 1955), 425; Joseph Pope, *Public Servant* (Toronto, 1960), 116. Pope, who would later serve as Canada's assistant secretary of state for external affairs, was responsible for Atlantic fisheries at the JHC meetings. He was quite upset that the large number of issues at hand distracted from the major points.

3. *New York Times,* 23 August 1898, and 27 September 1898.

4. Ibid., 23 and 24 November 1898. In this case, U.S. and Canadian naval officers conducted independent appraisals of the sealing fleet. Both sides' estimates were in the $500,000 range, far below expectations. Even so, they disagreed on whether or not to include vessels that were no longer in use for sealing because of the decline of the herd.

5. *New York Times,* 21 September 1898.

6. Charles Fairbanks to Laurier, 18 July 1901, in Oscar Skelton, ed., *The Life and Letters of Sir Wilfrid Laurier* (New York, 1922), 2:56.

7. J. Castell Hopkins, *The Canadian Annual Review of Public Affairs, 1906* (Toronto, 1906), 88–90. For the sockeye salmon it is always best to compare runs that correspond to the four-year life cycle; therefore, the size of the 1902 catch is the best comparison for 1906.

8. Petition from Southampton to Minister of Marine and Fisheries, 14 October 1905, File 1241, Pt. 1, Records of the Ministry of Marine and Fisheries, Record Group 23, National Archives of Canada, Ottawa (hereafter RG 23).

9. R. Prefontaine, Minister, to Southampton, 26 October 1905, File 1241, Pt. 1, RG 23.

10. Southampton citizens to John Tolmie, 11 October 1906; R. N. Venning, memorandum, 29 October 1906, File 1241, Pt. 2, RG 23.

11. S. F. Haserot et al. to the Cleveland Chamber of Commerce, 9 June 1910, File 711.428, General Records of the Department of State, Record Group 59, United States National Archives, Washington, D.C. (hereafter RG 59).

12. Ibid.

13. A. Kelly Evans was a very active utilitarian conservationist in Ontario. For an example of his work in promoting a comprehensive plan for the province, see "Ontario Game and Fisheries Commission, 1909–10: Interim Report," in the hunting journal *Rod and Gun in Canada,* Vol. 12, No. 3 (August 1910), 313–56.

14. W. E. Meehan, American Fisheries Society, to Lord Grey, 16 October 1907, File 3214, RG 23.

15. Richard Leopold, *Elihu Root and the Conservative Tradition* (Boston, 1954), is the standard biography of Root and account of his tenure as secretary of state.

16. Ibid., 55.

17. Elihu Root to Sir Mortimer Durand, 15 March 1906, Records of the Ministry of External Affairs, Series F-4, Vol. 1002, Record Group 25, National Archives of Canada, Ottawa (hereafter RG 25). Note that Root and his successors did settle the Newfoundland fishing question and establish the International Joint Commission for the boundary.

18. Durand to Sir Edward Grey, 19 March 1906, ibid.

19. David Starr Jordan, *The Days of a Man* (Yonkers-on-Hudson, N.Y., 1922), 2:258.

20. Jordan, 2:270. Anderson's replacement in the Taft administration, Henry Hoyt, disagreed with Anderson on this point, but he died in November 1909 on his way to Ottawa to discuss the treaty with Laurier. After Hoyt's death, Anderson resumed his former position.

21. Earl Grey to Durand, 23 April 1906, F-4, Vol. 1002, RG 25. Rainy River and Rainy River Lake flowed from Lake of the Woods.

22. Root to Durand, 6 June 1906, ibid.; and Chandler Anderson, undated memorandum (probably September 1907), File 8275, Microfilm M862, Roll 602, RG 59.

23. Root to Durand, 6 June 1906, F-4, Vol. 1002, RG 25.

24. Earl Grey to the Secretary of State for the Colonies, Lord Elgin, ibid.

25. Apparently, neither Anderson nor Root was too familiar with the Rathbun-Wakeham report, which clearly demonstrated the inadequacy of Georgian Bay regulations. Chandler Anderson, undated memorandum (probably September 1907), File 8275, Microfilm M862, Roll 602, RG 59.

26. James Bryce to Sir Edward Grey, 12 December 1907, F-4, Vol. 1002, RG 25.

27. Memorandum from Root to Bryce, February, 1908, ibid.

28. Earl Grey to Bryce, 5 March 1908, ibid.

29. Earl Grey to Durand, 23 April 1906, ibid.; Chandler Anderson, undated memorandum (probably September 1907), File 8275, RG 59.

30. Newspaper clippings in File 3328, Microfilm M862, Roll 311, RG 59.

31. Richard Rathbun and William Wakeham, "Report of the Joint Commission Relative to the Preservation of the Fisheries in Waters Contiguous to Canada and the United States," 54th Congress, 2d sess., House Document 315, p. 403.

32. Redfield Proctor to Root, 2 April 1907, and Root to Bryce, 11 April 1907, File 3328, Microfilm M862, Roll 311, RG 59.

33. Acting Secretary Robert Bacon to Hughes, 9 December 1907, ibid.

34. H. C. Thomas, Commissioner, Vermont Department of Fisheries and Game, to Proctor, 11 January 1908, ibid.

35. Bryce to Lord Grey, 15 January 1908, File 3214, RG 23.

36. Bryce to Root, 12 March 1908, F-4, Vol. 1002, RG 25.

37. Root to Bryce, 16 March 1908, ibid.

38. C. P. Lucas, Colonial Office, to Sir Edward Grey, 27 March 1908, ibid.

39. Alvey A. Adee to Hugh Smith, Bureau of Fisheries, 25 June 1908, File 8275, Microfilm M862, Roll 602, RG 59.

40. Bryce to Lord Grey, 28 May 1908, F-4, Vol. 1002, RG 25.

41. George Bowers to Root, 28 May 1908, File 8275, Microfilm M862, Roll 602, RG 59.

42. Jordan, 1:51–52, 365–69.

43. Jordan to Senator Frank Flint (R-CA), 11 January 1908, Vol. 53, Roll 149, David Starr Jordan Papers, microfilm edition, Stanford University Libraries, Stanford, California.

44. Jordan, 1:545.

45. Hopkins, 321; J. Castell Hopkins, *The Canadian Annual Review of Public Affairs, 1908* (Toronto, 1908), 284, 526; Bryce to Root, 3 June 1908, File 8275, RG 59.

46. Root to Jordan, 3 June 1908, Correspondence, Roll 59, Jordan Papers.

47. Jordan to Root, 16 June 1908, File 8275, RG 59. Note that Jordan remained as president of Stanford, devoting much of his time to the fisheries commission.

48. Jordan to Root, 17 June 1908, ibid.

49. Jordan to Bacon, 24 August 1908, ibid.

50. Jordan, 2:258; Jordan to Robert Bacon, 24 August 1908, File 8275, RG 59; J. Babcock, assistant commissioner of fisheries, British Columbia, to Jordan, 26 October 1908, Correspondence, Roll 60, Jordan Papers.

51. Jordan to Samuel Bastedo, 1 October 1908, Jordan to Barton W. Evermann, 20 and 23 October 1908, Vol. 51, Roll 148; and Bastedo to Jordan, 9 October 1908, Correspondence, Roll 60, Jordan Papers.

52. Jordan to Bastedo, 17 October 1908, Vol. 51, Roll 148, Jordan Papers.

53. Jordan to Bacon, 24 August 1908, File 8275, RG 59; note that there are two letters from Jordan to Bacon with the same date but different contents.

54. Chandler Anderson, Memorandum to the State Department, September 1908, File 8275, RG 59.

55. Jordan to Evermann, 10 September 1908, Vol. 51, Roll 148, Jordan Papers.

56. Jordan to Evermann, 5 December 1908; Jordan to Anderson, 24 October 1908; and Jordan to Bastedo, 17 October 1908, Vol. 51, Roll 148, Jordan Papers.

57. Jordan wrote many books and articles on the subject of reforms, including *The Call of the Nation: A Plea for Taking Politics out of Politics* (Boston, 1910).

58. Jordan to J. S. Whipple, New York Commissioner of Fisheries, 27 October 1908, Vol. 51, Roll 148, Jordan Papers.

59. Hopkins, *Canadian Annual Review,* 1906, 92.

60. Report of the Commission Appointed by the Dominion Government to Investigate the Fisheries of Lake Erie, 16 February 1909, Correspondence, Roll 62, Jordan Papers.

61. E. E. Prince, "International Fisheries Commission: Report of Progress," 14 December 1908, File 3214, RG 23.

62. Jordan to Root, 17 October 1908, File 8275, RG 59.

63. John Burnham to James Whipple, 19 October 1908, Box 3, File Correspondence, 1901–08, John Burnham Papers, American Heritage Center, University of Wyoming, Laramie.

64. Senator Knute Nelson to Root, 14 November 1908, File 8275, RG 59.

65. J. H. Todd to L. P. Brodeur, 14 November 1908, File 3214, RG 23.

66. Bacon to Strauss, 12 and 17 November 1908, File 8275, RG 59.

67. Paul Marschalk to Jordan, 28 November 1908, ibid.

68. E. E. Prince, "International Fisheries Commission: Report of Progress," 14 December 1908, File 3214, RG 23; Prince Memorandum to Brodeur, 17 December 1908, File 3214, RG 23; Root to Bryce, 21 December 1908, File 8275, RG 59.

69. Jordan to Anderson, 19 December 1908, Vol. 51, Roll 148, Jordan Papers.

70. J. D. Taylor to Brodeur, 1 December 1908; and B. C. Packers Association to Prince, 18 December 1908, File 3214, RG 23; presumably they were offering to shut down for the lean years of 1910 and 1911, as the salmon run of 1909 promised to be huge.

71. Todd to Brodeur, 1 December 1908, File 3214, RG 23.

72. Fraser River Canners' Association to Brodeur, 11 December 1908, File 3214, RG 23.

73. Jordan telegram to Root, 20 December 1908, File 8275, RG 59; Brodeur to the Fraser River Canners' Association, 24 December 1908, and Prince to Brodeur, 30 December 1908, File 3214, RG 23.

74. Jordan to Root, 1 January 1909, File 8275, RG 59; Jordan to Anderson, 9 January 1909, Vol. 53, Roll 149, Jordan Papers.

75. Jordan to Evermann, 2 February 1909, Vol. 54, Roll 149, Jordan Papers.

76. Jordan to Anderson, 18 March 1909, ibid.

77. Jordan to Carlos Avery, Minnesota Fish Commissioner, 22 March 1909; and Jordan to Adee, 17 March 1909, Vol. 56, Roll 150, Jordan Papers.

78. Prince to Evermann, 27 March 1909, File 3214, RG 23.

79. Brodeur to Prince, 1 April 1909, ibid.

80. Prince's notes from the Vancouver meeting, untitled, 7 April 1909, ibid.

81. Jordan, *Days of a Man*, 2:257.

82. Jordan to Prince, 8 April 1909, Vol. 56, Roll 150; and Jordan to Anderson, 17, 22, and 28 April 1909, Letterbook 57, Roll 151, Jordan Papers.

83. Jordan, *Days of a Man*, 2:269.

84. Jordan to Anderson, 19 April 1909, Letterbook 57, Roll 151, Jordan Papers.

85. Draft Regulations, dated 29 May 1909, F-4, Vol. 1002, RG 25.

86. Jordan to Huntington Wilson, 6 April 1910, Letterbook 63, Roll 153, Jordan Papers.

87. Jordan to Adee, 22 April 1909, Letterbook 57, Roll 151, Jordan Papers.

3 / THE ONE THAT GOT AWAY

1. A good place to start a study of the personalities and policies of the Taft administration's foreign policy is Walter V. Scholes and Marie V. Scholes, *The Foreign Policies of the Taft Administration* (Columbia, Mo., 1970); especially chapter 1. One point worth noting is the potential confusion about Francis Huntington Wilson. During this time period, he signed most of his correspondence as Huntington Wilson, but the Scholes use the name he adopted later in life, Francis Huntington-Wilson.

2. Chandler Anderson to Philander Knox, 29 April 1909, File 8275, Record Group 59, General Records of the Department of State, United States National Archives, Washington, D.C. (hereafter RG 59).

3. Anderson to David Starr Jordan, 30 April 1909, File 8275, RG 59; Jordan to Barton W. Evermann, 18 October 1909, Letterbook 61, Roll 152, David Starr Jordan Papers, microfilm edition, Stanford University Libraries, Stanford California.

4. L. P. Brodeur to Knox, 9 June 1909, Records of the Ministry of Marine and Fisheries, File 3214, Record Group 23, National Archives of Canada, Ottawa (hereafter RG 23); Knox to Brodeur, 25 June 1909, File 8275, RG 59. Traditionally, someone in the Canadian cabinet would use the offices of the governor general and British Embassy in Washington to communicate such a request. Given that both Lord Grey and Ambassador Bryce were interested in the treaty, perhaps Brodeur would have been wise to follow standard procedure.

5. Charles Bullymore to Jordan, 29 May 1909; W. M. McCormick to Jordan, 22 June 1909; and H. R. Warden, General Manager, Booth Fisheries Company, to Jordan, 1 June 1909, Correspondence, Roll 63, Jordan Papers. The Booth Fisheries Company had widespread operations, including its Canadian subsidiary, the Dominion Fishing Company.

6. Ferdinand Hansen to Jordan, 13 July 1909, ibid. Support from dealers like Hansen indicated that some fish merchants were able and willing to consider the long-term benefits of the regulations.

7. Since January, Jordan had planned to spend the summer in the field; Jordan to Root, 1 January 1909, File 8275, RG 59.

8. Jordan to Knox, 19 August 1909, File 8275, RG 59. Jordan to Anderson, 6 September 1909, Letterbook 60, Roll 151; Jordan to Anderson, 21 October 1909, Letterbook 61, Roll 152; and Jordan to Evermann, 18 October 1909, Letterbook 61, Roll 152, all in Jordan Papers.

9. Jordan to Evermann, 9 September 1909, Letterbook 60, Roll 151, Jordan Papers.

10. Jordan to E. E. Prince, 21 October 1909, ibid.

11. In fact, the *Congressional Record* shows no record of debate on the bill.

12. David Starr Jordan, *Days of a Man* (Yonkers-on-Hudson, N.Y., 1922), 2:271. The Pinchot-Ballinger affair arose from a dispute between the Chief Forester and Secretary of Interior William Ballinger over the proper use of federal lands that had been designated as sites for power plants. While the details of the incident are complex, it was clear that Taft fired Pinchot for lobbying Congress. Ballinger bore the brunt of the public outcry. Alpheus T. Mason's *Bureaucracy Convicts Itself: The Ballinger-Pinchot Controversy of 1910* (New York, 1941) offers the standard assessment that Ballinger was spineless, if not corrupt. James Penick, Jr. (*Progressive Politics and Conservation: The Ballinger-Pinchot Affair* [Cambridge, 1968]) offers a more balanced view, arguing that Pinchot and Ballinger had different views of the nation's best interests.

13. Jordan to Evermann, 28 February 1910, Letterbook 63, Roll 153, Jordan Papers.

14. Prince to James Bryce, 7 March 1910, File 3214, RG 23.

15. Theodore Burton to Knox, 15 January 1910, File 8275, RG 59.

16. Burton to Huntington Wilson, 5 March 1910, File 711.428, RG 59.

17. Senator Charles Dick to Jordan, 28 February 1910, ibid.

18. Jordan to Wilson, 26 February 1910, File 8275, RG 59.

19. C. S. Pierce to Knox, 18 February 1910, ibid.

20. George Whitehouse to Jordan, 18 February 1910, ibid.

21. Jordan to Evermann, 3 and 7 March 1910, Letterbook 63, Roll 153, Jordan Papers.

22. Prince, "Memorandum, RE: United States Request to Change One of the International Fishery Regulations," 4 March 1910, and Prince to Bryce, 7 March 1910, File 3214, RG 23; Jordan to Lewis Gisborne, 22 March 1910, Jordan to Prince, 14 March 1910, and Jordan to Prince, 19 March 1910, Letterbook 63, Roll 153, Jordan Papers; Prince to Jordan, 26 May 1910 and 16 June 1910, Correspondence, Rolls 67 and 68, Jordan Papers.

23. In Canadian Parliamentary debates, the M.P.s agreed that two-thirds of Canadian fishermen on the Great Lakes worked for American companies. In addition, American companies controlled most of the fishing on Lake of the Woods, Lake Winnipeg, Lake Manitoba, and Lake Winnipegosis. *Debates, House of Commons,*

Dominion of Canada, 1909–1910, 11th Parliament, 2d Session, 26 April 1910, Vol. 50, Pt. 4, Column 8065.

24. Kerr and McCord, Attorneys, to Senator Wesley Jones, 16 March 1910, File 711.428, RG 59.

25. Charles Dorr and Hadley to Senator Piles, 8 April 1910, File 8275, RG 59.

26. Jordan to Anderson, 27 May 1910, Letterbook 66, Roll 153, Jordan Papers.

27. Kerr and McCord to Knox, 27 April 1910, File 711.428, RG 59; Charles Dorr to Jordan, 10 May 1910, Correspondence, Roll 67, Jordan Papers.

28. Jordan to Prince, 30 April 1910, Letterbook 66, Roll 153, ibid.; and Jordan to Wilson 2 June 1910, File 8275, RG 59.

29. The complete transcript of the debate is in *Debates, House of Commons, Dominion of Canada, 1909–1910,* 11th Parliament, 2d Sess., Vol. 50, Pt. 4, beginning 23 March 1910, Column 5906, and continuing on 26 April 1910, Column 8033.

30. Ibid., 26 April 1910, Vol. 50, Pt. 4, Column 8041.

31. Ibid., Column 8039.

32. Ibid., Columns 8064–65.

33. Prince to Jordan, 20 June 1910, Correspondence, Roll 68, Jordan Papers.

34. Prince to Jordan, 24 June 1910, ibid.

35. Jordan to Prince, 19 September 1910, ibid.

36. Prince, "Memorandum RE: United States Request to Change One of the International Fishery Regulations."

37. Prince to Bryce, 7 March 1910, File 3214, RG 23.

38. Prince, "Memorandum RE: Suggested Modification of International Fishery Regulations," 27 May 1910, ibid.

39. Brodeur to William Harrison Bradley, 3 August 1910, and Bradley to Knox, 17 August 1910, File 711.428, RG 59.

40. Brodeur to Jordan, 13 December 1910, ibid.

41. Jordan to Adee, 12 December 1910, ibid. In January 1910, Adee had asked Jordan if he could collect some Pacific coast minerals and marine plants for him to study on his microscope, a request that Jordan fulfilled.

42. Jordan to Anderson, 17 December 1910, ibid.

43. Jordan, undated letter fragment from late December 1910, Correspondence, Roll 69, Jordan Papers.

44. This paragraph and the one that follows come from a report that Jordan drafted in late December for the State Department. He sent it on 11 January 1911, File 711.428/239, RG 59.

45. Knox to Jordan, 20 and 26 January 1911, and Jordan to Knox, 28 January 1911, File 711.428, RG 59.

46. Jordan to Knox, 4 February 1911, ibid.

47. Prince to Jordan, 31 March 1911, Correspondence, Roll 72, Jordan Papers.

48. *Congressional Record,* 61st Congress, 3d Sess., 10 February 1911, Vol. 46, Pt. 2: 2288; Knox to Taft, 7 February 1911, File 711.428, RG 59.

49. State Department Counselor Report, "In re International Fisheries Regulations," 8 February 1911, File 711.428, RG 59.

50. *Debates, House of Commons, Dominion of Canada, 1910–1911,* 11th Parliament, 3d Session, 10 March 1911, Vol. 51, Pt. 3, Columns 5035, 5217–5232.

51. J. H. Todd to William Templeman, Minister of Internal Revenue, 31 March 1911, File 3214, RG 23.

52. Charles Bullymore to Department of State, 4 February 1911, and Bullymore to Knox, 25 February 1911, File 711.428, RG 59.

53. Bullymore to Jordan, 20 March 1911, Correspondence, Roll 71, Jordan Papers.

54. Bullymore to Jordan, 18 April 1911, Correspondence, Roll 72, Jordan Papers.

55. Jordan to Bullymore, 12 April 1911, ibid.

56. Jordan to Bullymore, 13 April 1911, ibid.

57. Knox to Jordan, 19 April 1911, File 711.428, RG 59.

58. Wilson to Jordan, 21 April 1911, ibid.

59. Jordan to Evermann, 15 May 1911, Correspondence, Roll 72, Jordan Papers.

60. Jordan to Bullymore, 8 May 1911, ibid.

61. Jordan to Rathbun, 11 May 1911, ibid.

62. Jordan to Nagel, 29 December 1911, File 66239, Record Group 40, General Records of the Department of Commerce, United States National Archives, Washington, D.C. (hereafter RG 40).

63. Jordan to Nagel, 1 January 1912, ibid.

64. Jordan to Nagel, 27 January 1912, ibid.

65. Jordan to Woodrow Wilson, 20 December 1912, File 711.428, RG 59.

66. Charles Nagel to Knox, 23 August 1912, File 66239, RG 40.

67. *Congressional Record,* 62d Congress, 1st Sess., 17 and 22 May 1911, Vol. 47, Pt. 2:1267, 1433. Smith's official report to the Foreign Relations Committee is in United States, 61st Congress, 3d Sess., S. Rep. 1176, "Fisheries in Waters Contiguous to the United States and Canada."

68. Bryce to Sir Edward Grey, 6 June 1911, Records of the Ministry of External Affairs, Series F-4, Vol. 1002, Record Group 25, National Archives of Canada, Ottawa (hereafter RG 25).

69. Bryce to Knox, 17 June 1911, ibid.

70. Bryce to Knox, 1 August 1911, ibid.

71. At one point in 1910, the American Tariff Commission came to the British Embassy "hat in hand," looking for any reason to keep the minimum tariff in place. One thing they did demand was that the embassy exclude the State Department from any of the discussions, which prompted one British official to write, "The present State Department is more out of touch with other departments than usual, which is

saying much." George Young to Lord Grey, 18 March 1910, "Commercial Relations with the United States," F-4, Vol. 1002, RG 25. The standard account of the reciprocal trade issue is L. Ethan Ellis, *Reciprocity, 1911* (New Haven, Conn., 1939). A revisionist version is Robert Hannigan's "Reciprocity 1911: Continentalism and American Welt-politik," *Diplomatic History*, Vol. 4 (Winter 1980), 1–18. Hannigan argued that Taft and his allies wanted to develop a North American bloc, with Canada and Mexico feeding natural resources to the American industrial machine.

72. One of the sticking points throughout the negotiations was a new provincial export duty on lumber and wood pulp. Newspaper editors were especially concerned about the impact of that measure, and they pressured the Taft administration to work on their behalf. Bryce, however, pointed out that Quebec and Ontario saw the tariff as a means of conserving their own resources. Bryce to Lord Grey, 3 February 1910, F-4, Vol. 1002, RG 25.

73. "Summary of the Work and Present Position of the International Fisheries Commission," received by the Governor General, 14 March 1912, G 21, Vol. 94, No. 192b, vol. 1(a), Record Group 7, Records of the Governor General's Office, National Archives of Canada, Ottawa.

74. Bryce to Sir Robert Borden, 3 May 1913, File 3214, RG 23.

75. Jordan to Woodrow Wilson, 20 December 1912, File 711.428, RG 59.

76. Jordan to William Jennings Bryan, 11 March 1913, ibid. Less than two years earlier, Jordan had called Taft "as great a man of peace . . . as Carnegie and I put together."

77. Prince to Hugh Smith, 19 August 1913, File 3214, Pt. 2, RG 23.

78. Prince to Charles Cooke, State Department, 27 September 1913, File 711.428, RG 59.

79. "Draft Pro-Memoriam to the United States Government" from Ambassador Sir Cecil Spring Rice, 18 June 1913 (sent on 26 November), F-4, Vol. 1002, RG 25.

80. "Memorandum for the Minister" from Prince, 11 December 1913, File 3214, Pt. 2, RG 23.

81. C. H. Wilson to Woodrow Wilson, 13 December 1913, and C. H. Wilson to Bryan, 10 January 1914, File 711.428, RG 59.

82. *Congressional Record*, 63rd Congress, 2d Sess., 10, 12, and 27 February 1914, Vol. 51, Pt. 3: 3248, 3426, 4026–29.

83. J. B. Moore to Bryan, 24 February 1914, File 711.428, RG 59.

84. Spring Rice to the Governor General, the Duke of Connaught, 25 February 1914, F-4, Vol. 1002, RG 25.

85. Herner gave no basis for this figure, which was double the estimate made by Senator Burton. William Herner to Bryan, 2 March 1914, File 711.428, RG 59.

86. Frank Wright, President of Carlisle Packing Company, to Woodrow Wilson, 16 March 1914, ibid.

87. E. Chester Jones to State Department, 27 March 1914, ibid.

88. *Congressional Record,* 63rd Congress, 2d Sess., 27 February 1914, Vol. 51, Pt. 3, p. 4026.

89. Ibid., 4027.

90. Ibid., 4027–28.

91. Ibid., 2 March 1914, 51, Pt. 3, pp. 4173–74.

92. Ibid., 4174–78.

93. Spring Rice to Edward Grey, 14 May 1914, F-4, vol. 1002, RG 25.

94. Connaught to Spring Rice, 8 October 1914, ibid. Spring Rice to Bryan, 19 October 1914, File 711.428, RG 59.

95. Smith to Bryan, 8 March 1915, File 66239, RG 40.

96. Jordan to Woodrow Wilson, 20 December 1912, File 711.428, RG 59.

4 / CONFLICT IN THE BERING SEA

1. Samuel Flagg Bemis, *A Diplomatic History of the United States* (New York, 1955), 413.

2. William T. Hornaday, *Thirty Years War for Wild Life* (1931; rpt., New York, 1970), 171. Hornaday was the most skilled public relations conservationist of his time, and he took an active role in protecting the seal beginning in 1907.

3. The next several paragraphs are based on a collection of historical and scientific works. A good source of general information about the fur seal is Victor Scheffer's *Year of the Seal* (New York, 1970), which combines Scheffer's extensive scientific experience with a compelling story. The historian Briton Busch's *War against the Seals* (Montreal, 1985) is the most comprehensive history of the sealing industry. The first scientific study of the animals was Henry W. Elliott's *Seal-islands of Alaska* (1876; rpt., Kingston, Ont., 1976), written after he studied the islands in the early 1870s. A more thorough government report was that of David Starr Jordan, *Report of Fur-Seal Investigations* (Washington, 1898). More recent scientific studies include the National Advisory Committee on Oceans and the Atmosphere (NACOA), *North Pacific Fur Seals: Current Problems and Opportunities Concerning Conservation and Management* (Washington, 1985); F. H. C. Taylor, et al., *Distribution and Food Habits of the Fur Seals of the North Pacific Ocean* (Washington, 1955); and the North Pacific Fur Seal Commission, *Report on Investigations from 1967 through 1972* (Washington, 1975).

4. Aldo Leopold, *Game Management* (1933; reprint, Madison, Wis., 1986), 42.

5. Busch, 99, 128.

6. NACOA, 28–29; Hornaday, "The Rescued Fur Seal Industry," *Science,* Vol. 23 (July 1920), 81–82; Busch, 128. Busch also reported that skins taken at sea were always worth less than those taken on land.

7. Elliott, "The Seal-islands of Alaska," in Jordan and George A. Clark, eds., *Seal and Salmon Fisheries and General Resources of Alaska,* Vol. 3 (Washington, 1898), 54.

8. Jordan and Clark, 3:692; Taylor, et al., 34–39, 57–58; North Pacific Fur Seal Commission, 30.

9. William Metcalf to Theodore Roosevelt, 2 January 1906, Records of the Department of Commerce and Labor, File 66001, Folder 1, Record Group 40, United States National Archives, Washington, D.C. (hereafter RG 40). One should note that as of 1985 the NACOA had to admit that scientists were unable to answer some very basic questions about seal/human interactions.

10. The Aleuts lived in conditions of servitude. Although they received some pay for their work, they had no means of leaving the islands or getting any other work. The U.S. government commission that reported on sealing in 1985 compared the Pribilovian Aleuts' previous existence to slavery (NACOA, *North Pacific Fur Seals*). Busch (pp. 115–18, 125–26) also discusses the plight of the Aleuts and the history of Russian sealing.

11. Elliott to William Windom, Secretary of the Treasury, 21 November 1890, Box 44, Seal Fisheries in Alaska, 1874–1912, RG 40. Elliott's *Seal-islands* is the most complete English-language source on the Russian era of control, although it is based on some questionable sources, principally the account of the one-time bishop of Alaska and later primate of the Russian church, Innocent Veniaminof.

12. Busch, 101–103; Jordan, *Fur Seal Investigations,* 1:25.

13. Busch, 107.

14. Busch, 110–11. A text of the lease can be found in Elliott's "Report upon the Condition of the Fur-seal Rookeries of the Pribilof Islands of Alaska," in Jordan and Clark, 3:451–52.

15. Busch, 110–12. This thorough killing of the young males led Henry Elliott to begin his protest against the entire sealing industry.

16. C. Hart Merriam and Thomas Mendenhall were the first scientists to subject pelagic sealing to a rigorous study. Their report can be found in *Fur Seal Arbitration: Proceedings of the Tribunal of Arbitration, Convened at Paris* (Washington, 1895), 2:307–433. Also see Jordan and Clark, "Truth About the Fur Seals of the Pribilof Islands," Department of Commerce and Labor, Bureau of Fisheries, Economic Circular No. 4, 20 December, 1912, File 66013, RG 40. The percentage of seals recovered depended largely on the method of sealing used. The use of rifles, for instance, caused much more waste than did spears.

17. *New York Times,* 8 June 1884.

18. Salisbury to Pauncefote, 28 March 1890, quoted in Charles S. Campbell, Jr., *Anglo-American Understanding, 1898–1903* (Baltimore, 1957), 81. Campbell, "The Anglo-American Crisis in the Bering Sea, 1890–1891," *Mississippi Valley Historical Review,* Vol. 66 (Dec. 1961), 395–410. The diplomatic correspondence can be found

in U.S. Department of State, *Foreign Relations of the United States, 1890* (Washington, 1891), 358–508 (hereafter, *FRUS*), and *FRUS, 1891* (Washington, 1892), 530–643. For some reason, *FRUS, 1892* does not have any material on the Bering Sea dispute. For a complete account of these negotiations, see Charles Tansill, *Canadian-American Relations, 1875–1911* (New Haven, Conn., 1937), 267–95.

19. Campbell, "Anglo-American Crisis." A copy of the NACC contract is in File 66001, Folder 20, RG 40. Note that for most of the term of the lease, the government limited the NACC to 15,000 seals.

20. Elliott never backed down from the 4,500,000 figure, which he first put forth in *The Seal-islands of Alaska;* for instance, Elliott to Secretary of Commerce and Labor Metcalf, 8 January 1904, Box 44, File 1874–1904, RG 40. For a different view of Elliott's work, see "Mr. Chamberlain's Letter," undated, in the George A. Clark Fur Seal Controversy Papers, within the David Starr Jordan Papers, microfilm edition, Stanford University Libraries, Stanford, California, and Jordan's assessment in *Seal and Salmon Fisheries,* 3:696–97.

21. General O. O. Howard, internal memorandum, undated, Box 44, File 1911, Seal Fisheries in Alaska, 1874–1912, RG 40.

22. Elliott to Secretary William Windom, 21 November 1890, Box 44, File 1874–1904, RG 40. Another copy can be found in Jordan and Clark's *Seal and Salmon Fisheries,* Vol. 3.

23. Windom to John Foster, 24 February 1893, Box 44, File 1874–1904, RG 40. The evidence linking Elliott to the ACC is weak, especially given Elliott's suggestion that the NACC deserved a refund from the government. Elliott denied ever having been an employee of the company, but several government officials claimed otherwise.

24. James Thomas Gay, "Henry W. Elliott: Crusading Conservationist," (*The Alaska Journal,* Vol. 3 [1973], 211–16), portrays Elliott in a more favorable light, comparing him to modern environmentalists. On the other hand, Briton Busch argues that Elliott hurt his cause with his inability to admit his mistakes. Busch, 119–21.

25. Campbell, "The Bering Sea Settlements of 1892," *Pacific Historical Review,* Vol. 32, No. 4 (1963), 347–68; Chandler Anderson, "Canadian Questions: Alaskan Fur Seals," 1906, File 99, General Records of the Department of State, Record Group 59, United States National Archives, Washington, D.C. (hereafter RG 59).

26. *Fur Seal Arbitration,* 3:308–11; for more on Merriam, see Keir Sterling, *Last of the Naturalists: The Career of C. Hart Merriam* (New York, 1977).

27. *Fur Seal Arbitration,* 3:345–66.

28. Anderson, 8–12.

29. The complete account of the tribunal, in sixteen volumes, can be found in *Fur Seal Arbitration.* In particular, Foster's report opening Volume 1 lays out the American position and reasons for defeat. The arbitrators were Justice John Harlan and Senator John Morgan for the United States, Lord Hannen for Britain, Minister

of Justice Sir John Thompson for Canada, Baron Alphonse de Courcel for France, Marquis Visconti Venosta for Italy, and Mr. Gregers Gram for Sweden and Norway.

30. Foster to Gresham, *Fur Seal Arbitration,* 1:10–11.

31. The *New York Times* presented a good brief summary of the arguments at the tribunal (15 July 1893).

32. For instance, Hornaday called the ruling "the greatest licking of our lives, diplomatically," Hornaday to Elliott, 16 July 1910, Letterbook 8, William T. Hornaday Papers, Library of Congress, Washington, D.C.

33. The summary of the tribunal's deliberations is in *Fur Seal Arbitration,* 1:51–61.

34. *New York Times,* 16 August 1893.

35. Campbell, *Anglo-American Understanding,* 86. The attitudes of Canadian sealers toward the diplomatic activity can be found in National Archives of Canada, Record Group 33/107, Claims by Pelagic Sealers arising out of the Washington Treaty, 7 July 1911; and the regulations made under the Paris award, which came into force in 1894.

36. *New York Times,* 17 August 1893. Elliott, Jordan, and the *Times* editors all agreed that the American claim to ownership was ridiculous and detrimental to American diplomacy. George A. Clark, "The Report of the Recent Fur Seal Conference," late 1897, in the Clark Fur Seal Papers.

37. Leonhard Stejneger, "The Asiatic Fur-Seal Islands and Fur Seal Industry," in Jordan's *Report of Fur Seal Investigations,* 4:323–27.

38. In 1895, Great Britain and the United States came close to war over the appropriate way to handle a boundary dispute between Venezuela and British Guiana, but they resolved their differences by establishing an arbitration tribunal. Ernest May, *Imperial Democracy: The Emergence of America as a Great Power* (1961; rpt., Chicago, 1991), 33–66.

39. Campbell, *Anglo-American Understanding,* 81–86.

40. Jordan, *Days of a Man,* 2:545, 571; and Chandler Anderson, "Canadian Questions: Alaskan Fur Seals," 1906, File 99, RG 59. Jordan's colleagues included Stejneger and Frederic Lucas from the Smithsonian, and Charles Townsend from the New York Aquarium.

41. Jordan and Clark's *Seal and Salmon Fisheries,* volume 3, which contains both Elliott's 1890 report and Jordan's rebuttal from 1898, illuminates the differences in their approach.

42. David Starr Jordan, *Matka and Kotik; A Tale of the Mist-islands* (San Francisco, 1897).

43. Jordan, *Report of Fur Seal Investigations.*

44. Jordan and Clark, 3:713.

45. George A. Clark, "The Report of the Recent Fur Seal Conference," late 1897, in the Clark Fur Seal Papers. Years later, Townsend and Macoun agreed to meet, but

Townsend insisted that "all seal talk will be barred." Macoun, however, reported to his superiors that he could use his contact with Townsend to acquire privileged information about the American diplomatic position! Townsend to Macoun, 6 January 1910, and Macoun to Pope, 19 April 1911, Vol. 1108, File 40, Vol. II, Pt. 1, Records of the Department of External Affairs, Record Group 25, National Archives of Canada, Ottawa (hereafter RG 25).

46. "Résumé of Discussion at the International Fur Seal Conference," 25 October 1897, in the Clark Fur Seal Papers. Further diplomatic correspondence is in *FRUS, 1897.*

47. "Résumé of Discussion at the International Fur Seal Conference," 25 October 1897.

48. Comments of the Japanese delegate, Mr. Fujita, ibid.

49. "Résumé of Discussion at the International Fur Seal Conference," 27 October 1897, in the Clark Fur Seal Papers; and Secretary of Commerce and Labor Charles Nagel and Counselor Chandler Anderson to Secretary of State Philander Knox, 13 May 1912, File 711.417/227, RG 59.

50. "Memorandum Regarding the Fur Seals," given to McKinley 11 March 1897, and a similar, untitled document given to Sherman on the same day, in Clark Fur Seal Papers.

51. Chandler Anderson, "Canadian Questions: Alaskan Fur Seals," 1906, File 99, RG 59; and Campbell, *Anglo-American Understanding,* 86–87.

52. The British members of the subcommittee were Sir Louis Davies and Lord Herschell; Campbell, *Anglo-American Understanding,* 91–92; also *New York Times,* 27 September 1898, and 23 November 1898.

53. Nagel and Anderson to Knox, 13 May 1912, File 711.417/227, RG 59. Campbell wrote that Britain requested only $600,000, while Clark reported that the United States offered $250,000, and Canada asked for $500,000. I believe that Nagel and Anderson had more reliable access to the official records of the negotiations.

54. Sir Joseph Pope (*Public Servant* [Toronto, 1961], 116) argued that Laurier agreed to the conference with the understanding that there would be a compromise on the two Alaska issues.

55. George Clark, "The Future of the Alaska Fur Seal Industry," after September 1898, Clark Fur Seal Papers.

56. Campbell, *Anglo-American Understanding,* 93.

57. "Résumé of Discussion at the International Fur Seal Conference," 25 October 1897.

58. Jordan's speculations on the equilibrium theory can be found in ibid. and in *Report of Fur Seal Investigations,* 1:156–60. In later years, his willingness to consider the theory became a point of contention between the Elliott and Jordan factions.

59. The figure from the land catch comes from Busch, 153. As to pelagic sealing, the Canadian government admitted to almost 550,000 seals caught between 1886

and 1898, "Pelagic Sealing Catches by Canadian Vessels," Vol. 1108, File 40, Vol. 2, Pt. 1, RG 25.

5 / CONCILIATION AND CONSERVATION

1. R. N. Venning to L. P. Brodeur, 17 December 1908, vol. 1093, File 31-1909, Pelagic Sealing, Records of the Department of External Affairs, Record Group 25, National Archives of Canada, Ottawa (hereafter RG 25). Hay's service as ambassador to London 1897–98 no doubt encouraged his efforts to remove sources of friction. C. C. Tansill, *Canadian-American Relations, 1875–1911* (New Haven, Conn., 1943), 162–66, describes Hay's attitude toward Canada and Great Britain.

2. R. Venning to R. Prefontaine, 29 October 1903, Vol. 153, File 425, Records of the Ministry of Marine and Fisheries, Record Group 23, National Archives of Canada, Ottawa (hereafter RG 23); Chandler Anderson, "Canadian Questions: Alaskan Fur Seals," 1906, File 99, General Records of the Department of State, Record Group 59, United States National Archives, Washington, D.C. (hereafter RG 59).

3. Elliott to Secretary Metcalf, 8 January 1904, Box 44, Seal Fisheries in Alaska, 1874–1912, File 1904, Records of the Department of Commerce and Labor, Record Group 40, United States National Archives, Washington, D.C. (hereafter RG 40).

4. Before British Columbia entered the Dominion in 1871, it was administered by a governor, not a governor general; Elliott's confusion after nearly 40 years is understandable. Elliott to William Loeb, Secretary to the President, 6 December 1904; Elliott to Hay, 11 March 1905; and Elliott to Loeb, 20 March 1905; Box 44, File 1904-5, RG 40.

5. Dillingham originally proposed his amendment to S. 3355 on 12 January 1904; *Congressional Record*, 58th Congress, 2d Sess., 12 January 1904, Vol. 43, Pt. 1: 613. Although it never passed, Dillingham and his allies liked to keep the amendment on hand to encourage the Canadians to negotiate.

6. Secretary Charles Nagel and Solicitor Chandler Anderson to Secretary Philander Knox, 13 May 1912, File 711.417, RG 59.

7. Reports of the Privy Council, 31 March 1905 and 21 July 1905, RG 25.

8. Elliott to Loeb, 9 December 1906, Box 44, File 1906, RG 40. Even as late as December 1906, Root endorsed Dillingham's resolution as a "useful" tool for the State Department. Root to Dillingham, 14 December 1906, File 99, RG 59.

9. Nagel and Anderson to Knox, 13 May 1912, File 711.417, RG 59.

10. Elliott to Hay, 11 March 1905, Box 44, File 1905, RG 40.

11. A series of letters (Box 44, File 1905, RG 40) between Elliott and Hay reveals how Elliott's need for recognition and self-promotion as the preeminent seal expert ruined his relationship with Hay. In particular, Elliott tried to charge the department $5,000 for a series of sketches he had made during his earlier journeys to the islands. Even in his last year, 1930, Elliott took credit for coauthoring the Hay-

Durand agreement, which he still maintained was based on joint control; his account is in William T. Hornaday, *Thirty Years War for Wild Life* (1931; rpt., New York, 1970), 173–81.

12. Jordan agreed with Elliott on the need for international control, and in his autobiography he claims that in 1897 he urged Washington to cede the island St. George to the Canadians in order to establish the basis for cooperation. David Starr Jordan, *Days of a Man* (Yonkers-on-Hudson, N.Y., 1922), 1:604.

13. Peter Neary, "Grey, Bryce, and the Settlement of Canadian-American Differences, 1905–1911," *Canadian Historical Review*, Vol. 49, No. 4 (1968) 357–80.

14. Roderick Nash, *Wilderness and the American Mind*, 3d ed. (New Haven, 1982), 152; Richard Leopold, *Elihu Root and the Conservative Tradition* (Boston, 1954), is the best work on Root's career, especially his tenure as secretary of state. Root's active role in all three treaties in this study is ample evidence that he recognized the importance of conservation activities.

15. Nagel and Anderson to Knox, 13 May 1912, File 711.417, RG 59; Tansill, 368–69.

16. Extract from Laurier's letter to Lord Grey, 25 September 1906, File 99, RG 59; Root received the letter from the British Ambassador on 6 December. *Toronto Globe*, 30 April 1907 in V. 1093, File 31, March–Dec. 1909, RG 25.

17. Elliott to Hornaday, 29 February 1908, Correspondence, Box 51, Folder Jan.–Feb. 1908, William T. Hornaday Papers, Library of Congress, Washington, D.C.; Elliott, "The Depredation of the Seal Rookeries," in *Pacific Fisherman*, August 1909.

18. Hornaday to Nagel, 27 May 1910, Charles Nagel Papers, Yale University Library, Manuscripts and Archives, New Haven, Connecticut. Neither the Yale nor the U.S. National archives have information on Lembkey's background, but his annual reports in the Congressional Serial Sets reveal a civil servant who followed orders to the letter. Unlike other government officials, Lembkey did not hesitate to hammer back at Elliott (Box 44, 9 November 1906, RG 40). On the question of overharvesting, even Jordan's assistant George Clark concluded that Lembkey had failed in his obligation to reserve enough young males. Clark to George Bowers, 30 October 1911, George A. Clark Fur Seal Controversy Papers, in David Starr Jordan Papers, microfilm edition, Stanford University Libraries, Stanford, California.

19. Elliott to Hornaday, 12 February 1908, and 16 June 1909, Correspondence, Boxes 51 and 53, Hornaday Papers.

20. Metcalf to Roosevelt, 2 January 1906, File 66001, Folder 1, RG 40.

21. Boscowitz to Assistant Secretary Robert Bacon, 2 October 1907, and Root to Boscowitz, 4 November 1907, File 99, RG 59.

22. Boscowitz to the Governor General, 28 July 1908, Vol. 153, File 425, Pt. 12, RG 23.

23. Ibid.

24. A summation of the RCS report for 1908 is in George Bowers to Nagel,

9 March 1909, File 66003, Folder 2, RG 40. Each of the annual RCS reports can be found in RG 40, although they are scattered throughout the files.

25. Lembkey to Metcalf, 15 October 1906, File 66012, Miscellaneous, RG 40; confirmation can be found in Solicitor E. H. Sims to Metcalf, 6 August 1906, File 66007, Japanese Raids on the Seal Islands, RG 40.

26. Bowers to Nagel, 9 March 1909, File 66003, Folder 2, Bering Sea Patrol, RG 40.

27. Lembkey Memorandum and Strauss to Root, 28 September 1907, File 66008, Matters Pertaining to the Victoria Sealing Fleet, RG 40.

28. The *Times* predicted that, if the United States could ensure the adherence of other nations, then the seal would be saved because the Paris rules would eventually drive Canadian sealers out of business, *New York Times,* 19 August 1893.

29. As part of the settlement of the Russo-Japanese War, the Japanese acquired the southern half of Sakhalin Island and smaller surrounding islands, including Robben Island and the Kuriles.

30. "Behring Sea Sealing," Mr. Howard, British Embassy, to Robert Bacon, 20 July 1908, File 99, RG 59.

31. Montgomery Schuyler, Ambassador to Russia, to Root, 11 August and 4 September 1908, and P. A. Jay, Chargé in Tokyo, to Root, 5 October 1908, ibid.

32. Editorials from the *Japan Times,* 9 August 1908, and *Japan Daily Mail,* 20 August 1908, ibid.

33. Root to Ambassador Baron Kogoro Takahira, 21 January 1909, File 99, RG 59.

34. R. N. Venning to L. P. Brodeur, Minister of Marine and Fisheries, 17 December 1908, Vol. 1093, File 31, RG 25.

35. The best source on the origins of the External Affairs Department is John Hilliker, *Canada's Department of External Affairs,* Vol. 1: *The Early Years, 1909–1946* (Montreal, 1990).

36. Bryce to Lord Grey, 5 May 1909, Vol. 1093, File 31, RG 25.

37. Pope to Secretary of State Charles Murphy, October 1909, ibid.

38. Whitelaw Reid to Alvey Adee, 5 November 1909, File 99, RG 59.

39. E. H. Edwards to his commanding officer, 13 September 1909, and Louis Mallet, Foreign Office, to the Colonial Office, 9 November 1909, Vol. 1093, File 99, RG 25; Pope to Charles Murphy, 28 May 1911, File 40, pt. 3, RG 25; see also Briton Busch, *War against the Seals* (Montreal, 1985), 113, 119, 143–44.

40. Pope's Memorandum on the United States Proposal to Suppress Pelagic Sealing, December 1909; and Pope to Laurier, 29 November 1909, Vol. 1093, File 31, RG 25.

41. Strauss to FSAB, 15 January and 6 February, 1909, File 66001, Folder 1, Personnel of the Fur Seal Board, RG 40. It is important to note that while Jordan was the chairman of the FSAB, he was also working with Professor E. E. Prince on the boundary waters fishing regulations.

42. The substance of Clark's report is in Hugh Smith, Acting Commissioner of Fisheries, to Nagel, 31 August 1909, in the Nagel Papers. It should be noted that Clark did suspect that, as Elliott charged, the NACC was killing male seals that were too young. His persistence in advocating an internal investigation eventually led to a falling-out between him and the government fisheries officials.

43. "Recommendations of the Fur Seal Advisory Board," 23 November 1909, File 66001, Folder 1, RG 40.

44. David Starr Jordan, *The Call of the Nation: A Plea for Taking Politics out of Politics* (Boston, 1910), 41.

45. Anderson to Henry Hoyt, State Department Counselor, 22 November 1909 and 7 August 1910, File 711.417, RG 59. Anderson did not elaborate on his reasons, but one can infer from his simultaneous work on the boundary water fisheries, Bering Sea fur seals, and Newfoundland fisheries arbitration that he had lost his patience with fishery biologists!

46. Nagel to Taft, 11 March 1910, Box 3, Folder 37, Nagel Papers; Nagel's testimony to the Committee on Conservation of Natural Resources, 22 March 1910, United States, 61st Congress, Senate Document 605.

47. Senate bill 7242 in the 61st Congress. Hornaday, *Thirty Years War for Wild Life,* 171–83; Hornaday's testimony to the Committee on Conservation of Natural Resources, 26 February 1910, United States, 61st Congress, Senate Document 605.

48. An example of the thinking of the FSAB is Frederic Lucas to Nagel, 17 August 1911, in which he argued that the suspension of land killing would be a waste. Box 6, Folder 86, Nagel Papers. Anderson to Hoyt, 3 July 1910, File 711.417, RG 59.

49. Hornaday bombarded Nagel with letters, including one 18 May 1910 (Box 3, Folder 44) and "An Open Letter and Exhibits from the Camp-Fire Club of America, in behalf of the Fur Seal," 24 July 1910, both in the Nagel Papers.

50. Memo to Knox, 15 March 1910, Box 3, Folder 37, Nagel Papers.

51. Hornaday to Nagel, 18 May 1910. On the Pinchot-Ballinger controversy, see chap. 3, note 12, above.

52. Hornaday's testimony to the Committee on Conservation of Natural Resources, 26 February 1910.

53. Lord Grey to Bryce, 28 February 1910; and Pope to Lord Grey, 6 May 1910, Vol. 1100, File 65-1910, RG 25.

54. Bryce to Lord Grey's Administrator, Mr. Girouard, 11 July 1910; and Lord Crewe to Lord Grey, 2 September 1910, Vol. 1100, File 65-1910, Pt. 2, RG 25; note that Britain's interest was at least partially related to London's role as the center of the fur industry.

55. Found to Pope, 3 December 1910; and Pope to Laurier, 5 December 1910, Vol. 1100, File 65-1910, Pt. 2, RG 25.

56. For a copy of the treaty, see *FRUS, 1911* (Washington, 1918), 256–59.

57. Pope to Bryce, 5 June 1911, Vol. 1108, File "Negotiations with the Japanese," RG 25.

58. The terms of the first American offer are in Anderson to Bryce, 15 April 1911, Vol. 1108, File 40, Vol. 2, Pt. 1, RG 25. There are at least four descriptions of the actual course of the negotiations available: first, the official protocols, about which Pope said "nobody appears to attach any weight to the protocols, or to what they say or do not say," are in File 711.417, RG 59, and in the Nagel Papers; second, Pope kept exhaustive records of the negotiations, which are in Vol. 1108–9, RG 25; third, those same files also hold some of Bryce's reports back to Edward Grey; fourth, Nagel and Anderson wrote a thirty-four-page report on the negotiations for Knox, in File 711.417/227, RG 59.

59. Bryce to Sir Edward Grey, 23 May 1911, Vol. 153, File 425, Pt. 14, RG 23; Uchida's statement in the Protocols, 16 May 1911, p. 7, Nagel Papers.

60. Pope to Secretary of State Charles Murphy, 28 May 1911, Vol. 1108, File 40, RG 25. Pope sent about twenty long, confidential letters to Murphy, keeping him fully informed of the progress of the negotiations. These letters form the best record of the negotiations available.

61. Nagel and Anderson to Knox, 13 May 1912, File 711.417/227, RG 59.

62. Protocols of Negotiations, 22 May 1911, p. 15, Nagel Papers.

63. Pope to Murphy, marked "Private and Confidential," 23 May 1911, Vol. 1108, File 40, Vol. 2, Pt. 2, RG 25. On many days, Pope sent two letters to Murphy, one in measured tones for the official records and one more bluntly assessing the positions and behavior of his fellow diplomats.

64. Nagel and Anderson to Knox, 12 May 1911, File 711.417/227, RG 59; Pope to Murphy, 6 June 1911, Vol. 1109, File 40, Pt. 2, RG 25.

65. Pope to Murphy, 6 June 1911, Vol. 1109, File 40, Pt. 2, RG 25.

66. Pope to Bryce, 5 June 1911; "Table Showing the Anticipated Number of Fur-Seals Killed," Furnished by the Japanese Ambassador; and Pope to Uchida, 10 June 1911, Vol. 1108, File "Negotiations with the Japanese," RG 25.

67. Pope to Uchida, 10 June 1911, ibid.

68. Uchida to Pope, 11 June 1911, Vol. 1109, File 40, Pt. 2, RG 25.

69. Taft telegram to Ambassador O'Brien, 12 June 1911, File 711.417, RG 59; Pope to Murphy, 12 and 18 June 1911, Vol. 1109, File 40, Pt. 2, RG 25; *New York Daily Tribune*, 14 June 1911, Vol. 1109, File 40, Pt. 2, "newspaper clippings," RG 25.

70. The historian Thomas Bailey contended that a Japanese desire to improve relations with the United States was one of three reasons why Tokyo sent delegates to the convention. "The North Pacific Sealing Convention of 1911," *Pacific Historical Review*, Vol. 4, No. 1 (1935), 1–14. In his study of U.S.-Japanese interactions from 1897–1911, *Pacific Estrangement* (Cambridge, 1972), the historian Akira Iriye indicates, in part, that Japanese leaders wanted to live up to the expectations from the

Russo-Japanese War that Japan had joined the ranks of progressive states. He also points out the importance of the 1911 commercial agreement, which restored Japan's tariff autonomy, to which Taft was obliquely referring.

71. A copy of the treaty can be found in *FRUS, 1911* (Washington, 1918).

72. A. Mitchell Innes to Edward Grey, 28 August 1912, Vol. 153, File 425, Pt. 14, RG 23.

73. The complete record of the hearings, all 892 pages, is in *Hearings before the Committee on Expenditures in the Department of Commerce, House of Representatives, Investigation of the Fur-seal Industry of Alaska* (Washington, 1914).

74. "Bowers Hits Hard," *Washington Star,* 12 August 1911; and "Brings Trained Seal to Committee Room," *Washington Star,* 21 August 1911, in File 66001, Folder 26, "Press Clippings," RG 40.

75. *Congressional Record,* 62d Congress, 2d Sess., 7, 14, and 28 February 1912, Vol. 48, Pt. 2–3: 1812–21, 2047–65, 2549.

76. Jordan and Clark, "Truth About the Fur Seals," 5; and Hornaday, "Open Letter and Exhibits."

77. Jordan to Sulzer, 5 February 1912, and Jordan to Hitchcock, 10 April 1912, Clark Fur Seal Papers; Charles Sheldon, Boone and Crockett Club, to the Senate, 8 April 1912, File 66013, RG 40.

78. Knox to Senator Henry Cabot Lodge, 18 July 1912, File 711.417, RG 59; Anderson to Nagel, 30 November 1912, File 66013, Folder 1, "North Pacific Sealing Convention," RG 40.

79. Memorandum from the Imperial Japanese Embassy to the State Department, 7 September 1912, File 711.417, RG 59; Pope to Bryce, 9 July 1911, Vol. 1109, File 40, Pt. 2, RG 25; Bryce to Edward Grey, 27 September 1912, Vol. 153, File 425, Pt. 14, RG 23.

80. Hitchcock to Jordan, 3 April 1912, Clark Fur Seal Papers.

81. Alvin C. Glueck, Jr., "Canada's Splendid Bargain: The North Pacific Fur Seal Convention of 1911," *Canadian Historical Review,* Vol. 63, No. 2 (June 1982), 179–201.

82. Chargé d'Affaires Wheeler, in St. Petersburg, to Knox, 1 July 1911; U.S. consul general in Yokohama to Knox, 21 June 1911; Alvey Adee to Taft, 9 October 1912, File 711.417, RG 59.

83. Pope to Murphy, 12 June 1911, Vol. 1109, File 40, Pt. 3, RG 25.

6 / OF MALLARDS AND MEN

1. An interesting discussion about how people value different species can be found in Bryan G. Norton, ed. *The Preservation of Species: The Value of Biological Diversity* (Princeton, 1986). Felton Gibbons and Deborah Strom in *Neighbors to the Birds: A History of Birdwatching in America* (New York, 1988) provide an in-depth explanation of the appeal of birds.

2. "U.S. Studies Bird Migration," *New York Times*, 20 June 1915. The first attempt to synthesize the data came in 1935 with Frederic Lincoln's *Migration of Birds*, rev. ed. (Washington, 1979).

3. Garrett Hardin, "The Tragedy of the Commons," *Science*, Vol. 162 (13 December 1968), 1243–48.

4. Gibbons and Strom, 149–55. Unlike the American states, the Canadian provinces did not seem to be in competition with one another, although provincial laws still had their shortcomings.

5. John Burnham, "Take the Game from Game Hogs," Box 30, File "Take the Game from Game Hogs," John Burnham Papers, American Heritage Center, University of Wyoming, Laramie; W. C. Hazelton, "A Lucky Half-Hour with the Blue-Wings on the Des Plaines River," in Hazelton, ed., *Duck Shooting and Hunting Sketches* (Chicago, 1916). Similar stories can be found in other anthologies and in the hunting magazines of the day.

6. Harold Grieg, "Duck Shooting in British Columbia," in *Rod and Gun in Canada*, Vol. 12, No. 8 (January 1911), 1027.

7. T. Gilbert Pearson, "Bird Reservations," *Proceedings of the Seventh Annual Meeting of the Canadian Conservation Commission* (Montreal, 1916), 53–58.

8. William T. Hornaday, *Our Vanishing Wild Life* (New York, 1913), 94–103; see also Helen Ossa, *They Saved Our Birds: The Battle Won and the War to Win* (New York, 1982). Because there is no good account of the market hunters, information about them must be gleaned from their opponents, such as Hornaday and the writers in the Audubon magazine *Bird-Lore*.

9. *New York Times*, 8 October 1908; Mershon to George Grinnell, 23 March 1914, Folder 100, George Bird Grinnell Papers, Manuscripts and Archives, Yale University Library, New Haven, Conn.

10. "Our Medicine Bag," *Rod and Gun in Canada*, Vol. 11, No. 12 (May 1910), 1234; George Hopper, "Ducking on the Susquehanna Flats, Past and Present," in W. C. Hazelton, *Tales of Duck and Goose Shooting* (Chicago, 1916), 30–31.

11. William T. Hornaday, *The Statement of the Permanent Wild Life Protection Fund, 1913–1914* (New York, 1915), 81.

12. This assessment refers to the leaders on this particular fight: T. Gilbert Pearson, William T. Hornaday, John Burnham, Frank Chapman, Mabel Wright, E. W. Nelson, George Grinnell, and E. H. Forbush.

13. "Our Medicine Bag," *Rod and Gun in Canada*, Vol. 11, No. 8 (January 1910), 721. Hornaday's *Our Vanishing Wild Life* was basically one long diatribe against current hunting practices.

14. Maitland DeSormo, *John Bird Burnham: Klondiker, Adirondacker, and Eminent Conservationist* (Saranac Lake, N.Y., 1978), 147; John Reiger's *American Sportsmen and the Origins of Conservation* (New York, 1975) argues that, in fact, sportsmen deserve nearly all of the credit for developing conservationism.

15. Fred Cadham, "Duck Shooting in Manitoba," in *Rod and Gun in Canada*, Vol. 11, No. 9 (February 1910), 747.

16. As usual, one of the best sources on Roosevelt was the old Bull Moose himself: "Bird Reserves at the Mouth of the Mississippi," in Paul Schullery, ed., *Theodore Roosevelt: Wilderness Writings* (Salt Lake City, 1986), 215. Also see Theodore Roosevelt, *An Autobiography* (1913; rpt., New York, 1985), 408–36.

17. Quoted in Thomas Dunlap, *Saving America's Wildlife* (Princeton, N.J., 1988), 25.

18. The best source on this first Audubon Society is Frank Graham, *Audubon Ark: A History of the Audubon Society* (New York, 1987), 3–12. A facsimile of Grinnell's first *Audubon* magazine (February 1887, Vol. 1, No. 1) can be found in the modern *Audubon*, Vol. 89, No. 2 (March 1987).

19. Various reports, American Ornithologists' Union Records, Box 1, Folder 15 "Committee on the Protection of North American Birds," Smithsonian Institution Archives, Washington, D.C.

20. American Ornithologists' Union, *Fifty Years' Progress of American Ornithology* (New York, 1933); Keir Sterling, *Last of the Naturalists: The Career of C. Hart Merriam* (New York, 1977), chapters 3 and 4.

21. Lisa Mighetto, *Wild Animals and American Environmental Ethics* (Tucson, Ariz., 1991), 54–57.

22. John Burroughs, *Wake-Robin* (Boston, 1871) and *Bird Stories from Burroughs: Sketches of Bird Life Taken from the Works of John Burroughs* (New York, 1909), 51.

23. 161 United States Reports 519 (1896), 520–35.

24. Ibid., 520.

25. Ibid., 534.

26. Graham, 18–19.

27. Graham, 19; Hornaday estimated that 80 percent of the national work for wildlife was done in New York City (*The Statement of the Permanent Wild Life Protection Fund, 1915–16*, [New York, 1917], 18).

28. *Bird-Lore*, Vol. 1, No. 6 (November 1899), 205. As the "Official Organ of the Audubon Societies," this magazine carried attacks on milliners in almost every issue. In addition, Hornaday lent his support to the cause and popularized the fact that egret feathers were worth their weight in gold. A good source on the issue is Robin W. Doughty, *Feather Fashions and Bird Preservation: A Study in Nature Protection* (Berkeley, Calif., 1975).

29. George K. Cherrie, "The Egret Hunters of Venezuela," *Bird-Lore*, Vol. 2, No. 2 (March 1900), 50; Graham, 18; T. Gilbert Pearson, *Adventures in Bird Protection* (New York, 1937), 264; William Dutcher, "The Snowy Heron," National Committee of Audubon Societies, Educational Leaflet No. 7. The annual files of wardens' reports in the National Audubon Society Collection, Rare Books and Manuscripts Division,

New York Public Library (hereafter Audubon records), detail the various difficulties that the Audubon Association had in protecting egret colonies from aggressive poachers.

30. E. T. Couterman to Burnham, 24 September 1908, and Wm. H. Weston to Burnham, 29 Sept. 1908, Box 3, File "Correspondence, 1901–08," Burnham Papers.

31. Jenks Cameron, *The Bureau of Biological Survey: Its History, Activities and Organization* (Baltimore, Md., 1929), 70–83; Michael Bean, *The Evolution of National Wildlife Law* (Urbana, Ill., 1983), 20–22.

32. According to Hornaday, public demand for Lacey's bill was so intense that congressmen actually begged Lacey to bring it up for debate and a vote, but this could be another example of Hornaday's literary inclinations overriding his sense of accuracy. Hornaday to Sheldon, 28 September 1912, Box 4, File "Correspondence, Sept.–Dec., 1911," Burnham Papers.

33. Graham, 31, 44; Gibbons and Strom, 149–74; Pearson, 130–32.

34. Gibbons and Strom, 181. Copies of the leaflets can be found in *Bird-Lore,* which carried a different one in each issue. Just about every file in the Audubon records for this period contains letters from school officials or parents trying to get copies of the leaflets or get help in establishing a local branch of the Junior Audubon program.

35. Burnham, "Gilbert Pearson," speech from 1935, Box 37, Folder "Gilbert Pearson," Burnham Papers.

36. Mabel Osgood Wright, *Citizen Bird* (New York, 1898); Frank Chapman, *The Travels of Birds* (New York, 1916).

37. Mabel Osgood Wright, *Birdcraft: A Field Book of Two Hundred Song, Game, and Water Birds* (New York, 1899); Frank Chapman, *Bird Studies with a Camera* (New York, 1903); Herbert K. Job, *Wild Wings: Adventures of a Camera-Hunter among the Larger Wild Birds of North America on Sea and Land* (Boston, 1905); Reginald H. Howe, Jr., *On the Birds' Highway* (Boston, 1907).

38. Two poachers murdered the warden Guy Bradley in 1905 when he caught them hunting egrets in Florida's Cape Sable region. The defendants successfully claimed self-defense, and there were no eyewitnesses to contradict their story. In reporting his death, *Bird-Lore* called Bradley "the first martyr in the cause of bird protection." *Bird-Lore,* Vol. 7, No. 4 (July 1905), 218; Gibbons and Strom, 133.

39. John Phillips, *Migratory Bird Protection in North America* (Cambridge, Mass., 1934), 8; Grinnell to Shiras, 30 April 1921, George Shiras Papers, in Edward Nelson Papers, Smithsonian Institution Archives, Washington, D.C.

40. Pearson, 276.

41. Phillips (p. 9) and Graham (p. 92) both give Pearson credit for including non-game birds, but Hornaday claimed responsibility in his account. Hornaday, *Thirty Years War for Wild Life* (New York, 1931), 161–63.

42. Hornaday, *Thirty Years War for Wild Life,* 164; Gibbons and Strom also reported that Ford ordered 600 car dealers to lobby Congress on behalf of the bill (p. 157).

43. The NAAS originally accepted the money but reversed course under pressure from its membership. William S. Haskell, *The American Game Protective and Propagation Association: A History* (New York, 1937), 7–8; note that Haskell was the organization's attorney from its inception. George Grinnell wrote a more candid version of the AGPPA's origins (untitled memorandum, 27 May 1926, Folder 53 "1924–29," Grinnell Papers). Burnham to C. L. Reierson, Remington Arms UMC, 4 December 1916, Box 5, Folder "Correspondence, Dec. 1916," Burnham Papers.

44. Nelson to Pearson, 13 June 1915, Audubon records, Box 75, Folder "1915 D.C."; and Roosevelt to Burnham, 19 September 1911, Box 4, Folder "Correspondence 1911," Burnham Papers.

45. DeSormo, 25; L. P. Smith, Vice-President, Ithaca Gun Company to Burnham, 11 June 1918, Box 6, Folder "Correspondence Jan–July 1918," Burnham Papers.

46. C. Gordon Hewitt to Hornaday, 7 November 1916, Box 60, William T. Hornaday Papers, Library of Congress, Washington, D.C.; William Hornaday, *Our Vanishing Wild Life* (New York, 1913); McLean to Hornaday, 23 January 1913, Box 57, Hornaday Papers.

47. George McLean, "To Protect Migratory Game and Insectivorous Birds in the United States," Committee on Forest Reservations and the Protection of Game, S. Rep. 675, 62d Cong., 2d Sess.

48. Ibid.

49. James Trefethen, *An American Crusade for Wildlife* (New York, 1975), 154; Hornaday to Charles Sheldon, 28 September 1912, Box 4, Correspondence, File Sept.–Dec. 1911, Burnham Papers.

50. C. D. Clark to Howard Eaton, 15 January 1913, Box 70, Folder "Howard Eaton," Audubon records.

51. DeSormo, 180–81; Phillips, 10–12. Both of these accounts are based on John Burnham's recollection of events.

52. S. Res. 428, 62d Congress, 14 January 1913.

53. DeSormo, 180.

54. Hornaday to Captain Radclyffe, 22 March 1913, Box 80, Letterbook 11, Hornaday Papers; Pearson, 279.

55. Graham to Harkin, 18 March 1913, Vol. 114, File WL.U. 10[1], Records of the Canadian Wildlife Service, Record Group 109, National Archives of Canada, Ottawa (hereafter RG 109).

56. Foster, 127–31; J. H. Fleming to Harkin, 18 June 1913, RG 109.

57. Graham to W. W. Cory, Deputy Minister of Interior, 22 March 1913, RG 109. Conservationists in both countries used a wide range of estimates of crop damages, but E. H. Forbush's figure of $800,000,000 was by far the most commonly cited.

58. C. Gordon Hewitt, *Conservation of Wild Life in Canada* (New York, 1921), 7.

59. Taverner to Graham, 22 March 1913, RG 109.

60. Brooks to Harkin, 1 June 1913; Fleming to Harkin, 18 June 1913; and Saunders to Harkin, 5 December 1913, all in RG 109; Foster, 130–36.

61. Haskell, 23.

7 / COORDINATING SCIENCE, DIPLOMACY, AND PUBLIC RELATIONS

1. Henry Oldys to George Grinnell, 4 January 1913, Folder 184 "Migratory Bird Legislation, 1907–1919," George Bird Grinnell Papers, Manuscripts and Archives, Yale University Library, New Haven, Connecticut.

2. A. L. Hamilton, letter to the editor, 5 May 1913, *New York Times;* one can find thorough coverage of the issue on the *Times*'s op-ed pages throughout 1913. The editors were blatantly pro-Hornaday, and their editorials show strong support for conservation.

3. Hornaday circular "What the Feather Trade's 'Amendment' Really Means to the Birds of the World," 20 June 1913, Box 20, File "Conservation — Birds," William T. Hornaday Papers, Library of Congress, Washington, D.C.; Hornaday, "Women: The Juggernaut of the Bird World," *New York Times,* 23 February 1913; Hornaday, letter to the editor, *New York Times,* 31 May 1913; T. Gilbert Pearson, *Adventures in Bird Protection* (New York, 1937), 261–67.

4. Hornaday, *Thirty Years War for Wild Life* (New York, 1931), 199–201; Oldys to Grinnell, 10 February 1918, File "NAAS, 1917–35," Grinnell Papers.

5. Harcourt to the Dominion Privy Council, 31 July 1913, and Circular submitted to Commonweal, 1 October 1913, Vol. 416, File 11358, Record Group 7 G21, Records of the Governor General's Office, National Archives of Canada, Ottawa (hereafter RG7 G21).

6. Wallace to Wilson, 9 April 1913, File 800.6232, General Records of the Department of State, Record Group 59, United States National Archives, Washington, D.C. (hereafter RG 59).

7. Ibid.

8. Wilson to Bryan, 19 April 1913, and Alvey Adee to the secretary of agriculture, 15 April 1913, File 800.6232, RG 59.

9. Acting Secretary of Agriculture Beverly Galloway to Bryan, 2 May 1913, File 800.6232, RG 59.

10. H. W. Henshaw, chief of the Biological Service, to William Dutcher, 5 May 1910, General Correspondence, Records of the Department of Agriculture, Bureau of Biological Survey, Record Group 22, United States National Archives, Washington, D.C. (hereafter RG 22); Nelson's field journals for his research in Mexico are located

in the Edward W. Nelson Papers, Smithsonian Institution Archives, Washington, D.C.; Wallace to Wilson, 9 April 1913.

11. Good accounts of the Wilson-Huerta struggle are in Ramon Ruiz, *The Great Rebellion: Mexico, 1905–1924* (New York, 1980) and Lloyd Gardner, *Safe for Democracy* (New York, 1984), chapters 2–4.

12. H. S. Beattie to Hornaday, early February 1919, File 800.6232/101, RG 59. Note that Hornaday solicited the report, presumably because Beattie had extensive experience in Mexico; on American attitudes toward Mexican conservation in 1936, see for instance Edward Goldman to Ira Gabrielson, 25 January 1936, Box 45, Game Protection — Mexican Treaty, RG 22.

13. Solicitor Joseph Folk to Mr. Van Dyne, 22 May 1913; J. B. Moore, State Department counselor, to the Department of Agriculture, 26 May 1913; and Galloway to Bryan, 29 May 1913, File 800.6232, RG 59.

14. In 1913, the AGPPA dropped "Propagation" from its name.

15. Burnham to Bryan, 9 July 1913, and Galloway to Bryan, 30 July 1913, File 800.6232, RG 59; John Phillips, *Migratory Bird Protection in North America* (Cambridge, Mass., 1934), 13.

16. Janet Foster, *Working for Wildlife* (Toronto, 1978), 3–15.

17. Burnham to Lord Eustace Percy, British Embassy, 15 May 1914, Vol. 114, File WL.U. 10 [1], Canadian Wildlife Service, Record Group 109, National Archives of Canada, Ottawa (hereafter RG 109).

18. Grinnell to Pearson, 10 October 1913, Series 1, Reel 17, Grinnell Papers.

19. *New York Times,* 20 June 1914. After the Senate agreed to a similar appropriation in 1914, the editors wrote, "It is a sorry sight to see grave Senators prostituting their services to the game hogs" (29 April 1914).

20. E. T. Grether, editor of the *St. Louis Globe-Democrat,* to Burnham, 17 December 1915; Pearson to Stanley Hanson, 3 July 1916, National Audubon Society Collection, Rare Books and Manuscripts Division, New York Public Library (hereafter Audubon records).

21. *New York Times,* 9 November 1913, 12 November 1913, 17 November 1913, 3 December 1913, 22 December 1913; and Hornaday to Pearson, 29 November 1913, Letterbook 11, Box 80, Hornaday Papers.

22. T. S. Palmer to Grinnell, 3 January 1914, Folder 107 "T.S. Palmer, 1901–25," Grinnell Papers.

23. Charles Ditto to Bryan, 14 August 1913, File 800.6232, RG 59; on the formation of the ISPA, which largely confined itself to Missouri and neighboring states, see Hornaday, *The Statement of the Permanent Wild Life Protection Fund, 1913–14* (New York, 1915), 53. Hornaday termed the group's first meeting "incendiary and seditious."

24. G. W. Field to Hornaday, 28 May 1916, File "W. T. Hornaday," Nelson Papers.

25. Nelson to Burnham, 10 August 1916, and Lawyer to Burnham, 7 September 1916, Box 6, Folder "Correspondence July–Dec. 1916," John Burnham Papers, American Heritage Center, University of Wyoming, Laramie.

26. Pearson, 280; the legal citations for these cases are *State v. Sawyer*, 113 Maine 458; *United States v. Shauver*, 214 Federal Reports 154; and 221 Federal Reports 288.

27. McLean to Pearson, 16 September 1915, Box 75, Folder "1915, D.C.," Audubon records; McLean had introduced a similar resolution in 1911 without result. E. S. Corwin, "Game Protection and the Constitution," *Michigan Law Review*, Vol. 14, No. 8 (June 1916), 614–25.

28. Acting secretary, USDA (illegible, but possibly Beverly Galloway) to Bryan, 3 January 1914, File 800.6232, RG 59; Phillips, 13.

29. Apparently, no copy of this draft has survived. One can deduce its contents by comparing a later draft with reports such as the one from Spring Rice to Sir Edward Grey, 30 April 1914, Vol. 419, File 12734, "Migratory Bird Protection," RG 7 G21.

30. Wallace to McLean, 5 February 1914; Polk to Smith, 6 February 1914; Moore to Ambassador Sir Cecil Spring Rice, 16 February 1914, File 800.6232, RG 59.

31. Spring Rice to Bryan, 24 February 1914, File 800.6232, RG 59; Spring Rice to Grey, 24 February 1914, RG 109.

32. Spring Rice to Sir Edward Grey, 30 April 1914, RG 109.

33. Hewitt, "International Treaty for the Protection of Migratory Birds," internal memorandum written in August 1916, RG 109.

34. Hornaday, *The Statement of the Permanent Wild Life Protection Fund, 1917–19* (New York, 1920), 15; Graham to Harkin, 20 January 1916, RG 109; Burnham to Nelson, 22 April 1932, File "John Burnham," Nelson Papers.

35. *Ottawa Journal*, 11 December 1913; *Montreal Star*, 21 January 1914; "Resolution Adopted by the Commission on Conservation," 20 January 1914, RG 109; Graham to Harkin, 19 December 1913, RG 109.

36. E. T. D. Chambers, North American Fish and Game Association, to Harkin, 26 January 1914, and Harkin to W. W. Cory, deputy minister of interior, 23 January 1914, RG 109.

37. Pope to the minister of interior, 18 March 1914, RG 109.

38. G. W. Brown to Thomas Mulvey, undersecretary of state, 2 May 1914, and F. Langelier, lieutenant governor, Quebec, to the secretary of state, 13 July 1914, RG 109. The letters from the lieutenant governors are all together, despite the disparity in dates.

39. Provincial Secretary H. E. Brown to Lieutenant Governor Thomas Patterson, 12 May 1914, RG 109.

40. Patterson to Pope, 28 July 1914, RG 109.

41. Pope to Joseph Coté, assistant deputy minister of interior, 19 August 1914, and Harkin to Coté, 21 August 1914, RG 109.

42. Harkin to J. G. Mitchell, 7 April 1915, RG 109.

43. Privy Council Report 1247, and Spring Rice to the governor general, 12 February 1916, RG 109.

44. Grether to Burnham, 17 December 1915, File "John Burnham," Nelson Papers.

45. Nelson to Charles Sheldon, 19 April and 1 June 1915; Sheldon to Nelson, 24 May 1915, Box 4, File "Charles Sheldon," RG 22.

46. Hornaday, "Game Protection and the Biological Survey," *Forest and Stream,* Vol. 20 (October 1915), 632.

47. Pearson, 281; Nelson to Sheldon, 13 October 1915, Box 4, File "Charles Sheldon," RG 22; McLean to Pearson, 13 May 1914, Box 71, Folder "1914, D.C.," Audubon records; Pearson to Underwood, 30 July 1915 and Underwood's reply, 2 August 1915, Box 75, Folder "1915, D.C.," Audubon records.

48. Hewitt to Pearson, 21 January 1916, Box 82, Folder "Canada, 1916," Audubon records; Hewitt to Harkin, 28 January 1916, RG 109.

49. Other writers have given Hewitt, Nelson, and Burnham credit for locating the treaty, but Spring Rice singled out "the Director of the New York Zoological Park." Spring Rice to the governor general, 12 February 1916, RG 109.

50. Spring Rice to Lansing, the governor general, and Sir Edward Grey, all 12 February 1916, RG 109.

51. McLean to Pearson, 28 February 1916, Box 78, Folder "District of Columbia, C–M," Audubon records. *Bird-Lore, Forest and Stream,* and the *New York Times* all ignored this development, and there is no record of comment by Hornaday, Burnham, Nelson, or Pearson.

52. Privy Council to the minister of interior, 7 March 1916, RG 109; F. K. Nielsen, assistant solicitor, to Mr. Smith, 14 March 1916, File 800.6232, RG 59.

53. Hewitt, Memorandum on the Revised Draft Convention for the Protection of Migratory Birds, 11 April 1916, RG 109. On Nelson's two changes see Phillips, 14–15.

54. Burnham, "Statement," undated, but sometime in the summer of 1916, Box 29, Folder "Migratory Bird Law," Burnham Papers.

55. Burnham's story is recounted in Phillips, 16–18.

56. Phillips, 18; Burnham to Nelson, 8 June 1916, File "John Burnham," Nelson Papers.

57. Nelson to Sheldon, 31 March and 23 May 1916, File "Charles Sheldon," RG 22.

58. Pearson to Nelson, 25 April 1916; Field to Hornaday, 28 May 1916; Nelson to Pearson, 16 May 1916, Box 78, Folder "District of Columbia, N–O," Audubon records.

59. Pearson remembered that the board voted unanimously, but Forbush stated that he voted against and Hornaday left before the vote was taken, Pearson to Forbush, 2 June, and Forbush's reply, 3 June 1916, Box 80, Folder "E. H. Forbush #2," Audubon records.

60. Forbush to Pearson, 28 April 1916, Box 80, Folder "E. H. Forbush, #2," Audubon records.

61. Forbush to Pearson, 1 May 1916, and Field to H. W. Henshaw, 18 June 1916, Box 80, Folder "E. H. Forbush, #2," Audubon records; *Forest and Stream,* Vol. 21 (September 1916), 1158.

62. Privy Council Report 1537, 29 June 1916; Spring Rice to Lansing, 5 July 1916, File 800.6232, RG 59.

63. F. K. Nielsen to Mr. Smith, 10 July 1916, File 800.6232, RG 59; Forbush to Nelson, 25 July 1916, File "E. H. Forbush," Nelson Papers; Phillips to Mr. Johnson, 10 August 1916, File 800.6232, RG 59.

64. Nielsen to Smith, 10 August 1916, and Lansing to Wilson, 17 August 1916, File 800.6232, RG 59.

65. Hornaday did not identify the senator who supposedly spoke these words; Hornaday to Nelson, 31 August 1916, File "W. T. Hornaday," Nelson Papers.

66. Harriet U. Andrews to Wilson, 25 August 1916, File 800.6232, RG 59. Andrews's letter was one of about a dozen from Missouri preserved in the department's files.

67. C. W. Limick, U.S. Ammunition Company, to Wilson, 22 August 1916, File 800.6232, RG 59.

68. Hewitt to Nelson, 8 September 1916, File "Misc. letters," Nelson Papers.

69. Hornaday to President Woodrow Wilson, 30 August 1916, File 800.6232, RG 59.

8 / PROTECTING THE NATIONAL INTEREST

1. Pearson to Mrs. Frederick Thompson, 19 December 1916, Box 80, Folder "N.Y.," National Audubon Society Collection, Rare Books and Manuscript Division, New York Public Library (hereafter Audubon records). On the relationship with Shipp, see Box 79, "Thomas R. Shipp & Co." Folder, Audubon records.

2. M. J. Murphy to Pearson, 8 December 1916, Box 79, "Shipp & Co." Folder, Audubon records.

3. Pearson to Thompson, 19 December 1916, Box 80, Folder "N.Y.," Audubon records.

4. John Phillips, *Migratory Bird Protection in North America* (Cambridge, Mass., 1934), 21–22; Pearson to McLean, 15 December 1916, Box 78, Folder "District of Columbia, I–O," Audubon records.

5. McLean to Pearson, 13 December 1916, Box 78, Folder "District of Columbia, I–O," Audubon records; Pearson to Nelson, 15 December 1916, File "T. Gilbert Pearson," E. W. Nelson Papers, Smithsonian Institution Archives, Washington, D.C.

6. The various records do not tell us why Smith did not introduce the bill, but Hitchcock did have some experience working with conservation issues, such as the fur seal treaty.

7. "Saving Thousands of Birds by Law," *New York Herald,* 30 January 1917, Box 183, "Clippings," Audubon records.

8. Pearson to Hewitt, 28 March 1917, Box 87, Folder "Canada, 1917," Audubon records.

9. Greeley et al. to Wilson, 23 January 1917, and "Resolution of the Boone and Crockett Club," 8 February 1917, File 800.6232, General Records of the Department of State, Record Group 59, United States National Archives, Washington, D.C. (hereafter RG 59); Burnham to *Forest and Stream,* January 1917, p. 278.

10. Forbush to Ford, 16 January 1917, and Ford's general secretary, E. G. Liebold, to Wilson's secretary, Joseph Tumulty, 19 January 1917, File 800.6232, RG 59.

11. Huddleston to Earle Brothers Grocers, 31 January 1917, Box 82, Folder "Alabama, 1917," Audubon records; Lansing to Flood and Gore, 25 January 1917, File 800.6232, RG 59. For the record, Huddleston opposed the bill in 1918.

12. United States, 64th Congresss, 2d Sess., House Report 1430, "Protection of Migratory Birds," 6 February 1917.

13. Wallace to Houston, 15 February 1917, Box 82, Folder "Alabama, 1917," Audubon records.

14. Houston to Lansing, 20 February 1917, File 800.6232/64, RG 59; this letter provided an unusually detailed account of the path of the treaty, which helped to convey Houston's frustration about Congress's delay.

15. Undated memorandum (middle February 1917) from the assistant secretary, File 800.6232, RG 59.

16. United States, 64th Congress, 2d Sess., Senate Report 1102 "Protection of Migratory Birds," 20 February 1917; Hornaday, *The Statement of the Permanent Wild Life Protection Fund, 1915–16* (New York, 1917), 140.

17. Lansing to Wilson, Lansing to Flood, and Lansing to Smith, all 23 February 1917, and Wilson to Lansing, 27 February 1917, File 800.6232, RG 59.

18. Houston to Lansing, 20 February 1917, ibid.

19. *Congressional Record,* 65th Congress, 3d Sess., 24 May 1918, 56, Pt. 7:7029.

20. The letters used here all come from the State Department records, File 800.6232, RG 59.

21. M. L. Alexander to Wilson, 13 June 1917; J. B. Hauer (California) to Wilson, 3 May 1917; A. J. Rasmussen (Wisconsin) to Wilson, 19 May 1917; Ernest Mead (Virginia) to Wilson, 30 April 1917; and Robert Lawrence (New York) to Wilson, 14 May 1917, all in File 800.6232, RG 59.

22. *Forest and Stream,* June 1917, p. 262.

23. As examples, see Tillie Hollmann to Wilson, 2 May 1917, and Robert Terry, Treasurer, Audubon Society of Missouri, to Wilson, 25 April 1917, File 800.6232, RG 59.

24. Forbush to Wilson, 24 April 1917, and A. H. Hollinger to Wilson, 1 May 1917, ibid.

25. James to Wilson, 12 June 1917; Benjamin Gratz to Wilson, 28 April 1917; and George K. Andrews to Wilson, 27 April 1917, all ibid.

26. McCrea to Wilson, 30 May and 3 October 1917, ibid.

27. John E. Traeger to Adolph Sabath, 21 March 1918, and Peter Hoffmann to Adolph Sabath, 22 March 1918, Box 6, Folder "Correspondence, Jan.–July 1918," John Burnham Papers, American Heritage Center, University of Wyoming, Laramie.

28. Pratt to Wilson, 27 April 1917, and Badé to Wilson, 10 May 1917, File 800.6232, RG 59.

29. The most commonly cited number was Forbush's estimate of $800,000,000. E. H. Forbush, *Useful Birds and their Protection* (Boston, 1907), 36.

30. *Bird-Lore,* Vol. 19, No. 4 (July 1917), 232.

31. For more on Hoover's work with food conservation, see David Kennedy, *Over Here: The First World War and American Society* (New York, 1980), 117–19.

32. Kennedy, 253–56.

33. United States, 65th Congress, 1st Sess., Senate Report 27, "Protection of Migratory Birds," 20 April 1917.

34. *Congressional Record,* 65th Congress, 1st Sess., 28 June 1917, Vol. 55, Pt. 5: 4399–4402.

35. *Congressional Record,* 65th Congress, 1st Sess., 9 July 1917, Vol. 55, Pt. 5:4811–15.

36. *Congressional Record,* 65th Congress, 1st Sess., 9 July 1917, Vol. 55, Pt. 5:4818–20. On the question of insects running rampant if not for birds, Smith cited studies that purported to show that the offspring of one pair of gypsy moths could defoliate the continent in eight years and that in one year one pair of hop aphids could produce ten sextillion offspring.

37. *Congressional Record,* 65th Congress, 1st Sess., 30 July 1917, Vol. 55, Pt. 6:5543–47.

38. Burnham to Nelson, 31 July 1917, Folder "John Bird Burnham, 1915–1919," Nelson Papers; Burnham to Baruch, 17 May 1917, Box 6, Folder "Correspondence, May–July 1917," Burnham Papers.

39. Pearson to Hoover, 5 November 1917, Box 83, Folder "District of Columbia," Audubon records. The membership figure of 300,000 is almost hard to believe, but Pearson clearly stated it.

40. Pearson to Hewitt, 11 January 1918, Box 87, Folder "Canada, 1917," Audubon records; Chapman, "A Warning!" *Bird-Lore,* Vol. 20, No. 1 (January 1918), 70.

41. Burnham to William Phillips, 4 December 1917; Lansing to Flood, 8 December 1917; Hornaday to House, 29 December 1917, all in File 800.6232, RG 59; also McLean to Pearson, 18 December 1917, Box 83, Folder "District of Columbia," Audubon records.

42. United States, 65th Congress, 2d Sess., House Report 243, "Protection of Migratory Birds," 17 January 1918.

43. Pearson to Hewitt, 18 January 1918, Box 87, Folder "Canada, 1917," Audubon records.

44. McLean to Wilson, 30 April 1918; Wilson to Lansing, 1 May 1918; and Phillips to Flood, 4 May 1918, File 800.6232, all in RG 59.

45. Burnham to "My dear Sir," 2 May 1918, Box 6, Folder "Correspondence, Jan.-July, 1918," Burnham Papers; *Congressional Record,* 65th Congress, 2d Sess., 24 May 1918, Vol. 56, Pt. 7:7029.

46. *Congressional Record,* 65th Congress, 2d Sess., 4 June 1918, Vol. 56, Pt. 7:7357.

47. Ibid., Pt. 7:7359-60.

48. Ibid., Pt. 7:7363, 7367; and 6 June 1918, Vol. 56, Pt. 8:7445, 7448.

49. Ibid., Pt. 7:7365-67.

50. Ibid., 6 June 1918, Vol. 56, Pt. 8:7446-7.

51. Ibid., 4 June 1918, Vol. 56, Pt. 7:7361, 7369-70; Stedman was easily the most persuasive and devoted advocate for bird protection in the House, yet I have not found any mention of him in the conservationists' writings.

52. Grinnell to Burnham, 8 March 1918, David Smouse to Burnham, 14 June 1918, and Burnham to Glen Buck, 7 June 1918, Box 6, File "Correspondence, Jan.-July 1918," Burnham Papers.

53. *Debates, House of Commons, Dominion of Canada,* 7th Sess., 12th Parliament, 21 June and 21 July 1917, Vol. 3, column 2525, and Vol. 4, columns 3657-63.

54. Deputy Minister of Interior W. W. Cory to Hewitt, 26 July 1917, Vol. 114, File WL.U. 10 [1], Canadian Wildlife Service, Record Group 109, National Archives of Canada, Ottawa (hereafter RG 109).

55. "Protection of Birds," *Montreal Gazette,* 10 August 1917, and "A Treaty for the Protection of Migratory Birds in Canada," *Montreal Herald,* 11 August 1917, Vol. 114, WL.U. 10 [1], RG 109.

56. Harkin, undated memorandum, Vol. 114, WL. U. 10 [2], RG 109.

57. Hewitt to Harkin, 15 March 1918, and C. J. Kerr to Harkin, 24 October 1918, ibid.; and "Bill to Amend the Migratory Bird Conservation Act," undated, but post-March 1920, Vol. 114, WL. U. 10 [3], RG 109.

58. Janet Foster, *Working for Wildlife* (Toronto, 1978), 147.

59. Phillips, 22; the records of MBTA prosecutions can be found in Record Group 22, Records of the Bureau of Biological Survey, United States National Archives. It is unclear whether the prosecution records reflect the nature of the law-breaking or a concentration of enforcement efforts.

60. William Haskell, *The American Game Protective and Propagation Association: A History* (New York, 1937), 27-30. It seems likely that Holland would have recognized McAllister, so the false name story seems implausible. There is also some question as to whether or not the incident was staged to furnish a test case. If Haskell's account, which probably came directly from Holland, is accurate, then McAllister seemed more interested in good hunting than in being a martyr.

61. *United States Reports,* Vol. 252, pp. 416–18.

62. Ibid., 419–21.

63. Ibid., 424–28.

64. Ibid., 431–35. Felix Frankfurter described Holmes's decision as "one of the finest pearls you've ever cut. . . . It's a thrilling piece." Frankfurter to Holmes, 15 May 1920, in Robert Mennel and Christine Compston, eds., *Holmes and Frankfurter: Their Correspondence, 1912–1934* (Hanover, N.H., 1996), 89.

EPILOGUE

1. For more on the IPSFC, see John Roos, *Restoring Fraser River Salmon: A History of the International Pacific Salmon Fisheries Commission* (Vancouver, 1991); "Canada Slashes Salmon Fishery," *Seattle Post-Intelligencer,* 5 July 1995.

2. Philip Shabecoff, "Urgent Effort to Save Ducks Begins in U.S. and Canada," *New York Times,* 9 February 1988.

3. Richard Benedick, *Ozone Diplomacy: New Directions in Safeguarding the Planet* (Cambridge, Mass., 1990), includes a similar, but more detailed, list of lessons drawn from his experience in the 1980s with the international efforts to protect the ozone layer (pp. 204–208).

Bibliography

ARCHIVAL COLLECTIONS

United States National Archives, Washington, D.C.
  Records of the Department of Agriculture, Bureau of Biological Survey (Record Group 22)
  Records of the Department of Commerce and Labor (Record Group 40)
  General Records of the Department of State (Record Group 59)
National Archives of Canada, Ottawa
  Claims by Pelagic Sealers Arising out of the Washington Treaty of 7th July 1911 (Record Group 33/107)
  Records of the Canadian Wildlife Service (Record Group 109)
  Records of the Department of External Affairs (Record Group 25)
  Records of the Governor General's Office (Record Group 7, G21)
  Records of the Ministry of Marine and Fisheries (Record Group 23)
New York Public Library, Rare Books and Manuscripts
  National Audubon Society Collection
Smithsonian Institution Archives, Washington, D.C.
  Records of the American Ornithologists' Union

PERSONAL PAPERS

John Burnham Papers. American Heritage Center, University of Wyoming, Laramie.
George A. Clark Fur Seal Controversy Papers, in David Starr Jordan Papers. Microfilm edition. Stanford University Libraries, Stanford, California.
George Bird Grinnell Papers. Manuscripts and Archives, Yale University Library, New Haven, Connecticut.
William T. Hornaday Papers. Library of Congress, Washington, D.C.
David Starr Jordan Papers. Microfilm edition. Stanford University Libraries, Stanford, California.
Charles Nagel Papers. Manuscripts and Archives, Yale University Library, New Haven, Connecticut.
Edward W. Nelson Papers. Smithsonian Institution Archives, Washington, D.C.
Richard Rathbun Papers. Manuscripts and Archives, Cornell University Libraries, Ithaca, New York.

George Shiras Papers. In Edward W. Nelson Papers, Smithsonian Institution Archives, Washington, D.C.

PUBLISHED DOCUMENTS

Canada. *Debates, House of Commons, Dominion of Canada, 1909–1910.* 2d Sess., 11th Parliament, Vol. 50.

Canada. *Debates, House of Commons, Dominion of Canada, 1910–1911.* 3d Sess., 11th Parliament, Vol. 51.

Canada. *Debates, House of Commons, Dominion of Canada, 1917.* 7th Sess., 12th Parliament, Vol. 58.

United States Congress. *Congressional Record,* 58th Congress, 2d Sess., Vol. 43.

United States Congress. *Congressional Record,* 61st Congress, 3d Sess., Vol. 46.

United States Congress. *Congressional Record,* 62d Congress, 1st Sess., Vol. 47.

United States Congress. *Congressional Record,* 62d Congress, 2d Sess., Vol. 48.

United States Congress. *Congressional Record,* 63d Congress, 2d Sess., Vol. 51.

United States Congress. *Congressional Record,* 65th Congress, 1st Sess., Vol. 55.

United States Congress. *Congressional Record,* 65th Congress, 2d Sess., Vol. 56.

United States Congress. *Congressional Record,* 65th Congress, 3d Sess., Vol. 57.

United States Congress. *Hearings Before the Committee on Expenditures in the Department of Commerce and Labor, House of Representatives. Investigation of the Fur-seal Industry of Alaska.* Washington, D.C. 1914.

United States Congress. 54th Congress, 2d Sess., "Report of the Joint Commission Relative to the Preservation of the Fisheries in Waters Contiguous to Canada and the United States." House Document 315.

United States Congress. 61st Congress, 2d Sess., "Fur-Seal Fisheries: Hearings Before the Committee on Conservation of National Resources." Senate Document 605.

United States Congress. 61st Congress, 3d Sess., "Fisheries in Waters Contiguous to the United States and Canada." Senate Report 1176.

United States Congress. 62nd Congress, 2d Sess., "To Protect Migratory Game and Insectivorous Birds in the United States." Senate Report 675.

United States Congress. 64th Congress, 2d Sess., "Protection of Migratory Birds." Senate Report 1102.

United States Congress. 64th Congress, 2d Sess., "Protection of Migratory Birds." House Report 1430.

United States Congress. 65th Congress, 1st Sess., "Protection of Migratory Birds." Senate Report 27.

United States Congress. 65th Congress, 2d Sess., "Protection of Migratory Birds." House Report 243.

United States Department of State. *Papers Relating to the Foreign Relations of the United States, 1890.* Washington, D.C., 1891.

United States Department of State. *Papers Relating to the Foreign Relations of the United States, 1891.* Washington, D.C., 1892.

United States Department of State. *Papers Relating to the Foreign Relations of the United States, 1897.* Washington, D.C., 1898.

United States Department of State. *Papers Relating to the Foreign Relations of the United States, 1911.* Washington, D.C., 1918.

United States Department of State. *Fur Seal Arbitration: Proceedings of the Tribunal of Arbitration, Convened at Paris.* Washington, D.C., 1895.

United States Supreme Court. *United States Reports.* Vol. 161, Washington, D.C., 1896.

United States Supreme Court. *United States Reports.* Vol. 252, Washington, D.C., 1920.

BOOKS, ARTICLES, AND THESES

American Ornithologists' Union. *Fifty Years' Progress of American Ornithology.* New York: Special Publication of the American Ornithologists' Union, 1933.

Ashworth, William. *The Late, Great Lakes: An Environmental History.* New York: Alfred A. Knopf, 1986.

Avery, Mary. *Washington: A History of the Evergreen State.* Seattle: University of Washington Press, 1961.

Bailey, James A., ed. *Readings in Wildlife Conservation.* Washington, D.C.: The Wildlife Society, 1974.

Bailey, Thomas. "The North Pacific Sealing Convention of 1911." *Pacific Historical Review* 4 (March 1935): 1–14.

Beale, Howard K. *Theodore Roosevelt and the Rise of America to World Power.* Baltimore: The Johns Hopkins University Press, 1956.

Bean, Michael. *The Evolution of National Wildlife Law.* Urbana: Praeger, 1983.

Bemis, Samuel Flagg. *A Diplomatic History of the United States.* New York: Holt, 1955.

Benedick, Richard. *Ozone Diplomacy: New Directions in Safeguarding the Planet.* Cambridge: Harvard University Press, 1991.

Bogue, Margaret Beattie. "To Save the Fish: Canada, the United States, the Great Lakes, and the Joint Commission of 1892." *Journal of American History* 79 (March 1993): 1429–54.

Bogue, Margaret Beattie, and Virginia A. Palmer. *Around the Shores of Lake Superior: A Guide to Historic Sites.* Madison: University of Wisconsin Press, 1979.

Burroughs, John. *Bird Stories from Burroughs: Sketches of Bird Life Taken from the Works of John Burroughs.* New York: Houghton Mifflin, 1909.

———. *Wake-Robin.* New York: Hurd and Houghton, 1871.

Busch, Briton. *The War against the Seals: A History of the North American Seal Fishery.* Montreal: McGill-Queen's University Press, 1985.

Caldwell, Lynton Keith. *International Environmental Policy: Emergence and Dimensions.* Durham, N.C.: Duke University Press, 1984.

Cameron, Jenks. *The Bureau of Biological Survey: Its History, Activities and Organization.* Baltimore: The Johns Hopkins University Press, 1929.

Campbell, Charles S., Jr. "The Anglo-American Crisis in the Bering Sea, 1890–1891." *Mississippi Valley Historical Review* 66 (December 1961): 395–410.

―――. *Anglo-American Understanding, 1898–1903.* Baltimore: The Johns Hopkins University Press, 1957.

―――. "The Bering Sea Settlements of 1892." *Pacific Historical Review* 32 (November 1963): 347–68.

Carroll, John E. *Environmental Diplomacy: An Examination and a Prospective of Canadian-U.S. Transboundary Environmental Relations.* Ann Arbor: University of Michigan Press, 1983.

Chacko, Chirakaikaran J. *The International Joint Commission between the United States of America and the Dominion of Canada.* 1932. Reprint edition, New York: AMS Press, 1968.

Chapman, Frank. *Bird Studies with a Camera.* New York: D. Appleton and Company, 1903.

―――. *The Travels of Birds.* New York: D. Appleton and Company, 1916.

Chasan, Daniel Jack. *The Water Link: A History of Puget Sound as a Resource.* Seattle: University of Washington Press, 1981.

Corwin, E. S. "Game Protection and the Constitution." *Michigan Law Review* 14 (June 1916): 614–25.

Cutright, Paul R. *Theodore Roosevelt: The Making of a Conservationist.* Urbana: University of Illinois Press, 1985.

DeSormo, Maitland. *John Bird Burnham: Klondiker, Adirondacker, and Eminent Conservationist.* Saranac Lake, N.Y.: Adirondack Yesteryears, 1978.

Devine, Michael. *John W. Foster: Politics and Diplomacy in the Imperial Era, 1873–1917.* Athens: Ohio University Press, 1981.

Doughty, Robin. *Feather Fashions and Bird Preservation: A Study in Nature Protection.* Berkeley: University of California Press, 1975.

Dunlap, Thomas. *Saving America's Wildlife.* Princeton, N.J.: Princeton University Press, 1988.

Elliott, Henry W. *The Seal-islands of Alaska.* 1876. Reprint edition, Kingston, Ontario: Limestone Press, 1976.

Ellis, L. Ethan. *Reciprocity 1911: A Study in Canadian-American Relations.* New Haven: Yale University Press, 1939.

Everhart, W. Harry, and William D. Youngs. *Principles of Fishery Science.* 2d ed. Ithaca: Cornell University Press, 1981.

Falconer, Robert. *The United States as a Neighbor, from a Canadian Point of View.* New York: Macmillan, 1925.

Flores, Dan. "Bison Ecology and Bison Diplomacy: The Southern Plains from 1800 to 1850." *Journal of American History* 78 (October 1980): 465–85.

Forbush, Edward H. *Useful Birds and their Protection.* Boston: Massachusetts State Board of Agriculture, 1907.

Foster, Janet. *Working for Wildlife: The Beginning of Preservation in Canada.* Toronto: University of Toronto Press, 1978.

Fox, Stephen. *John Muir and His Legacy: The American Conservation Movement.* Boston: Little, Brown, and Company, 1981.

Gardner, Lloyd. *Safe for Democracy: Anglo-American Response to Revolution, 1913–1923.* New York: Oxford University Press, 1984.

Gay, James Thomas. "Henry W. Elliott: Crusading Conservationist." *The Alaska Journal* 3 (1973): 211–16.

Gibbons, Felton, and Deborah Strom. *Neighbors to the Birds: A History of Birdwatching in America.* New York: W. W. Norton, 1988.

Glueck, Alvin C., Jr. "Canada's Splendid Bargain: The North Pacific Fur Seal Convention of 1911." *Canadian Historical Review* 63 (June 1982): 179–201.

Graham, Frank. *Audubon Ark: A History of the Audubon Society.* New York: Alfred A. Knopf, 1987.

Halliday, T. R. "The Extinction of the Passenger Pigeon *Ectopistes migratorious* and Its Relevance to Contemporary Conservation." *Biological Conservation* 17 (2 February 1980): 157–62.

Hannigan, Robert E. "Reciprocity 1911: Continentalism and American Weltpolitik." *Diplomatic History* 4 (Winter 1980): 1–18.

Hardin, Garrett. "The Tragedy of the Commons." *Science* 162 (13 December 1968): 1243–48.

Haskell, William S. *The American Game Protective and Propagation Association: A History.* New York: Special Publication of the AGPA, 1937.

Hatcher, Harlan. *The Great Lakes.* London: Oxford University Press, 1944.

———. *Lake Erie.* Indianapolis: Bobbs-Merrill, 1945.

Hayden, Sherman Strong. *The International Protection of Wildlife: An Examination of Treaties and Other Agreements for the Preservation of Birds and Mammals.* New York: Columbia University Press, 1942.

Hays, Samuel. *Conservation and the Gospel of Efficiency: The Progressive Conservation Movement, 1890–1920.* Cambridge, Mass.: Harvard University Press, 1959.

Hazelton, W. C., ed. *Duck Shooting and Hunting Sketches.* Chicago: Eastman Brothers, 1916.

———. *Tales of Duck and Goose Shooting.* Chicago: Eastman Brothers, 1916.

Hewitt, C. Gordon. *Conservation of Wild Life in Canada.* New York: Scribner's Sons, 1921.

Hilliker, John. *Canada's Department of External Affairs.* Vol. 1: *The Early Years, 1909–1946.* Montreal: McGill-Queen's University Press, 1990.

Hobsbawm, Eric. *The Age of Empire, 1875–1914.* New York: Vintage Books, 1989.

Hopkins, J. Castell. *The Canadian Annual Review of Public Affairs, 1906.* Toronto: The Annual Review Publishing Company, 1906.

———. *The Canadian Annual Review of Public Affairs, 1908.* Toronto: The Annual Review Publishing Company, 1908.

Hornaday, William Temple. *Our Vanishing Wild Life.* New York: Scribner's Sons, 1913.

———. "The Rescued Fur Seal Industry." *Science* 52 (23 July 1920): 81–82.

———. *The Statement of the Permanent Wild Life Protection Fund, 1913–1914.* New York: New York Zoological Society, 1915.

———. *The Statement of the Permanent Wild Life Protection Fund, 1915–1916.* New York: New York Zoological Society, 1917.

———. *The Statement of the Permanent Wild Life Protection Fund, 1917–1919.* New York: New York Zoological Society, 1920.

———. *Thirty Years War for Wild Life: Gains and Losses in the Thankless Task.* New York: Scribner's Sons, 1931; reprint edition, New York: Arno Press, 1971.

Howe, Reginald H., Jr. *On the Birds' Highway.* Boston: Small, Maynard, and Company, 1899.

Innis, Harold. *The Cod Fisheries: The History of an International Economy.* New Haven: Yale University Press, 1940.

Iriye, Akira. *Pacific Estrangement: Japanese and American Expansion, 1879–1911.* Cambridge, Mass.: Harvard University Press, 1972.

Isenberg, Andrew C. "Indians, Whites, and the Buffalo: An Ecological History of the Great Plains, 1750–1900." Ph.D. dissertation, Northwestern University, 1992.

Job, Herbert K. *Wild Wings: Adventures of a Camera-Hunter among the Larger Wild Birds of North America on Sea and Land.* Boston: Houghton Mifflin, 1905.

Johnson, Robert Underwood. "The Neglect of Beauty in the Conservation Movement." *Century* 79 (1910); in Roderick Nash, ed. *American Environmentalism: Readings in Conservation History.* 3d ed. New York, 1990.

Jordan, David Starr. *The Call of the Nation: A Plea for Taking Politics out of Politics.* Boston: Beacon Press, 1910.

———. *Days of a Man, Being Memories of a Naturalist, Teacher, and Minor Prophet of Democracy.* Yonkers-on-Hudson, N.Y.: World Book Company, 1922.

———. *Matka and Kotik; A Tale of the Mist-islands.* San Francisco: Whitaker and Ray, 1897.

———. *Report of Fur Seal Investigations.* Washington, D.C.: Government Printing Office, 1898.

Jordan, David Starr, and George A. Clark, eds. *Seal and Salmon Fisheries and General Resources of Alaska.* Washington, D.C.: Government Printing Office, 1898.

Jordan, David Starr, and Barton W. Evermann. *American Food and Game Fishes.* New York: Doubleday, Page and Company, 1908.

Jordan, David Starr, and Edwin Chapin Starks. *The Fishes of Puget Sound*. Palo Alto: Stanford University Publications, 1895.

Kennedy, David M. *Over Here: The First World War and American Society*. New York: Oxford University Press, 1980.

Kennedy, Paul. *The Rise and Fall of the Great Powers: Economic Change and Military Conflict from 1500 to 2000*. New York: Random House, 1987.

LaFeber, Walter. *The American Age: United States Foreign Policy at Home and Abroad since 1750*. New York: W. W. Norton, 1994.

Landon, Fred. *Lake Huron*. Indianapolis: Bobbs-Merrill, 1945.

Leopold, Aldo. *Game Management*. 1933. Reprint edition, Madison: University of Wisconsin Press, 1986.

———. "Wildlife in American Culture." In James A. Bailey, ed. *Readings in Wildlife Conservation*. Washington, D.C.: The Wildlife Society, 1974.

Leopold, Richard. *Elihu Root and the Conservative Tradition*. Boston: Little, Brown, and Company, 1954.

Lincoln, Frederic. *Migration of Birds*. Revised edition. Washington, D.C.: Government Printing Office, 1979.

Lyster, Simon. *International Wildlife Law: An Analysis of International Treaties Concerned with the Conservation of Wildlife*. Cambridge, England: Grotius Publishers, 1985.

Mason, Alpheus T. *Democracy Convicts Itself: The Ballinger-Pinchot Controversy of 1910*. New York: Viking Press, 1941.

May, Ernest. *Imperial Democracy: The Emergence of America as a Great Power*. 1961. Reprint edition, Chicago: Imprint Publications, 1991.

McEvoy, Arthur F. *The Fisherman's Problem: Ecology and Law in the California Fisheries*. New York: Cambridge University Press, 1986.

Mennel, Robert M., and Christine L. Compston, eds. *Holmes and Frankfurter: Their Correspondence, 1912–1934*. Hanover, N.H.: University Press of New England, 1996.

Merck, Frederick, ed. *Fur Trade and Empire: George Simpson's Journal*. Cambridge, Mass.: Harvard University Press, 1931.

Mighetto, Lisa. *Wild Animals and American Environmental Ethics*. Tucson: University of Arizona Press, 1991.

Moffett, Samuel. *The Americanization of Canada*. New York: Columbia University Press, 1907.

Nash, Roderick, ed. *American Environmentalism: Readings in Conservation History*. 3d ed. New York: McGraw Hill, 1990.

———. *Wilderness and the American Mind*. 3d ed. New Haven: Yale University Press, 1982.

National Advisory Committee on Oceans and the Atmosphere. *North Pacific Fur*

Seals: Current Problems and Opportunities Concerning Conservation and Management. Washington, D.C.: Government Printing Office, 1985.

Neary, Peter. "Grey, Bryce and the Settlement of Canadian-American Differences, 1905–1911." *Canadian Historical Review* 49 (December 1968): 357–80.

Newell, Dianne. *The Development of the Pacific Salmon-Canning Industry: A Grown Man's Game.* Montreal: McGill-Queen's University Press, 1989.

North Pacific Fur Seal Commission. *Report on Investigations from 1967 through 1972.* Washington, D.C.: Government Printing Office, 1975.

Norton, Bryan G., ed. *The Preservation of Species: The Value of Biological Diversity.* Princeton, N.J.: Princeton University Press, 1986.

Nute, Grace Lee. *Lake Superior.* Indianapolis: Bobbs-Merrill, 1945.

Ossa, Helen. *They Saved Our Birds: The Battle Won and the War to Win.* New York: Hippocrene Books, 1982.

Pearson, T. Gilbert. *Adventures in Bird Protection.* Special Publication of the American Committee for International Wildlife Protection. New York: Appleton-Century, 1937.

———. "Bird Reservations." In *Proceedings of the Seventh Annual Meeting of the Canadian Conservation Commission, 1916.* Montreal: Federated Press, 53–58.

Penick, James, Jr. *Progressive Politics and Conservation: The Ballinger-Pinchot Affair.* Chicago: University of Chicago Press, 1968.

Penlington, Norman. *The Alaska Boundary Dispute: A Critical Reappraisal.* Toronto: McGraw-Hill Ryerson, 1972.

Perkins, Bradford. *The Great Rapprochement: England and the United States, 1895–1914.* New York: Atheneum, 1968.

Phillips, John. *Migratory Bird Protection in North America.* Special Publication of the American Committee for International Wildlife Protection. Vol. 1, No. 4. Cambridge, Mass., 1934.

Pope, Joseph. *Public Servant: The Memoirs of Sir Joseph Pope.* Toronto: Oxford University Press, 1960.

Reiger, John. *American Sportsmen and the Origins of Conservation.* New York: Winchester Press, 1975.

Roos, John E. *Restoring Fraser River Salmon: A History of the International Pacific Salmon Fisheries Commission.* Vancouver, B.C.: Pacific Salmon Commission, 1991.

Roosevelt, Theodore. *An Autobiography.* 1913. Reprint edition, New York: Da Capo, 1985.

Ruiz, Ramon. *The Great Rebellion: Mexico, 1905–1924.* New York: W. W. Norton, 1980.

Sand, Peter H., ed. *The Effectiveness of International Environmental Agreements: A Survey of Existing Legal Instruments.* Cambridge, England: Grotius Publishers, 1992.

Scheffer, Victor. *The Year of the Seal.* New York: Scribner's, 1970.

Scholes, Walter V., and Marie V. Scholes. *The Foreign Policies of the Taft Administration.* Columbia: University of Missouri Press, 1970.

Schorger, A. W. *The Passenger Pigeon: Its Natural History and Extinction.* Norman: University of Oklahoma Press, 1973.

Schullery, Paul, ed. *Theodore Roosevelt: Wilderness Writings.* Salt Lake City: Peregrine Smith Books, 1986.

Skelton, Oscar, ed. *The Life and Letters of Sir Wilfrid Laurier.* New York: Century Company, 1922.

Stein, Julie. *Archaeology of San Juan Island.* Seattle: University of Washington Press, forthcoming 1999.

Stejneger, Leonhard. "The Asiatic Fur-Seals and Fur Seal Industry." In David Starr Jordan, *Report of Fur Seal Investigations,* Vol. 4. Washington, D.C.: Government Printing Office, 1898.

Sterling, Keir. *Last of the Naturalists: The Career of C. Hart Merriam.* New York: Arno Press, 1977.

Tansill, Charles C. *Canadian-American Relations, 1875–1911.* New Haven: Yale University Press, 1943.

Taylor, F. H. C., et al. *Distribution and Food Habits of the Fur Seals of the North Pacific Ocean.* Washington, D.C.: Government Printing Office, 1955.

Tober, James A. *Who Owns the Wildlife? The Political Economy of Conservation in Nineteenth-Century America.* Westport, Conn.: Greenwood Press, 1981.

Trefethen, James. *An American Crusade for Wildlife.* New York: Winchester Press, 1975.

Weller, Phil. *Fresh Water Seas: Saving the Great Lakes.* Toronto: Between the Lines Press, 1990.

White, Richard. *Land Use, Environment, and Social Change: The Shaping of Island County, Washington.* Seattle: University of Washington Press, 1980.

Wright, Mabel Osgood. *Birdcraft: A Field Book of Two Hundred Song, Game, and Water Birds.* New York: Macmillan, 1899.

————. *Citizen Bird: Scenes from Bird-Life in Plain English for Beginners.* New York: Macmillan, 1897.

NEWSPAPERS AND MAGAZINES

Audubon
Bird-Lore
California Fish and Game
Forest and Stream
Japan Daily Mail
Japan Times
Montreal Gazette

Bibliography

Montreal Herald
Montreal Star
New York Herald
New York Times
Ottawa Journal
Pacific Fisherman
Rod and Gun in Canada
Seattle Post-Intelligencer
Toronto Globe
Washington Star

Index